Soldier and State
in Africa

SOLDIER
AND
STATE
in Africa

a comparative analysis
of military intervention
and political change

edited by
CLAUDE E. WELCH, JR.

Northwestern University Press
Evanston   1970

Contents

Introduction   vii

1. The Roots and Implications of Military Intervention,
   by CLAUDE E. WELCH, JR.   1

   Introduction to Chapter 2
2. The Military and Politics: Dahomey and Upper Volta,
   by W. A. E. SKURNIK   62

   Introduction to Chapter 3
3. Congo-Kinshasa: General Mobutu and Two Political
   Generations, by JEAN-CLAUDE WILLAME,
   compiled and translated by CLAUDE E. WELCH, JR.   124

   Introduction to Chapter 4
4. Arms and Politics in Ghana,
   by JON KRAUS   154

   Introduction to Chapter 5
5. The Algerian Army in Politics,
   by I. WILLIAM ZARTMAN   224

   Introduction to Chapter 6
6. The Military and Political Change in Africa,
   by PIERRE L. VAN DEN BERGHE   252

   Appendixes

A. Armed Strength and Defense Expenditures of African States in
   1966   267

B. Violence and Military Involvement in African Politics from
   Independence through 1968   270

   Selected Bibliography   302

   Glossary of Acronyms   310

   Index   313

Introduction

"AFRICAN ARMIES Move in When Politicians Fail," a headline trumpeted in the New York *Times* early in 1966. It appeared that the brave promises of economic, social, and political well-being voiced by political leaders could not be fulfilled. As the *Times* reporter noted, one theme prevailed in the coups and mutinies that had occurred to that date: "growing disillusionment in Africa with the old established nationalists who won widespread respect in the fight for independence but are now losing it by their misconduct in office."[1] Even *Pravda* echoed this thought: "As a rule, the interference of the army in politics in African countries is determined by breaches of stability within the ruling party, by its inability to solve one highly important problem or another, problems of great urgency for the population."[2]

This book analyzes two major areas: the factors leading to military involvement in politics, and the impact of military-based rule upon individual African states. Why did military involvement occur? Subsequent chapters point to political interference with the armed forces and weaknesses within the civilian regimes as the most significant factors leading to intervention. In some fashion, officers came to believe that the government was meddling unduly in matters best left to the military itself. This feeling of untoward interference was often linked to the belief that the government had lost popular support. Its legitimacy had been undermined; it was the duty of the armed services to correct a deteriorating situation. Members of the military thus obtained a "disposition to intervene," as S. E. Finer has noted.[3] They became imbued with the sense of an

---

1. *New York Times*, January 2, 1966.
2. Quoted in *Current Digest of the Soviet Press*, XVIII, no. 44 (1966), 28.
3. S. E. Finer, *The Man on Horseback: The Role of the Military in Politics* (London: Pall Mall, 1962), pp. 23–71.

identity separate from that of the civilian government; they felt they had a unique duty to safeguard the national interest undermined by the politicians in control. Opportunities to intervene occurred in many forms—widespread strikes or demonstrations against the government, severe economic difficulties, the undesired dependence of the government upon the armed forces to maintain control over a rapidly deteriorating situation.

Can the various military rulers succeed better than their civilian predecessors in coping with these issues, or might an extended period of further coups and counter-coups bedevil the prospects for political development? The answers to these questions must necessarily be tentative. Our perspective is limited in time. The first military-based government south of the Sahara was established in the Sudan just over a decade ago, and collapsed in 1964. Evidence of trends is scattered and fragmentary. Few theorists have developed models of political change within which the military regimes of tropical Africa might be fitted. Scholarly analysis of intervention and its effects, particularly by Africans, has been relatively scanty. Many of the African states in which takeovers have occurred could not be analysed in time to meet the deadline for this book—particularly Mali and Nigeria. The chapters of this book thus do not provide a full-fledged theory of political change under military governments, but the various case studies offer tentative generalizations for deeper comparative analysis. Hopefully, *Soldier and State in Africa* suggests further research.

Many thoughtful comments have been made as this manuscript passed through its stages of development. I am particularly grateful to those props of professional life, advanced graduate students, who contributed to the manuscript: Gordon J. Idang, Shelah Gilbert Leader, and Robert C. Vogt of SUNY/Buffalo for their research assistance; Cornelia Dopkins of SUNY/Buffalo and Valerie P. Bennett of Boston University for their comments upon the draft manuscript. I wish to thank Bea Langan, Elizabeth McCluskey, Joyce Peacock, and Lucille Peterson for combining the complex chores of typing with the other duties and pressures of the Dean's office. The index shows the skill of Mary Bellhouse. And, on behalf of all the contributors to this book, a weary word of gratitude to wives and children, who endured long hours while we labored to unite depth of analysis with reasonable style and reasonable timeliness.

C.E.W.

Soldier and State
in Africa

1.

The Roots
and Implications
of Military
Intervention

CLAUDE E. WELCH, JR.
State University of New York at Buffalo

POLITICAL VIOLENCE is no stranger to Africa. One scholar recently estimated that 300 to 400 acts of political violence occurred in the sub-Saharan region from 1946 to 1964.[1] In few of these, however,

Part of this chapter originally appeared, in a shortened form, in the *Journal of Modern African Studies*, V, no. 3 (1967), published by Cambridge University Press. The author is grateful to the Research Foundation of the State University of New York and to the Committee on African Studies of the State University of New York at Buffalo for financial assistance.
1. Victor T. Le Vine, "The Course of Political Violence in Africa," in *French-Speaking Africa: The Search for Identity*, ed. William H. Lewis (New York: Walker, 1965), p. 63. Cf. Eckstein's estimate that in the 1946–59 period, 1,200 unequivocal instances of guerrilla wars, localized rioting, widely dispersed turmoil, organized and apparently unorganized terrorism, mutinies, and coups d'état occurred throughout the world (Harry Eckstein, ed., *Internal War: Problems and Approaches* [New York: Free Press, 1964], p. 3).

were African soldiers the direct initiators.[2] The "man on horseback" familiar to students of Latin American history or the military president common in Middle Eastern history did not play any significant role in African states in the 18 years after World War II. It seemed as though the new countries of post-colonial Africa would escape the dreary round of coup and counter-coup typical of Latin America, the Middle East, and Southeast Asia. Such, at least, was the hope.

Direct military intervention, aimed at unseating civilian governments and replacing them with ruling councils drawn largely from the army, is a relatively recent phenomenon in Africa. With the exception of the Sudan (where officers led by General Ibrahim Abboud seized control in November, 1958), no supplanting of civilian authority by a military junta occurred until June 19, 1965 (Algeria). Then, in rapid succession, the governments of Congo-Kinshasa (November 25, 1965), Dahomey (December 22, 1965), Central African Republic (January 1, 1966), Upper Volta (January 3, 1966), Nigeria (January 15, 1966), Ghana (February 24, 1966), Nigeria once again (July 29, 1966), Burundi (November 28, 1966), Togo (January 13, 1967), Sierra Leone (March 22, 1967), Congo-Brazzaville (August 4, 1968), and Mali (November 19, 1968) all fell victims to coups d'état. What factors affected the timing of these coups? What salient differences can be observed between the relative quiescence of African armies before mid-1965 and the subsequent outright seizures of control? Might the forces that helped topple civilian authority cause a subsequent downfall of military government, as occurred in the Sudan in October, 1964? Should we view army intervention with alarm, as inherently detrimental to the best interests of African states, or should we concur with a noted authority who suggested that "frequent coups are a sign of change and progress"?[3] It verges on truism to call the African military one of the prime determinants of contemporary political change. Yet how will the various armies and their leaders exercise the power they assume? This book seeks to illuminate these questions by analyzing military intervention in five African states, the background to the coups as well as the directions of political change in

2. Grundy counts 64 instances of successful military coups d'état, military secessions, or military actions instrumental in bringing about governmental changes, and attempted military takeovers, secessions, and mutinies that failed to gain control but were disclosed (Kenneth W. Grundy, *Conflicting Images of the Military in Africa* [Nairobi: East Africa Publishing House, 1968]).

3. Samuel P. Huntington, ed., *Changing Patterns of Military Politics* (New York: Free Press, 1962), p. 40.

Algeria, Congo-Kinshasa, Dahomey, Ghana, and Upper Volta. Our concern is with the comparative analysis of political change, focusing upon the specific problem of coups d'état.

Students of African political change almost totally neglected the role of the military until the uprisings noted earlier made the omission distressingly obvious. Writings on African armies were practically nonexistent.[4] The armed forces were not considered to have the potential to become a meaningful independent political force. Major emphasis rested, rather, upon "charismatic leadership," "institutional political transfer," "mass parties," and similar slogans used by political scientists. Africa was the continent of the "political kingdom" or the "primacy of politics," not the continent of the army *caudillo* and frequent coups. Patterns of political change in Africa made knowledge of the military seem irrelevant. Two factors accounted for this lack of attention: the manner in which colonial territories gained independence, and the historical heritage of African armies.

Most African states gained independence through constitutional negotiation, through pressure exerted by party leaders against colonial powers relatively willing to withdraw. Self-government did not come through military action. Tropical Africa (leaving aside the territories still under Portuguese control) had no Bolívar, San Martín, or Ho Chi Minh. The so-called "African revolution" thus differed from many other great political changes: hegemony was handed over without large-scale civilian uprisings, campaigns of civil disobedience, or other techniques of political violence, in most cases. Algeria provided the exception, and the tensions born of revolution greatly disrupted post-independence political change.

As a result of the peaceful transfer of power, pressed by nationalist movements, African leaders tended to ascribe extraordinary powers of social, economic, and political transformation to political parties. They were to function as "mobilization systems," recreating African society and its economic underpinnings along new lines.[5] The political kingdom offered the key to further advance, for "all things shall be added to it," according to the slogan popularized by Kwame Nkrumah. In such a setting the military appeared unessential, perhaps irrelevant. However, the failure of political parties to

4. To take one instance, a state department bibliography, "Role of the Military in Less Developed Countries, January 1958–February 1964," contains references to four articles dealing with Africa, contrasted with 37 items on Latin America and 33 on the Middle East. There are no references to Africa in the bibliography in Huntington, *Changing Patterns*.

5. David E. Apter, *The Politics of Modernization* (Chicago: University of Chicago Press, 1965), pp. 357–90.

3

achieve their objectives of change and to maintain widespread popular enthusiasm helped prepare the way for army intervention.

Broadly speaking, African leaders confronted two major post-independence challenges, nation-building and state-building. Nation-building required the inculcation of political loyalties to the system as a whole, transcending the bounds of kinship, language, and locale. "The African nationalist," Rupert Emerson wrote in 1960, "still has before him almost the entire task of creating the nations in whose name he professes to speak."[6] National unity became the "supreme value and goal."[7] Since political parties had demonstrated their efficacy in the achievement of independence, why not continue to rely upon them in the post-independence reforging of society? The task of state-building involved a distinct series of challenges. Here, emphasis rested upon efficient administration, economic development, further specialization and expansion of the civil service —not upon fealty to the major political leader or mobilization of popular enthusiasm within a political party framework. Nation-building appeared to rest largely upon the political party, state-building upon the bureaucracy.

What role did African armies play in nation-building and state-building before seizure of control became widespread? The answer is simple. They usually remained on the sidelines. African leaders depended upon parties and administrative hierarchies, not upon the relatively small forces inherited from the departed colonial power. Hence, scholarly neglect of the political significance of African armies stemmed from many factors. Standing forces were the creations of the colonial power; in the evolution toward independence they did not participate directly, although the impact of demobilized soldiers on the growth of political awareness must not be denied.[8] But this impact was made by individuals, not by the

6. Rupert Emerson, *From Empire to Nation: The Rise to Self-Assertion of Asian and African Peoples* (Cambridge: Harvard University Press, 1960), p. 94.

7. James S. Coleman and Carl G. Rosberg, Jr., eds., *Political Parties and National Integration in Tropical Africa* (Berkeley and Los Angeles: University of California Press, 1964), p. 663.

8. A key event in Ghana's political history, for example, was the march on Christiansborg Castle, led by members of the Ex-Servicemen's Union on February 28, 1948. Riots broke out after the marchers were dispersed (and two killed) by police gunfire; the outbreak of violence led to the Watson Commission Report, of tremendous significance in the hastening of constitutional progress. See David E. Apter, *Ghana in Transition* (New York: Atheneum, 1963), pp. 167 ff.; and Dennis Austin, *Politics in Ghana, 1946–1960* (London: Oxford University Press, for the Royal Institute of International Affairs, 1964), pp. 73 ff. The relationship of the Ex-Servicemen's Union to the Convention People's Party is described by Eugene P. A. Schleh, "The Post-

military as a corporate group, or by ex-servicemen's unions linked to nationalist movements. Resentment against colonial rule was thus channeled through political parties, not through military uprisings. Wishful thinking may also have contributed to the lack of attention. No doubt many scholars hoped Africa might avoid, in its political change, the vicious cycle of coup and counter-coup that earlier had rocked Latin America, the Middle East, and Southeast Asia. What they forgot for the moment was the lesson expressed by Thomas Hobbes: Politics resembles a game of cards; hence, players must agree upon trumps. In politics, if no other card is agreed upon, clubs become trumps.[9] Such was the case in tropical Africa in the mid-1960's.

THREE TYPES OF INVOLVEMENT

In tracing military intervention in Africa, one can distinguish three types. The first type, relative passivity and abstention from political interference, was usually confined to the immediate post-independence period. The armies remained under substantial expatriate influence, which precluded (or certainly made more difficult) any meddling in politics. This was the period of the "nonpolitical army,"[10] in which a commander such as General Alexander could proclaim, "in the armed forces we were practically free from this taint [of politics]."[11] The second type of involvement saw

War Careers of Ex-Servicemen in Ghana and Uganda," *Journal of Modern African Studies,* VI (1968), 210–12. Demobilized veterans in Nigeria helped carry the gospel of nationalism to the "bush": more than 100,000 Nigerians served in World War II—30,000 of them outside their native country. See James S. Coleman, *Nigeria, Background to Nationalism* (Berkeley and Los Angeles: University of California Press, 1958), p. 254; and Frederick A. O. Schwarz, Jr., *Nigeria: The Tribes, the Nation, or the Race: The Politics of Independence* (Cambridge: M.I.T. Press, 1965), pp. 57–58. See also Donald Rothchild, "The Effects of Mobilization in British Africa," Duquesne University, Institute of African Affairs, reprint no. 2. However, as Olusanya notes, ex-soldiers did not play a significant note in Nigerian politics prior to independence due to fragmentation and poor leadership. See G. O. Olusanya, "The Role of Ex-Servicemen in Nigerian Politics," *Journal of Modern African Studies,* VI (1968), 221–32.

9. Cited in Dankwart A. Rustow, "The Military in Middle Eastern Society and Politics," in *The Military in the Middle East: Problems in Society and Government,* ed. Sydney Nettleton Fisher (Columbus: Ohio State University Press, for the Mershon Center for Education in National Security, 1963), p. 4.

10. For a caustic view of the "nonpolitical army" in Ghana, see Geoffrey Bing, *Reap the Whirlwind: An Account of Kwame Nkrumah's Ghana from 1950 to 1966* (London: Macgibbon & Kee, 1968), pp. 416–38.

11. H. T. Alexander, *African Tightrope: My Two Years as Nkrumah's Chief of Staff* (New York: Praeger, 1966), p. 20.

5

resentment against European officers and African political leaders explode in mutinies. These outbursts were not intended—at least directly—to unseat the government in control. They were aimed rather at forcing the government to adopt certain policies, notably higher pay, pension privileges, or immediate Africanization of the officer corps. Coups d'état, the third type, brought full-scale military involvement in politics. The occupants of presidential palaces were removed, possibly executed; into their offices moved the initiators of the intervention, intent on "restoring" the country to "normal" patterns.

Military Non-Involvement:
The Politics of Decolonization

Independence brought changes in the political and administrative sectors of African governments far more rapidly than in the military sector. The pace of Africanization differed dramatically. Few were the nationalist parties in which expatriates played any role. The replacement of European cadres in the civil service by Africans was a first order of priority for newly independent states; this task was eased by accelerated retirement and pension schemes and by absorption into the domestic civil service of the former colonial power. In the armed services, however, the replacement of Europeans in command positions was relatively leisurely—at least until mutiny or political decision to diminish reliance on foreign officers came about.

No army in tropical Africa, apart from the Sudanese, had a significant proportion of African officers when independence was granted.[12] In Ghana, which enjoyed perhaps the highest educational level of the sub-Saharan countries, only 10 per cent of the officers were African in 1957.[13] In 1951, the new commander of the West Africa Frontier Force decided to dispense with British non-commissioned officers and ensure African majors "within ten years."[14] Such a statement seemed almost revolutionary at the

---

12. James S. Coleman and Belmont Brice, Jr., "The Role of the Military in Sub-Saharan Africa," in *The Role of the Military in Underdeveloped Countries,* ed. John J. Johnson (Princeton: Princeton University Press, 1962), pp. 366–67.

13. *Ibid.,* p. 370. Gutteridge notes that in January, 1961, three months after Nigeria gained independence, 81 out of about 300 officers in the Nigerian Army were Africans, the most senior being a lieutenant colonel. See William F. Gutteridge, "Military Elites in Ghana and Nigeria," *African Forum,* II (1966), 37.

14. Sir John Smyth, *"Bolo" Whistler: The Life of General Sir Lasher Whistler: A Study in Leadership* (London: Frederick Muller, 1967), p. 199.

time. The Force Publique in the former Belgian Congo had no Africans in command positions in 1960: there were but three African sergeant-majors in an army of 24,000 soldiers and noncommissioned officers, 542 officers, and 566 junior officers.[15] Not until 1959 did an African from British East Africa receive an appointment to Sandhurst.[16]

The late start in Africanization can be attributed to the pace of post–World War II political change in Africa, which far exceeded the pace envisaged by the colonial administrations.[17] Until independence was clearly recognized as the objective—in the short-run, not in the distant future—of constitutional evolution, there was little value in replacing Europeans with possibly less-experienced Africans. The supply of Africans with the requisite educational background was limited.[18] And, at a more subtle level, the loyalty of European officers to their home country could be taken for granted. Control over the armed services was never turned over to African supervision before self-government was granted.

The armies of contemporary Africa are the direct descendents of forces created by the colonial administration. Pre-colonial raiding forces or palace armies were disbanded, or placed under severe restrictions. The prime duty of the colonial army was internal pacification, not international involvement. Border defense involved some troops, but since most frontiers in Africa separated non-antagonistic colonial powers, the main objective was prevention of smuggling.[19] Tropical Africa was isolated from direct involvement in the world wars, save for action undertaken by British and French forces against Kamerun, Tanganyika, and Togo in World War I. I do not wish to minimize the contributions made by African soldiers to the Allies: in World War II 166,000 inhabitants of British Africa

15. Coleman and Brice, "The Role of the Military," p. 379; Catherine Hoskyns, *The Congo since Independence, January 1960–December 1961* (London: Oxford University Press, for the Royal Institute of International Affairs, 1965), p. 59.

16. Coleman and Brice, "The Role of the Military," p. 373.

17. On the eve of World War II, the British secretary of state for the colonies commented: "It may take generations or even centuries for the peoples in some parts of the Colonial Empire to achieve self-government." Clearly he had Africa in mind. Quoted in Kenneth Robinson, "World Opinion and Colonial Status," *International Organization*, VIII (1954), 468.

18. For example, the twenty spaces available, after the 1953 Lagos conference, for West Africans at Sandhurst were rarely fully used, since British selection boards were not satisfied with the quality of applicants.

19. Exceptions included the frontiers of the former German colonies (Kamerun, Tanganyika, Togo, and South-West Africa), and the frontiers dividing French West Africa from British territories during the period of Vichy rule, mid-1940 to early 1942.

and 141,000 inhabitants of French West Africa served outside their home countries.[20] There is evidence that France looked upon her tropical dependencies as reservoirs of manpower, to be drawn upon in the event of general war.[21] Even taking account of these external commitments, however, the armies of colonial Africa were adjuncts of the administration, used to suppress domestic violence. They supplemented police forces in restoring calm—often by shows of force, a reputation for rapacity, and occasionally outright brutality. Soldiers were often recruited from "martial" tribes, then stationed far from their place of origin, often among traditional enemies. Ill-trained and ill-disciplined in many instances, colonial armies "were often regarded by the local population with deep distrust, as hated tools of the white conqueror."[22] The Force Publique in the former Belgian Congo, characterized by Willame in Chapter 3 as a "blind instrument of repression," built up a reputation for "toughness, efficiency, and some brutality."[23]

In the colonial period, the armies of Africa were kept small. Garrisons of European soldiers were stationed at strategic locations (e.g., Dakar and Fort Lamy); and with air transport facilities, additional troops could quickly be brought from the metropolitan country. However, the main reason for the restricted size was the limited role given the African military at times of international peace. Border patrolling, suppression of occasional internal unrest, and symbolizing the presence of the colonial power composed the major tasks of the small armed forces. The 24,000 soldiers in the Force Publique made up the largest army in any colonial territory of tropical Africa—and they represented less than 0.2 per cent of the population of the Belgian Congo.

The armies of colonial Africa were, in a sense, occupying forces. Characterized by complete subordination to the administration, they carried out admininstration by other means—not politics by other means, as Clausewitz suggested. Limited size, active distrust by the population of some territories, and an orientation toward

20. Lord Hailey, *An African Survey,* revised 1956 (London: Oxford University Press, for the Royal Institute of International Affairs, 1957), p. 253.

21. The mandate treaties for Togoland and Cameroon under French administration permitted troops raised in the mandated area, in the case of a general war, to repel attack or defend territory outside the mandated area—despite an attempt by the League of Nations to prevent the establishment of fortifications or military training in the areas under international supervision. Also see Coleman and Brice, "The Role of the Military," pp. 376–79.

22. Pierre van den Berghe, "The Role of the Army in Contemporary Africa," *Africa Report,* March 1965, p. 14.

23. Hoskyns, *The Congo Since Independence,* p. 59.

internal control rather than external involvement (leaving aside the world wars) typified the military forces of the sub-Saharan area before independence. The "legacies of imperial history," as Gutteridge stressed, form the essential background, the basis from which adjustments were made after the departure of the colonial power.[24]

Military conservatism makes reorganization in a short period nearly impossible—save in settings (to be discussed subsequently) where officers embodying traditions and methods of organization are forcibly removed. Few African leaders embarked upon drastic military reorganization immediately after attaining self-government. If assured of obedience, the new heads of state often wished to continue the organization of the armed forces essentially unchanged. Much of this stability resulted, however, from the presence of European officers. Africanization of command positions was accelerated, but it was nearly impossible—and possibly politically inexpedient—to remove expatriates on the spot. Although politicians supported Africanization in principle, the uncertainties of the post-independence period gave them second thoughts about firing experienced Europeans. President Nkrumah of Ghana, for example, retained a British chief of staff for more than four years after independence, despite pressures for naming an African to the position. Even so mercurial a leader as Patrice Lumumba of the former Belgian Congo felt the need for continuity in the army—that is to say, retention of European officers. "We are not, just because the Congo is independent, going to turn a second-class soldier into a general."[25] Even more forceful was his demand made to the Congo Executive College two months before independence:

> it is essential that the Force Publique, the only force available, stays intact. It must pass under the command of the Congolese Government exactly as it is—with its officer class, its junior officers, its traditions, its discipline, its unique hierarchy and above all its morale unshaken. This is not the moment to disorientate the Force by innovations, for an army in the process of organization or reorganization is not in a fit state to carry out its duties.[26]

Continuity entailed limitations on immediate promotion—a stricture many Congolese soldiers were unwilling to accept.

The contrast in the pace of Africanization between the civil

24. William F. Gutteridge, *Military Institutions and Power in the New States* (New York: Praeger, 1965), pp. 15–25.
25. Hoskyns, *The Congo Since Independence*, p. 60.
26. *Ibid.*

service and the officer corps was striking in many African states. As noted earlier, a mere 10 per cent of officers in the Ghanaian Army were Africans in 1957. Three years earlier, however, close to 40 per cent of senior officers in the Ghanaian civil service were Africans.[27] Analogous disproportions in the rate of advancement existed elsewhere, and helped account for the outbreak of mutinies, discussed in the following section.

Budgets for the armies of Africa, small in the period of colonial administration, remained limited after independence. Even as late as 1966, 17 of the 28 states of East, Central, and West Africa devoted less than 10 per cent of total government expenditure to the military. (See Appendix A.) Several factors helped to keep costs down. In the terminal period of colonial rule, European powers were unwilling to spend more than a bare minimum on defense for the African dependencies. The limited size of pre-independence forces and the retention of European officers may have inhibited lobbying or pressure for increased appropriations. The conception of the army as the former tool of colonial interests made it easy for politicians to scrimp on military spending. Limited resources were better spent on such popular objectives as education, health, and expansion of other public services. Even after independence, the former colonial power continued to bear many costs, particularly through providing equipment and training, and, in ex-French territories, by furnishing officers directly. In fact, until the officer corps was largely Africanized, until the former colonial power had disavowed its willingness to intervene in the event of insurrection, and until the aura of unity surrounding the dominant party had been broken, pressure from the military upon politicians—and consequently the funds devoted to military expenses—remained low.

Let us examine the ties retained between African armies and the former colonial powers in greater detail. It stands to reason that, if officers plotting to overthrow a government expect their efforts may be thwarted by external intervention, they would be less likely to initiate action than officers to whom the threat of intervention was negligible, other conditions being equal. The case studies in this book bear out this contention. Direct action by the former colonial powers (as occurred in Gabon and East Africa) halted mutinies or attempted coups; conversely, the denial of external assistance enabled many officers to depose elected officials. The possibility of external involvement seems thus a variable in both the planning and the carrying out of military action against African governments.

Most of the states of former French West Africa and French

27. Austin, *Politics in Ghana,* p. 158.

Equatorial Africa negotiated bilateral treaties with France shortly after independence. These agreements permitted extensive interconnections between French and African armies—to the point of allowing France both to "intervene directly" and to establish French bases and military installations. African governments could appeal for French assistance in maintaining the "organization of their own armies," a clause under which the Mba government of Gabon received assistance against an attempted seizure of control. In addition to public affirmations of military support, the French government is alleged to have signed numerous secret treaties, under which French troops could participate in maintaining public order in ex-colonies. Military links of a regional nature were embodied in the Union africaine et malgache de défense (UAMD), created in September 1961. The contracting states, which included all former French African colonies (except Guinea, Mali, and Upper Volta) plus France, agreed to come to the defense of any threatened member; a headquarters and machinery for periodic consultation were set up.[28]

British defense agreements with previous African dependencies were made exclusively on a bilateral basis; there was no regional organization comparable to the French-sponsored UAMD. However, the basic thrust of the treaties provided for the same contingencies as French agreements: mutual defense, provision of equipment, seconding of officers for training, a gradual phasing out of metropolitan troops stationed in Africa.[29] The mutiny of the Force Publique less than a week after independence ended hopes for military stability in the former Belgian Congo. Once the Force had been reintegrated following the turmoil of 1960–62 (for details, see Chapter 3), the Belgian government furnished officers and equipment, essential to the army's effectiveness.

These brief observations point inescapably to the conclusion that African armies, in the immediate post-independence period, were

28. *Africa Report,* January 1964, p. 10.
29. That many of these objectives could be achieved without formal treaty was demonstrated by Anglo-Nigerian relations. A month after independence, an "innocuous but very unpopular" defense pact was signed; it was abrogated in January, 1962, following a storm of protest from leaders of the Action Group, the major opposition party. However, as Sklar and Whitaker point out, "its provisions were sufficiently unobtrusive to be sustained afterwards without benefit of that document" (Richard L. Sklar and C. S. Whitaker, Jr., "The Federal Republic of Nigeria," in *National Unity and Regionalism in Eight African States,* ed. Gwendolen M. Carter [Ithaca: Cornell University Press, 1966], p. 134). The "innocuous but very unpopular" phrase appears in James S. Coleman, "The Foreign Policy of Nigeria," in *Foreign Policies in a World of Change,* ed. Joseph E. Black and Kenneth W. Thompson (New York: Harper & Row, 1963), p. 396.

not "national" armies. Organization and equipment depended heavily on external sources. Most of the trappings of the colonial period were simply carried over, save in states where self-government brought rupture from the former administering country.[30] Defense pacts, the dominance of Europeans in the officer corps, and a relatively slow-paced Africanization of command positions contrasted with Africanization of the civil service, helped perpetuate the image of the army as expatriate-controlled. Armies were not viewed, then, as institutions in which Africans took pride. They were remnants of a time of "national" shame, in the eyes of prominent politicians. This makes an interesting contrast with the states of Latin America, where independence came through armed struggle, and "the leaders of the revolutionary armies moved easily and naturally into the political vacuum created by the disappearance of royal authority. Thus at the very beginning of nationhood the armed forces [of Latin America] assumed extramilitary (that is, political) functions."[31] Only in Algeria, and to a much more limited extent in Morocco, Tunisia, Cameroon, and Kenya, did bands of guerrilla fighters carry forward the quest for independence.

The colonialist tinge of the African military contrasted strongly with the populist image of African nationalist movements and the political parties to which they gave rise. Political parties sought to reach all parts of the population, to fire them with anticolonial fervor; armies remained in their barracks, cut off from direct participation in nationalist activities, and occasionally fought against guerrilla groups favoring self-government. Political parties often attracted the best-educated, the young modernizers who had studied abroad; the armies were seen as refuges for up-country illiterates. European officers held tight control over the military; budding African politicians often barred Europeans from membership in their organizations. Armies were instruments of oppression, parties means of liberation. If Africa was the continent of the "political kingdom," it was because politicians, not soldiers, gained the credit for driving out colonial rule.

30. Guinea is an obvious instance. After the *Non* vote in the referendum of September 28, 1958, which resulted in the country's independence, the French government "almost at once began to repatriate Guineans then serving in its army." All French troops were withdrawn by November 30, 1958, and the Guinea government eschewed any French assistance in training. For a dithyrambic view of the reorientation of the Guinean army, see Victor D. Du Bois, "The Role of the Army in Guinea," *Africa Report*, January 1963, pp. 3–5, from which the quotations are taken.

31. Edwin Lieuwin, *Arms and Politics in Latin America*, rev. ed. (New York: Praeger, 1961), p. 19.

The relatively low priority accorded military expenditures in African states is shown clearly in national budgets.[32] Far more palpable to political leaders than pressure for more guns was the demand for social welfare—for schools and dispensaries, for new roads and piped water. The well-known "revolution of rising expectations" affected African political leaders who, even in the absence of popular demands, "undertook to bring about a fundamental change in the situation through government action."[33] Party militants pressed for due reward, reflected in a burgeoning of the civil service and inordinate salary increases. The 1962 budget of Senegal, to take one example, was five times that of 1957; in Dahomey, the budget doubled from 1958 to 1961.[34] In 1961, the "political class" in the former Belgian Congo received salary hikes of 380 per cent, while schoolteachers, civil servants, and other government employees gained respective increases of 96, 93, and 115 per cent.[35] Available funds could not cover all demands, however, and the general rise in government expenditures often did not affect the armed forces. The most striking instance of the dangers of cutting off the military occurred in Togo, where President Sylvanus Olympio refused to pension off demobilized soldiers—and lost his life as a result.

Independence thus found party leaders in control, while members of the armies remained on the sidelines. Political enthusiasm ran high. A "band-wagon" effect helped mobilize support—or at least votes—behind the major party. "As participation was extended," Zolberg notes, "a large number of people hitherto uninvolved in

32. Of course, there are exceptions to this generalization. The major factors of variation appear to be external military assistance and revanchist claims, plus the presence of a revolutionary army largely responsible for achieving independence. These considerations apply to Ethiopia and Somalia, Morocco and Algeria. The white-ruled states of southern Africa obviously sought, through increased military expenditures, to stave off threats from former colonial territories. If the states of North Africa are not included, the $322,000,000 spent by the Republic of South Africa for its armed services in 1965 was 16 per cent more than the *total* military expenses of 28 states in Central, East, and West Africa. See Appendix A.

33. Aristide R. Zolberg, *Creating Political Order: The Party-States of West Africa* (Chicago: Rand McNally, 1966), p. 40.

34. Five-eighths of the 1958 operating budget of Dahomey (3,210,000,000 C.F.A. francs) went to pay personnel; even with 10 per cent salary cuts for civil service members in early 1961, the budget totaled 6,338,000,000 C.F.A. francs ($25.5 million). Virginia Thompson, "Dahomey," in *Five African States: Responses to Diversity,* ed. Gwendolen M. Carter (Ithaca: Cornell University Press, 1963), pp. 195–96.

35. Edouard Bustin, "The Congo," in *Five African States,* ed. Carter, p. 137. Bustin notes that the pay increases given Congolese soldiers were an astronomical 450 per cent—a clear indication of the increased bargaining strength of the military following the July, 1960, mutiny.

politics identified with the dominant party unless there was a strong reason—usually involving primary group ties—for not doing so."[36] This awakening of political consciousness and flocking toward the dominant party should not be confused with either nation-building or state-building. Residual cleavages, based on primordial ties of ethnicity, language, religion, way of life, or even lineage, furnished the basis for a we-they distinction and hence an unintegrated, syncretic society.[37] Yet many African leaders believed that the dominant political party, as microcosm of the building nation, could make the transition toward social integration quick and painless. Self-government gave them a sense of euphoria: political leaders may have developed an inflated idea of their ability to bring about fundamental alterations in the social and economic fabric of their new states. During this period, the armies of Africa lacked channels to make their wishes known, owing to the continued influence of the former colonial power. Accordingly, politicians tended to ignore the soldiers and work on more familiar constituencies. The distribution of post-independence largess seemed to pass the military by. For the time being, at least, party leaders controlled the trumps.

Mutinies and Steps Toward Involvement

Direct military involvement in the political life of African states came initially through mutinies. Their proximate cause appears to have been dissatisfaction within the ranks over such internal issues as promotions and pay scales. Though they had a direct impact upon politics, the mutinies were not directly political.[38] In other words, these revolts primarily represented insubordination to officers, not direct rebellion seeking to displace elected officials. The causes were intrinsic to the army, not extrinsic to the political system. And, as such, post-independence mutinies arose over conditions similar to those that had prompted many mutinies during the colonial period.

Africanization of the officer corps had barely started in most sub-Saharan states when the colonial power withdrew. The European commanders viewed their duty as assuring continuity in a period of profound stress. The most candid expression of this view came from

36. Zolberg, *Creating Political Order*, p. 21.
37. Aristide R. Zolberg, "The Structure of Political Conflict in the New States of Tropical Africa," *American Political Science Review*, LXII, no. 1 (1968), 71.
38. A similar distinction is drawn by Ali Mazrui and Donald Rothchild. See "The Soldier and the State in East Africa: Some Theoretical Conclusions on the Army Mutinies of 1964," *Western Political Quarterly*, XX (1967), 87.

General Emile Janssens, commander of the Force Publique in the former Belgian Congo. A few days after independence, he addressed a sullen group of officers and soldiers at the Leopoldville military camp. The Congolese troops "had the impression that independence had passed them by."[39] This impression was seemingly confirmed when General Janssens wrote on a blackboard "Before independence = after independence."[40] This infuriated the soldiers, who rebelled and dismissed all European officers. The first significant mutiny against an independent African state had started.

The self-confidence of General Janssens was more than matched by the confidence of Prime Minister Julius Nyerere of Tanganyika. Shortly after the Congo mutiny, Nyerere declared: "These things cannot happen here. First, we have a strong organisation, TANU [Tanganyika African National Union]. The Congo did not have that kind of organisation. . . . There is not the slightest chance that the forces of law and order in Tanganyika will mutiny."[41] Three-and-a-half years later, after Nyerere had devoted considerable attention to reorganizing TANU and assuring military loyalty, the 1st Batallion of the Tanganyika Rifles rose against their British officers and marched into Dar es Salaam, demanding higher pay and total Africanization of the officer corps. The vaunted strength of TANU and its respected leader seemed to crumble when confronted by a handful of mutinous troops. To be certain, the mutineers had before them the example of the successful revolutionaries in Zanzibar, which "probably did act as a spark to the army's pent-up sense of injustice and frustration."[42] Even so, the chain reaction of mutinies in East Africa testifies to the depth of resentment felt by African soldiers against their European officers.

To draw a clear division between mutinies and coups d'état is a hazardous task. The events in Togo of January, 1963, illustrate aspects of both intra-army mutinies and broader military involvement in politics aimed at changing government personnel. The Togolese insurrection centered around President Sylvanus Olympio, a crusty, no-nonsense former businessman who led his small country of 1½ million inhabitants to independence in April, 1960. Olympio had an unusual background and unusual ideas, contrasted with other prominent African politicians of the period. Descended from "Brazilians" who had settled in Dahomey in the mid-nineteenth

39. Hoskyns, *The Congo Since Independence,* p. 87.
40. *Ibid.,* p. 88.
41. Quoted in Mazrui and Rothchild, "The Soldier and the State in East Africa," p. 82.
42. Frere Ginwala, "The Tanganyika Mutiny," *World Today,* March 1964, p. 94.

century, he was educated at the University of Vienna and the London School of Economics after World War I, after which he entered commerce. His financial acumen, urbane character, and undoubted competence helped make him general manager in Togo of the United Africa Company in 1936. Olympio resigned his position, following World War II, to devote full efforts to politics; his primary objective was the removal of the restrictive bonds of French administration.[43]

As leader of independent Togo, Olympio pursued a course of financial austerity. He balanced current expenditures without resorting to external economic assistance. One of the main victims of Olympio's financial retrenchment was the small army inherited from the French administration, along with 300 Togolese veterans demobilized from the French army after independence. Togolese who had fought for France, Olympio felt, had no greater claim on their home country than any other unemployed Togolese. His distaste for the veterans could scarcely be concealed. When a petition on their behalf was given Olympio on January 12, 1963, he rebuffed the soldiers, calling them "mercenaries." Late the same night, a group of the disgruntled veterans surrounded the president's house. Dawn the following morning found Olympio dead—shot by mutinous soldiers in the garden of the nearby American Embassy.

Having assassinated the president, the Togolese mutineers did not know what next to do; Olympio's death appears to have been unpremeditated. The soldiers did not attempt to form a government; they called upon opposition politicians who had left Togo. The new president, Nicolas Grunitzky, quickly appeased the soldiers and unemployed veterans by advocating the establishment of two new companies, possibly even tripling the size of the military. The leaders of the insurrection castigated Olympio for failing to give attention to "daily increasing unemployment"; he manifested attitudes of "profound contempt for the military" and authoritarian paternalism.[44] Olympio's slights against the armed forces and his

43. Detailed information on the political history of Togoland under French administration can be gleaned from voluminous reports submitted to the United Nations by the French government, from reports of U.N. Visiting Missions, and from debates in the Trusteeship Council and the Fourth Committee of the General Assembly. For briefer treatment, see James S. Coleman, "Togoland," *International Conciliation*, CIX (1956); François Luchaire, "Le Togo français, de la tutelle à l'autonomie," *Revue juridique et politique de l'Union Française*, XI (1957), 1–46, 501–87; and Claude E. Welch, Jr., *Dream of Unity: Pan-Africanism and Political Unification in West Africa* (Ithaca: Cornell University Press, 1966), pp. 23–147, *passim*.

44. Quoted in Helen Kitchen, "Filling the Togo Vacuum," *Africa Report*, February 1963, p. 7.

desire to pare nonessential expenditures ironically brought about the policies he had hoped to avoid. Grunitzky, having taken office under the shadow of military intervention, had to appease the armed forces; therefore he cast aside the policy of austerity his brother-in-law, Sylvanus Olympio, had briefly implemented.

As a footnote to the Togo story, the cabinet of President Grunitzky lasted less than four years. On January 13, 1967, the veterans who had eliminated Olympio unceremoniously ousted Grunitzky and set up a military regime. The first intervention found the soldiers in a quandary, not knowing where or how to turn for political leadership, save to former opposition politicians. The second uprising—clearly a coup d'état—showed that the military had far clearer ideas of what to do. The unsure reaction of January, 1963, was a mutiny with significant political repercussions, not a full-blown seizure of control vesting leadership in a military cabinet. To events of this nature we must now turn.

Military Involvement in Politics: The Seizure of Control

The military seizures of control that rocked the sub-Saharan area from mid-1965 on cannot be attributed to a single factor. The complexity of events belies simple, unicausal analysis. Many political systems were involved, each with distinct heritages and problems. To assume that "popular discontent" or "economic stagnation" or "neocolonialist interference" brought about the coups d'état does not do justice to the unique combinations of circumstances. Rather than search for a sole cause, we must examine a series of factors, the salience of whose components differs from one African state to another.

Significant factors that helped promote military intervention may be summarized in this form:

1. Declining prestige of the major political party, as exemplified by
   a. increased reliance upon force to achieve compliance,
   b. a stress upon unanimity in the face of centrifugal forces, and
   c. a consequent denial of effective political choice.
2. Schism among prominent politicians, thus weakening the broadly based nationalist movement that had hastened the departure of the former colonial power.

3. Lessened likelihood of external intervention in the event of military uprising.
4. "Contagion" from seizures of control by the military in other African countries.
5. Domestic social antagonisms, most obviously manifested in countries where a minority group exercised control (e.g., the Arabs in Zanzibar, the Watusi in Burundi).
6. Economic malaise, leading to "austerity" policies most affecting articulate, urbanized sectors of the population (members of labor unions, civil servants).
7. Corruption and inefficiency of government and party officials, a corruption especially noticeable under conditions of economic decline.
8. Heightened awareness within the army of its power to influence or displace political leaders.

Let us consider these factors in greater detail.

DECLINING PARTY PRESTIGE

Enthusiasm for the dominant party flagged rapidly in many African states, following the initial spurt of organizational enthusiasm and the jubilation of self-government.[45] The waning was in part psychological. Independence may have aroused unwarrantedly high expectations. The "golden age" would be ushered in; in some remote regions, self-government was interpreted as an end to taxes, communal labor, and other unpleasant aspects of administrative control. Such hopes obviously could not be fulfilled. Economic squeeze also contributed to the loss of party fervor. But the major agent of declining prestige of political parties was internal. The tactics and organization of parties appropriate for anti-colonial activities were not necessarily appropriate for the tasks of governance after independence. Failure in the structural adaptation of political parties made them considerably less effective instruments in a self-governing African state.

It may seem paradoxical to call a dominant party a coalition, or, in Zolberg's apt phrase, a "heterogeneous monolith."[46] However,

45. Zolberg, *Creating Political Order*, p. 22.
46. Aristide R. Zolberg, "Politics in the Ivory Coast," *West Africa*, July 30, August 6, and August 29, 1960, pp. 847, 883, 939. In his outstanding book on the Ivory Coast, Zolberg notes that "the growth of territorial nationalism was accompanied by the renascence of ethnic subnationalism." Aristide R. Zolberg, *One-Party Government in the Ivory Coast* (Princeton: Princeton University Press, 1964), p. 143.

the "band-wagon" effect described previously meant that many African political parties were little more than loosely bound cartels of upwardly mobile office-seekers. By 1962, Austin has maintained, the Convention People's Party of Ghana was a "massive propaganda machine without an effective appeal to sustain it."[47] The resignation of Nyerere as prime minister of Tanganyika in 1962, to devote his full attention to the reorganization of TANU, testified to the seriousness with which he viewed a decline in party enthusiasm. Difficulties arose from the limits of the changes that political groups could effect. Loyalty to a dominant party, its leader, and the "nation" it purportedly embodied could not be readily internalized in the face of conflicting, ethnically based loyalties. For most newly enfranchised Africans an understanding of politics could not be disentangled from traditional outlooks and antagonisms. The broad, anticolonial nationalist movements had succeeded, in varying degrees, in juxtaposing what one might call the "subnational nationalisms" of ethnic groups. With independence achieved and its novelty gone, however, cracks appeared in the "heterogeneous monolith." The united front showed clear signs of disintegration, of a loss of vigor. Primordial attachments remained strong, despite the success of the nationalist movements in winning independence. Indeed, the extension of political awareness through party activities may have exacerbated group tensions. Greater political awareness brought through participation, Geertz has noted, "does indeed tend to lead to the stimulation and maintenance of a very intense popular interest in the affairs of government. But . . . much of this interest takes the form of an obsessive concern with the relation of one's tribe, region, sect, or whatever to a center of power."[48] To regain the apparent unity of anticolonial struggle was a problem with which most African leaders struggled after independence. Agreement had to be created once again—and it was to be revived through the achievement of unanimity.

Two steps are involved in this task, according to Zolberg: erasing all traces of political opposition; and modifying both dominant party and government through the creation of a new institutional order.[49] The methods by which opposition parties have been harassed and eventually removed from public attention have been

47. Austin, *Politics in Ghana,* p. 418.
48. Clifford Geertz, "The Integrative Revolution: Primordial Sentiments and Civil Politics in the New States," in *Old Societies and New States,* ed. Clifford Geertz (New York: Free Press, 1963), pp. 119–20.
49. Zolberg, *Creating Political Order,* pp. 66 ff.

analyzed elsewhere in detail.[50] Essentially what was involved were civil actions against politicians—legal restrictions on their activi- ties, manipulation of electoral machinery and regulations, rewards for "crossing the carpet"—rather than widespread campaigns of intimidation undertaken against supporters of opposition groups. By removing the spokesmen for "subnational nationalisms," Afri- can political leaders hoped to eliminate detrimental parochial tend- encies. However, given the deeply rooted nature of ethnic identity and its stimulation through political participation, such measures may only have worsened the situation. It is in this context that politicians turned increasingly to the use of force to attain goals of integration unreachable through persuasion.

There are many connections between politics and the control of force. Following Max Weber, numerous political scientists have seen the legitimate control of coercion as the distinctive characteristic of a government or political system.[51] Ultimate collective sanctions are vested in and exercised by the state. Yet we are intuitively aware that force is used relatively infrequently in most political systems, which persist rather through habit, tacit obedience, and regular compliance; only infrequently is coercion utilized. Analysts have pointed to the similarities exhibited by banks and political systems. Banks keep on hand only a fraction of their customers' deposits; a "run on the bank" would quickly exhaust available funds. Money does not lie idle, for it is the "base on which a complex structure of credit is erected."[52] In political systems, the command of force exercised by the government might break down with a "run on the bank"—with the funds in this case being the "power" controlled by the political system. The analogy has been expressed by Karl Deutsch in this fashion:

> Banks often lend out several times as much money as they have received in deposits—since they rely on their customers not all demanding back their deposits at one and the same time. In much the same way, governments can promise to back with sanctions many more of their binding decisions, rules, and laws, and to do so against many more people than any government could possibly do if all people started disobeying it at one and the same time.

50. See, *inter alia*, the country studies and concluding chapter of Coleman and Rosberg, *Political Parties and National Integration in Tropical Africa;* Martin L. Kilson, "Authoritarian and Single-Party Tendencies in African Politics," *World Politics*, XV (1963), 262–94; and Zolberg, *Creating Political Order*, pp. 66–92.
51. H. H. Geerth and C. Wright Mills, eds., *From Max Weber: Essays in Sociology* (New York: Oxford University Press, 1946), p. 78.
52. Talcott Parsons, "Some Reflections on the Place of Force in Social Process," in *Internal War,* ed. Eckstein, p. 44.

Governments, like banks, thus base their operation on the fact that the popular expectations favorable to them—that one ought to leave one's money in the bank and that one ought to obey the law and the police—are highly coordinated, so that most individuals most of the time can count on everybody else to do as they do.[53]

Once expectations of regular obedience are broken, as Hobbes eloquently expressed, man's life becomes "solitary, poor, nasty, brutish and short." So too, perhaps, with political systems.

The attempted elimination of political opposition entailed the use of force, which in turn affected political life in African states. The following points, drawn from Zolberg, illustrate the complexities of the shift from "power" to "force."[54]

1. Governments may fall into the snare of believing that harsh treatment will eliminate disruptive demands. However, the governments may become more vulnerable to other threats, since the limited capital of force is used up—and not readily replenished. In other words, the probability of a "run on the bank" within an African political system is increased.

2. Increasing use of force enhances the significance of police, military, and other groups capable of its exercise. By contrast, the significance of political parties, civil services, or similar institutions declines.

3. If groups or individuals lack the opportunity for legitimate political activity—that is, the exercise of the power to express their demands—they are tempted to use force to press these demands.

A brief examination of events in Ghana confirms these points. The government of Kwame Nkrumah restricted opposition politicians by a wide variety of means. The Ghanaian population, as Kraus notes, was denied effective political choice. The attempt to restrict claims on the system resulted not in a lessening of claims but in a decrease in the extent to which they were effectively communicated, with attendant frustration and discontent with the system. Army and police leadership represented the only institutional groups capable of posing a serious threat to the Nkrumah regime. Heavy-handed efforts to stamp out opposition in Ghana caused the Convention People's Party to lose the aura of legitimacy it once had com-

53. Karl W. Deutsch, *The Nerves of Government: Models of Political Communication and Control* (New York: Free Press, 1963), p. 121.

54. Zolberg, "The Structure of Political Conflict," pp. 73–77. I have omitted Professor Zolberg's point about the problem of legitimacy: he notes that the shift to force "enhances the problem of the legitimacy of the rulers in the eyes of those to whom the implementation of force must necessarily be entrusted."

manded; no longer could it assure regular coordination. The increasing severity of sanctions helped set up a vicious circle, in which force was both used and used up. Parsons has described the situation of "power deflation" in the following terms:

> Essentially a constitutional regime is marked, on the one hand, by restraint in the expectation of fulfillment of various demands and, on the other, by restraint in the coercion of the opposition by those in power. In particular, the leadership refrain from abridging the freedom to displace the incumbents from power, not only by maintaining the electoral rules, but by upholding the other normal components of political freedom like freedoms of the press, of assembly, and so forth. The opposition must be free to influence the voters, although neither they nor the incumbents should coerce or bribe them.
>
> It is when, in the vicious circle of power deflation, these restraints are broken in the interaction between incumbents and opposition that the makings of a revolutionary situation are present.[55]

"Power deflation" certainly promoted the Nigerian coup d'état of January, 1966. In the Western Region, steps taken against the Action Group (the governing party of the region until mid-1963) brought the area to the brink of civil war. Following a party split in May, 1962, a state of emergency was declared by the Nigerian federal government. The leader of the Action Group was convicted of conspiracy in the arms plot.[56] A regional election in late 1965 was marred by blatant rigging. Wholesale political violence erupted. The breakdown of public confidence manifested in looting, arson, and murder bore witness to "power deflation."

No precise, quantifiable catalogue of the characteristics of "power deflation" has been developed. Extrapolating from the countries surveyed in this volume, the following seem significant: a sharp increase in deaths attributable to domestic group violence; rampant electoral manipulation; a greater military participation ratio (the ratio of uniformed armed forces and the total population);[57] the oft-

55. Parsons, "Some Reflections," pp. 65–66.

56. Richard L. Sklar, "Nigerian Politics: The Ordeal of Chief Awolowo, 1960–65," in *Politics in Africa: Seven Cases,* ed. Gwendolen M. Carter (New York: Harcourt, Brace & World, 1966), pp. 119–62; John P. Mackintosh, *Nigerian Government and Politics* (London: Allen and Unwin, 1966), pp. 427–60.

57. Chalmers Johnson, *Revolutionary Change* (Boston: Little, Brown, 1966), pp. 126–27. The ratio was originally developed by Stanislaw Andreski, *Military Organization and Society,* 2d ed. (Berkeley and Los Angeles: University of California Press, 1968).

discussed transfer of allegiance of intellectuals;[58] a ritualization of political life, as discussed by Willame; a rise in ideological appeals, in which ethnic identification forms a major component; heightened dependence of political leaders upon police, gendarmerie, or army support; and various symptoms of social disequilibrium. Further research must be undertaken to ascertain the precise significance of these and related factors, however.

POLITICAL SCHISMS

The quest for unanimity, sought by the leaders of the dominant party, must be examined in a different context. Maintaining the cohesion of the party entailed a reformulation of party-state relations, in which an increasing emphasis upon individual leadership emerged. In few African political parties has collective decision-making prevailed—if it ever existed. The reins of control have often been garnered by a single leader. However, in states in which political rivalry could not be contained within the framework of a single party, the likelihood of coups d'état increased. Often the military would be solicited to intervene; on other occasions, splits among top political leaders furnished the pretext for military incursions into politics. Four examples illustrate this point.

1. The first significant army intervention in tropical Africa occurred November 17, 1958, with the assumption of control in the Sudan by General Ibrahim Abboud. In a context of political wrangling and constitutional uncertainty, Abboud was invited to intervene by the Prime Minister, Abdallah Khalil, to stave off a possible growth in Egyptian influence. Clearly, the weakness of the government coalition brought military intervention "to save the country from political ruin"—more precisely, from ruin by politicians.[59]

2. General Joseph Mobutu's first intervention into Congolese politics came in September, 1960. Prime Minister Patrice Lumumba and President Joseph Kasavubu had found themselves in a constitutional impasse: Kasavubu relieved Lumumba of his duties, an action whose legality Lumumba denied. As government activity shuddered to a halt, Mobutu stepped in to neutralize all politicians and assume power, for a period of slightly over three months. He insisted his action constituted a "peaceful revolution," not a coup

58. Crane Brinton, *The Anatomy of Revolution,* rev. ed. (New York: Vintage, 1965), pp. 39–49.
59. Yusuf Fadl Hasan, "The Sudanese Revolution of October 1964," *Journal of Modern African Studies,* V (1967), 494.

d'état.[60] The government would be run by "technicians," by which Mobutu meant Congolese university graduates and students.

3. Colonel Christophe Soglo attempted to heal the long-standing split in Dahomean politics in October, 1963, by temporarily replacing President Hubert Maga.[61] However, the long-standing tensions among regionally based politicians in Dahomey could not be effaced, and as Skurnik notes in Chapter 2, the formation of a single party (the Parti Démocratique Dahoméen) failed to resolve the unstable situation.

4. The abortive coup d'état in Gabon in February, 1964, resulted in part from long-standing divisions between President Leon Mba and Jean-Hilaire Aubame, the premier of the short-lived provisional governmnent.[62] The two men, rivals since the elections to the first Constituent Assembly in 1945, polarized Gabonese politics. To gain power, Aubame could turn only to the army. The Comité Revolutionaire included his sympathizers in the armed forces, whose basic error was neglecting the closing of the Libreville airport, where French troops landed to restore Mba.

Disgust with squabbling politicians clearly prompted these actions. Soglo put his views forcefully:

> The trouble with our country, as you know, is separatism and regionalism with all their threats of division. The political leaders are not bad; they are men with great qualities who have rendered considerable service to their country, but they have proved that they cannot rise above their personal quarrels. . . . Our objective is to introduce into this country a new style of politics in which the people will rally around a program and not around personalities.[63]

Abboud called his action "a turning point from chaos towards stability and from corruption towards efficient rule."[64] To set the government aright by eliminating the schism and regionalism encouraged by conflicting leadership thus was cited to justify military intervention. In other words, soldiers like Soglo and Mobutu were prompted to seize control to restore equilibrium, which they felt

60. Hoskyns, *The Congo Since Independence,* p. 214.
61. The regional tensions are extensively discussed by Thompson, "Dahomey," pp. 207–35.
62. John A. Ballard, "Four Equatorial States," in *National Unity and Regionalism in Eight African States,* ed. Carter, pp. 253–61; Charles and Alice Darlington, *African Betrayal* (New York: David McKay, 1967); Brian Weinstein, *Gabon: Nation-Building on the Ogooué* (Cambridge: M.I.T. Press, 1966), pp. 175–76.
63. Quoted in *Africa Report,* February 1966, p. 15.
64. Hasan, "The Sudanese Revolution," p. 495.

had been disrupted by personality conflicts. Their goal was "caretaker" administration—not sweeping change but minor adaptation. Minor shifts in personnel and policy would be undertaken; the *status quo* would be restored. Freed of the disequilibrium supposedly resulting from political machinations, the whole political system would return to normalcy—or so the interveners asserted.

POSSIBILITY OF EXTERNAL INTERVENTION

The plotters of coups d'état must always calculate the likelihood of international response against their planned takeover.[65] In Africa, fear of external intervention to prevent military seizure of control—particularly fear of intervention by the former colonial power—has been a significant variable in the cases under consideration.

The role of European officers has already been examined. It is reasonable to assume that their presence moderates the willingness of African officers and soldiers to embark upon coups d'état when the expatriates are obviously committed to upholding the African government concerned.

More important, however, is the risk of massive intervention from the ex-administering country in the event of an attempted seizure of control. British forces rapidly quelled the mutinies in Kenya and Tanganyika, upon request; French troops crushed the uprising in Gabon, once again upon request. (It does not appear that President Olympio requested French assistance in halting the mutiny that brought his death.)

From the limited evidence available, it appears that the British and French governments have been relatively circumspect. They have intervened only upon request of the duly constituted government (though how well established Mba's government was is an open question), where a show of force (as by disarming mutineers) would restore calm. The former colonial powers have not intervened in cases of popularly supported revolutionary upheaval (e.g., Zanzibar or the overthrow of President Fulbert Youlou in Congo-Brazzaville), in relatively popular coups in which politicians are removed from office but not executed (Central African Republic, Dahomey, and Upper Volta), or in violent coups carried out with great rapidity (Togo and Nigeria).

---

65. A sound strategy for coups, Major Goodspeed has commented, involves assessment of the sympathies of the country's armed forces, the state of public opinion, and the international situation. D. J. Goodspeed, *The Conspirators: A Study of the Coup d'État* (New York: Viking, 1962), p. 210. The six seizures of control analyzed in this book are European.

25

How likely are the Belgian, British, and French governments to become embroiled in protecting future African politicians from the ire of discontented armed forces? Not very likely, it would seem, save in cases in which very substantial investments and numerous citizens were involved, and in which international political considerations—that is to say, the Cold War—obtrude. The use of paratroops against Stanleyville in 1964 fulfilled these criteria, but a repetition of the surrounding circumstances appears unlikely. European troop deployments in Africa have been cut dramatically. "As far as the major powers are concerned," Gutteridge has commented, "on the whole their military involvement in Africa is limited by the fact that the continent is not of prime concern for their own security. Only for France do bases in Africa constitute a major part of her strategic scheme, and she is progressively withdrawing from the area."[66] The 16,000 French troops stationed in Africa at the start of 1966 were considerably reduced with the closing of bases; should any of the eleven countries with which France has defense agreements call for assistance, units for intervention would come from the 11th Infantry Division, generally based in southwest France and Britanny.[67] The British government after March, 1966, maintained only 2,000 soldiers in Africa.[68] No Belgian troops are stationed south of the Sahara, although advisers have been provided for the armies of Burundi, Congo-Kinshasa, and Rwanda.[69] Almost all American troops in Africa (5,500 of 6,000) are stationed in Ethiopia and Libya.[70] Despite the rapid mobility offered by modern aircraft, and the retention of some French troops, the capacity of the former colonial powers to intervene has declined considerably —as well, perhaps, as their desire to become involved in what they view as domestic political crises. And, further, if a coup is rapid and the removal of politicians complete, intervention by the former colonial power would be nugatory. Leaders of coups learn quickly the value of " 'twere well it were done quickly."

CONTAGION

Three weeks after the assassination of President Olympio, Colonel David Thompson, commanding officer of Liberia's National

66. David Wood, "The Armed Forces of African States," Institute for Strategic Studies, Adelphi Papers, no. 27 (London: 1966), p. 3.
67. *Ibid.*, p. 26.
68. *Ibid.*, p. 27.
69. *Ibid.*, pp. 19, 22.
70. *Ibid.*, p. 27.

Guard, was arrested on suspicion of plotting a coup d'état. "If only 250 Togolese soldiers could overthrow their government, a Liberian Army of 5,000 could seize power easily," Colonel Thompson is alleged to have argued.[71] Successful seizure of control in one state may touch off a series of coups. The Zanzibar uprising may have helped trigger the East African mutinies; similarly, the intervention of Soglo in December, 1965, may have helped touch off coups in the Central African Republic, Upper Volta, Nigeria, and Ghana.

Contagion must be considered on two levels: the personal links among African officers in different countries, and the increasing extent of interstate ties. Shared experiences in the French army provided the leaders of intervention in the Central African Republic, Dahomey, Togo, and Upper Volta (respectively Bokassa, Soglo, Eyadema, and Lamizana) with potentially significant individual ties. All four served in Indochina. It is quite likely that the success of one in winning political control prompted the others to consider intervention—though no conclusive evidence can be adduced. Since independence, contacts among African leaders have multiplied. As Zartman has noted, political alignments in western Africa have been marked by a continual search for alliances.[72] The distinctions between English-speaking Africa and *Afrique francophone* have apparently diminished; ideological cleavages have made interstate relations in Africa a kaleidoscope of shifting alliances. Close alignments exist within the United Nations, as shown by sophisticated analyses of voting.[73] Further, shared problems of development have encouraged greater commonality of purpose among African political leaders: positions tagged as radical, moderate, or conservative "have been overlaid by pragmatic responses to the problems of state-building. . . . The very magnitude of the problems narrows the range of realistic responses and in so doing encourages a rough consensus among the several African states."[74] As Africa has increasingly become a subsystem in world politics, reciprocal influences among African states have multiplied. These reciprocal influences include the germ of military intervention.

71. Kitchen, "Filling the Togo Vacuum," p. 9.
72. I. William Zartman, *International Relations in the New Africa* (Englewood Cliffs: Prentice-Hall, 1966), p. 26.
73. Hayward R. Alker, Jr., "Dimensions of Conflict in the General Assembly," *American Political Science Review*, LVIII (1964), 642–57. Also see Thomas Hovet, Jr., *Africa in the United Nations* (Evanston: Northwestern University Press, 1963).
74. Robert C. Good, "Changing Patterns of African International Relations," *American Political Science Review*, LVIII (1964), p. 641.

Reference has already been made to conditions of social disequilibrium affecting attempts at army seizure of control. When members of the armed forces perceive the government to be dominated by members of an ethnic group hostile to the interests of members of another ethnic group which is heavily represented within the military, grievances based on tribe or region may quickly develop. Often army intervention may be pushed by the clash of "primordial sentiments." To be certain, this factor is connected closely with the phenomenon of army consciousness, which is analyzed subsequently; however, brief consideration must be given to ethnic factors.

Many grievances were involved in the Nigerian coup d'état of January, 1966. One of these grievances was the belief among Ibo officers that the federal government was pursuing policies often at variance with the best interests of the Ibo population. Of the 81 African officers in the Nigerian army in January, 1961, a significant number were Ibo.[75] There was little doubt, Gutteridge noted, "that some of the young Ibo officers joined the army as the result of suggestions from political quarters."[76] Politics in Nigeria thus impinged directly upon the ethnic composition of the officer corps. The ethnic imbalance of the officer corps (Ibos constitute at most 15 per cent of Nigeria's population of 56 million) was not untypical of post-independence Africa. Officers were drawn generally from areas in which education was relatively widespread; disparities resulted in large measure from the uneven distribution of schools in African states.[77] Ethnic imbalance resulted also from historical and cultural factors, for, as Gutteridge pointed out, the Yorubas were prejudiced against the army for historical reasons; Muslim resistance to education in Northern Nigeria certainly slowed down the pace with which trained men could be able to take up military positions.[78]

75. Gutteridge, "Military Elites," p. 37. He asserts that three-fourths were Ibos, and that "most of the Ibos came from a particularly well-developed group of secondary schools in the Onitsha area of the Eastern Region and thus had a strong sense of solidarity." However, unpublished research carried out by Martin J. Dent indicates that, of the 45 officers in the Nigerian establishment at independence, 26 were Ibo and two Ibibio.

76. Gutteridge, "Military Elites," p. 39.

77. Coleman and Brice, "The Role of the Military," p. 400. I do not accept without qualifications their assertion that "the educated class, from which army officers are necessarily recruited, represents a fairly comprehensive cross section of society." The uneven impact of missionary educational activity, noted in the following sentence, introduced a major ethnic skewing.

78. Gutteridge, "Military Elites," pp. 37–38.

Occasional military interventions in Africa have gained impetus from conditions of marked social disparity. Outstanding in this respect was Zanzibar, where a revolutionary militia under "Field Marshal" John Okello overthrew a minority government based upon the Arabs and Shirazis.

STAGNATING ECONOMIC SITUATION

Rising government budgets do not indicate increasing prosperity. The dramatic increase in the expenditures of African states in the late colonial and immediate post-colonial period reflected the strong desire of political leaders to spread social benefits widely and rapidly. Universal primary education, for example, was a goal with obvious attractions—but one involving tremendous costs in relationship to overall resources. An economic squeeze resulted, compounded by shifts in world prices for commodities, such as cocoa, on which many African countries depended for export earnings. The termination of preferential marketing agreements (especially between France and her former dependencies), as well as absolute declines in the quantity of goods exported (as noted in Skurnik's chapter on Dahomey and Upper Volta), further weakened the economic position of African states. A seemingly insatiable demand for consumer goods, manufactured items, and machinery essential for even the rudiments of industrialization heightened the need for foreign exchange. Lacking ready reserves, or a sufficiently growing quantity of exports to cover these needs, African states found themselves in an economic quandary. Few avoided inflation. Deficits were the rule, not the exception.[79] Governments became involved with "suppliers' credits," loans of dubious economic validity, and stopgap schemes for economic betterment.

Yet the demands could not be stilled. The economically privileged parts of contemporary African society—the civil servants, the trade unionists, and above all the politicians—benefited to the greatest extent from government pay hikes. Even so, their inflated aspirations could not always be satisfied. Discontent with salaries in Dahomey and Upper Volta helped ignite the civil disturbances that preceded the coups d'état; the precarious economic position of Ghana before the anti-Nkrumah coup has been documented by Kraus.

79. In Congo-Kinshasa, to take an admittedly extreme example, the central government in 1962 estimated it would receive approximately 4 billion francs, while expenditures totaled more than 19 billion francs. Bustin, "The Congo," p. 138, n. 133.

Revolutions are made by the relatively privileged, not by the downtrodden.[80] The privileged of modern Africa are the educated. They gained most from independence, especially through the expansion of benefits brought by Africanization and salary increases. When the flow of these perquisites was interrupted through financial necessity, however, the discontent of the educated could not be easily contained. And, as the following chapters indicate, efforts to impose economic austerity often failed to accomplish their purpose. To utilize Willame's commentary, the slashes in civil service salaries made necessary for economic stability may have been "irrational," since they merely encouraged discontent.

The economic history of Ghana under Nkrumah provides many lessons in the perils of attempting rapid industrial growth. Economic development meant industrial development through the establishment of purportedly more efficient state firms and state farms, the imposition of exchange controls and import licenses (both temptations for corruption), large-scale government expenditures for development, and a host of similar devices. To finance these costs required higher taxes—an act never popular with any population in the world. Let us look briefly at the 1961 budget. Government revenues derived from cocoa exports were falling, due to changes in world market prices; however, President Nkrumah and his cabinet were strongly behind a program of rapid industrialization, the Second Development Plan. To finance this program, "voluntary contributions" made by cocoa farmers were increased, as 16 per cent of the price paid producers was withheld. Import duties rose sharply. Income taxes were introduced in the upper economic brackets. A compulsory savings scheme required all persons earning over $336 annually to accept 5 per cent of their wages in National Investment Bonds. For the average Ghanaian, with an income of $174 per year, the burden of direct and indirect taxes of $42 per year imposed extraordinary burdens.[81] The result was widespread discontent, a major strike in the port city of Sekondi Takoradi, and threats from President Nkrumah about penalties to be meted out to

80. Brinton's observations on revolutions seem apposite here. In his comparative analysis, he suggests that revolutions occurred in societies "on the whole on the upgrade economically before the revolution came, and the revolutionary movements seem to originate in the discontents of not unprosperous people who feel restraint, cramp, annoyance, rather than downright crushing oppression. Certainly these revolutions are not started by down-and-outers, by starving, miserable people" (*The Anatomy of Revolution*, p. 250).

81. These figures have been drawn from St. Clair Drake and Leslie Alexander Lacy, "Government Versus the Unions: The Sekondi-Takoradi Strike, 1961," in *Politics in Africa*, ed. Carter, pp. 75–78.

strikers. The economic situation of Ghana continued to deteriorate after 1961—the result primarily of extravagant government expenditures. One must not underestimate the value, in the long run, of the enterprises encouraged under the Nkrumah government. However, in the straitened economic conditions of the early 1960's, the utilization of limited resources on projects such as "Job 600"— and the $20 million hotel built for visiting heads of state at the 1965 meeting of the Organization of African Unity—undermined confidence in the Convention People's Party and its leaders. Ghanaians expected a far more comfortable life after independence than the CPP provided. The milking of funds from the cocoa farmers aroused major dislike; corruption further poisoned the atmosphere. I do not wish to claim that economic difficulties, by themselves, brought about the overthrow of Nkrumah. However, the drop in the standard of living, occasioned by inflation, wage restraints, and a chronic shortage of both imported goods and domestically produced foodstuffs, gravely undermined the legitimacy of the Ghanaian government. As General Ankrah announced a few days after the coup d'ètat: "Incomes are falling, the cost of living is rising, unemployment has struck many families . . . We are very close to famine and starvation."[82] Such, most assuredly, was not the economic setting most Ghanaians had envisioned when self-government was won.

CORRUPTION

The puritanical tendencies of military leaders have often been commented upon. Their distaste for ostentation has served as a rationalization—and I suspect as a reason—for intervention. To clear up the affairs of state and restore fiscal integrity and responsibility are themes frequently expounded upon by the leaders of coups d'état. General Ankrah, for example, accused President Nkrumah of bringing Ghana "to the brink of economic disaster by mismanagement, waste and unwise spending."[83] Attempts to reduce government spending, undertaken by all the new military leaders under review in this volume, may be viewed as a response to a belief in widespread corruption. Similarly, the banning of political parties (another typical step following intervention) was partially intended to cut down opportunities for corruption.

82. *Africa Research Bulletin,* III, no. 2 (1966), cols. 467BC.
83. *Ibid.*

Seizure of control by military juntas normally does not occur when officers recognize civilian control of the armed forces as legitimate. For intervention to take place, members of the military must distinguish between the "national interest" of the country and the policies espoused by the government in power. The denial of the legitimacy of the duly constituted civilian government is the first—*and probably the most important*—step in military seizure of power. The "disposition to intervene," as Finer has suggested, is based on a distinction between "national interest" and the practices followed by the government.[84] If the armed forces are to remain in their barracks and not attempt to displace the political leadership, they must accept civilian supremacy. According to Finer's analysis, however, the "low political culture" typical of most African countries encourages military takeovers. In such states, the populations may have little attachment to or comprehension of existing political institutions. Civilian organizations—especially political parties—suffer from numerous weaknesses, especially those stemming from the lack of widespread consensus about the "rules of the game" or even the extent of the political community.[85] Public attachment to political institutions remains shallow. Accordingly, coups d'état may be extremely popular—as appears to have been the case in most of the states examined in this book.

The "disposition to intervene" arises in part from the unique technological and organizational position of the armed forces. The military pride themselves on their efficiency and *esprit de corps.* Their centralization, hierarchy, discipline, and intercommunication —quite apart from their control of modern weaponry—set them apart from most institutions within a given society. Recruits into the armed forces generally receive intensive training, instilling in them a sense of the unique heritage and duty the army embodies. As many analysts of the role of the military in new states have observed, this indoctrination may prove extremely beneficial in implanting "a sense of citizenship and an appreciation of political action."[86] Yet this indoctrination may serve just as well to implant loyalty to the army as an institution set apart from its political

84. S. E. Finer, *The Man on Horseback: The Role of the Military in Politics* (London: Pall Mall, 1962), pp. 23–60.
85. David Easton, "An Approach to the Analysis of Political Systems," *World Politics,* IX, no. 3 (1957), 383–400.
86. Lucian W. Pye, "Armies in the Process of Political Modernization," in *The Role of the Military,* ed. Johnson, p. 83.

system. There may be the emergence, as Willame documents for Congo-Kinshasa, of a strong sense of the honor and duty of the military, including the duty to intervene to correct the misdeeds of politicians. When military seizure of control is rationalized by coup leaders, in the words of a main plotter against Nkrumah, as "necessary to save our country and our people," the "disposition to intervene" is clearly present.[87]

Antagonism between military and civilian leaders was aroused by the factors previously listed—the declining prestige and legitimacy of the dominant party, schism among political leaders, unstable social situations, corruption, and economic adversity. Far more significant, however, was political interference in the internal affairs of the army. There is little the professional soldier less appreciates than meddling in his bailiwick. As a specialist in the use of violence, the army officer considers himself equipped with a competence no civilian could match.[88] Once again, the instance of Ghana is apt. President Nkrumah imposed numerous controls upon the Ghanaian army and police, including first arming then disarming the police, sporadic attempts to associate the armed forces more closely with the Convention People's Party, the assumption by the president of control over army intelligence, the forced retirement of Generals Ankrah and Otu in mid-1965, the use of informers within the ranks, and the development of a Presidential Guard (POGR) under Nkrumah's direct command, lavishly equipped at the expense of the needs of the regular army, and advised by Soviet security specialists. (It should be noted, on the other hand, that this elaborate intelligence network may have staved off earlier plots against Nkrumah.) The announced intent of forming a civilian militia, purportedly to fight against Rhodesia after the unilateral declaration of independence, clearly ran counter to the professional judgment of the officer corps. The Ghana army, in the words of Major Afrifa, "was virtually at the mercy of the politicians who treated it with arrogance and open contempt. . . . Because of bad planning, economic mismanagement and political interference, this army was rendered incapable, ill-equipped, and had virtually been reduced to

---

87. Colonel A. A. Afrifa, *The Ghana Coup, 24th February 1966* (New York: Humanities Press, 1966), p. 37.

88. "What does the military officer do when he is ordered by a statesman to take a measure which is militarily absurd when judged by professional standards and which is strictly within the military realm without any political implications? . . . The presumption of superior professional competence which existed in the case of a military superior giving a questionable order does not exist when the statesman enters military affairs. Here the

a rabble."[89] Heavy-handed efforts at extending political control over the armed services—to make them reliable instruments in Nkrumah's pursuit of development under CPP aegis—only turned the officers against their civilian commander-in-chief, Kwame Nkrumah.

Summary

The preceding analysis has presented the complexities of discovering "causes" for military intervention. To pick out a single factor as The Cause of a coup d'état is nearly impossible. Military intervention has resulted from the combination of many factors. In the coups surveyed in this volume, economic, cultural, and political reasons were intertwined; the declining prestige of political parties and growing consciousness among the military of their power obviously played significant roles. The diminished likelihood of external intervention and the effects of contagion must be added to a sense of grievance within the army as part of the background. When and how coups have occurred differs greatly. There seems to be no uniform circumstances under which military seizure of control has come about—save that the popularity of the government had noticeably declined among the politically relevant strata of the population, and that the army seemed to illustrate an awareness of its unique duty to protect the "national interest" as perceived by its officers. Once they have distinguished between the policies pursued by the civilian government and the policies desired by the armed forces, the "disposition to intervene" exists.

The "disposition to intervene" is thus *prompted* by evidence of political weakness, but it is ultimately *acted upon* as a result of slights upon the armed forces or the belief that the country—and its military—would be better served by direct military control. Such a formulation partially answers the question "Why did intervention occur in country X but not country Y, when both suffered from corruption, political schisms, and the general weakness of the governing party?" Political instability in Africa is endemic and perhaps unavoidable.[90] *Whether the situation is altered by military intervention depends largely upon the attitude of the armed forces, notably the officer corps.* The desire to protect professional auton-

---

existence of professional standards justifies military disobedience." Samuel P. Huntington, *The Soldier and the State: The Theory and Politics of Civil-Military Relations* (New York: Vintage, 1964), p. 77.

89. Afrifa, *The Ghana Coup*, pp. 100, 102.

90. James O'Connell, "The Inevitability of Instability," *Journal of Modern African Studies*, V (1967), 181–91.

omy provides perhaps the most widespread and potent motive for intervention.[91] Hence, the wise African statesman will respect the sphere of professional decision-making, even while seeking to link the armed forces to a shared sense of national purpose; he will seek to foster, over an extended period, a sense of military professionalism, as defined by Huntington.[92] But the blunt fact is that many politicians did not forestall the growth of the "disposition to intervene." We should, therefore, examine the ways in which officers who seize control exercise their new-found powers.

THE AFRICAN MILITARY
AND POLITICAL CHANGE

Once civilian governments have been ousted, the leaders of military intervention seek to justify their seizure of control. To "prove" that installation of an army regime was necessary is a first order of business. But the newly installed rulers must go a step further, and proclaim their goals for the country. Possibly the most important theme sounded by the military leaders has been "national reconstruction." Though wording varies, the import remains identical: Politicians have failed to resolve the fundamental economic, political, and social problems confronting the state; only a transitional period of military rule can purge the political system of its inadequacies. And, of course, only a period of military rule can restore the professional autonomy of the armed forces.

Rhetoric must not be confused with probability of action, however. The promises of renovation and rebuilding may prove hollow. Can a military-based government cope any more successfully with the difficulties which civilian regimes encountered? Are some of these problems susceptible to solution by means congenial to the governing military junta, in ways that escaped the preceding civilian regime? What are the ways in which a military background might contribute to nation-building and to state-building?

To answer these complex questions, we must examine the process of political change—its directions, its causes, its implications. Using a threefold definition of political development ("purposeful political change in certain directions"), I shall consider how military rule could theoretically contribute to political development, then illustrate how the difficulty of building political legitimacy complicates

91. Finer, *The Man on Horseback*, p. 47.
92. Huntington, *The Soldier and the State, passim,* esp. pp. 70–79.

the tasks of military-based governments. The final section of this chapter turns to the prospects for military withdrawal from active political involvement.

Theoretical Connections:
Political Development and Military Rule

The constituent elements of political development have been subject to heated debate among scholars.[93] Three major aspects recur in most definitions:

1. An increased centralization of power in the state, coupled with the weakening of traditional sources of authority.
2. The differentiation and specialization of political institutions.
3. Increased popular participation in politics, and greater identification with the political system as a whole.[94]

CENTRALIZATION OF POWER

As organizations, armed forces are characterized by centralization, discipline, hierarchy, communication, and *esprit de corps*.[95] To function effectively, they require a clearly defined chain of command, with adequate communications to ensure that orders are carried out, and with means of disciplinary control. Effective military organization, almost by definition, demands a high degree of centralization.

93. Apter, *The Politics of Modernization;* James S. Coleman, ed., *Education and Political Development* (Princeton: Princeton University Press, 1965); John H. Kautsky, ed., *Political Change in Underdeveloped Countries: Nationalism and Communism* (New York: Wiley, 1962); Joseph LaPalombara, ed., *Bureaucracy and Political Development* (Princeton: Princeton University Press, 1963); Joseph LaPalombara and Myron Weiner, eds., *Political Parties and Political Development* (Princeton: Princeton University Press, 1966); Marion J. Levy, Jr., *Modernization and the Structure of Societies* (Princeton: Princeton University Press, 1966); A. F. K. Organski, *The Stages of Political Development* (New York: Knopf, 1965); Lucian W. Pye, *Aspects of Political Development* (Boston: Little, Brown, 1965); Lucian W. Pye, ed., *Communications and Political Development* (Princeton: Princeton University Press, 1963); Lucian W. Pye and Sidney Verba, eds., *Political Culture and Political Development* (Princeton: Princeton University Press, 1965); Robert E. Ward and Dankwart A. Rustow, eds., *Political Modernization in Japan and Turkey* (Princeton: Princeton University Press, 1964); Edward Shils, *Political Development in the New States* (The Hague: Mouton, 1962); K. H. Silvert, ed., *Expectant Peoples: Nationalism and Development* (New York: Random House, 1963); Claude E. Welch, Jr., ed., *Political Modernization: A Reader in Comparative Political Change* (Belmont, Calif.: Wadsworth, 1967).
94. Welch, *Political Modernization*, p. 7.
95. Finer, *The Man on Horseback*, p. 7.

Many scholars have equated "modern" government with centralized and highly organized government. Huntington has argued in the following manner:

> Political modernization . . . involves the rationalization of authority: the replacement of a large number of traditional, religious, familial, and ethnic political authorities by a single, secular, national political authority. . . . It means national integration and the centralization or accumulation of power in recognized national law-making institutions.[96]

Centralization of power, it would appear, accords well with patterns of organization familiar to the military. In organizational terms, thus, the armed forces appear to be a paragon of a "modernized" political system.

Such an appearance is deceiving, however, unless one realizes that centralization is effective only if the right of the central entity to rule is widely accepted. The key word in Huntington's definition is authority. Without entering into the disputations that have surrounded this word, authority may be defined as the acceptance of certain individuals or offices as possessing a legitimate right to leadership.[97] The exercise of authority presupposes "a community of opinions, values and beliefs, as well as of interests and needs."[98] Applied to the context of military intervention in politics, the question of authority centers on the act of seizing control: Is this regarded as usurpation, or as a rightful act? In other words, by their ousting of the civilian government, do the armed forces become the legitimate wielders of authority? Can the military develop the "community of opinions, values and beliefs, as well as of interests and needs" that constitutes authority?

For a tentative answer, let us turn briefly to Hobbes's analogy between politics and a game of cards. In both, Hobbes suggested, the participants must agree upon what constitutes legitimate power —what is authority, which cards are trumps. If no card is agreed upon, then clubs—force of arms—become trumps. Where confusion

96. Samuel P. Huntington, "Political Modernization: America vs. Europe" *World Politics,* XVIII (1966), 378.

97. Carl J. Friedrich, ed., *Authority* (Cambridge: Harvard University Press, 1958).

98. Carl J. Friedrich, *Man and His Government* (New York: McGraw-Hill, 1963), p. 244. Dahl defines authority as the influence of a leader clothed with legitimacy; legitimacy is the belief that structures, procedures, acts, decisions, policies, officials, or leaders of government possess "the quality of 'rightness,' propriety, or moral goodness and should be accepted because of this quality" (Robert A. Dahl, *Modern Political Analysis* [Englewood Cliffs: Prentice-Hall, 1963], p. 19).

prevails over the source of authority, the possibility of military intervention increases significantly; should intervention occur, the leaders of the coup will attempt to convert their power into authority.[99] Their prospects for success depend upon developing political institutions with a capacity for effective change—a point to which we shall return.

Weakening of traditional sources of authority does not necessarily result from centralization of government functions. To replace traditional, religious, familial, and ethnic political authorities by a single, secular, national political authority obviously requires time, favorable conditions, communications based upon similar values, and a growth in mutual confidence.[100] In the absence of favorable conditions, attempts at centralization may touch off major countervailing forces. Tensions may be exacerbated; would-be centralization can bring disintegration.

To put the matter simply, the "modern" organizational characteristics of the armed forces—centralization, discipline, hierarchy, communications, and *esprit de corps*—may readily break down under the stresses of military intervention. Clearest evidence for this collapse comes from what may be deemed "second-stage" coups d'état, in which junior officers turn against those senior officers who previously had seized political control. Three such coups in West Africa manifested the collapse of effective military discipline. The Nigerian uprising of July 29, 1966, led by Northerners in an anti-South (especially anti-Ibo) vendetta, resulted in the deaths of Fajuyi (military governor of the Western Region), Ironsi (supreme commander), W. A. Okafor, and Okoro; other target officers, including Gowon, Njokwu, and Ojukwu, barely escaped. An analogous breakdown of the chain of command occurred in the abortive

---

99. Dahl, *Modern Political Analysis,* pp. 31–32.
100. Karl W. Deutsch *et al.,* "Political Community and the North Atlantic Area," in *International Political Communities: An Anthology* (Garden City: Doubleday, 1966), pages 1–91. Deutsch and his associates list nine essential conditions for the creation of an "amalgamated security-community": (1) mutual compatibility of main values; (2) a distinctive way of life; (3) expectations of stronger economic ties or gains; (4) a marked increase in political and administrative capabilities of at least some participating units; (5) superior economic growth on the part of at least some participating units; (6) unbroken links of social communication, both geographically between territories and sociologically between different social strata; (7) a broadening of the political elite; (8) mobility of persons, at least among the politically relevant strata; and (9) a multiplicity of ranges of communication and transaction. The authors note three other conditions which may be essential: (10) a compensation of flows of communications and transactions; (11) a not-too-infrequent interchange of group roles; and (12) considerable mutual predictability of behavior (pp. 37–38).

uprising in Ghana on April 17, 1967. Lieutenants Arthur and Yeboah and a small detachment seized Flagstaff House and slew General Kotoka; General Ankrah fled in time from Osu Castle, which was also taken by the insurgents. The ouster of General Soglo in Dahomey, December 17, 1967, bore witness to pronounced tension between two generations of army officers. Clearly, Soglo had lost the respect of the "young Turks," who showed, by his dismissal, a severe weakening of military discipline. In these cases, the authority of civilians had been broken by previous intervention; extending the same principle, junior officers acted upon their belief, in these "second-stage" coups d'état, that senior officers no longer exercised rightful command. The loss of authority can as readily afflict commanding officers as presidents. The semblance of centralization accordingly must not be mistaken for an effective central, unitary authority that receives unquestioning obedience.

DIFFERENTIATION AND SPECIALIZATION

In a traditional setting the many functions carried out within a society may be "fused," in Riggs's phrase.[101] A modern setting, on the other hand, is characterized by differentiation among these functions and the development of particular structures (institutions) for their accomplishment. Clearly, the armed services epitomize such differentiation of function and specialization of structure. A modern army is not a temporary band of marauders, nor a disorganized militia. Its *raison d'être* is the rational utilization of violence; its organization reflects the application of modern techniques.[102]

The high degree of specialization within the armed services contrasts not only with the "fused" traditional social setting, but also with other "modern" groups. Few political parties in Africa, for example, can match the centralization, discipline, hierarchy, *esprit de corps*, and speed of communications manifested by even the smallest professional armies on that continent. Qualitatively, the organizational strength of the military sets it apart from other groups. Command of weaponry is not the sole distinguishing factor of African armies vis-à-vis civilian organizations; the very organizational characteristics of armies are distinctive.

Many commentators on the role of the military in developing

101. Fred W. Riggs, *Administration in Developing Countries: The Theory of Prismatic Society* (Boston: Houghton Mifflin, 1964), p. 23.
102. Lucian Pye notes, for example, that "modern armies are essentially industrial-type entities" ("Armies in the Process of Political Modernization," p. 76).

countries have focused upon the impact of army training upon both officers and recruits. It stands to reason that extended military service, under certain conditions, will weaken an individual's primary identification with his village, region, and ethnic group. An African soldier must likely learn a new language, serve in areas hundreds of miles from his home, and associate with men of different ethnic backgrounds. He may acquire technological skills unknown to the average villager. Specialized training courses for officers (and particularly those taken outside Africa) further remove them from the traditional setting. Pye argues that

> the good soldier is also to some degree a modernized man. Thus it is that the armies in the newly emergent countries come to play key roles in the process by which traditional ways give way to more Westernized ideas and practices. . . . the acculturative process in the army tends to be focused on acquiring technical skills that are of particular value for economic development. . . . Politically the most significant feature of the process of acculturation within the army is that it usually provides some form of training in citizenship.[103]

Janowitz speaks of the military offering training for technical and administrative skills, as well as basic literacy and citizenship.[104] Lerner and Robinson note that the Turkish army became "a major agency of social change" precisely because it spread among Turkish rural youth "a new sense of [national] identity—and new skills and concepts as well as new machines."[105] But do these observations apply with equal force to tropical Africa?

To answer this question, we must distinguish between the overall organization of the armed services and the effect upon individuals of experience within them. The armies of tropical Africa are small and relatively simple in organization. Contrasted with the large, complex standing armies of many states of Southeast Asia, Latin America, or the Middle East, the armed forces of sub-Saharan Africa currently exist at a completely different order of magnitude. Taking eastern, western, central, and black-ruled southern Africa together, only two states (Congo-Kinshasa and Ethiopia) had armies larger than 19,000 in 1966—and both countries had received

103. *Ibid.*, pp. 80–83.
104. Morris Janowitz, *The Military in the Political Development of New Nations,* reprinted in *Garrisons and Government: Politics and the Military in New States,* ed. Wilson C. McWilliams (San Francisco: Chandler, 1967), p. 74; cf. Pye, "Armies in the Process of Political Modernization," pp. 76 ff.
105. Daniel Lerner and Richard D. Robinson, "Swords and Ploughshares: The Turkish Army as a Modernizing Force," *World Politics,* XIII (1960), pp. 19–44.

extensive external assistance to build these forces. (See Appendix A for detailed figures.) Putting the matter in another way, the ratio of military to civilian population in tropical Africa is about 1 per 1,131—compared to 15 per thousand in the United States, 10 for the United Kingdom and the Middle East, and 5 for the Maghreb states.[106] Further, African armed forces consist almost entirely of infantry. The few specialized units (air forces, paratroop units, navies) are highly dependent on foreign military assistance and training, if not on expatriate personnel.[107] There is accordingly no African counterpart to the complex organization of the Burmese army noted by Pye: an engineer and signal corps, plus special sections on chemical warfare, psychological warfare, and even a historical and archaeological section.[108] Though the rudiments of modern organization exist within African armed forces, they certainly do not exist on the same level as in armed forces elsewhere in the *Tiers Monde*.

Universal military training comparable to Turkey or Israel does not exist in tropical Africa. Although the efforts of the National Service in Tanzania[109] or the Service Civique in the Ivory Coast, for example, should not be underestimated, these undertakings differ in scale. Military service in most African states is voluntary and long-term. The small size of the armies, coupled with length of service, practically precludes substantial impact upon the population as a whole. Few soldiers are demobilized each year. Little transferability or spill-over of skills occurs. Further, one cannot assume that membership in an ethnically heterogeneous army necessarily fosters a "national" outlook. Few African armies are representative, in their membership, of major ethnic groups. The Kamba and Kalenjin of Kenya, though numbering respectively 9.5 and 11 per cent of the population, nevertheless each furnished 34 per cent of the army in 1961;[110] the Kikuyu, despite their dominance in the civil service and political realm, were barred by British decision from serving in the military during the Emergency, and furnished an insignificant fraction of the men in the ranks. It is difficult to

106. Kenneth W. Grundy, "On Machiavelli and the Mercenaries," *Journal of Modern African Studies,* VI (1968), p. 299.
107. *Ibid.*
108. Pye, "Armies in the Process of Political Modernization," p. 106.
109. Henry Bienen, *Tanzania: Party Transformation and Economic Development* (Princeton: Princeton University Press, 1967), pp. 375–77.
110. Population percentages calculated from figures given in Carl G. Rosberg, Jr., and John Nottingham, *The Myth of Mau Mau: Nationalism in Kenya* (New York: Praeger, for the Hoover Institution on War, Revolution and Peace, 1966), pp. 2–6; army percentages from Gutteridge, *Military Institutions and Power,* p. 80.

envisage the armed services serving to diminish ethnic distinctions with such skewed recruitment; the military may implicitly appear to represent the interests of one or a few tribes, rather than the state as a whole.

Hence, the argument that specialties and "national" outlooks can readily be carried over from the armed forces to the entire population cannot be convincingly substantiated in the African context. Organizational complexity does not as yet characterize most African armies—and "modern" skills are not necessarily diffused from the military to the civilian realm.

POPULAR PARTICIPATION AND IDENTIFICATION

The extent of political participation can readily be altered by military regimes; the degree of popular identification with the political system is not susceptible to easy manipulation.

In the creation of political systems, perhaps the most important task is that of fostering popular identification. People who physically are members of a given political system should come to feel psychologically members of that system.[111] This identification may be enhanced by greater opportunities for symbolic participation. Officers in control accordingly may turn to referenda (particularly on new constitutions) as an innocuous means of transforming participation into identification. However, enhanced opportunities for participation may not lead to a "national" type of identification. Instead it may lead to

> an obsessive concern with the relation of one's tribe, region, sect, or whatever to a center of power that, while growing rapidly more active, is not easily either insulated from the web of primordial attachments, as was the remote colonial regime, or assimilated to them as are the workaday authority systems of the "little community." Thus, it is the very process of the formation of a sovereign civil state that, among other things, stimulates sentiments of parochialism, communalism, racialism, and so on, because it introduces into society a valuable new prize over which to fight and a frightening new force with which to contend.[112]

Popular identification with the political system as a whole cannot be legislated into existence. "Some realms of life cannot be directly affected in an enduring way through the machinery of govern-

111. Sidney Verba, "Comparative Political Culture," in *Political Culture and Political Development*, ed. Pye and Verba, p. 529.
112. Clifford Geertz, "The Integrative Revolution: Primordial Sentiments and Civil Politics in the New States," in Welch, *Political Modernization*, p. 177.

ment."[113] To be certain, the overthrow of an unpopular civilian dictator may bring great initial credit to the perpetrators of military intervention; installation of a genuinely popular army member as head of state may similarly result in public approbation. The vagaries of popular opinion, however, and the threat of ethnically based parochialism make widespread popular identification with the new regime an unlikely direct product of military intervention. The fostering of legitimacy requires far more than a displacement of political personnel by officers; it requires a difficult, long-range effort.

SUMMARY

Let us recapitulate the three major aspects of political development. As organizations, the armed forces of African states illustrate only a limited degree of centralized authority and functional specialization. Seizure of control by the military may result from confusion over the source of authority within the state. There is no guarantee that the new leaders resulting from a coup d'état will be viewed by the people as exercising *legitimate* authority—a possibility that, in Hobbes's terms, opens the way for further disputes and use of force. The growth of identification with the political system (surely a key part of legitimacy) may well depend on factors largely outside the area of direct governmental control. There is no guarantee that military training will affect, in the short run, the perceptions and behavior of most inhabitants of the state concerned. Political development requires a combination of skillful leadership, fortuitous circumstances, national unity, and political capacity—a combination which is certainly not characteristic of most of contemporary Africa. Only by enhancing the legitimacy of governing institutions and their capacity can effective political development come about.

Political Development and Institutional Capacities

To examine political change adequately, we must remain continually aware of the capacity of political institutions to satisfy demands.[114] To measure this capacity is an ambitious task. Ca-

113. Morroe Berger, *The Military Elite and Social Change: Egypt since Napoleon,* reprinted in *Garrisons and Government,* ed. McWilliams, p. 225.
114. I am arguing here along lines analogous to Professor Spiro's concern with the "development of politics," namely that "expansion of the capacity of the political system to process a heavier volume of problems, to discuss a greater range of issues, to forge new goals as old ones are being approached, and

pacity depends upon numerous interrelated variables, the combination of which obviously alters over time in all states. At the risk of oversimplification, however, let us consider capacity in terms of (1) "legitimate organizational strength," and (2) sufficient resources to carry out tasks.[115] The key factor is authority—an admittedly nebulous but central term in the analysis of the capacity of political institutions.

Political institutions exercise authority by exercising control that is seen as rightful, correct, or legitimate. Authority implies a recognition of common purposes, and a belief in the inherent rightness of leadership of some sort. Most citizens must be willing to bridle private or personal impulses for the sake of general social objectives. Rapoport comments cogently that this organizational strength characterizes both civilian and military life: recognition of a "rule of law" in the civilian realm and discipline in the army both channel individual desires toward a common good.[116]

In many states, both Western and non-Western, nationalism provided cohesiveness and purpose. A sense of unity was enhanced by historical ties, defence against an external enemy, commonality of tradition, language and territory, and the "intimate interconnections"[117] of state and nation. A sense of community emerged: This is "our" state; we are its people; those are "our" leaders. Governments were recognized as legitimate; their authority rested not upon coercion and force of arms but upon expectations of compliance and obedience.

It has frequently been stressed that African states are riven with differences arising from conflicting "primordial sentiments." As the subtitle of a recent book inquired, should Nigeria be considered in terms of tribes, people, or race? The fact is often expressed in the antinomy of "tribalism" and "nationalism"—admittedly inadequate and possibly misleading terms to characterize complex phenomena. More appropriately, one should say that ethnic loyalties

---

to make more people conscious of the possibilities of change-through-politics" (Herbert J. Spiro, "The Military in Sub-Saharan Africa" in *Garrisons and Government*, ed. McWilliams, p. 271).

115. Huntington, in his provocative critique of theories of political development, focuses upon institutional capacities in terms of scope of support and level of institutionalization, the latter being measured by the adaptability, complexity, autonomy, and coherence of its organizations and procedures. Samuel P. Huntington, "Political Development and Political Decay," *World Politics*, XVII (1965), pp. 386–430; reprinted in Welch, *Political Modernization*, pp. 207–45.

116. David C. Rapoport, "A Comparative Theory of Military and Political Types," in *Changing Patterns of Military Politics*, ed. Huntington, p. 79.

117. Emerson, *From Empire to Nation*, p. 104.

for most Africans are not yet fully complemented by identification with the country as a whole: Aizo, Fon, or Bariba rather than Dahomey; Bamileke, Bassa, or Bulu rather than Cameroon. Recognizing the limited extent of "national" loyalties, or, in somewhat different terms, the low level of national political integration, African political leaders have often viewed the state, or a dominant party, as the "architect" of the nation.[118] However, between concept and implementation, theory often goes astray. The inefficiency of the government and the decay of the dominant party into little more than a machine for distributing spoils reduce the necessary element of institutional strength.[119] Social mobilization in ethnically heterogeneous African states often reinforces particularistic tendencies.[120] Nigeria has been established—but not Nigerians. Accordingly, to build political authority upon the shallow foundations of Nigerian, Dahomean, or any other "nationalism" in Africa runs serious risks. Overly hasty efforts at centralization of government control may bring disintegration.

Obviously, it would be preposterous to assert that nationalism as a factor underlying political authority in African states cannot be enhanced. The major question, rather, is whether African governments *under military auspices* will have greater likelihood than their civilian predecessors in developing nationalism as a basic support for political authority.

The answer, simply, is No. The copious literature on integration generally argues that nation-building requires extended time and favorable conditions.[121] As a process, nation-building cannot be unduly hurried. Ethnic and cultural divisions appear remarkably durable, be they in Belgium or in Congo-Kinshasa, in the United States or in Nigeria. Since integration ultimately may depend more upon time than upon short-term government policies, hasty admin-

---

118. Léopold Sédar Senghor, *Nation et voie africaine du socialisme* (Paris: Présence Africaine, 1960), p. 24.

119. Austin notes, for example, that the CPP turned into a massive propaganda machine; the privileges of a large number of beneficiaries depended on its survival. Dennis Austin, *Politics in Ghana 1946–60*, p. 418.

120. Karl W. Deutsch, "Social Mobilization and Political Development," *American Political Science Review*, LV (1961), 493–514; Geertz, "The Integrative Revolution," pp. 167–87.

121. Claude Ake, *A Theory of Political Integration* (Homewood, Ill.: Dorsey, 1967); Karl W. Deutsch, *Nationalism and Social Communication: An Inquiry into the Foundations of Nationality*, 2d ed. (Cambridge: M.I.T. Press, 1966); Geertz, "The Integrative Revolution"; Immanuel Wallerstein, "Ethnicity and National Integration in West Africa," *Cahiers d'études africaines*, III (1960), 129–39; W. Howard Wriggins, "Impediments to Unity in New Nations: The Case of Ceylon," *American Political Science Review*, LV (1961), 313–20.

istrative actions may impede nation-building. The short-lived Ironsi regime offers such evidence. Under pressure from younger officers and intellectuals, in large measure Ibos, General Ironsi decreed the abolition of the four regions, destroying the federal system in order to

> remove the last vestiges of the intense regionalism of the recent past and to produce that cohesion in the governmental structure which is so necessary in achieving and maintaining the paramount objective of the National Military Government and, indeed, of every true Nigerian, namely, national unity.[122]

The higher ranks of the civil service were joined into a national public service, an act that aroused tremendous Northern antagonism. Within two days, mobs in the North started to attack Ibos, whose slaughter and flight testified to an overly hasty effort at centralization. "National unity" in Nigeria had yet to supersede tribally based antagonisms—and the vendetta launched in the North enhanced the Ibo solidarity built through modernization.[123]

Granted that the ethnic divisions of African states impede the growth of political legitimacy based upon nationalism, are there other bases on which military-dominated governments might seek to achieve legitimacy? The jubilation that accompanied the overthrow of Nkrumah and other unpopular politicians would appear to indicate widespread approbation for various coups. Harlley, Kotoka, and their cohorts profited from "popular exhaustion and tacit or active support for the dismantling of sclerosed political institutions."[124] By removing venal and autocratic rulers—whether by incarceration, assassination, or exile—the military rulers emphasized the break with the past. Political parties were banned, on the basis of the corruption and authoritarianism of their previous leaders. One may ask, however, whether this distaste for politicians and support for the military will persist for more than a few months.

No groups of rulers can long base their claims for legitimacy on acrimony and memory of previous injustices. If the new military governors of African countries intend to remain in power for an extended period they must seek to build the capacity of governing institutions, in terms both of legitimate organizational strength and skillful use of resources. There are three interlocking ways that

122. *Africa Research Bulletin*, III, no. 5 (1966), cols. 534BC.
123. Paul Anber (pseud.), "Modernization and Political Disintegration: Nigeria and the Ibos," *Journal of Modern African Studies*, V, no. 2 (1967), 163–79.
124. Roger Murray, "Militarism in Africa," *New Left Review*, no. 38 (1966), p. 57.

African military rulers might seek to achieve legitimacy: (1) gain or create social and political basis of support; (2) avoid recourse to excessive use of force; (3) build effectiveness over an extended period.

Given the contemporary characteristics of both African states and their military establishments, none of these means will likely bring about legitimacy. "Prolonged effectiveness over a number of generations," Lipset notes, "may give legitimacy to a political system. In the modern world, such effectiveness means, primarily, constant economic development."[125] This pathway to legitimacy is not feasible for governing African juntas. Both the uncertainty of economic development in Africa and the timespan emphasized by Lipset imply that short-run effectiveness will not be translated into widespread support for military governments.

The tendency to resort to violence exists in all military-dominated governments.[126] After all, how else did the military gain control? Devised to use force in the most efficient manner, armies may more readily turn to violence than to palaver, to repression rather than to compromise. Bargaining and compromise are not familiar skills to military leaders. In scorning politicians, they may scorn the techniques well-known to politicians, such as the artful ethnic balance. Military life does not necessarily provide relevant, simple formulas for a viable political system; army leaders must learn politics through experience.[127] If they cannot learn these skills, they run the risk of popular disaffection that, communicated to ambitious, restless junior officers, may lead to "second-stage" coups or to abrupt withdrawal from political life. For instance, the gyrations of the Dahomean armed forces in mid-1968 testified to the political innocence of most officers, particularly the "Young Turks" grouped around Kouandété. Faced with unimpeachable evidence of the failure of their electoral schemes, the military abruptly withdrew, as shown by Skurnik in Chapter 2.

The most feasible means of building legitimacy rests in careful cultivation of a strong basis of popular support. Military rulers, like their civilian predecessors, must construct a coalition of supporting groups, create political parties with widespread appeal, develop strength among significant parts of the population. Many coup

125. Seymour Martin Lipset, *Political Man: The Social Bases of Politics* (Garden City: Doubleday, 1963), p. 70.

126. H. Daalder, *The Role of the Military in the Emerging Countries* (The Hague: Mouton, 1962), quoted in *Garrisons and Government,* ed. McWilliams, p. 26.

127. Morris Janowitz, *The Military in the Political Development of New Nations: An Essay in Comparative Analysis* (Chicago: University of Chicago Press, 1964), pp. 104–5.

leaders have sought legitimacy by naming civilian advisory councils, often in response to mounting discontent with policies imposed by the military governments. In Ghana, for example, a civilian "political committee" was named on June 30, 1966, four months after Nkrumah's ouster, when austerity policies were causing increasing unrest. The Gowon regime in Nigeria created a civilian advisory council in June, 1967; its creation was intended to smooth the creation of twelve states within a shifting federal framework.

The role of civilian councils is significant only if they are seen as harbingers of a civilian-controlled government. In Dahomey the civilian Committee for National Renovation was dissolved in June, 1967, when its members, in the eyes of Soglo, seemed more concerned with revivification of regional splits and divisive political tendencies than with national unity. In Ghana and Nigeria a great deal of pressure was necessary to bring civilians into the cabinet, and this sharing of power resulted from emergency conditions (devaluation of the cedi; Biafran secession and the creation of new states) that necessitated enhanced support. Civilian advisory councils should not be regarded as nuclei of future governments, but as tactical allies of the military rulers, essential for increasing their authority.

Of necessity, army-dominated African governments have worked closely with civil servants.[128] It is tempting to assert that the similar technocratic orientation and organizational hierarchy of army officers and civil servants bring both groups into natural alliance. Their concern with state-building—with rational use of resources, with complex bureaucratic surveillance, with governmental efficiency more than effectiveness—testifies to an affinity of outlook. Much of this affinity, however, arises from distrust of politicians. To paint the picture in starkest terms, politicians concern themselves primarily with nation-building (popular support and identification), members of the civil service and the armed forces with state-building (efficient utilization of resources). The Ironsi government focused upon civil service unification, to its detriment, ignoring the intense ethnic pressures against this move;

128. Chief Awolowo has expressed this affinity strongly. To quote his recent *Thoughts on Nigerian Constitution:* "It has been said that governments may come, and governments may go, but the Civil Service remains for ever. It is a most merciful thing indeed that the Civil Service remains largely unaffected by the vicissitudes of politics. What a tragedy, for instance, it would have been if the recent reverses in the fortunes of politicians had hit the civil servants more or less equally! The smooth take-over by the army would have been impossible. There would have been a chaotic collapse of public administration, with harsh and injurious effects on the welfare of people" (Obafemi Awolowo, *Thoughts on Nigerian Constitution* [Ibadan: Oxford University Press, 1966], p. 73).

the Kouandété regime was so preoccupied with speed and efficiency that it failed to comprehend the significance of group participation in decision-making. Had the respective leaders given heed to politically conscious advisers, their period of rule might have ended less abruptly.

Military leaders have other options. Rather than draw upon the ranks of former politicians and highly placed civil servants, they can create new political parties under their direct auspices to foster legitimacy. In other words, instead of the support given to politicians participating in an elite coalition, army officers may seek their own foundations of popular support. General Mobutu, for example, announced in April, 1967, his intention of creating and leading the "Mouvement populaire de la Révolution," intended to organize the popular masses for education, instruction, and training. But the prospects for the rapid creation of a strong party structure are negligible. In the face of widespread apathy, attempts to build legitimacy through persuasion, party activity, and economic development involve huge expenditures of effort without significant short-run impact. The series of failures to create a broadly based political movement in the United Arab Republic, despite intensive efforts by President Nasser, clearly indicates the limitations on building legitimacy through party auspices.[129]

To rule effectively, having once achieved power, military leaders must develop political organizations of civilian types, or work out viable relations with civilian political groups.[130] There are no other paths toward political development. Military governments will confront the same problems of ethnicity and economic stagnation that confronted civilian governments. The centralized authority and functional specialization of armies may promote intervention, but they do not enhance the possibilities for effective governance based upon legitimate governmental strength. The military rulers of Africa often lack bargaining skills. Their impatience with politicians—their "politics of wanting to be above politics"—leads them to distrust the slow, difficult process of coalition-building.[131] Having banned political parties, and likely lacking the abilities to build parties afresh, the African military may well not promote political development. They cannot build legitimate political institutions through the use of force; they cannot transplant their organizational style to the civilian realm; they are not equipped to bring

129. P. J. Vatikiotis, *The Egyptian Army in Politics: Pattern for New Nations?* (Bloomington: Indiana University Press, 1961).
130. Janowitz, *The Military in the Political Development of New Nations,* p. 1.
131. *Ibid.,* p. 65

stability, modernization, or political participation; and they lack sufficient flexibility and innovativeness to govern effectively.[132] Indeed, once members of the armed services recognize their inherent limitations in governing, the prospects for a return to civilian rule brighten.

AN END TO MILITARY INVOLVEMENT IN POLITICS?

It is notoriously easier for the armed forces to seize control than to give it up. Having taken the reigns of power in order to bring certain changes—an end to political meddling in military affairs; a government freed from corruption; an opportunity for wider political choice—the ruling officers may be reluctant to return to the barracks without strong assurance the civilian regime will not revert to its previous ways. Such assurances can never be absolute. Hence, the return to the barracks may be deferred, again and again, pending conviction on the part of the governing military group that their reforms will not be undone. Having tasted the power, excitement, and rewards of political life, officers may be personally reluctant to step aside. Second thoughts and procrastination about handing over to civilians thus become common phenomena in the history of military-dominated governments. Withdrawal often does not occur through a simple desire to restore civilian rule, but through a transformation of the military itself.

Military withdrawal from political involvement, in simplest terms, comes about in two ways. First, governance leads to division within the armed forces. Torn between a professional ethic that respects civilian supremacy and a desire to protect professional autonomy by forestalling political interference, officers may fall into two camps, those who would carry forth the duties of the armed services by eschewing direct political involvement, and those who would retain military autonomy by precluding significant civilian control. As this split is resolved, so is the extent of military involvement in politics. When the advocates of withdrawal gain the upper hand, withdrawal may occur. Second, over time, a military-dominated government may so transform itself as to become practically indistinguishable from a civilian regime. Officers shed their uniforms for business suits; they participate with gusto in electoral campaigns; they build political parties and a foundation for legitimate political authority. Generals become presidents through subtle alchemy—as Mustafa Kemal became President Kemal Ataturk

132. Spiro, "The Military in Sub-Saharan Africa," p. 266.

("Father of the Turks").[133] Internal divisions and subtle transformation: such are the two main ways in which the armed services
become disengaged from active, direct political involvement. Let us
examine both in detail.

Voluntary Withdrawal: Two Examples

Two tropical African states—Dahomey and Sierra Leone—restored civilian rule in 1968 after an interlude of military rule. In
both instances, withdrawal occurred after young officers and men in
the ranks overthrew their superiors, who earlier had seized control
from civilians.

If military regimes set themselves up as doctors of the body
politic, they risk being infected by the ills from which the previous
civilian governments suffered; or, should the patient fail to improve,
the physician may be discharged. There is thus a dual danger. On
the one hand, the military regimes may fall prey to corruption,
unwarranted use of force, electoral or ethnic manipulation, or the
denial of political rights—all weaknesses that helped justify (or, at
least, rationalize) the toppling of the civilian government. To avoid
such "infection" the army may prefer withdrawal. On the other
hand, the popular welcome that may have accompanied the military
takeover may soon be exhausted. The medicine prescribed for the
cure may well prove unpalatable. Accordingly, the pro-withdrawal
school may persuade their colleagues of the need to retreat. Let us
illustrate these points by briefly examining Dahomey and Sierra
Leone.

In Dahomey, as Skurnik illustrates later in this volume, economic
vicissitudes. trade union unrest, and the bitter heritage of strong
regional tensions exacerbated by excessive centralization led to a
brief intervention late in 1963 by Colonel Soglo, who returned power
to civilians after general elections in January, 1964. In late 1965,
Soglo intervened twice, first transferring power from the premier to
the speaker of the National Assembly, then assuming full military
control. The economic crisis continued unresolved, and tensions in-

---

133. Among many studies of the impact of Ataturk and the Turkish
military upon political change, the following are most useful: Kemal H.
Karpat, *Turkey's Politics: The Transition to a Multi-Party System* (Prince-
ton: Princeton University Press, 1959); Daniel Lerner and Richard D.
Robinson, "Swords and Ploughshares: The Turkish Army as a Modernizing
Force"; Richard D. Robinson, *The First Turkish Republic: A Case Study in
National Development* (Cambridge: Harvard University Press, 1963); Dank-
wart A. Rustow, "The Army and the Founding of the Turkish Republic,"
World Politics, XI (1959), pp. 513–52; and Dankwart A. Rustow, "The
Military," in *Political Modernization in Japan and Turkey,* ed. Ward and
Rustow, pp. 352–88.

creased within the armed forces. On December 16, 1967, Soglo was himself ousted by a group of young officers who promised to hold general elections within six months and return the country to civilian rule. The young officers complained that Soglo had failed to achieve the basic objectives:

> to put a stop to absurd quarrels between rivals by appeasing the people and restoring respect for the sense of duty which many Dahomean citizens were beginning to ignore; to remedy the economic and financial ills from which the country was suffering and to reconcile the children of Dahomey and enable them to reassume control of the management of their country's affairs in order, harmony and newly restored fraternity.

These hopes had not been fulfilled. "The very people who we had promised to defend and protect now hate and despise us." As Radio Cotonou broadcast:

> This is why we, the young cadres of the army, aware that the role of the whole army was in question; considering that our seniors in the army had disappointed the people and betrayed the national army; aware that it is the duty of us, the young army cadres, to restore the situation as well as the authority and dignity of the nation; decided in the higher interests of the nation to dissolve the government of General Soglo and the military committees of vigilance, to create a revolutionary military committee, to form within 24 hours a provisional government responsible for day-to-day state affairs, and to create a constitutional committee.[134]

Colonel Alley declared that elections would be held within six months, "no matter what the consequences." A draft constitution providing for a modified presidential regime was approved by Dahomean citizens on March 31, 1968. The early months of 1968 witnessed intense disputes among army leaders. Splits centered upon distaste, pure and simple, for governing; upon different outlooks concerning the role of prominent ex-politicians; upon policies toward strike-prone trade unions; and upon personal animosities magnified by prevailing circumstances. A disastrous presidential election May 5, in which only 27 per cent of the registered voters participated, touched off even greater internal quarrels. Confronted with union intransigence and with disagreement about future actions and the nature of civilian leadership, a pro-withdrawal faction favoring a relatively neutral civilian as head of the government carried the argument. On August 1, 1968, two weeks after the inauguration of appointed President Emile Zinsou, the military

---

134. *Africa Research Bulletin,* IV, no. 12 (1967), col. 927C.

government of Dahomey was dissolved. Younger officers' impatience had led them to intervene and promise civilian rule—but their bungling of the transition made the shift abrupt and graceless.

The first coup in Sierra Leone grew out of the results of "democracy." After a bitterly contested election in May, 1967, the opposition African Peoples Congress (APC) apparently ousted the ruling Sierra Leone People's Party (SLPP). When the leader of the APC, Siaka Stevens, had been sworn in as prime minister, however, Brigadier David Lansana intervened; in turn, he was supplanted within two days by a National Reformation Council (NRC) composed of young officers drawn from all ethnic groups. Subsequently, the Dove-Edwin report and government white paper noted,

> The whole of the Government's arrangements for the 1967 election was rigged and corrupt. . . . they were determined to use all means fair or foul to win and remain in office and if all failed to get Brigadier Lansana to take over. . . . [delay in reporting election results] could have developed into a tribal war if the National Reformation Council had not stepped in on March 23rd, 1967.[135]

Publication of the Dove-Edwin report in December, 1967, provided strong incentive for the Sierra Leone military to withdraw. The commission of inquiry criticized the many ways in which the SLPP had attempted to ensure a majority, such as having returning officers declare APC nomination papers invalid and raising the required deposit by 150 per cent. It declared that the APC won the election "on their own merit."[136] In its commentary on the report, the NRC announced the appointment of a Civilian Rule Committee, whose terms of reference were explicit:

> (a) The National Reformation Council has decided to hand over the Government of Sierra Leone to a civilian government.
> (b) The Civilian Rule Committee has been invited to deliberate and advise on the following:
> (i) The necessity for a fresh General Election;
> (ii) If (i) above is in the negative, the method of forming a National Government; if (i) above is in the affirmative, the stages in which the handover should be effected;
> (iii) Any other action which the Civilian Rule Committee considers necessary to effect a peaceful handover.[137]

These terms of reference foundered, however, on two unforeseen factors: growing unwillingness among members of the National

135. *Ibid.,* col. 929B.
136. *Ibid.,* V, no. 1 (1968), col. 950A.
137. *Ibid.,* IV, no. 12 (1967), col. 929C.

Reformation Council to step aside, and growing distaste for the NRC among the ranks. In what most appropriately is described as a mutiny with political repercussions, an Anti-Corruption Revolutionary Movement led by warrant officers imprisoned all but two of the commissioned officers of the Sierra Leone army and almost all police officers on April 17 and 18, 1968. Disgruntled with low pay and the apparent self-serving attitudes of the NRC, the rebellious soldiers announced that the thirteen month interlude of army and police rule would end and civilian supremacy would return. As a spokesman for the Anti-Corruption Revolutionary Movement commented:

> Little did we realize that the people we had chosen [in March, 1967] to direct our nation's affairs were more corrupt and selfish than the ousted civilian regime.
> It has since become absolutely clear that most of the so-called National Reformation Council members only wanted to benefit their selfish ends; the rank and file of the army and police have been ignored. All that was practised in both the army and the police were nepotism and blatant victimization.
> Fellow Sierra Leoneans, we cannot continue any longer under such adverse conditions. The so-called National Reformation Council members have greatly mismanaged the nation's affairs. They have failed to fulfill their boastful promise to both civilians and members of the armed forces. And above all, they want to remain in office indefinitely.
> Soldiers and police have no business in the running of this country. Our immediate aim is to return to civilian rule.[138]

A National Interim Council was quickly formed by army and police officers. Within ten days, Siaka Stevens was sworn in as prime minister. Sierra Leone returned to civilian rule still confronting ethnic tensions and economic vicissitudes that the NRC could not overcome. For months thereafter, army and police officers continued to languish in the Pademba Road prison.

Three variables eased military withdrawal from active political roles in Dahomey and Sierra Leone. First, the commanding officers were firm in their resolve to step aside. The Revolutionary Military Committee (Dahomey) and the National Interim Council (Sierra Leone) did not envisage indefinite periods of rule, but a time for quick surgery of economic, social and political problems under military rule and a time for convalescence under civilian auspices. They came to political power to remove themselves from it.

The second variable was a group of forceful, articulate civilians, who regularly reminded the ruling juntas of their rhetoric of withdrawal. In Dahomey, trade unionists and young intellectuals

138. *Ibid.,* V, no. 4 (1968), col. 1035C.

formed this group; in Sierra Leone, supporters of Siaka Stevens, plus members of the civil service and universities, did not look upon extended military rule with favor. The military's willingness to surrender control thus must be complemented by civilian desire to regain political power. The ease with which an APC-SLPP coalition government was installed under Siaka Stevens contrasts with the hasty scramble to inaugurate Zinsou and bar the "big three" from political prominence.

The third and most significant factor in withdrawal was the belief that military unity and effectiveness would be further impaired by remaining in control. The "professional" interests of the commanding officers—the cohesion, morale, and effectiveness of the army—conflicted with the demands inherent in political dominance. The Kouandété government was torn apart by its unavoidable involvement in disputes about the "big three." In Sierra Leone, members of the NRC neglected the morale of the ranks. Evidence of the distractions of politics, combined with their inexperience in leadership, certainly prompted the Anti-Corruption Revolutionary Movement briefly to take control, in order to withdraw.

Conscious Civilianization

To chronicle the transformation of a military-dominated government into a civilian-controlled government would take us outside Africa. As noted earlier in this chapter, intervention in the political life of African states has occurred relatively recently, for the history of these countries as independent entities covers, in most cases, scarcely a decade. Conscious civilianization, contrasted with voluntary withdrawal, takes place over an extended period of time. Although recent African history offers no instances of this subtle shift to "civilian" control, in which generals become presidents and base their authority upon public support rather than force of arms, the modalities of such a change must be examined.

The starting point for this process is the establishment of close ties between civilians and military leaders following the seizure of control. The extent of civilian participation in a military-dominated government admits of many degrees. The spectrum ranges from complete army control, in which all key governmental posts are occupied by officers, to behind-the-scenes manipulation, in which figurehead politicians carry out their activities under military surveillance. Most African states currently under military control fall near the center of this spectrum. Officers must make alliances with civilians to exercise and maintain control. When an army as miniscule as that of Sierra Leone (only 0.06 per cent of the total population) takes power, it can fill only a few top administrative posts with officers, without risking diluting its energies or neglecting army command functions. The ruling junta must exercise its would-be power through civilians, whether civil servants, traditional chiefs, or some other group. Alliances are both natural and necessary.

Civil servants and officers may share an instrumental outlook, a belief that society can be altered by application of certain administrative techniques—a concern, as noted previously, with "state-building." The organizational structure of the civil service accords with the organizational structure of the armed forces: both are bureaucracies, or "rational-legal authorities" in Weber's phrase. Similarity of outlook thus makes alliance easy. A close working relationship with the civil service has the further advantage, for the officers, of bringing in a relatively uncorrupt group long over-shadowed by politicians. Government employees threatened by party machinations have, in many African states, furnished strong support to newly installed military juntas. What more suitable pact than between groups that chafed under the inept control of venal politicians?

At a different level, the ruling officers may ally themselves with traditional chiefs, particularly in local governance. The chiefs represent a mixed blessing, for the support they command in rural areas must be weighed against the antipathy they arouse in some urban areas. However, for reasons that Feit has examined, military rulers may find it tactically appropriate to link themselves with the chiefs, in the process re-establishing the "administrative-traditional" framework that characterized the colonial period.[139]

Lacking from this constellation of forces, however, are highly significant social groups, notably trade unionists. As the turbulent history of Dahomey illustrates, such groups must not be disregarded in the civilianization of the regime. Without meaningful participation, they may turn to active opposition. It is simple for officers to seize control, difficult to withdraw. The success of civilianization depends upon the attitude of the armed forces, and often the result is that noted by Finer:

> Those armed forces that have tried to disengage from politics have had to hasten back as soon as their quondam political enemies came within sight of regaining power, while those that have elected to remain and rule have been ejected only by popular revolt, or by further military revolts of their own malcontents. In most cases the military that have intervened in politics are in a dilemma: whether their rule be indirect or whether it be direct,

139. Edward Feit, "Military Coups and Political Development: Some Lessons from Ghana and Nigeria," *World Politics*, XX (1968), 179–93.

they cannot withdraw from rulership nor can they fully legitimize it. They can neither stay nor go.[140]

If they are to go, members of the military must distinguish between the areas of civilian supremacy and professional autonomy. Members of the ruling military junta may divest themselves of their soldierly regalia and demeanor, to become full-fledged civilians. They may endeavor to set themselves in the Kemalist model: military heroes who decide to immerse themselves fully in the civilian realm, renouncing direct involvement in the armed forces. Ataturk carried out such a change—his was a "determination to civilianize the Turkish Republic that cut wide and deep"[141] but few of his would-be successors have proven successful.

Probably the closest imitator of Ataturk's actions in tropical Africa now is General Joseph Mobutu. Since seizing control in November, 1965, Mobutu has engaged in a subtle effort to draw the nationalist, Lumumbist mantle to himself. He has announced his intention of leading a "revolutionary" mass political movement. A draft constitution approved in June, 1967, stipulated parliamentary elections in 1968 and a presidential election at the end of 1970. Several observers have pointed out that timing of this election would allow Mobutu to reach the ripe age of 40, the minimum age for the president prescribed by the constitution. Mobutu thus appears to be attempting to make a personal transition from military hero to charismatic president—a tortuous transition that cannot, in and of itself, protect Congo-Kinshasa from dissension within the ranks, popular discontent, and the other difficulties officers face in confronting political responsibilities.

The main obstacle to conscious civilianization—like the major barrier to voluntary withdrawal—lies in tensions and rivalries internal to the armed forces. Coup begets counter-coup. The meteoric rise of a lieutenant colonel to unchallenged military and political power does not pass unnoticed. Those who seize control risk arousing jealousies, thereby becoming victims of the whirlwind they unleashed. Legitimacy once broken, cannot readily be restored. Since it is likely that the agents overthrowing a military dominated regime will themselves belong to the armed forces, the possibility of a dreary round of coups and counter-coups cannot be discounted. Coups may become the major mechanism for change of political personnel—after all, this practice is hardly unusual in the annals of history.

Civilian replacement of military-dominated governments thus

---

140. Finer, *The Man on Horseback*, p. 243.
141. Lerner and Robinson, "Swords and Ploughshares," p. 19.

depends ultimately upon the attitudes of influential members of the armed services. The military must choose to go, or they must choose to stay, with its attendant risks. They are the ultimate arbiters of the nature and pace of a return to civilian rule.

PATHS OF FUTURE CHANGE

There are certain advantages political leaders in Africa may use to their benefit in staving off military intervention, even where the scope for such intervention may be very great.[142] First, the current international climate of opinion, of which heads of state in Africa (and, hopefully, their chiefs of staff!) are acutely aware, condemns naked seizures of power and denial of democratic processes. In this respect, the international setting clearly differs from the dawn of independence in Latin America, when local *caudillos* could indulge in a *golpe de estado, cuartelazo,* and other forms of coup d'état without regard to external factors. To be "modern" is to respect civilian, democratic rule—and African leaders desperately wish their states to be "modern."

At this point in time, African armies are proportionately the smallest in the world. The peaceful assumption of independence by African countries, unlike the armed seizure of independence that characterized Latin America, did not enshrine the military as the cornerstone of significant political change. Would-be parallels drawn from Latin America or the Middle East, by omitting the differing circumstances of independence and the international context, are as likely to mislead as to illuminate.

Yet the danger remains that the coup d'état or similar wielding of force to achieve political ends will increasingly characterize African politics. Coups may be institutionalized as the means for bringing in new personnel—not for changing the basic constraints within which the political systems must operate. In order to stave off discontent within the armed forces, political leaders may turn to the time-honored tactic of expanding budget commitments to obtain ever more and better military equipment. But the relationship is two-sided, and may turn into a form of blackmail against political

142. Finer comments: "Where public attachment to civilian institutions is strong, military intervention in politics will be weak. . . . By the same token, where public attachment to civilian institutions is weak or non-existent, military intervention in politics will find wide scope—both in manner and in substance. . . . Where the parties or trade unions are feeble and few, where the procedure for the transfer of power is irregular or even nonexistent, where the location of supreme authority is a matter of acute disagreement or else of unconcern and indifference: there the military's political scope will be very wide" (*The Man on Horseback,* p. 21).

leaders fearful of dismissal.[143] Increased military spending may be viewed as a form of preventive action by a government. Why not "invest" in the good will of the armed services when violence (à la Togo and the assassination of Olympio) might be the result of not doing so? Good will cannot be purchased, however, if military grievances remain unresolved.

Let us draw together the threads of the argument. Military intervention has become commonplace in tropical Africa as members of the armed services became more conscious of the power they could wield in overturning what they saw as meddlesome, inefficient, unpopular, and dictatorial political parties and governments. The conception of civilian supremacy has not taken firm root in most African states. As a result, few constraints operate to preclude military intervention.

Contrasted with the relative ease of seizing control are the manifold problems of effective governance. Though military governments may embark upon control with the assurance of widespread popular enthusiasm, little can guarantee the maintenance of this climate of enthusiasm. The moment of rejoicing at the fall of an unpopular civilian regime may quickly give way to resentment against the policies military leaders feel compelled to adopt—just as the moment of rejoicing with the achievement of independence was followed by growing disenchantment with the dominant party. Economic policies may undercut popular support of military governments, particularly through deliberate deflation, unemployment, and cuts in civil service perquisites. Military rule does not automatically stamp out corruption, nor can it eliminate primordial sentiments in the interests of greater national unity. In short, coup leaders face the same difficulties over which their civilian predecessors stumbled—without necessarily benefiting from greater advantages.

The building of political institutions requires time, caution, and exemplary skill. The mass-based party helped arouse political awareness and participation; in the tasks of nation-building, it made a clear contribution. Military governments, owing to their "technocratic" orientation, may make greater contributions to state-building. But both nation-building and state-building are requisite to political development. Effective political institutions cannot be created de novo by coups d'état. The political development of African states depends upon the creation of effective, widely supported instruments of government. To this development, military leaders can make only a slight contribution. Such is the sobering lesson this chapter and this book attempts to convey.

143. *Ibid.*, pp. 118–28.

INTRODUCTION TO CHAPTER 2

JOINED BY 250 kilometers of common frontier and former association within the Federation of French West Africa, Dahomey and Upper Volta furnish many comparisons. Each is characterized by ethnic and regional tensions exacerbated by party conflicts, by economies split between traditional and modern sectors, and by volatile trade unions conscious of the power that organization brings and resentful of any measures to diminish their relative affluence. Though the amount of army involvement varies—by late 1968, Dahomean officers had been involved in four changes of government, including a hasty return to civilian rule, while only one military intervention had occurred in Upper Volta—the patterns of army rule show numerous similarities.

Central to Professor Skurnik's analysis are the "built-in professional limitations" officers confront in resolving political issues. Governance involves skills not taught at Saint Cyr or Sandhurst. Effective political action requires compromise, sensitivity to group interests, reasonable impartiality in resolving conflicting claims, a concern with support as well as efficiency. To be certain, changes can be ramrodded through, should the regime possess sufficient support and coercive resources. In their absence, however, efforts to achieve basic alterations will fail, as the precipitous withdrawal of Dahomean officers in July, 1968, illustrates.

Marching on the parade ground or going into action, the armed forces appear unified, cohesive, committed to certain objectives. Manipulating the organs of government, however, the armed forces may fall prey to internal differences. Political involvement may unleash a host of policy, personal, generational, and ethnic tensions.

60

It was this fragmentation, Professor Skurnik notes, that led to the hasty disengagement of the Kouandété government in Dahomey. Perhaps victim of trying to impose too much upon Dahomean citizens, the armed forces found withdrawal the only satisfactory means of preserving professional unity.

The comparisons drawn by Professor Skurnik thus suggest that military leadership cannot bring fundamental changes, due to centrifugal tendencies within the armed forces. Dahomey and Upper Volta cannot, at this moment, follow the policy prescription set down a decade ago:

> Utilize the organizational strength of the national armies and leadership potential of their officer corps as temporary kernels of national integration, around which the other constructive forces of the various societies could rally, during a short period of breakthrough from present stagnation into a genuine developmental take-off.[1]

The first requisite is a *national* army free from ethnic and regional overtones; this necessity has yet to be achieved in the two states. In fairness to the ruling juntas, one must point out that they were faced with extremely complex economic and political issues; their strategies of efficiency simply could not satisfy the intellectuals and trade unionists instrumental in bringing military involvement in politics. But this point leads to a simple conclusion. Neither in Upper Volta nor in Dahomey did the military transform the political system and the tensions that had plagued it. The governing officers were weakened by the same forces that had earlier affected the civilian regimes.

C. E. W.

1. Guy J. Pauker, "Southeast Asia as a Problem Area in the Next Decade," *World Politics*, XI, no. 3 (1959), 342.

2.

The Military and Politics:

Dahomey and Upper Volta

W. A. E. SKURNIK
University of Colorado

POLITICAL BACKGROUND TO INSTABILITY

THE FORMAL POLITICAL HISTORY of Upper Volta and Dahomey, both before and after independence, is a colorful and confusing kaleidoscope which, if observed with the naked eye, can result only in dizziness. An attempt to single out the myriad unique elements is instructive, but yields no reliable generalization regarding behavior patterns.

Any interpretive scheme provided by outsiders conceals risks of oversimplification; however, the overall pattern of political dy-

I wish to acknowledge financial assistance from the University of Denver, which enabled me to do field research in Dahomey and Upper Volta as a research associate of the Graduate School of International Studies/Social Science Council during the summer of 1967. My thanks go also to Messrs. Antoine André for documentary help and stimulating discussions, and Dov Ronen for his perceptive comments on a previous draft.

namics in these countries appears to have been one leading from pluralism through "truncated" pluralism to domination by a single leader, thereby eliminating pluralistic expectations. This pattern was accompanied by a process of disaffection which grew in strength as domination neared. The process of centralization culminated in efforts to monopolize decision-making. Having written—and signed —their momentous pages in history, incumbent leaders looked upon independence as the terminus, rather than the beginning, of their ascent to lofty pinnacles from which nothing could ever topple them.

No single issue can be isolated as most potent in "causing" the final break, although a cursory reading of issues which may be termed "immediate causes" from the point of view of chronology could be interpreted in that light. What caused the final breakdown was the cumulative impact of a variety of issues, which reached a point of no return when the legitimacy of the incumbent government approached zero, and needed only a relatively slight disturbance to be consumed by disaffection transformed into open opposition.

Upper Volta

In Upper Volta, the political background which led to military intervention in 1966 may be conveniently separated into two phases. The first phase witnessed tensions arising from the displacement of the Mossi traditional structure by the new, secular, fragmented political structure of the "modern" state. The second phase was characterized by the crystallization of the secular elements into competing factions, regionally based and gathered around leadership groups; it ended with one of these factions in control of the new state machinery.

After the end of World War II, Mossi chiefs believed that the time had come for "Mossi self-government"; they successfully advocated the return of the "Upper Ivory Coast" to Upper Volta, a transfer which took place in 1947. But the erosion of Mossi authority had already begun. It was manifest in the narrow defeat of their candidates in "Upper Ivory Coast" by Houphouet-Boigny's Parti Démocratique in 1946. It was further accelerated by three developments:

1. The emergence of a group of younger, educated Mossi in Ouahigouya who based their political campaign on a long-standing split between northern and western Mossi. Under the leadership of Gérard Ouédraogo and of a French Captain, Michel Dorange, who

represented the interests of the Ouahigouya Mossi veterans of the French armed forces, they formed the Mouvement Démocratique Voltaique (MDV) and openly attacked the traditional, ascriptive authority of the Mossi emperor in Ouagadougou.

2. The withdrawal of Nazi Boni from an earlier "Voltaic" coalition to form a party supported by the Bobo ethnic minority in the west in order to oppose a Houphouet-sponsored section of the Rassemblement Démocratique Africain (RDA) in that region.

3. The successive failures of Joseph Conombo, a supporter of the Ouagadougou Mossi, to align his Parti Social d'Education des Masses (PSEMA) with the winning side.

Between internal autonomy in 1957 and national independence in 1960, the political struggle was no longer between the strong Mossi hierarchy in Ouagadougou and its adversaries: it concentrated on regionally based secular political parties. The first African national executive, installed in 1957, was based on a coalition between the RDA, the MDV, and PSEMA, and headed by Ouezzin Coulibaly, a compromise candidate suggested by Houphouet-Boigny. Moreover, the Territorial Assembly benefited from only 52 per cent of the registered voters' ballots and was badly split: the RDA emerged with 37 of the 70 seats, the MDV with 26, Nazi Boni's Mouvement Populaire Africain with 5, and independent splinter groups with 2.

The fragile coalition split apart when its non-RDA partners (Boni, Conombo, and Gérard Ouédraogo), uneasy at Coulibaly's close relations with the Ivory Coast, withdrew and asked for the government's resignation. Coulibaly, however, refused, and was upheld as prime minister by the French government, after making skillful use of a constitutional ambiguity.[1] The subsequent reversal of four pivotal MDV members, among whom was Agriculture Minister Maurice Yaméogo, restored a slight pro-Coulibaly majority in the legislature, and Yaméogo was rewarded by becoming interior minister.

Another crisis followed the untimely death of Coulibaly in an airplane crash in September, 1958. The Mossi emperor, the Moro Naba, made an unsuccessful bid for political influence by converging some 3,000 warriors on the legislature to demand a "union gov-

1. Article 2 of Decree 57–459 of April 4, 1957, merely mentioned that the African executives may resign "if they believe that they no longer enjoy the confidence of the Territorial Assembly." The lack of clarity in case of conflict between the executive and the assembly tended to encourage ministers to maintain their position in spite of majority opposition in the assembly. Such was the case in Upper Volta only a few months after the decree was promulgated. For details, see Gil Dugué, *Vers les États-Unis d'Afrique* (Dakar: Lettres Africaines, 1960), pp. 25–35.

ernment," i.e., a new coalition with ample room for Joseph Conombo and his followers. The assembly nonetheless proceeded to elect an RDA candidate as its president and agreed to ask Maurice Yaméogo, handpicked by Coulibaly as his successor, to become the new head of government in Upper Volta.

Political developments after independence were dominated by the new single party launched in 1959 by Maurice Yaméogo, the Union Démocratique Voltaique (UDV). As a result, the political structure was transformed from a creature with several heads into a creature with one apparently healthy head and several undernourished heads in danger of atrophy.

Yaméogo's consolidation of formal power followed the general outlines discussed by Aristide Zolberg.[2] The Yaméogo regime traversed the three-month period needed for a constitutional referendum held on March 15, 1959, and the election of a legislature with the crutch of a national emergency. For that election, which took place on April 19, 1959, the three opposition parties combined into a short-lived Mouvement de Regroupement Voltaique. But Yaméogo adjusted electoral laws so that his party, having received about 62 per cent of the votes cast, obtained 70 of the 75 seats in the Legislative Assembly, and he appointed a government of 16 ministers excluding any opposition leader. One last, unsuccessful effort at organizing effective political opposition was made by Nazi Boni after the election; he created a Parti National Voltaique which was promptly dissolved by the government, then formed a Parti Républicain de Liberté which, in the name of national unity, was likewise dissolved.[3]

Since most politically active people were civil servants, it was easy for President Yaméogo to transfer recalcitrant employees to outlying areas. The more important "opposition" leaders either suffered "administrative internment" (like Joseph Ouédraogo, a union leader who helped Yaméogo's political start, on the grounds that he advocated a genuine coalition government), were exiled (like Nazi Boni), or sent abroad as ambassadors (like Henri Guissou to West Germany). Others were simply sidetracked through a reorganization of local governments, whose elected heads were replaced by appointed officials.

Toward the end of 1965, Yaméogo decided to put the final touches

---

2. *Creating Political Order: The Party States of West Africa* (Chicago: Rand McNally, 1966).

3. In 1963, Yaméogo created a special Security Court modeled after that of the Ivory Coast whose members, appointed by the president of the republic, could arrest and try anyone without appeal.

to his plans for complete control over the formal political process. He dismissed five cabinet members, appointed a cousin, Denis Yaméogo, as interior minister, and took over the defense portfolio himself. Prior to the forthcoming election—the first national election since April, 1959—he modified electoral laws so that he would be re-elected one month before the legislators. Yaméogo thus won an official 99.77 per cent majority and drew up the single list of candidates for the National Assembly, in the process retiring large numbers of his earlier supporters. The effect of Yaméogo's centralization policy was to isolate himself from supporters and increasingly narrow the base of his own legitimacy.

Supporters and detractors of Maurice Yaméogo agree that, by 1965, a general malaise had resulted from his excessive centralization of authority and had been exacerbated by palpable, though muted, dissatisfaction with the government's handling of several key issues. One such issue concerned Upper Volta's relations with the Ivory Coast: there was a widespread belief that Yaméogo tended to see the Voltaic national interest as a function of his personal relation with President Houphouet-Boigny. Yaméogo was criticized, for instance, for not supporting more effectively the interests of some half million Voltaic citizens—about 10 per cent of the population— who earn their living in the Ivory Coast as semiskilled and unskilled labor. Fears of being "sold down the forest" crystallized when Houphouet proposed common citizenship for the countries of the Conseil de l'Entente (Dahomey, Upper Volta, Niger, and the Ivory Coast). Trade unions representing civil servants, as well as opponents of the regime, argued that, unless salaries of Voltaic civil servants were increased to match those of their Ivoirien colleagues, single nationality would tend to abolish national frontiers and hence empty Upper Volta's administration.

In the same vein, there was unhappiness at the failure of the trade agreement with Ghana signed in 1963. Yaméogo's critics contend that the agreement could have worked, but that it was entered into only because of a temporary disagreement between Yaméogo and Houphouet and that the government did nothing to prevent local French business from boycotting Ghanaian goods. Upper Volta's subsequent *rapprochement* with Mali and Guinea was ascribed to the same ephemeral motives. When the quarrel was patched up, Yaméogo rushed into the other extreme and acted as Houphouet's spokesman in inter-African quarrels which did not concern Upper Volta. During a Guinea-Ivory Coast crisis concerning an alleged plot to overthrow Touré, for instance, it was said that, whereas the Ivory Coast remained silent, Yaméogo answered Guinea's charges and hurled insults at President Touré.

Another issue which aroused widespread criticism concerned a relatively innocuous event: President Yaméogo's divorce and subsequent remarriage. That Yaméogo exchanged his popular "traditional" wife for a young Ivoirien beauty was not what elicited adverse comment. Rather, it was the manner in which this was done, *viz.*, the humiliation and maltreatment of his first wife (and others), which resulted in a boycott of both the wedding ceremony and the inauguration of the "neo-baroque" Party House—dedicated to Houphouet—by the Roman Catholic hierarchy.

A third issue concerned the retention of the president's cousin, Denis Yaméogo, in the cabinet. The latter's qualifications for office, aside from family ties, appear to have been inadequate education and a penchant for pugilism. Rumor had it that his boxing talent was used to persuade union leaders and others of the nobility of government policy.

A fourth issue was the construction, at enormous expense and with French funds, of modern public buildings to serve as a showcase of an independent modern Upper Volta. No one can deny that these are objects of pride and tend to function as symbols of national integration. Nonetheless, given the resources and needs of Upper Volta, many believed that foreign aid could have been invested in a more productive manner; a poor country erecting what the government proudly called the skeleton of a modern city in Ouagadougou and a luxurious presidential palace in the president's home town of Koudougou displays a questionable sense of values in the allocation of scarce resources.

The events in Ouagadougou which culminated in the fall of the Yaméogo regime and its replacement by the army were precipitated by new austerity measures which the unions found unacceptable. The chronology of events between December 27, 1965, and January 3, 1966, is worth scrutinizing in some detail for what it reveals about the fragility of Upper Volta's political system. What happened, briefly, was that government leaders were unprepared and inept; that unions leaders had lost faith in Yaméogo; that a small, illegal splinter party took advantage of the opportunity to make common cause with the unions; and that the armed forces remained benevolently neutral until they had no choice but to intervene.

Upper Volta's new budget, to be approved by the fresh, obedient legislature, included a 20 per cent cut in government workers' salaries over $60 per month, an increase of personal income taxes for monthly salaries of $40, and a reduction of family allowances for children. President Yaméogo was determined to go through with his austerity budget and let it be known that any attempt to modify his plans would fail.

Against the background of the general malaise discussed above, union leaders found the measures unacceptable, to a large extent because their confidence in the Yaméogo government had been exhausted. The unions contended that a president seriously concerned with his country's economic welfare should not have flown to Brazil on an expensive honeymoon at taxpayers' expense. At first they tried to pressure the legislature into not passing the budget. When this did not work, the two central labor organizations and several autonomous unions, representing nearly all public employees, established a Joint Union Committee and elected Joseph Ouédraogo president. The committee carried its grievances to the executive but met with a complete refusal to discuss the issue.

On December 31, 1965, union leaders decided to take more drastic steps after having been dispersed from a meeting by police with tear gas. They agreed to call for a general strike on Monday, January 3, 1966; while high government officials celebrated New Year's Eve, some 500 union messengers spread the news of the strike through Ouagadougou. Another crucial union decision was to tell Lieutenant Colonel Sangoulé Lamizana, armed forces chief of staff, that relations between unions and government had reached a point of no return which could be settled only by the government's resignation.

In spite of the government's declaration of a national state of emergency, the general strike was an unqualified success. It was joined, and at times led, by the Mouvement de Libération Nationale (MLN), an unlawful splinter party created in 1958, whose intellectual, "radical" orientation had stood in the way of securing meaningful popular support. On the morning of January 3, government employees did not report to work and the streets at first remained empty. About 8 A.M., under MLN teacher leadership, students from the Zinda Kaboré High School, the girls' High School, and the Ouagadougou Normal School began marching toward army headquarters, some carrying placards reading "Bread, Water, Democracy." The students were soon joined by other demonstrators including youthful street vendors and unemployed (the "Monoprix" boys). Eyewitnesses testify that this was a demonstration with a smile and a taste for adventure delighting its young participants. Cries of "the army to power" were heard occasionally. Demonstrators also called for an end to "the 20%" and, when the armed forces showed no hostility and withdrew quietly from several strategic points in the city, the emboldened demonstrators advanced in the direction of the government buildings.

When the people reached the last, and strongest, military barrier they stopped, but police units dispersed them with tear gas. Soldiers ignored orders to open fire. Then the demonstrators, in a well-planned move, formed three "columns." One attempted to enter the president's office but was barred, another reached and vandalized the interior minister's residence, and the third entered the national assembly building. There, according to the official account, "the rooms and especially the bar were invaded, and bottles of whisky, beer, and champagne were consumed."[4]

Following time out for lunch and a siesta, potential demonstrators were summoned to army headquarters by freely circulating soundtrucks. Estimates of the crowd which gathered around 2:30 P.M. vary, but all agree on a minimum of 25,000. This time the chant asking for an army takeover was general, and some, in an obvious reference to the previous national and municipal elections, carried signs reading "We, the 0.02%."

The government appears to have been taken by surprise by the gravity of events. It responded in an *ad hoc* fashion to challenges as they appeared. At first the interim president of the republic refused to see a delegation from the Joint Union Committee—Maurice Yaméogo having flown to Abidjan for a conference with Entente leaders.[5] When Ouédraogo addressed a letter to Yaméogo, with a carbon copy to Colonel Lamizana, Interior Minister Denis Yamoégo called the union leaders to his office. The minister left the union leaders standing and showered them with verbal abuse. That same evening, December 31, he assured the president that everything was under control.

The government's next response was to attempt to prevent the strike. It arrested some 100 union leaders, but could not find the top leaders who remained in hiding; word had been passed around, presumably by the interior minister, that they would be shot when found. President Yaméogo tried to discredit union leadership by

---

4. *Carrefour africain* (Ouagadougou), January 2–9, 1966.

5. Unconfirmed reports assert that Entente leaders agreed to a Yaméogo proposal to transform the Entente into a confederation. Houphouet-Boigny would be its president and take up residence at the confederal capital of Ouagadougou. Although these reports originated with reporters attending the Entente meeting, they may also have been planted by Yaméogo supporters to improve their leader's image.

raising the specter of external interference. In a radio broadcast on January 1, he declared:

> A Communist inspired subversion has entered the country with a son of the land, presently in flight, as its leader. I am speaking of Joseph Ouédraogo.
>
> Under the cover of union demands, he has indoctrinated a few workers who tend to disturb order in the capital. Joseph Ouédraogo wants to deliver our country to Ghana, hence to Peking China. The evidence is in our possession.[6]

Yaméogo appealed to workers to ignore the coming general strike, thus unwittingly publicizing the event. Further, he declared a state of emergency in the capital (extended to the nation the next day), asked the people to retain confidence in the armed forces who would protect them from foreign enemies, and asked religious leaders (i.e., the Mossi emperor) to help prevent the strike.

When the demonstrators filled the streets on January 3, President Yaméogo expected police and armed forces to contain them, by force if necessary. There were telephone consultations with other Entente leaders regarding the possibility of using the secret antisubversion agreements to airlift troops to Ouagadougou. Presumably this was not thought necessary. According to some, Houphouet-Boigny offered Yaméogo the funds needed to rescind the austerity measures. Yaméogo sought to negotiate with union leaders but by that time they would talk only to the army. After 9 of the 13 cabinet members withdrew to their homes, the president dispatched Lamizana to announce to the people, at 6:30 P.M., his decision to leave austerity out of the budget. The people responded by asking for Yaméogo's dismissal, which was announced some three hours later, again by Lamizana, to the jubilant demonstrators. They returned home only after Lamizana also told them that he had taken over the government.

Army officers were not unsympathetic to the unions' views or to the possibility of a military takeover. Union leaders had kept Lamizana au courant of their attempts to reach an understanding with the government; according to some reports, they had cultivated several officers and sought to extract a commitment for help. Some officers were attracted by an army coup: armed forces had recently taken over the governments of Dahomey and the Central African Republic. On the whole, however, the officers counseled patience. Army intervention must be justified by more than union

6. *Carrefour africain,* January 2–9, 1966.

grievances. In the meantime they were mindful of possible untoward consequences were they to open fire on demonstrators. Their benevolent neutrality, then, encouraged union leaders to create the conditions under which army officers could intervene without violating their notion of legitimacy.

Dahomey

Dahomey's political history was marked by the progressive, relative decline of the early predominance of one leader and by adjustments of national politics to ethnically based regionalism. Dahomey's pluralism, however, was never expressed fully in politics. It was truncated by a succession of biregional coalitions whose leaders, having sidetracked one region, spent their energies on eclipsing each other.

Dahomeans refer nostalgically to the period immediately after World War II when the country was "united" under the leadership of Sourou Migan Apithy.[7] His pre-eminence in Dahomean politics, however, was short-lived. His support came primarily from the area of the old kingdom of Porto Novo, urban *evolués*, and the small but influential Roman Catholic hierarchy.

The gradual extension of the franchise allowed other groups to participate in the political process. The first region to challenge Apithy's supremacy was the north, populated by ethnic groups with a distinct social and economic structure. By 1951, north and south were about equal in voter support, so that Apithy was joined by Hubert Maga, a northern school teacher, as deputy in the French legislature.

The next group to benefit fortuitously from further extensions of the franchise were the Fon people, heirs to the prestigious Abomey kingdom, who emerged as a serious political force in 1956. With the support of Houphouet-Boigny's RDA, Justin Tometin Ahomadegbé secured some 40,000 votes, nearly all Fon, (compared with 65,000

---

7. In fact, he remains a prestigious figure in that country. He was intimately associated with the emergence of "modern" political life, with the formation of electoral committees to support his candidacy and that of the Reverend Father Aupiais for election to the French Constituent Assembly in August 1945. After his now famous injunction that the future of Africa be decided not in Paris but in Africa, he represented Dahomey in French legislatures, founded the loose, Paris-based coalition of African deputies called Indépendants d'outre-mer, and later became his country's first chief executive.

votes for Apithy and 60,000 for Maga) during the 1956 election for the French National Assembly.

Apithy tried to retain his predominance and tailored electoral laws to that purpose. The first African government of Dahomey, in 1957, was a coalition led by Apithy, including Maga and some independent forces. Shortly afterward, Apithy formed a new government without either Maga or Ahomadegbé but with the help of some northern dissidents. This attempt to govern alone, however, marked the end of Apithy's supremacy. It caused a crisis which was reinforced when Ahomadegbé obtained a plurality of popular votes in the election of the Constituent Assembly in 1959. The crisis was "settled" once again by Ivory Coast's Houphouet, a long-time antagonist of Apithy. Hubert Maga, as a compromise candidate, became the new premier, Apithy remained in the cabinet, and Ahomadegbé was left in "opposition."

If there were any expectations that Maga and Apithy would cooperate harmoniously after their political parties merged into the Parti Dahoméen Unifié (PDU) in November, 1960, these were soon abandoned. Theirs was an uneasy, suspicious alliance, and the subsequent events were more like a farcical seesaw than an attempt to collaborate in the national interest. Maga attempted to centralize authority, and Apithy responded by embarrassing and warning his coalition partner.

Maga began by reducing local, grass-root support for his opponents. He dissolved the elected municipal council of the five largest cities and replaced them by centrally appointed prefects responsible to the ministry of interior. Apithy traveled to East European capitals to cement closer ties, and entered into commercial and diplomatic agreements—at a time when the Maga government was involved in negotiations with Western nations.

Apithy also began courting progressive intellectuals concentrated in the schools of Porto Novo. Maga retaliated against the intellectuals in a manner which, ironically, helped to undermine the legitimacy of his government. When René Dossa, editor of the official newspaper, *L'Aube nouvelle,* wrote an article generally critical of single-party regimes in Africa, he was imprisoned and only released ten days later following the intercession of the justice minister. When some high school teachers, headed by Professor Stanislas Spéro Adotévi, distributed tracts critical of Maga, they were drafted into the army for 24 days. Mr. Adotévi was welcomed to the barracks as an eminent personality and asked by the officers if he would not conduct some courses and thus contribute to the soldiers' education. Adotévi was glad to oblige and lectured on philosophy, literature, and civics, reportedly emphasizing revolutionary theory and the proper functions of governments. Thus part of the armed forces became conscious that their civilian superiors were not necessarily above reproach and that soldiers, as citizens, were able to evaluate a government in the light of criteria other than the need for unity.

Maga subsequently sidetracked Apithy by appointing him ambassador to France, thus courting the alienation of Porto Novo in addition to that of Abomey. This move theoretically placed Apithy under the authority of any cabinet member, and the new ambassador did not fail to point out, in his accreditation speech, that "this occasion is without precedent in that the Vice-President of a Republic is at the same time his own [resident diplomatic] representative in another state."[8]

By 1963, it was clear that Maga continued his attempts at centralizing authority while at the same time courting Ahomadegbé and isolating Apithy. During the PDU congress in September, a 25-member political bureau was elected by acclamation from a single list of carefully selected Maga supporters. A reconciliation with Ahomadegbé was engineered, first by appointing an Ahomadegbé supporter to his cabinet, next by releasing some 300 political prisoners, then by granting a pardon to Ahomadegbé and others previously convicted on trumped-up charges of plotting against the state. Ahomadegbé, during a speech at the PDU congress, confirmed his readiness to work for the Maga government.

Apithy's reaction was instantaneous. He made an unscheduled speech and warned Maga that continued cooperation under the circumstances was not possible. A "systematic uniformization" of politics, said Apithy, invited the kind of instability found in Togo and other African states; future stability in Dahomey required a "judicious balance among the diverse regions, men and tendencies." He then addressed a warning to Maga:

> I am giving you my formal guarantee that, as long as the rules of the game are respected, my participation in the present effort will only grow. But if, and I hope this will not happen, the terms of our common contract were to be observed only through fear and distrust, and if intrigue should become too strong, then, in spite of myself, I would retire from the political scene and wish Dahomey the best of luck.
>
> This is the place to ask ourselves if each has played the game

8. "Lettre de créance présentée par M. Sourou Migan Apithy au Général de Gaulle," typescript (Porto Novo: n.d.), p. 1.

honestly. If not, there is still time. *Before long, it will be too late.*
My position is thus clearly defined: single party, yes; regionalist
or personal power, no.[9]

Political dissension grew after the PDU congress. There were
rumors of plans to transfer the national museum from Abomey to
the south, and grumbling about the enormous cost of erecting
"palaces" for the Conseil de l'Entente and the presidency of the republic. Tensions between Maga and Apithy increased when the
latter resigned from the PDU in protest over Maga's packing of the
party executive, and thus gave the signal to Porto Novo that something had to give. To make matters worse, the president of the
National Assembly, Valentin Djibodé Aplogan, who enjoyed some
independent support in Alladah but generally leaned toward
Apithy, opened the legislature's session in October, 1963, by criticizing the government for obstinacy and reluctance to introduce
reforms.

It was against this background of hostility and suspicion that the
"affaire Bohiki" emerged and provided a catalyst for Maga's opposition. Christophe Bohiki, a deputy in the National Assembly, had
been allegedly implicated in the murder of a prominent Apithy
supporter. Apithy was understandably sensitive to the need for
bringing Bohiki to justice, but the assembly and the Maga government protected Bohiki. After several months of mediation, the
assembly agreed to lift Bohiki's parliamentary immunity but insisted that he not be arrested. When Bohiki was nonetheless arrested, the assembly asked for his immediate release.

As a result, demonstrators appeared in the streets of Porto Novo
demanding justice. They removed the national flag from over the
city hall while chanting *"Vive la France!"* and they called for the
armed forces to take over the government. Taking advantage of the
disorders, the Union Générale des Travailleurs du Dahomey
(UGTD), the national central labor organization, called for a
general strike (for reasons discussed below); the strike took place
on October 26, and union leaders joined in the demands for an army
takeover. On the following day, Colonel Christophe Soglo, armed
forces chief of staff, announced that the government was dissolved
in order to avert a civil war.

The two-month interlude between the dissolution of the Maga
government and the election of a new one was dominated by three

9. "Intervention du camarade Apithy au premier congrès du Parti Dahoméen de l'Unité (PDU), 30 Septembre 1963," typescript (Porto Novo:
n.d.), p. 3, emphasis added.

developments: (1) the army-supported reconciliation among Dahomey's "big three" leaders, (2) the unions' bid for influence which resulted in Maga's retirement, and (3) the creation of new political institutions. At first Colonel Soglo created a provisional government headed by himself and including Messrs. Ahomadegbé, Apithy, and Maga. The unions, however, demanded the dissolution of the legislature, the creation of a national and of regional revolutionary committees with union membership, Maga's political retirement, and a parliamentary political system. Maga was dismissed from the provisional government following an incident at Porto Novo, when a few northern warriors fired on soldiers, and discovery of a "plot" for the assassination of Soglo, Apithy, and Ahomadegbé.

The Ahomadegbé-Apithy coalition lasted two years, from January, 1964, to December, 1965. The convulsions which punctuated the second Dahomean republic were distressingly similar to those of the first. The first republic had collapsed, but the players had emerged relatively unscathed and there were no sanctions to deter the new team from indulging in the tactics of old; the only effective national arbiter had made a brief appearance, admonished the players, and quietly withdrawn from the field.

Very little distinguished the "new" political institutions from those which they replaced. To paper over the party differences, a new single party, a Parti Démocratique Dahoméen (PDD) was fashioned out of two of the country's three political forces—those of Apithy and Ahomadegbé. Apithy became president of the republic, but his partner controlled the government as premier and vice-president.[10] Once again, a new Dahomean regime started with truncated pluralism, and with Apithy playing second fiddle.

The second republic witnessed the same drama as did the first, though with a changed cast of characters: two leaders at the top, after agreeing to neutralize the missing partner, maneuvered to "neutralize" each other. And since Ahomadegbé pulled more strings, neutralization eventually struck Apithy.

Apithy, faced with a partner who controlled government, legisla-

10. On the surface, the new arrangement provided for a "balance" of powers. The premier chose his cabinet, but with the approval of the president of the republic. The head of state was authorized to declare a state of emergency, and to appoint important officials such as the president of the Supreme Court, but with cabinet approval. The lineup of political strength, however, made it clear that Ahomadegbé had the edge; he controlled a majority of the National Assembly and of the PDD, and thus could maneuver to revise the constitution or to impeach the president of the republic since the body authorized to try the head of state, the High Court of Justice, was a creature of the legislature.

ture, and single party, nonetheless sought to redress the balance. His tactics were essentially the same as before. What he lacked in political influence he attempted to gain by courting progressive intellectuals and embarrassing the government abroad. Whereas Ahomadegbé was committed to the Entente and the larger French-speaking group, Apithy, on an official visit to Ghana, brought his host assurances of support concerning a continental African government, the liberation of Africa, and the fight against neocolonialism. While Ahomadegbé cooperated with West Germany, Apithy told the East Germans that Dahomey's sympathies were with them. Whereas Ahomadegbé maintained close relations with Taiwan and sent General Soglo to Taipei shortly after President de Gaulle recognized Peking, Apithy was instrumental in engineering his country's recognition of the People's Republic of China (for a time Cotonou hosted the delegations of both countries, who ignored each other as best they could).

The prime minister's distrust of Apithy increased when an Apithy sympathizer, V. D. Aplogan, created the Rassemblement des Impératifs Nationaux (RIN) as a splinter party while remaining an important member of the PDD and president of the Supreme Court. Ahomadegbé, mindful of Aplogan's role in undermining the previous government, reacted by dissolving the RIN, expelling him from the PDD, and dismissing him from the judiciary.

The immediate cause of the second republic's downfall was a dispute between president and premier concerning the choice of a new president of the Supreme Court.[11] Ahomadegbé at first sought unsuccessfully to bring the Supreme Court under the jurisdiction of his justice minister. Next he tried, again unsuccessfully, to enlist the help of the legislature to authorize him to appoint that official. President Apithy responded by putting his premier on notice that he would not promulgate such a law.

Following a visit to France by Apithy, which aroused fresh suspicions in the mind of the premier in view of the president's excellent Paris connections, Ahomadegbé decided to neutralize Apithy once and for all by removing him from his post. His efforts this time were successful and amounted to a coup d'état. On November 24, 1965,

---

11. The political importance of the president of the Supreme Court derived from two constitutional provisions. One stated that, in case of vacancy of the presidency of the republic, the vice-president temporarily assumed that office; the other stated that the Supreme Court decided when the president of the republic was permanently prevented from assuming his office, a step to be followed by new elections. See arts. 17, 25, 89, and 91, *Constitution de la République du Dahomey* (Porto Novo: Imprimerie Nationale, n.d.).

the Prime Minister convinced the PDD national executive, the cabinet, and the legislature in a joint session to expel Apithy from the party. Three days later, Ahomadegbé convened a "People's Assembly" including the above bodies plus union representatives. This extraconstitutional body dismissed Apithy from the presidency of the republic, named Ahomadegbé in his place, and called upon the legislature to draft a new constitution. President Apithy refused to resign and to vacate his office located in Porto Novo. When on November 28, the cabinet appointed a president of the Supreme Court, thousands of demonstrators took to the streets in Porto Novo.

As in 1963, the popular rebellion in Porto Novo and demands for an army takeover were joined by the unions. Dahomey's labor organizations were dissatisfied for three main reasons: (1) austerity measures which cut down their members' income; (2) politicians' quarrels which prevented them from paying proper attention to economic issues; and (3) lack of participation in the formulation of national economic policy.

Union grievances in 1963 were expressed in a number of specific issues. One was the Maga government's attempt to control them after having created, in 1961, a central, national union, the UGTD. Another was rooted in a misunderstanding about a 10 per cent salary tax instituted in 1961 as part of an austerity program.[12] Third, living standards of urban workers had declined as a result of higher prices and a freeze on salary increases. Finally, unions were concerned about rising unemployment and advocated absorbing more people into an already plethoric civil service. Perhaps most important, union leaders were convinced that the government was not living up to its responsibilities. As one union speaker put it in October, 1963, "we have always heard the slogan of austerity; we have accepted it. We have decided to collaborate, but has the government ever considered us as real collaborators?"[13]

Union grievances were not much different in 1965. It is true that the government had made some concessions. It had replaced a 10 per cent salary cut for public employees with a 5 per cent "investment tax" on salaries in excess of $80 per month—that is, for most civil servants—ended the wage freeze, and curtailed government expenses. By mid-1965, however, the government was faced with

---

12. Whereas unions believed that the money was being put aside for economic investment, the government did not explain that "savings" were in fact nonexistent since the "tax" was only a reduction in government expenditures.

13. *Afrique nouvelle* (Dakar), November 7, 1963.

serious economic and financial difficulties and sounded the alarm, in preparation for further austerity measures. Budgetary deficits, in spite of French aid, totalled over \$12 million (or nearly half of the total national budget), and declining exports covered a bare 40 per cent of the cost of imports. The government therefore suggested, and the assembly approved, a 25 per cent cut in government workers' salaries.

Union counterproposals, which struck the government as ineffective and unpatriotic, suggested: (1) reducing the number of government agencies, weakly arguing that, although these would not wipe out the national deficit, they would at least prepare the people psychologically for future sacrifices; (2) maintaining consumer imports since local production would not satisfy demand; and (3) rescinding salary cuts—they were unacceptable since they would further diminish purchasing power.

Moreover, unions were frustrated because they lacked an effective voice in making national decisions. The former head of the UGTD, Théophile Paoletti, was in Ahomadegbé's cabinet, but his presence there had proved ineffective. This was due in part to the lack of cohesion of labor unions which were divided into three central and a dozen smaller, autonomous groups after the Maga-sponsored UGTD was dissolved. Also, union membership threatened to become disenchanted with leaders and demanded action. The unions, during the traditional May Day meetings, reminded the government that it was not immune from the fate which befell its predecessor:

> It is incumbent upon us to be ready to remedy the certain failings of the party, to the extent that it mistakes itself for the government. The time has come to reaffirm our complete independence toward the government. The PDD may be a single party, but it is a long way from being a true mass party. The government cannot expect any true collaboration from us.[14]

In July, 1965, unions called for a general strike to protest the planned austerity measures. The strike failed, however, and several union leaders were imprisoned. The Porto Novo crisis gave unions the opportunity they were waiting for, and thus they made common cause with Apithy's supporters against Ahomadegbé.

The prime minister tried in vain to re-establish order in Porto Novo. When the local gendarmerie appeared powerless, he ordered the army to intervene, and Major Aho—Ahomadegbé's choice for replacing Soglo as chief of staff of the armed forces—dispatched

14. *Ibid.*, May 20, 1965.

some troops to the rebellious city. It is not entirely clear why the soldiers disobeyed Ahomadegbé's order to fire into the crowds.[15] They may have been influenced by Professor Adotévi's lectures, by the large number of women and children in the crowd, and by doubts regarding the legitimacy of orders issued by a civilian rather than by their commanding general. Be that as it may, the soldiers' doubts were resolved when General Soglo arrived and countermanded the prime minister.[16]

Eyewitnesses, as well as government officials, recount that Ahomadegbé gave Soglo a public dressing-down and that Soglo, without responding, returned to army headquarters in Cotonou.[17] On the morning of November 29, the army dismissed both Ahomadegbé and Apithy from their posts and appointed Tahirou Congacou, an outwardly shy northerner who was president of the National Assembly, as head of a provisional government.[18] As in 1963, the combined pressure of Porto Noviens and unions led to an army takeover which took place on December 22, 1965. General Soglo, as the new president of the republic, dissolved the legislature, municipal and regional councils, the hastily recreated political parties of the "big three," and suspended the constitution.[19]

15. Ahomadegbé reportedly put a pistol into his belt and rode to Porto Novo in an army jeep, like a commander leading troops into battle. Apocryphal or not, the story was widely circulated and earned the prime minister a good deal of ridicule.

16. Soglo, learning of Ahomadegbé's actions, officially pretended ignorance and drove to Porto Novo with his wife in his private car. He talked briefly with Ahomadegbé upon his arrival. Soglo and the premier were not on the best of terms, and the latter evidently failed to convince the general of the need to open fire on the demonstrators.

17. The officers, gathered by Lieutenant Colonel Alley, were waiting for Soglo and immediately conferred about the situation. Soglo, under the sting of public humiliation, issued orders to arrest the prime minister as a public menace, but his colleagues counseled restraint. During the late afternoon, Ahomadegbé paid army headquarters a surprise visit, but was told that the army would let him know their decision when the time came.

18. Article 17 of the Dahomean constitution of January 11, 1964, provides that, should the offices of the president of the republic and of the premier be vacant, the government be taken over provisionally by the president of the National Assembly. Mr. Congacou's provisional government included only four others, technicians in their early thirties: Emmanuel Tétégan, Jean Saka, Médé Moussa Yaya, and Antoine Boya.

19. Porto Noviens and unions continued demonstrations and asked that the National Assembly be dissolved as unrepresentative, that Congacou be dismissed for his role in the "People's Assembly," that national and regional revolutionary committees be formed including workers, youth, students, and army veterans, and that the army take power. The political parties created barely a week after the formation of Congacou's provisional government were: the Alliance Démocratique Dahoméenne for Ahomadegbé, the Union Nationale Dahoméenne for Maga, and the Convention Nationale Dahomé-

ECONOMIC FACTORS

Three major economic problems have bedeviled the two countries since independence, the first being the lack of connection between a large, traditional sector and the new smaller, modern sector of the economy. In Upper Volta, traditional commerce in rural areas is well organized, and its structure resists state control. Much of the country's wealth (some 80 per cent of the value of her exports) comes from cattle, which are sold to the Ivory Coast, Ghana, Togo, and Dahomey. In Dahomey, post-independence governments have revived a "return to the land" movement intended to inspire modernization. But the private and public schemes, including an armed forces program of pioneer units, were largely experimental and have not yet produced satisfactory results.[20] The major obstacle remains one of attitudes; little headway can be made in solving this problem as long as farmers value the number of their wives and children more highly than they do acquisition of some material possessions. There is no evidence that governments have undertaken the kind of sociopsychological study which would yield crucial insights for tackling this problem.

The second major economic problem concerns external trade.[21] Dahomey's trade imbalance grew from $12.5 million in 1960 to $20.5 million five years later. According to the first finance minister of the 1965 Soglo regime, Dahomey had the distinction of being the only state in former French West Africa whose exports had declined since independence, a decline estimated at between 10 and 50 per cent in

enne for Apithy. The party executives included Messrs. Ahomadegbé, Gabriel Lozès, Alexandre Adandé, Adrien Degbé, and Théophile Paoletti for the ADD; Paul and René Darboux, Arouna Mama, and Bertin Borna for the UND; and Dr. Léandre Amlon and V. D. Aplogan for the CND. To add to the confusion, the National Assembly split into two factions which met separately in Cotonou and Porto Novo.

20. See E. Costa, "Back to the Land: The Campaign Against Unemployment in Dahomey," *International Labour Review*, XCIII, no. 1 (1966), 29–49; and Julien Quirino-Lanhounmey, "Le Développement communautaire en Afrique noire: Leçons d'une expérience au Dahomey," *Politique étrangère*, XXIX, no. 2 (1964), 161–80.

21. Statistical material for this section is extracted from the following sources: for Upper Volta, (1) *Bulletin mensuel d'information statistique et économique* (Ouagadougou: Direction de la statistique et de mécanographie, January 1967); (2) *Marchés tropicaux et méditerranéens*, April 15, 1967, p. 1089; and (3) *Mémento de l'économie africaine* (Paris: Ediafric, 1967), pp. 195–217. For Dahomey, *Bulletin économique et statistique* (Cotonou: Direction des affaires économiques, October 1966); and *Mémento de l'économie africaine*, pp. 141–59.

the very cash crops which provide the country with most of its revenue. Whereas the value of exports covered 59 per cent of the value of imports in 1960, by 1965 that percentage had fallen to 39. Moreover, Dahomey remained heavily dependent on France, which accounted for 70 per cent of total exports and 55 per cent of total imports.

Upper Volta's trade position was not quite so bad. Although her exports still covered less than half of her imports, the percentage of the coverage nonetheless grew from 40.7 in 1962 to 47.4 two years later. Moreover, these indicators obscure a number of important improvements. The country is nearly self-sufficient in staples and is able to export some surpluses—whereas Dahomey has to import consumer goods to satisfy the relatively large urban bourgeoisie. Upper Volta's production of staples such as millet, sorghum, and corn nearly doubled between 1962 and 1964 during the interim national development plan, a goal not expected to be reached until about 1980. Moreover, Upper Volta's dependence on France was greatly reduced. Chief clients for exports, in descending order of importance, were the Ivory Coast, Ghana, and France (with only 18 per cent of the total in 1964); chief suppliers, in that same order, are France (50 per cent), the Ivory Coast, Mali, Ghana, and Senegal. Trade with Ghana can, and probably will, be improved since one of its major obstacles was the opposition of resident French merchants.

The rapid growth of national budgets beyond internal resources, and the consequent chronic budgetary imbalance, made up the third chief economic problem. Upper Volta's budget jumped from $20.8 million in 1959 to $37.6 million in 1964. French subsidies made up the deficits, which amounted to $4.6 million in 1964. Dahomey's budget rose from $21.6 million in 1960 to $33 million in 1965, and French budgetary subsidies have amounted to approximately $4 million per year. Soon after the formation of Dahomey's military regime in 1965, Finance Minister Nicéphore Soglo candidly admitted that "Dahomey is presently unable to assume the burdens flowing from accession to international dignity."[22]

By 1965, Dahomey's total national debt came to slightly more than that year's budget, one-fourth being owed to the resident French business community. In addition, both countries spent more than half of their national budget on civil servants' salaries. This problem was particularly acute in Dahomey, where the national and local civil service swelled from 12,000 in 1960 to over 18,000 in 1965,

22. *Afrique nouvelle,* May 5, 1966.

largely as a result of forced repatriation of Dahomeans from other African countries,[23] of the departure of French armed forces and the consequent loss of revenue, and of normal recruitment.

As budgetary deficits were made up by French subsidies, so trade deficits tended to be made up by external assistance and, in the case of Upper Volta, by the French government's pensions to veterans of the French armed forces which amounted to about $8 million per year. French public aid to Upper Volta from 1959 to 1966 was only slightly below the 1961 Voltaic budget; assistance from France and from the Common Market during that same period totaled some $42 million. Post-independence foreign assistance to Dahomey, chiefly from France and Western Europe, totaled $56 million by 1966, excluding French budget subsidies.

Finally, the growth rate of both countries' population was estimated at around 2.5 per cent per year so that it is expected to double within 20 years. This population increase, and its youth, may be expected to increase the unemployment problem (about 30,000 in Cotonou alone) and to present new political challenges in the near future. The resultant economic and political strains may well be beyond the capacity of any government to handle. Perhaps one of the most crucial handicaps to the solution of pressing economic problems has been what the French have called a *politique de facilité*, encouraged in part by French aid policy which subsidized a financial status quo and therefore discouraged greater indigenous efforts to search for solutions.

The problem is perhaps not so pressing in Upper Volta as in Dahomey, owing to the acute shortage of Voltaic cadres and skilled workers. But Dahomey has to contend with two kinds of "older" elites (the "Dahomeans" and those repatriated from elsewhere in

23. The French looked upon Dahomey as a manpower pool for the federal administrative services in French West and Equatorial Africa. Inhabitants of coastal agglomerations (chiefly Cotonou, Porto Novo, and Ouidah) were particularly receptive to educational opportunities, and Dahomey's resources in administrative cadres and professional people exceed her needs at this time. Suzanne Bozon, in "Les Dahoméens en Afrique noire," *Revue française de science politique*, XVII, no. 4 (1967), 718–26, suggests that the destruction of the traditional Fon hierarchy accounts for receptivity to change; but the degree of "destruction" of the Fon hierarchy is not universally accepted, and other, indigenous factors may be more helpful in explaining receptivity. The forcible "repatriation" of Dahomeans from other African countries, before and after independence, resulted from the educational achievements which were regarded as a threat by other countries' elites; Mlle. Bozon reports that fears of Dahomeans' presumed powers of witchcraft, reinforced by their lack of integration into their foreign surroundings, were additional factors.

Africa) who vie with each other and make the integration of the younger set that much more difficult. Many of the latter set find opportunities with international organizations and thus drain valuable talent away from home where it is most needed. The unemployed—and underemployed—in both Upper Volta and Dahomey have used times of overt political instability to join the ranks of demonstrators. Their potency as an independent factor, however, must not be exaggerated at the present because they tend to have working relatives and friends who help them survive, and they have no structure to articulate and aggregate their interests. Unions could appeal to them only by offering the security of jobs, but these are already filled by their protective members.

The first priority of the Soglo regime's policy was the economic recovery of Dahomey. As President Soglo declared shortly before his dismissal in 1967, "for the time being, our only objective is the economic recovery of our country."[24] Soglo's policy reflected not only the economic distress highlighted by official fears lest Dahomey be "erased from the map of independent states";[25] it reflected also the continued dependence upon French help which in turn depended upon serious, visible Dahomean management efforts. Mindful of French criticism of an African penchant for taking external help for granted, the government emphasized the importance of self-help. Dahomeans were officially encouraged to read such formerly banned works as René Dumont's *L'Afrique noire est mal partie*, and members of the new government engaged in a public relations exercise by spending some time working with peasants planting crops and building feeder roads and bridges.

Economic policy toward recovery contained three major aspects. The first was the increase of agricultural production and diversification. For this purpose, the new five-year development plan beginning in 1966 allotted one-third of total funds to rural development; a little less than one-third was allocated for the development of local processing industry.

Second, economic policy emphasized the need for external assistance. The 1966–70 development plan assumed the need for massive aid, Dahomey's own resources being sufficient for only 11 per cent of total anticipated investment. Special efforts were made to convince the French government that Dahomey, this time, was willing and able to make the effort required. As a result of the close personal contacts of Dr. Zinsou in Paris and, to some extent, those between

24. *Europe France-outre-mer,* October 1967, p. 13.
25. *Afrique nouvelle,* May 5, 1966.

Generals Soglo and de Gaulle, the Soglo government was able to secure additional French aid commitments.

The third aspect of economic policy consisted of financial rigor and austerity measures in order to balance the national budget within a reasonably foreseeable future. In spite of grave misgivings on the part of unions, the government enacted a series of austerity measures shortly after coming to office. It increased taxes on consumer goods, reduced a number of government worker indemnities by 50 per cent, decreased family allotments to a maximum of six children and, most important, increased an across-the-board "national solidarity tax" from 10 to 25 per cent of all salaries and applied it to employees in the private sector for the first time.

As may be expected, the results of Soglo's economic policy was something less than spectacular in the first two years: it laid the groundwork for further improvements while wrestling with immediate pressing problems. Agricultural production rose in some instances, but exports declined to an all-time low since independence; the trade deficit increased from $20.6 million in 1965 to $22.8 million in 1966, covering only 31.3 per cent of 1966 imports. The budget deficit was reduced to about half the 1965 figure of $5.2 million in one year; but it remained higher than anticipated, primarily because of overly optimistic revenue estimates.[26]

Economic policy in Upper Volta followed essentially the same lines as in Dahomey. The military government asked a team of French specialists to draw up a national development plan, the first for the state, which was completed by mid-1967.[27] As in Dahomey, emphasis was placed on agriculture and on small-scale industrialization, especially in connection with the manganese deposits at Tambao.

Lamizana's fiscal policy reflected the no-nonsense attitude which pervades officialdom in the capital city of Ouagadougou. Finance Minister Tiémoko Marc Garango, the armed forces' comptroller-

26. In another vein, foreign economic policy was redirected and doors were opened for better future relations with neighboring African states; a joint Dahomey-Togo-Ghana agreement provides for the purchase of electric power from Ghana's Akosombo dam, the inoperative 1961 Dahomey-Ghana trade agreement was revived, and a new trade agreement signed with Nigeria providing for the importation of consumer goods and increasing use of the port of Cotonou. Moreover, Soglo's government signed a number of economic agreements with such diverse countries as Taiwan, Czechoslovakia, and Poland.

27. The government was criticized for the speed with which the plan was put together, and it appears that the French team made no effort to benefit from the experience of other African countries. The planning minister was taken to task by his own party, the MLN, for having allowed foreigners to plan Upper Volta's economic future.

general,[28] began by abolishing President Yaméogo's austerity measures and paring down government expenses. Thus he decreased indemnities and salaries for top officials, closed several Voltaic embassies abroad, and shut down the television station, a relative luxury which cost some $70,000 per year to operate.

Financial rigor, designed as much to impress foreign—i.e., French —investors as to help toward economic recovery, led to lower national budgets than under Yaméogo.[29] Garango's chief concern seemed to be to wipe out the budgetary deficit of $14 million and the debt of $4.6 million. Austerity measures were nonetheless reintroduced, though gradually and in accordance with plainly stated intentions. Among the important measures introduced were a "patriotic contribution" equivalent to one-half of one month's salary, select consumer levies, a reduction in family allowances for children, and an income tax of 3 per cent for salaries under $480 per year and of 10 to 15 per cent for salaries over that amount [30]

GOVERNMENT STRUCTURE

The Lamizana regime's formal government structure was relatively simple and reflected Upper Volta's relative abundance of military officers, the result in part of the large contingents of Mossi who served in the French and colonial armed forces. Policy was

28. His rank is that of *Intendant-Général*, for which there is no precise equivalent in the US armed forces and which may correspond to any rank between Captain and General.

29. Budgets stood at $36,562,000 for 1966, $33,500,000 for 1967, and $34,200,000 for 1968. Foreign aid, chiefly French, financed over 90 per cent of Upper Volta's investment needs, which average about $10 million annually.

30. The Lamizana government also took steps to repair and diversify international economic relations. Following negotiations in Bamako, Planning Minister Pierre Claver Damiba visited the Soviet Union early in 1967 and laid the groundwork for future economic and diplomatic ties. Finance Minister Garango visited Taiwan, Japan, and the Republic of Korea to increase mutual trade. Moreover, after the European Development Fund agreed to finance a hard surface road from Ouagadougou to Popo on the Ghana frontier, Generals Lamizana and Ankrah exchanged state visits in 1968. The two countries created joint committees to study an economic *rapprochement,* signed a border agreement termed a "charter" of good neighborly relations, and agreed for the first time to allow enterprising Ghanaian truck drivers to carry goods to several Voltaic cities. Other agreements concerned the purchase of electric power from Ghana and the extension of the repayment period for a previous Ghanaian loan. The presence in Upper Volta, during General Ankrah's visit, of the president of the Dakar Chamber of Commerce, M. Henri-Charles Gallenca, was a sign that Upper Volta's economic policy need not remain oriented toward Abidjan to the extent that it has been in the past.

defined by an Armed Forces Council which included the president of the republic, the chief of the general staff, and the cabinet. The executive included five civilians and eight military officers (increased to nine in April, 1967). To round out the structure, there was a quasi-legislative advisory body called the Consultative Committee, whose 41 members included 10 military officers (but no government official), and which was presided over by a military official.

The formal structure of the Soglo government reflected a gradual increase in military control. The cabinet created on December 24, 1965, included four military officers and ten civilians. The military were given some—but not all—of the most sensitive posts: defense, interior, and security. Well-trained civilian elites, only some of them with a clear political affiliation, were tapped for such crucial posts as foreign affairs, agriculture, and financial and economic affairs. As General Soglo explained: "For the first time Ministers were chosen for their competence. . . . The Minister of National Education is a professor, the one for Agriculture an agricultural engineer, the one for Health a physician."[31]

The executive was assisted at first by a mixed military/civilian National Renovation Committee (formerly elected regional councils were replaced by regional renovation committees). The national committee (NRC) included representatives from the officer corps, unions, religious communities, and other "interest" groups—a total of 36 members selected by Soglo at the end of December. The authority given to the NRC, however, compared unfavorably with that of the pre-independence territorial assemblies created by the French; it could merely "deliberate on fundamental principles" of social and economic problems, be consulted by and make suggestions to the cabinet, and ask for joint NRC-government meetings.[32]

Tensions between the NRC and military officers, arising in part from an NRC claim for more authority, resulted in its dissolution and replacement, in April, 1967, by a Military Vigilance Committee (MVC) made up of eleven officers and four noncommissioned officers. Officially, they were entrusted with the responsibility of supervising all government activities. Lieutenant Colonel Alley emphasized that decisions were to be made henceforth by the armed forces and pointed out that the civilian members of the cabinet were there only "because we believe that they are qualified."[33]

31. *Le Monde,* June 30, 1966.
32. "Le CNR: Une institution destinée à épauler l'action du gouvernement," typescript (Cotonou: n.d.).
33. *L'Aube nouvelle,* April 16, 1967.

POLITICAL FORCES

The military regimes had to deal with two political forces: those organized specifically for political action, and the trade unions. Upper Volta's government was confronted with two kinds of partisan political forces when it took over the reins of government. The first was Yaméogo's RDA machine, whose followers were long associated with and dependent upon the former president of the republic and attempted to salvage what they could from the badly bruised organization. Under the leadership of a new secretary-general, the RDA blamed Yaméogo for having used the party for personal ends against the wishes of the members. But the RDA rapidly split into two wings, one orthodox and the other tending toward "renovation." The leadership generally emphasized the need for a government which "represented" the popular masses and accordingly called for rapid elections, hoping to capitalize on the RDA rump to renew some personnel while leaving the party structure relatively intact.

The second partisan political force was made up of (a) small urban and/or regional parties banished into obscurity under Yaméogo and hastily reconstituted when the military took over, and (b) traditional forces seeking to reassert themselves.

Small urban and/or regional parties included the Parti du Regroupement Africain (PRA) and the Mouvement de Libération Nationale (MLN). Both had come into existence in 1958. The PRA was an outgrowth of Bobo regionalism and an alliance of convenience with the federalist forces before independence. It was reactivated by Nazi Boni from his long Dakar exile, favored a two-party system including the PRA and one other, and was clearly out of touch with the realities of 1966. Aside from offering the services of cadres unsullied by contamination with the Yaméogo regime and from proposing a vague economic recovery program, its leaders spoke of an "eclectic Africanism" and declared that "we want to assimilate completely French culture with which we are so happily impregnated in order to invigorate our own and affirm our personality."[34]

The MLN, by contrast, was better attuned to the needs of the day, but it suffered from an overly "intellectual" image which stood in the way of increasing its rather limited urban appeal. Under the

---

34. *Afrique nouvelle,* September 8, 1966.

leadership of a man of international renown, Joseph Ki Zerbo, the MLN called for a mobilization regime led by vigorous, imaginative youth contrasting with the sterile old guard of rival parties. In view of its narrow popular base, it emphasized the need for a collegial political system resulting from agreement at the top among the contending parties and based upon a "minimum" program. The MLN also favored bringing Yaméogo to trial as soon as possible so as to remove potential competition from RDA remnants. After an agreement at the top, it envisaged a campaign to "enlighten and educate" the rural masses to secure the popular support it lacked at the outset. In spite of past opposition to the Entente, the MLN favored nonalignment and friendship with all nations, and projected to the voters the blurred and distant image of a "Swiss or California type prosperity [so as] to merit at least the esteem of countries which want to help us, France in particular."[35]

Traditional forces included both Muslim minority and Mossi majority. The former found expression in an Ouagadougou-based Groupement d'Action Populaire (GAP) under the leadership of a veterinarian, Dr. Nouhoum Sigué. As it had few followers, GAP opposed the formation of a future single party, arguing that at least two parties were necessary for a democratic future.

Some 100 Mossi chiefs from all over Upper Volta met with the Mossi Emperor, the Moro Naba Kougri, in his Ouagadougou palace at the end of March, 1968. Apparently in an attempt to revitalize the Syndicat des Chefs Coutumiers, somnolent since its creation in 1953, they declared themselves to be indispensable to the nation and asked for the revocation of the arbitrary measures which Yaméogo had taken against them.

Lamizana's response to the country's political fragmentation was to undertake several serious efforts to reconcile the warring political factions. At first he encouraged the four political parties (RDA, PRA, MLN, and GAP) to unite and agree on their country's future political structure. It soon became clear, however, that each party sought to eliminate the others by tailoring its policies to its chances for success. Moreover, solicitation of support resulted in an "incident" which demonstrated the depth of the parties' mutual antagonisms as well as the attendant threats to political stability in Upper Volta. The incident was a violent clash between RDA and MLN supporters in Yaméogo's home town of Koudougou. MLN leaders had decided to hold what they called an "information" meeting in that city—probably a tactical error in view of the local strength of

35. *Ibid.*

RDA supporters who, confronted with the MLN delegation, showed up in large numbers and precipitated a riot. President Lamizana subsequently forbade all political activity and replaced the local administrator with an army officer.[36]

Realizing that the political parties would not come to an agreement if left to their own devices, Lamizana convened a series of roundtable discussions in September and October, 1966; he made it clear that, once they agreed, he would supervise elections and turn the government over to civilians. But the parties, once more, could agree only on meaningless generalities such as the desirability of at least two parties and of their participation in writing a new constitution. Some of them pointedly—and gratuitously—reminded the army that it should prepare a return to "democracy" and retire to their barracks. It was only after these events that Lamizana decided to sweep the political process aside and to remain in office for another four years.[37]

In both countries, political partisanship follows either traditional, near-sacral lines, or "modern," overlapping criteria of issues and opportunism. In Dahomey, political fragmentation is more acute and widespread than in Upper Volta. Long years of political partisanship among relatively equal regional supporters have bred narrow attitudes which pervade simple conversations, orient perceptions, and deflect efforts toward objectivity. Nearly every politically conscious citizen is also committed to the proposition that only *his* leader has the right answers and follows the correct policy. Some order their children to keep off a road because it was built by the opposition, others openly deplore a "Dahomean mentality" denoting intolerance and opposition for the sake of opposition.

The intensity and longevity of this type of partisanship may be illustrated by a few examples. In January, 1966, the Soglo regime discovered an alleged plot to overthrow the government; several

36. *Ibid.*, September 29, 1966.
37. His determination was reinforced, if anything, following an alleged attempt at a coup d'état by Yaméogo supporters in September 1967. The plotters, denounced by a union leader whose support they were courting, included Maurice Yaméogo's first wife, two of his sons, and the son of former Foreign Minister Koné Bégnon; they called themselves the "Club of Palace Children" and distributed tracts calling for the government's overthrow. At first the government reacted mildly, considering that this "ye-ye" crowd was inoffensive enough. But after subsequent investigations revealed plans to assassinate Lamizana and other government leaders, as well as union and RDA leader Joseph Ouédraogo, that a "Committee for the Liberation of Maurice Yaméogo" also allegedly involved a number of Voltaic diplomats stationed in Abidjan, and that the plotters had called for a civil war and contacted some army officers and other officials, the ringleaders were arrested.

leaders were arrested—including Gabriel Lozès, former PDD secretary-general and foreign minister in the Ahomadegbé cabinet, and former Cotonou Mayor Theodore Hessou—for having distributed tracts inviting the population to revolt.[38] In April, 1966, Soglo toured northern Dahomey to calm people fearful for their political future. In September he issued a stern warning after several Ahomadegbé supporters were arrested and denounced as responsible for creating a sense of crisis in major cities; the government established a special military tribunal to deal with troublemakers. In February, 1967, citizens in the northern city of Parakou talked about a forthcoming "battle of revenge," and the local prefect admitted that there was a "psychosis of general fear, hatred, and distrust."[39] Three months later, President Soglo told the nation:

> I am warning you for the last time against the illusions, the sterile agitation and the criminal maneuvers of those who want to lead us into ruin and misery and, instead of building, know only how to destroy.[40]

In addition to specific partisanship, there was evidence of a very fundamental disaffection from the post-independence political system, and that many Dahomeans questioned the usefulness of their "national" experience since 1960. As one African observer put it, "I would not be honest if I said that all Dahomeans are in agreement about independence."[41] Apathy and disorientation remained, and "one more or less waits for things to happen; one plots; one wants to oust the government without knowing exactly by whom and by what to replace it."[42] In such a frame of mind, few people recognized for long the legitimacy of any government, civilian or military. An editorial in the government newspaper, for example, complained in February, 1967, that

> in the young African states, "support" has entered political customs to such an extent that, at times, each *quartier* has its specialists in support messages, of course of the indefectible attachment variety . . . to all regimes.[43]

Upon taking over the government in 1965, Soglo could not align himself with the discredited regional leaders. Consequently he

38. *Le Monde*, January 29, 1966. Messrs. Lozès and Hessou were subsequently pardoned by President Soglo and released.
39. *Afrique nouvelle*, March 30, 1967.
40. *L'Aube nouvelle*, April 9, 1967.
41. *Afrique nouvelle*, September 30, 1966.
42. *Ibid.*
43. *L'Aube nouvelle*, February 19, 1967.

sought the cooperation of some members of the country's intellectual elite. The ten civilians whom he co-opted as cabinet members had no actual or damaging previous association with civilian regimes, although they may have had their preferences among the big three,[44] and were chosen ostensibly for their neutral, technocrat role in the new government.

At the beginning of the Soglo regime it looked as though the "technocrats" were just that. They were careful to dissociate themselves from whatever past reputation as "troublemakers" they may have had.[45] It soon became evident, however, that the military's expectations of neutrality on the part of the younger intellectuals were erroneous. Some civilians, in fact, tried to guide government policy toward a version of "African Socialism" with which the armed forces were not comfortable; military-civilian differences on that issue developed into a split which led the most committed among the civilians—Finance Minister Nicéphore Soglo, Rural Development Minister Moise Mensah, and Planning High Commissioner Christian Vieyra—to resign from the government.

Those who view themselves as the intellectual elite, mostly teachers, holders of college and graduate degrees, and some professional people, make up a relatively small though articulate group without much popular support. Regardless of whether they once joined in a political party, as with the MLN in Upper Volta, or remained outside without a single organization, their progressive views did not appeal to urban workers, most of whom are civil servants; slogans like "Africanization is a categorical imperative,"

44. Much speculation in Dahomey has surrounded the question of the "technocrats'" alignment with the "big three" regional leaders. On the surface, it is striking that among the ten civilians, six were sympathetic to Apithy, two to Maga. Moreover, of the six new cabinet members appointed between the end of 1966 and March, 1967, to replace those who resigned, three each were sympathizers of Maga aind Apithy. The absence of Ahomadegbé supporters could be—and was in some quarters—attributed to the animosity between Ahomadegbé and Soglo. But that interpretation appears to be misleading because the four or five civilian cabinet members believed to place the national interest above personal considerations happened to be from Porto Novo and thus harbored "regionally determined" sympathies for Apithy. Moreover, one "Maga sympathizer" appointed in March, 1967, had, for entirely personal reasons, contracted an alliance of convenience with Ahomadegbé and thus could have been termed an Ahomadegbé "supporter."

45. Thus René Dossa, who in 1958 was believed by the French to be an "extremist nationalist" and a Communist, called on his countrymen to "let us build our economy, enough of politics." Professor Adotévi, who in 1963 had been accused of founding a Marxist party and imprisoned by Maga, said that "the question is no longer to be an intellectual of the left or not, but to see with realism what can be useful to Dahomey." See Le Monde, June 30, 1966.

aside from their intrinsic merits, have not attracted the rural masses.

To compensate for this handicap they have sought to associate themselves, at crucial moments of instability, with other groups which seemed to present an effective challenge to constituted authority. Intellectuals in Dahomey forged links with some military leaders and were given some government responsibility after the 1965 military intervention. Intellectuals in Upper Volta had an opportunity to challenge the larger political parties by reviving their own party created in the late 1950's in response to a specific issue, a party largely inactive since that issue disappeared. However, Voltaic intellectuals failed to establish, or maintain, their place under the official sun. This failure may be attributed to two basic causes. One was that, when competition occurred in the context of party politics, the odds were against them. They had neither the organization, the membership, the revenue, nor the issues on which the larger parties had been able to capitalize. Moreover, the fiasco of Koudougou in September, 1966, strengthened widely held beliefs that the MLN was fine in the classroom but sadly lacking in sound judgment for the greater tasks of politics.

The intellectuals' accession to important government posts in Dahomey points to the second major reason for their failure. Their notions of the best road to progress found little echo among either unions or military leaders; if they had hoped to "control" army officers, as has been alleged, then they were proven wrong. Their resignation from the government resulted from fundamental disagreements about basic policy issues and from their failure to convince others; it reinforced their reputation of being "too theoretical." From what could be learned unofficially in conversations in August, 1967, they were resented as much for the content as for the form of their advice and suggestions.

As committed "technocrats" they favored taking at least some steps designed to mobilize popular support and to accent industrialization. They complained about the "nausea of easy independence," sought to create a development mystique, and participated actively during July and August, 1966, in a brain trust which submitted written policy recommendations to the government. Neither the discussions nor the report were ever made public among the government, the military, and the NRC. The plan recommended, *inter alia*, the nationalization of some public utilities so as to reduce chronic operating deficits, creation of a national lottery under government control, closing diplomatic posts in African countries. Reportedly, the recommendations also envisaged the creation of a new institution to control the government. From what could be learned, the officer corps rejected the plan although some favored it, and the resulting crisis led to the formation of the Military Vigilance Committee discussed below.

As a source of independent opposition, the intellectuals seem relatively harmless if only because of structural and ideological fragmentation. Many, if not most, have retired from government and returned to teaching and writing, or sought greener pastures with international organizations. Unless they are called upon once more as advisers to the powers that be, their influence seems destined to remain slight.

The very system embodied in the military regime created a number of additional frictions. Civilian cabinet members complained about military officers attending and participating in cabinet meetings; as we have seen, the NRC yearned for more authority, arguing that it was more representative than the armed forces; displaced politicians resented the loss of patronage and the arrival of upstart "technicians" ignorant about politics; the French-controlled business community chafed under the technicians' blunt ways; and nearly everybody complained about the military's highhandedness in performing their duties.[46]

The other major political force with which the military had to deal were the unions, whose influence derived from a number of factors. First, unions had graduated from the passive role-perceptions which they entertained during previous regimes. Consequently they made greater demands on government. Second, restless members forced additional militancy upon their leaders. And third, since political parties were forced to remain officially inactive, unions knew that they constituted the only "power base" left for the military to lean upon.

Confronted with the need for at least some organized popular

46. At one time, several high army officers returning from neighboring Togo refused to heed the Dahomean customs officials' insistence that they pay import duty on the whisky they were bringing back; at least one customs official was imprisoned. When Me. Bertin Borna took over as minister of financial and economic affairs after the dismissal of Nicéphore Soglo, a cousin of the general, Mr. Pierre Fourn, president of the Cotonou chamber of commerce, complained publicly that the previous minister took important measures without consulting him and implied that, as a result, 1966 was one of the worst business years in Dahomey's history. In May, 1967, Major Adandédjan was removed as security director. In September, 1966, Defense Minister Lieutenant Colonel Aho cut short a European trip to tour Dahomey's military camps following some rumors that army officers were too strict in implementing government policy; Aho was later dismissed from his post, allegedly for being responsible for the mistreatment of prisoners. See *Afrique nouvelle,* September 15, 1966; and *L'Aube nouvelle,* January 22, 1967.

support and with their simultaneous commitment to economic recovery, the armed forces have spoken loudly and carried a small stick. On the surface, government-union relations suggest a positive correlation between increased military control, on one hand, and a better climate for economic improvement, on the other. But that correlation was also function of the degree of mutual trust and of the military's willingness to seek union leaders' counsel; tensions remained and union support could not be taken for granted.

In Upper Volta, relations between unions and the military were closer than in Dahomey. It is true that government leaders warned the unions to stay out of politics. Finance Minister Damiba, for instance, has remonstrated with "the wealthy elite who often have a standard of living à l'américaine, and who, in addition to their waste and prestige expenses, transfer their savings outside the country."[47] President Lamizana, a few months after taking office, warned the unions that they must not

> substitute themselves for the authority of the state or the government. If we accept counsel and advice, these must not become unrealizable demands, much less shattering views which would embarrass our actions.[48]

In spite of these public pronouncements, there was a good deal of cooperation between unions and government. Union leaders obviously feared a return to the *ancien régime* and thus had a common interest with the armed forces, who were willing to consult them on important aspects of economic policy. Lower austerity measures than in Dahomey and better economic prospects also contributed to at least tolerable relations.

Tensions nonetheless remained, and union leaders concentrated on three demands: (1) removal of restrictions to free assembly; (2) abrogation of the "anti-economic" austerity measures on the grounds that they are counterproductive—lower purchasing power breeds business recession which in turn decreases government revenue; and (3) for political reasons, the trial of Yaméogo and his chief lieutenants. Only a few specific recommendations, however, were forthcoming out of union criticism, and some of these were adopted and implemented by the government.

47. *Afrique nouvelle,* October 20, 1966. Dominique Kaboré, civil service minister, took the service to task by saying that "negligence has created an atmosphere of insecurity and withdrawal. The decadence of the state, waste, abuse, favoritism, routine, and inertia have resulted in a sclerosis on which foundered our decaying civil service" (*ibid.,* September 1, 1966).
48. *Ibid.,* June 23, 1966.

Union leaders, moreover, considered the government's announcement of December, 1966, that it would remain in office for four more years the equivalent of a military coup d'état; they criticized the government for having broken its earlier promise to return to civilian rule as quickly as possible.[49]

In Dahomey, the Soglo regime's relations with the unions were less successful than in Upper Volta. Deeper tensions resulted from three major causes: (1) stern austerity measures which were extended to the private sector and thus gave unions a common grievance against the government; (2) economic stagnation which sapped the unions' confidence in the military regime and cast doubt on the usefulness of further sacrifices; and (3) gradual centralization of national decision-making authority in military hands (discussed in the next section). Union unrest was touched off by the dissolution of the National Renovation Committee in mid-1966; it gathered momentum during 1967, and culminated in a general strike at the end of that year which forced the government to make important concessions.

A strike by private employees in late 1966, protesting the extension of the 25 per cent salary cut, petered out in a few days because public employees still resented the previous lack of solidarity on the part of the private sector. Union determination to have the government end the salary cut surfaced again in August, 1967, when one important union declared that

> in matters political and social, the situation of the workers has never been so bad. The military-technocrat regime of General Soglo, extending its hand to all those which preceded it since independence, has surpassed them in cynicism.[50]

The government reacted firmly, announced that "authority must be re-established," and some union leaders went to prison. Another showdown was averted shortly afterward when the government took a union grievance to the courts.[51]

The next phase of the union-government confrontation began toward the end of 1967, after President Soglo had returned from

49. Tensions occasionally surfaced, such as on May 1, 1967, when the government feared a rebellion led by unions on their traditional May Day celebration and prepared for the worst by placing troops at strategic spots. Some residents canceled their weekend plans and loaded their cameras in anticipation of the forthcoming excitement. Although the atmosphere was tense, nothing happened, whether because of the military's preparations or union second thoughts.

50. *Afrique nouvelle,* September 14, 1967.

51. *Ibid.,* cf. *Jeune Afrique,* October 29, 1967, pp. 15–16.

Paris with the promise of increased French aid for the Dahomean economy. Primary school teachers struck on December 8, 1967, asking for an end to the 25 per cent salary cut and the restoration of housing indemnities; they were joined within a few days by the entire private sector and by the postal employees, and supported by the country's three large labor federations. Again the government at first reacted firmly by banning all trade union activity. But since the ban had no effect, the government backed down. When workers remained on strike after the useless ban was revoked, the armed forces chief of staff, Lieutenant Colonel Alphonse Alley, negotiated an agreement satisfactory to the unions. The government agreed to reconsider its austerity program and announced the formation of an *ad hoc* committee (with union representation) to study a new policy. The confrontation thus ended in a union victory and a government retreat—and, within a few days, in the deposition of the Soglo regime.

THE MILITARY:
CHARACTERISTICS AND ATTITUDES

A number of attitudes and norms helped determine the behavior of the armed forces. These may be classified into three categories: those concerning the length of their "intervention" in politics, those concerning the political system, and those regarding nationalism.

The military have viewed their role as that of a temporary stabilizer churned up by chronic instability. This was true as much in 1963 as in 1967. In 1963, as we have seen, Soglo took over only to retire to the barracks within three months. Quarrels among political leaders were seen as roadblocks to be removed by the jolt of rebellion and army control. Having formed a provisional government including the big three, Soglo announced that "the army brings its support *to the three leaders* . . . and does not ask to participate in the government to be formed subsequently."[52] In 1965, the army leaders' attitude shifted toward a somewhat more active army role and critical evaluation of their civilian superiors. They now tended to recognize openly the failure of civilian politicians. Soglo, for example, said that "after two years, the political leaders . . . have shown their inability to lead the country."[53] Nonetheless, both Soglo and Lamizana attempted to reconcile the very political

52. *Afrique nouvelle,* October 31, 1963, emphasis added.
53. *Ibid.,* December 30, 1965.

96

leaders whom they castigated with past failure. President Soglo, in fact, declined Houphouet's mediation seeking to bring about a Maga-Ahomadegbé coalition; the general insisted that genuine national cooperation would require three, not two, of the country's regional leaders.[54]

The military officers' initial reluctance to commit themselves to political leadership may have resulted in part from norms determined by the colonial situation: distance, silence, and the propitiation of the establishment. During the colonial period, armed forces were symbols of administrative authority, with loyalties pulling toward the "mother country" rather than toward their African locale. Moreover, French officer tradition—the contrary de Gaulle experience notwithstanding—rested on the notion of the armed forces army as *la grande muette*, a silent partner expected to stay out of politics. In addition, officers like Soglo, Lamizana, and Alley had to be pliable to play the game in the French-controlled services in order to advance through the ranks; consequently they were not burdened with well-articulated political objectives which would be serviceable in the post-independence national context in which they were called upon to function.

A thoroughly antipolitical attitude made up the second category of the military's attitudes. This attitude extended to individual political leaders and to the political process as well. Time spent on political quarrels is wasted and should be spent on economic development, which is threatened by the injection of irrelevant, "political" considerations. Farmers ought to be able to work in peace instead of being distracted by politics. Politicians are irresponsible upstarts who, unlike military professionals, have not absorbed the integrity required of high office and consequently could not be expected to perform any better than they did.[55]

Government responsibilities influenced the military's view of politics, at least to the extent that fundamental aspects of the system had to be changed. Both governments announced repeatedly that the normalization of political life must be preceded by a change in politicians' priorities. Thus, Soglo spoke of a "new political style,

54. The Ivory Coast president's intercession took place in Abidjan during an Entente meeting where Messrs. Ahomadegbé and Maga embraced and declared their willingness to work together in the future. General Soglo, who was present at the ceremony, did not commit himself in Abidjan but announced his opposition to such a move upon his return to Cotonou.

55. The transition in attitudes may not be so clear-cut as suggested here. Soglo, for instance, went through a period when he blamed the system rather than the men who symbolized it. But the attitudes presented above were confirmed during numerous interviews in the summer of 1967.

where men . . . unite around a program and not around a few personalities."[56] Lamizana said that a civilian government was possible only after the civilians had become "responsible and patriotic men who will know how to silence their personal dissensions and apply themselves to a minimum program acceptable to all."[57] A future legislature, he added, "will give you responsibilities whose existence you might not suspect, and you will perhaps have to make unpopular decisions of which you shall be the first victim."[58]

Their views on politics were influenced also by professional confidence and foreign example. Many officers regarded their takeover as a kind of African counterpart to the fifth French republic in the sense that an ailing, lame, corrupt, and ineffectual regime was replaced by a vigorous, healthy, new system led by incorruptible military officers. Comparison with France yielded faith in recovery through military intervention, such as when *L'Aube nouvelle* pointed out that, if General de Gaulle could rally the French people behind him at a time when he was in exile, then African military leaders should be able to do at least as much when serving at the head of their countries at home.

A discussion of the military's "nationalism" may usefully distinguish between normative and structural aspects of that phenomenon. Once the military had decided to neutralize dysfunctional subnational political conflict, their chief concern was the continuation of their countries' national existence. As head of the 1963 provisional government, Soglo explained that "the major reason for which the Dahomean armed forces have intervened was to safeguard the Republic as well as . . . the authority of the state."[59] For this reason it was essential that the entire nation associate itself with the forthcoming changes. One of his chief concerns in 1965 was that "we shall continue to appeal to all, whatever their political past, to help us in our task of national reconstruction."[60] Lamizana struck the same note shortly after his takeover when he said: "I am not from any village, city, or region; I am Voltaic; I say no more."[61] These statements betrayed more than the need for immediate popular support; they showed a dedication and concern for the nation as an abstraction. This was expressed by President Soglo when he said that "a nation [may be able to] recover from an

56. *Afrique nouvelle,* December 30, 1965.
57. *Ibid.,* June 23, 1966.
58. *Ibid.,* May 4, 1966.
59. *Ibid.,* November 14, 1963.
60. *Ibid.,* January 6, 1966.
61. *Ibid.,* February 2, 1966.

economic crisis . . . [but] it is impossible to heal the sickness of the soul which gnaws at her."[62] That the military were thinking in primarily national terms is evident also from the emphasis given to their announcement, near the end of 1966, that they would continue in office. When Alphonse Alley, Dahomey's Chief of Staff, declared that "there is no question, in present circumstances, that this government make room for a civilian government," he added:

> [Assuming that] the army is in a position to bring about the unity of the country, still divided among the traditional big three parties, it will be only when the grudges are silent and unity is achieved that we can think of elections.[63]

From what may be called a "structural" point of view, the armed forces of Dahomey and Upper Volta are national. First, they were created from scratch after independence. Dahomey's armed forces, for instance, came into being in July, 1960, its gendarmerie in September, 1961, and its air force three months later. Second, they were built up by nationals who, although they had previously served under the French flag, nonetheless opted to serve their new country. Thus Lieutenant Colonel Soglo became his country's first chief of the general staff in 1960 after resigning from his job as France's military adviser to the new Dahomean government and acquiring Dahomean citizenship. Similarly, Major Lamizana was Upper Volta's first head of the armed forces in 1961.[64]

62. *L'Aube nouvelle*, January 8, 1967.
63. *Afrique nouvelle*, May 12, 1966.
64. For details, see (1) for Upper Volta: (a) *Décret 282 PRES–I–GR, définissant l'organisation générale et le fonctionnement du corps de le Garde Républicaine, Journal officiel de la République de Haute Volta (JORHV)*, July 22, 1961; and (b) *Décret 101 PRES–CM, portant création et organisation de l'état-major des forces armées, JORHV*, April 7, 1962; and (2) for Dahomey: (a) *Loi 60–32*, July 28, 1960, creating the Dahomean armed forces; (b) *Arrêté 42 DSFA portant création d'un corps de troupe dit Gendarmerie Nationale, Journal officiel de la République du Dahomey (JORD)*, October 1, 1961; (c) *Arrêté 645 MAID/CTM portant création de l'Escadrille Nationale, JORD*, December 5, 1961; (d) *Arrêté 1 MAID/CTM portant organisation des Forces Armées Dahoméennes, JORD*, February 1, 1962; (e) *Loi 62–10 portant organisation générale de la défense nationale et des Forces Armées, JORD*, March 1, 1962; and (f) *Arrêté 39 GPRD/SGDN portant organisation des Forces Armées, JORD*, February 1, 1964.
Upper Volta's armed forces include 1,500 troops, 1,500 gendarmes, and some 300 civilian police; those of Dahomey consist of 1,700 troops, 1,200 gendarmes, a fledgling air force of 100 men, and 1,000 civilian police.
Dahomey's armed forces were reorganized in August, 1966. The chief of the general staff was made responsible for (a) the Service Group (including one garrison company and one staff company); (b) the National Gendarmerie (including six national companies and mobile units—one squad per administrative Department); (c) the Tactical Group (including two infantry

Third, officers and noncommissioned officers were rapidly Africanized after independence. They were either transferred from French and/or colonial forces or taken into service upon graduation from French military schools.[65] Fourth, the last French base—and soldier—was evacuated from both states by the end of 1964.

Finally, the likelihood of intervention by external military forces in the domestic affairs of either state was remote; there is no evidence that such intervention was contemplated at any time by France. As is well known, Dahomey has a defense agreement with the former metropole. Upper Volta refused to consider such an agreement because of the role played by the French garrison in Bobo-Dioulasso shortly before independence.[66]

The bilateral Dahomean-French agreement provides for mutual assistance in the preparation and execution of national defense. Presumably, France could honor a request for military intervention

---

battalions with a total of five combat companies; one support group consisting of an armored squadron, one commando unit, one engineers company, and one support company); and (d) one Pioneer Battalion. The assistant chief of the general staff was given responsibility for (a) the Air Force, (b) the Health Services, (c) General Services, (d) Materiel and Maintenance Services, and (e) Engineers and Construction Services. See *Décret 306 PR/ MISDN, portant réorganisation des Forces Armées Dahoméennes, JORD,* August 15, 1966.

The national gendarmerie was placed under the direct authority of the chief of staff as an "integral part of the Dahomean Armed Forces" on December 15, 1965, during the life of the provisional government headed by Tahirou Congacou. See *Décret 128, PR/DGN, relatif à la nouvelle articulation de le Gendarmerie Nationale, JORD,* January 15, 1966.

A further reorganization of the Dahomean armed forces was initiated by its new chief of staff, Major Alphonse Alley. The "military" function was concentrated in an elite paratroop commando, a kind of internal *force de frappe* which could cope with internal disorders throughout the country. The bulk of the armed forces was to serve (a) to help the population build and repair bridges and roads, and to fight fires and floods; and (b) as cadres for "Engineer Battalions" of some 30 peasants each from the same village, thus laying the groundwork for a pool of "civic service" oriented citizens paralleling the technical cadres for the modernization of agriculture. See *Afrique nouvelle,* May 12, 1966.

65. M. J. V. Bell reports that France instituted a "crash programme" for training African officers in 1956, and that by the time the African states became independent they had enough officers to cover two-thirds of their requirements. He notes also that, in 1964, there were some 1,500 Africans undergoing officer training in France. See his *Army and Nation in Sub-Saharan Africa,* Institute for Strategic Studies, Adelphi Papers, no. 21 (London: 1965), pp. 8–9.

66. According to Voltaic government officials, Maurice Yaméogo's refusal to sign a defense agreement with France resulted from a dispute between Yaméogo and the French governor, M. Masson. The latter had helped Yaméogo by supporting his candidacy as the African head of the government

should this come from a legal government unable to repel armed attack across its frontiers;[67] but such an attack seems hardly likely. Under the terms of the agreement, France could intervene also to restore and maintain domestic order. But this is no more than theoretical because of the untoward repercussions of previous French intervention in Gabon, of the confused nature and rapid development of political crises, and of the lack of clear strategic importance of both states for France. The French government has continued to provide moderate technical assistance and equipment for both states, but this cannot justify French military intervention.

Neither is foreign African military intervention a serious threat to either country. Both Dahomey and Upper Volta belong to the Union Africaine et Malgache de Défense (UAMD) whose head-quarters are in Ouagadougou, and have signed a multilateral defense agreement with the other members of the Entente. There were unconfirmed reports that the government of Niger supplied President Yaméogo with tear-gas grenades during the last stages of the January, 1966, rebellion; there were also rumors of impending intervention by troops from Togo, Niger, and other neighboring countries, and of an appeal by President Maga in 1965 for Togolese and Nigerian troops to help quell a union strike. These were, however, emphatically denied, and may have been attempts by threatened civilian governments to discredit the armed forces at a crucial

---

under the 1956 French enabling act, for which service Yaméogo reportedly promised to use his influence in Paris to retain Masson as French high commissioner. A subsequent dispute between the two men led to a Yaméogo request that Masson leave the country; the governor, however, ensconced himself in the French military base at Bobo-Dioulasso and began mobilizing the support of the Voltaic veterans under the leadership of Captain Michel Dorange in Ouahigouya. Yaméogo, in danger of losing important political support, called on Jacques Foccart (later to become secretary-general for African affairs in the French *Presidence de la République*) who removed Masson from his post. Although this incident sealed a longtime Yaméogo-Foccart "friendship"—Yaméogo has referred to Foccart as "Mon Blanc à Moi"—the conclusion drawn by Yaméogo was that the presence of French armed forces on Upper Volta soil could become a threat to the independence of the country. For the text and an interpretation of the agreements signed between France, Upper Volta, and Dahomey, consult Maurice Ligot, *Les Accords de coopération entre la France et les états africains et malgache d'expression française* (Paris: La Documentation Française, 1964).

67. As the last French soldiers were leaving Dahomey, turning over $2 million worth of equipment to the Dahomean armed forces, Dahomey's Premier declared that "we have assurances that [the French] would come back in force and in the shortest time if some *external* event were to threaten Dahomey's integrity" *Africa Report*, March 1965, p. 35, emphasis added.

moment of political unrest. The failure of inter-African security efforts to prevent both internal unrest and subversion from external sources is well known, and these cases were no exception.[68]

It cannot be said that the military have covered themselves with glory during the first two years of their civilian tenure. Built-in professional limitations—their limited objectives, biases against politics, and political innocence—prevented them from making an impact on the political system which they "inherited" from their predecessors. When the armed forces took over the government, they immediately lost the important trump of national arbitration, much as a new car depreciates as soon as it has been sold. Military government thus amounted to the removal of the only "balancer" in the political system capable of restoring order if order is widely challenged. The glamor of the armed forces' neutrality was tarnished further when they made the unpopular decision to remain in office. The military in political office thus became just another political regime, judged by the same criteria applied to preceding ones. It is true that physical coercion can be used to some extent, but also noteworthy that the military have not, as a rule, sat on their bayonets in confronting discontent.

The military faced apathy as well as resentment and impatience, and discovered that politics "uses" incumbents in unexpected ways. As we have seen, unrest was greater in Dahomey, mainly because of intense regional fragmentation, economic conditions, and austerity measures. In fact, the Dahomean regime demonstrated a certain lassitude, near the end of 1967, toward the political problems of the country. This was evident on several occasions when both Soglo and Alley visited the "big three" in Paris, reportedly to sound them out about the possibilities of their return to the government. The agreement reached with the trade unions in December, 1967, gave the military regime a black eye which only reinforced its weariness. As will be shown below, the inability of military professionals to initiate or allow the growth of political change was brought out even more sharply following the military *Putsch* in Dahomey in December, 1967.

68. Other rumors current in Ouagadougou affirmed that President Yaméogo considered calling for Ivoirien troops to maintain himself in power. If there is any substance to them, one may assume that Upper Volta's armed forces vetoed such a move on the grounds that they were quite capable of dealing with unrest, and that to suggest otherwise would be an affront to their professional competence.

THE MILITARY: DISUNITY

Although the contrast in the apparent unity of the officer corps in the two countries is striking, it would be a mistake to believe that Upper Volta's armed forces are monolithic. In Upper Volta, the officers have maintained a solid, outward front in their relations with the larger political system. This may be attributed to at least two factors: first, the officer corps was developed in part on a wide base of veterans of the French armed forces; and second, from the very beginning they not only controlled but also ran the government to a much greater extent than did their counterparts in Dahomey.

Occasional signs of disunity among the Voltaic officers have broken the surface. After discovery of the pro-Yaméogo attempted rebellion, for instance, it was learned that some army officers had been approached for support, and President Lamizana subsequently warned those "who have sworn to divide the army."[69] At the same time, the officer corps has been careful to remain united, as witness their December, 1966, decision to stay in office, signed by *"l'ensemble des officiers de l'armée voltaique."*[70] Serious problems have concerned elements of the gendarmerie whose national commander was dismissed, and the Garde Républicaine, against several members of which sanctions were taken after the Yaméogo "rebellion."

Dahomey's swift, bloodless military *Putsch* of December 17, 1967, was the result mostly of "generational" tensions in evidence since about the middle of 1966. It will be recalled that Soglo's cabinet included more civilians than military officers. Junior officers were dissatisfied with their relatively marginal role in public affairs, and sought gradually to acquire official responsibilities. They failed, in July, 1966, in a move to gain official access to the national decision-making machinery by proposing a Supreme Council of the Republic which would have given them equal status with the government and the National Renovation Council (NRC).

Another attempt to gain a place in the official sun in April, 1967, was a structural success; but it was based upon a compromise which left them more with the appearance than with the substance of authority. They succeeded in replacing the NRC with a Military

69. *Afrique nouvelle,* March 2, 1967.
70. *Ibid.,* December 15, 1966.

Vigilance Committee (MVC), whose members were appointed by the president of the republic on nomination from Alley. The MVC was to supervise the government's activities, although the senior officers had rejected the original suggestion that the MVC be empowered to dismiss the president of the republic—General Soglo—from his post. Alley was clearly in sympathy with some of their demands, and pointedly stated that "the real leader is he who can recognize his errors and draw lessons from previous faults."[71] A few months later the officers decided that they should be able to vote and resign their commission to enter government service.[72] Although the MVC was created primarily to placate the junior officers' drive for greater participation in national decisions, one of their complaints after the putsch was that "it was rapidly muzzled and paralyzed. Its role was confined to that of a roving comptroller . . . who meddles in everything but accomplishes nothing." Another complaint was that "no one ever listened to us," and "the fact that major decisions affecting the future of the country and serious military responsibilities were made within the family circle."[73]

It seems plausible that ethnic factors also played an important role in bringing about substantial disunity among the military leaders; their relative potency, however, cannot be ascertained without additional, more accurate information. It is likely that ethnic considerations were the servants of personal ambitions and rivalries. The oft-repeated charge by Maga's opponents that he "massively" recruited northerners for the armed forces and the gendarmerie seems vastly exaggerated, but it did condition the thinking of military leaders to some extent. To Northerners, it appeared that the Military Vigilance Committee was stacked with southerners (nine out of fifteen), and that three of them—Major Sinzogan as president, Major Adandédjan, and Captain Hachémé—controlled that committee. The trio, dubbed the "Abomey group," was apparently led by Major Adandédjan, who took pride in counting the Fon king Ghézo among his ancestors and who, although demoted by Soglo from the post of director of the security services to that of head of the general's military cabinet in May, 1967, remained sufficiently close to the center to give rise to continued suspicions. When the Young Turks took over in December, 1967,

71. *Ibid.,* May 4, 1967.
72. Previous military statutes stipulated that officers could neither vote nor seek elective office. See *Journal officiel de la République du Dahomey,* June 26, 1963, *Loi 63-5 sur le recrutement,* art. 39. The decision to revoke these stipulations was made in October, 1967; see *Afrique nouvelle,* October 12, 1967.
73. *L'Aube nouvelle,* December 24, 1967.

they were led by two northerners, and sidetracked both Adandédjan and Sinzogan. Another Fon, Major Chasme, was removed from his brief tenure as justice minister and, during his subsequent trial, openly complained of a northern conspiracy. No doubt northerners also remembered that, after the riots in Parakou in March, 1964, to protest the exclusion of prominent northerners from the Apithy-Ahomadegbé government, it was a Fon, Captain Hachémé, who was appointed military prefect and later accused of brutalities.

Several other, less potent reasons account for the Young Turks' rebellion. First, they resented at their elders' style. Most of the junior officers and some noncommissioned officers were recent graduates of French military academies and considered themselves as the armed forces' intellectuals. Attracted more by a Mobutu than by a Soglo, they resented, for example, along with many civilians, General Soglo's remark on his return from Paris in November, 1967, that Dahomeans behave so as to deserve the manna falling from Paris skies. Soglo was, in their eyes, an inoffensive teddy bear, but one who was not sufficiently attuned to the junior officers' pride in their new army and who, as a result of his long-time association with Frenchmen, allegedly shared some of the colonials' paternalism toward the new Dahomey.

Second, they bristled at their elders' "soft on unions" policy and viewed unions as unpatriotic, engaged in the selfish pursuit of narrow material interests. Whereas their superiors allowed their long experience in human affairs to mediate notions of military efficiency and thus to compromise with political forces, the junior officers were concerned with the maintenance of ideals in their pristine purity.

And third, junior officers were distraught by the general sense of failure which permeated not only the civilians but also the army officers. Their professional pride was at stake, and it chafed under vocal and strident criticism calling into question the armed forces' ability to run the country. As they expressed it in their proclamation: "The army was accused. It was said that the army had failed."[74]

The "old guard," including Soglo, Aho, and, to some extent, Alley, came up through the ranks, fought wars on three continents, and were incorporated into the new states' armed forces after independence, bringing with them, perhaps, a part of the French tradition of *la grande muette* internalized during long years of service in the French army. Soglo, 59, was known for his bonhomie, and he tended

74. *Ibid.*

toward compromise. As a substantial property owner he had a stake in a modicum of stability and looked forward to his retirement.[75] Perhaps the most interesting portrait of General Soglo as a political leader was sketched by a Dahomean barely three months before the *Putsch* which dismissed him as president of the republic:

> A rough and snappy friendship, a taste for humour and practical jokes, but also a sense of responsibility. Frequently in the streets of Cotonou, he stops his car and, with disdain for protocol, mingles with the crowd of passers-by to ask how people are, sometimes with friendly taps on the back.
>
> The man is not an intellectual and is vocal in his delight about it. He does not like the gymnastics . . . of the mind. He is a peasant with solid good sense and the instinct of a salmon. No one has ever seen him buried and obstinate in one direction at the expense of another. He has an open mind, without an ounce of dogmatism . . . he knows how to listen and, unfortunately, has the weakness to succumb to the magic of words, since he often sides with the most subtle tongue.[76]

Colonel Alley's career resembles that of Soglo in many ways.[77] Unlike Soglo, however, he was admired by junior officers. He was born in north-central Dahomey into a minority ethnic group but grew up in the south; he reportedly speaks several southern languages without a trace of an accent; consequently he tended to bridge, in the eyes of civilians and military alike, whatever role regional or ethnic divisions may play among the officers and soldiers. He enjoyed a reputation for being decisive—though not rigid.

75. His property includes real estate in Cotonou, including the buildings housing the US Embassy and the American Cultural Center. Christophe Soglo was born in Abomey in 1909 and volunteered for service in the French army at 21. He participated in the French 1939–40 campaign and won a citation for bravery. Under the Vichy regime he went to Morocco with the Régiment d'Infanterie Coloniale du Maroc, France's most decorated regiment. Later he served with the 6th Régiment de Tirailleurs Sénégalais and, as second lieutenant, took part in the landings on Corsica, Elba, and in Provence where he won another citation. Assigned to the General Staff of Colonial Troops at the end of World War II, he became military adviser to the French overseas minister in 1947. Promoted to captain in 1950, he was sent first to the Ivory Coast, then to Tonkin and to Cochin China, where he met his wealthy, half-caste wife and was decorated with the prestigious *croix de guerre*. A few years later he was promoted to major (*chef de bataillon*) and assigned in 1956 to Senegal as staff officer at the French military base near Dakar. In 1960 he was attached to the office of the French prime minister, then to the new government of Dahomey as military adviser.

76. Paulin Joachim, "Le Général Soglo, ou le provisoire qui dure," *Europe France-outre-mer*, 453 (1967), 14.

77. Born on April 9, 1937, he served in the French armed forces, advanced through the ranks, and fought in Vietnam, Algeria, and Morocco, later served in Dahomey where he was transferred at the rank of lieutenant in 1961.

He was credited with persuading unions, in 1963, to accept a presidential regime instead of the parliamentary system they advocated at the time. He was responsible, also, for settling the long series of union grievances by negotiating the agreement in December, 1967, following which the workers returned to their job. He was frequently the voice of the armed forces and was chosen to make policy announcements. It was he who expressed the army's confidence in its ability to measure up to the tasks it had set for itself: "What . . . [the military] are presently doing in Dahomey, no other government could do."[78]

In spite of Alley's sympathies for the junior officers, his role perceptions prevented him from siding with them all the way. As the chief of staff of the armed forces, he could not allow the junior officers to take over the government and engineered the compromise which resulted in the MVC. The Young Turks repeatedly asked him to dismiss General Soglo from the presidency of the republic, but his loyalty to his commander remained stronger and he refused, although he probably could have emerged at the head of his country's government.

THE MILITARY: CONFLICTING LOYALTIES

Dahomey's military *Putsch* did not benefit from the support of trade unions or civilian elites; it resulted solely from the cleavages among the officer corps. An open split among the officers became evident on December 16 when Major Maurice Kouandété refused to attend a meeting called by his chief of staff to consider future policy toward the unions. Taking advantage of the presence of troops in Cotonou—which neutralized possible pro-Soglo union demonstrations—Kouandété and Captain Mathieu Kérékou, ironically at the head of Alley's paratroop commando, placed Soglo, Alley, Major Benoit Cossi Sinzogan (head of the MVC), and Interior Minister Colonel Philippe Aho under house arrest. A spokesman of the "young cadres" subsequently read a proclamation in which he recited the usual platitudes about national interests, charged the Soglo regime with inefficiency and nepotism, and announced the creation of a constitutional committee to draft a new constitution which would be submitted to a popular referendum as soon as completed.[79]

78. *Afrique nouvelle,* May 12, 1966.
79. The proclamation also justified the *Putsch* as necessary to "remedy economic and financial ills which the country is suffering and to reconcile the children of Dahomey and enable them to assume control over the manage-

Judging from the difficulties encountered by the Young Turks in putting together a government, the *Putsch* was as swift as it was devoid of planning. A government was finally established on December 22 after nearly a week of confusion. The Young Turks received no apparent support from the "normal" civilian power base, the unions and elites. In fact, the young officers seemed surprised when Dr. Zinsou, after learning that he had been appointed foreign minister, refused to take the job; the unions immediately reiterated their demands that austerity measures be softened. With few exceptions, the new leaders operated a complete change of government personnel.[80] None of the officers or important members of either the NRC or the MVC were included in the new government or in the new Military Revolutionary Committee (MRC).

General Soglo complicated things for the junior officers when he flatly refused to resign as president. He was formally deposed amidst rumors of a counter-*Putsch* by loyalist military. The official silence of the French government, whose resident ambassador conveyed to Major Kouandété his concern for the safety of General Soglo, and the subsequent French decision to suspend all aid to Dahomey, dealt additional blows to the fresh regime.[81]

As the Kouandété-Alley regime was formed, the military barely averted an open split within the leadership of the armed forces by calling on the former "strong man" to serve as president of the republic. In addition to being tired of governing and to the "generational" cleavage discussed above, frictions among military leaders centered on a number of issues: future policy toward the unions, the best method to turn the government back to the civilians, individual animosities between officers which were magnified as a result of the swift change and differences about political philosophy as well as some officers' sympathy for one of the "big three" civilian, regional leaders.

In spite of their professed dislike for unions, the Young Turks

---

ment of their country's affairs in order, harmony, and newly restored fraternity." See *L'Aube nouvelle*, December 24, 1967. The reference to nepotism concerned General Soglo's cousin, Nicéphore Soglo, and his cousin by marriage, Christian Vieyra, both of whom became cabinet members in December, 1965, and resigned one year later.

80. The exceptions included Pascal Kabi Chabi Kao, a Northern civilian who remained in a new post of finance minister; Major Joseph Louis Chasme, quartermaster-general of the armed forces, who became justice minister; and Captain Ferdinand Johnson who remained as security chief.

81. It was reported that Kouandété gave the French ambassador assurances about Soglo's safety and suggested that the general seek political asylum in the French embassy. After spending a few days at the embassy, Soglo flew to Paris to plead for the restoration of aid; thence he continued to Abidjan to confer with President Houphouet-Boigny.

were in no position to alter the substance of the December, 1967, agreement with the Soglo regime. Kouandété issued a stern warning lest unions break with the military, but at the same entered into negotiations with the Joint Union Committee and associated the unions with drawing up the 1968 budget, which forecast an estimated $2 million deficit. Kouandété faced the threat of a general strike, widespread unemployment, a business recession, and the abrupt suspension of French aid. Since the national treasury did not have enough money to pay civil servants beyond a few months, there was no alternative to taking the unions into confidence and asking them for support.

In an attempt to brighten their tarnished image, the young officers inaugurated a series of trials of both civilian and military officials accused of corruption. The civilians affected included the prefects of at least four of the country's six administrative regions, the director of the national radio, and numerous lesser officials. Most prominent among the military officers was Major Chasme, who was dismissed from his post as justice minister and arraigned before the very judicial body which he had inaugurated one day prior to his dismissal.[82] Moreover, Captain Jean-Baptiste Hachémé, who had become president of the MRC in spite of having been Soglo's military cabinet head, was dismissed without any explanation and replaced by Captain Kérékou.[83]

These "purges" had two consequences, one favorable and the other unfavorable for the prestige of the armed forces. The dismissal of officers connected with the Soglo regime, as well as the trial of officers, laid bare for public view further evidence of disunity among the armed forces on other than professional grounds; it also smudged the armed forces' image as an institution lead by incorruptible, dedicated men contrasting with corrupt civilian leaders.

82. Prefects dismissed were from Atlantique, Ouémé, Mono, and Borgou; Captain Ferdinand Johnson, one of the few officers who had served the Soglo regime, was summarily dismissed from his post as head of national security. Also dismissed were Dr. Amlon, head of the national health service, and Noel Mensah, national radio director.

83. Available evidence suggests the possibility of ethnic or regional factors as an additional cause of the *Putsch,* somewhat in the manner of Nigeria. Both Kouandété and Kérékou are from the north, and Chasme reportedly stated, during a later trial, that the new regime wanted him out of the way because he was not from the north. This is entirely possible, but does not appear to have become operational in subsequent policy. The names of the new leaders indicate that northerners were in a minority. Recourse to the support of Alley and others probably prevented any "northern" policy. Moreover, Hubert Maga gave no indication of supporting the new government which he considered illegal and whose efforts to legitimize itself he strenuously opposed—unlike Ahomadegbé who favored the new government because Kouandété was the former chief of his military cabinet.

But the propaganda value of the trials initiated by the young officers earned them considerable good will. The trials, in fact, dominated the news in Dahomey at a time when South Africa was hanging some 40 Africans and when the USS Pueblo was hauled into a North Korean port. To the extent that the war against corruption may have been inspired by hopes of achieving a permanent impact on Dahomey's political system, it may have redounded to the credit of the "young cadres" of the armed forces.

The thrust of the Kouandété caretaker regime's activities was directed toward the restoration of civilian rule, an issue which provided it with the only solid and widespread popular approval which it enjoyed. As its policy toward the future political system unfolded, it became apparent that the military were concerned more with efficiency than with effectiveness—or perhaps more with what happened to the military as an institution than with the fortunes of the political system. The draft constitution which emerged from hurried deliberations of a civilian committee headed by the prestigious president of the Supreme Court, and which was approved by the military leaders, laid the foundations for a centralized presidential system. It provided for a single party, to be named Parti Démocratique Unifié; for a legislature whose members would serve without salary, compensation being provided through indemnities for the brief sessions; for the isolation of the Supreme Court from the influence of other government branches; and, in an attempt to protect citizens from arbitrary government, for the right of any individual to challenge executive and legislative decisions by asking the Supreme Court for a ruling. (Note the similarities with Ghana's draft constitution.)

Although the official results of the constitutional referendum held on March 31, 1968, were impressive, they amounted to nothing more than a temporary expression of confidence in the new military regime. Altogether, 82 per cent of the registered voters went to the polls, and 92.09 per cent of them (or 75.68 per cent of registered voters) approved the draft constitution, as indicated in Table 1.

As expected, most of the negative votes were cast in the Abomey area of the Zou Department, stronghold of Mr. Ahomadegbé, to protest the presidential system and the single party. Over half the total negative ballots (37,253) came from the Abomey Sous-Préfecture, most of the remainder being scattered along the coast, in the Ouémé and Atlantique departments where Ahomadegbé's organization remained influential.

The meaning of the referendum for much of the electorate may be summed up by the comment made by an elector on her way to the

TABLE 1

Results of the March 31, 1968, Constitutional Referendum

Registered Voters	1,118,468
Ballots Cast	924,168
Valid Ballots	919,206
Affirmative Votes	846,521
Negative Votes	71,695

SOURCE: *L'Aube nouvelle*, April 7, 1968. Note the discrepancy between valid ballots and the total affirmative and negative votes.

polling place: "To vote is very nice, but for whom and why?"[84] Dahomeans remained in the dark about the purpose of the exercise, partly because of the very brief "information" campaign which preceded it and partly because the constitutional issues embodied in the new document were too abstract for general understanding by the population.

The ineffectiveness of the military's policy could not have been demonstrated more dramatically than it was in connection with the presidential election held on May 5, 1968. Their declared objective was a break with the past. Consequently the military barred the "big three" and their former close associates from candidacy for the office of president of the republic, in the process invalidating a Supreme Court ruling declaring the ban unconstitutional. To allow the "big three" to run, the military declared, "would consecrate the atmosphere of hatred, of division, of distrust which surrounds us."[85]

Five candidates, none of whom had any popular backing, were allowed to run. Two of them, 78-year-old Paul Hazoumé and

84. One of the reporters for the government newspaper found that "some voted because they were asked; the referendum was for them a presidential election, or the return of a former leader with money from foreign countries. Some even talked about 7 billion CFA francs [$28 million] 'for our country.' Ask the twelve-year-old what he was doing at the polling place. His mother sent him to vote in her place. He votes as he likes. What did he understand about the referendum? His mother perhaps even less." Moreover, reports indicate that secrecy was not taken very seriously by voters or officials. Voters were given an envelope and two ballots, orange for yes and blue for no, then asked to choose a ballot and place it into the envelope in the secrecy of the booth. But many voters who took their responsibility seriously performed the operation publicly, others entered a room containing large piles of negative ballots on the floor which indicated how others had voted, whereas others' understanding of the issue ranged from support for their regional leader to the conviction that an affirmative ballot would mean help to secure lavish foreign investments for Dahomey's industry. See *L'Aube nouvelle*, April 14, 1968.

85. *Le Moniteur africain du commerce et de l'industrie*, April 11, 1968.

Eustache Prudencio, were relatively well known throughout the country. The others included a businessman and two civil servants unknown outside Dahomey.[86]

The military chose to ignore unmistakable signs of trouble prior to the election. When Maga and Apithy learned of the ban against their candidacy, they formed an alliance in Paris, which was translated into a "National Committee for the Defense of Democracy" at a Cotonou meeting of supporters of both regional leaders. The brief electoral campaign witnessed the almost immediate resurgence of regionalism and of the intensity of the voters' attachment to their regional leader. As the Dakar-based newspaper *Afrique nouvelle* pointed out in March, "Regardless of what the 'intellectuals' may say, the . . . masses will deposit—on election day—their idol's ballot in the box."[87] To make matters worse, both Maga and Apithy issued a call for a massive boycott of the election from their Paris exile, whereas Ahomadegbé told his supporters to contest. Followers of Apithy and Maga made it clear that their loyalties had not changed: Oké Assogba, former cabinet member, said that "to entrust the reins of this country to youth would be a juvenile error," and Noel Tota, former deputy, declared that "no one can deny to the former presidents their legitimate rights and duties as citizens."[88]

The results of the election were a disaster for the military. Only some 27 per cent of the country's registered voters went to the polls. Of the ballots cast, an impressive 84 per cent went to Dr. Adjou, reportedly because of the backing of Ahomadegbé supporters; but these ballots amounted to only 21.2 per cent of total registered voters. A departmental breakdown of the percentage of eligible voters who did vote demonstrated the effectiveness of instructions from the "big three." Thus, in the northern department of Atacora,

86. In addition to Mr. Hazoumé, the candidates were: Eustache Prudencio, teacher and writer; Jean-Baptiste Ganmadualo Vierin, a specialist in financial and economic affairs serving in Gabon; Karim Urbain da Sylva, owner of a printing plant and president of the Syndicat National des Commerçants et Industriels du Dahomey, a private sector union; and a physician, Dr. Basile Moumouni Adjou, working for the World Health Organization. The military rejected the candidacy of Léon Boissier-Palun, long-time intimate of President Senghor of Senegal, a native of Dahomey, who had just resigned from the presidency of the Senegalese Economic and Social Council.

87. *Afrique nouvelle,* March 7, 1968.

88. *L'Unité africaine,* February 29, 1968. Commenting on Dahomey's fragmentation under the front-page headline "We All Deserve to be Hanged," the official newspaper stated that "no one would object to the return of the big three if it were assumed that his idol would emerge victorious in the next election" (*L'Aube nouvelle,* January 20, 1968). The writer could have added that the "big three" could not be replaced so soon by candidates without popular appeal or organization.

that percentage was a bare .09, whereas it amounted to 49.82 per cent in the Zou department where Ahomadegbé strength is concentrated. The same can be shown by comparing important cities: in Abomey, 62.37 per cent of the voters went to the polls, whereas the percentages were 10.1 in Parakou and only 3.03 in Natitingou, both in the north.[89]

It is obvious that the military's policy was not only defeated, but it also brought about the very results it sought to avoid. In one sense, the Maga-Apithy coalition emerged as the victor from the electoral battle, and in another, Ahomadegbé showed his strength without even having chosen a candidate. Nonetheless, it is this writer's contention that the "big three" are not irrevocably entrenched in Dahomey's political system and therefore indispensable. The contest was between three leaders each of whom benefited from a solid following, on one hand, and five individuals who were relatively unknown and had no following to speak of. The outcome of this contest was, therefore, a foregone conclusion.

CONCLUSION

Politics in Dahomey and Upper Volta are those of transitional societies: traditional and modern elites, as well as such modern social groups as unions and party structures, clash without the benefit of mediation through routinized, legitimate decision-making processes. Politicization of new participants seems to pose threats to, rather than build support for, the national decision-making elites. In these circumstances, the military can only point the way toward further transition to a *modus vivendi* among the contending factions—provided that they understand this process and can themselves survive the strains on their own structure, or that they be assisted in their task by pre-existing centripetal forces. One of the major differences between the ability of the military in the two countries to provide a modicum of stability is the existence, in Upper Volta, of the traditions of the Mossi, an integrating factor absent in Dahomey.

A number of generalizations concerning the characteristics, capabilities, and handicaps of military regimes in black Africa emerge from this study. First, the "old guard" was better attuned to the political process than were the Young Turks. In spite of official policy banishing the political process at least temporarily, military

89. Percentage figures are adapted from reports in *Afrique nouvelle,* May 16, 1968, and *Le Moniteur africain du commerce et de l'industrie,* May 16, 1968.

regimes headed by "older" officers tended to seek and accept at least some advice from politicians and politically conscious groups. The younger officers, by contrast, tended to be impatient with the political system and wanted to change it rapidly, without the benefit of either much experience or understanding of that system.

Second, military regimes tended to be relatively conservative, in the sense that they were most comfortable with balanced budgets and with a political system that did not upset the *status quo*. This characteristic is probably as much the result of their training as of their sensitivity to the economic dependence of their country upon the continued good will of France. In Dahomey, the attempt to secure the help of progressive civilian elites ended in failure because of the military's distaste for the socialist changes which the progressives advocated. Moreover, what innovations the military brought about—a computer to control state finances, the extension of the military "pioneer" programs, or public relations schemes to increase agricultural production and government legitimacy—concerned more efficient ways of tackling problems within the existing social, political, and economic order.

Third, the military's concept of the legitimacy required for a transfer of political authority was more structured than that of civilian leaders who defined it as they pleased. Military officers, particularly the "old guard," were imbued with a high sense of decorum, procedure, and hierarchy that stood in the way of a forthright coup d'état. Personal friendships with civilian politicians may have influenced the officers' reluctance, and this reluctance was probably extended to other civilians in high office. The military seem to have done nothing to discourage maneuvers by the opposition to bring about a military takeover. But they needed visible popular backing before their concern with the legitimacy of a military coup was assuaged.

Fourth, the military were convinced that political problems were amenable to rational solutions, that reason was on their side, and that reason plus time sufficed to change ingrained political behavior. Reason, to the military, simply illuminated the idiosyncratic features of an irrational system: pursuit of personal gain, waste of public property, mediocrity of civilian leaders, complaisance about finances, in short, the egregious nature of the political process. Nothing could have been more natural for them than to park such a system on an abandoned lot, a public monument to its past, shabby existence. Though their assessment of politics changed as reluctance to intervene made room for duty to remain, it was still grounded in the notion that it must conform to their own definition before being allowed to resume its "normal" role; political behavior which did

114

not conform to the military's vision was abnormal behavior and had to be rooted out.

At the same time, the military believed that lifting the veil from people's eyes was enough not only to let them see things in the proper light but also to act accordingly. Sidetracking the political system anticipated an incubation process during which the people would recognize the futility of subnational allegiances and dedicate themselves to "national" goals and interests. Problems are solved best by rational methods, and reason conveys the self-evident values of dedication and sacrifice for the common good.

Fifth, and contrary to some expectations, the military in office made remarkable little use of their monopoly of force. This may be attributed to the fact that the stakes were too low to warrant its use. When confronting mobs, they exercised caution because of the presence of relatives, friends, women, and children; of their disagreement with civilian leaders' policies; and of their awareness that violence would be dysfunctional in terms of the popular support and good will required for economic recovery.

But the military did not hesitate to deploy troops and police in anticipation of possible violence resulting from planned demonstrations. No doubt they were aware of the deterrent effect of a show of strength. It is not at all clear, however, how they would have responded to actual, large-scale public—or union—demonstrations, or to widespread challenges to either their political authority or to the military as an institution, both situations in which the stakes would have been immeasurably higher.

Sixth, the term "armed forces" conveys an erroneous impression of homogeneity impervious to fragmentation. In fact, African armed forces are far from homogeneous. The following are some of the major causes for disunity within the armed forces—keeping in mind that these are not mutually exclusive: (1) partisanship for civilian political forces, (2) "generational" tensions, (3) government policy, (4) regional or ethnic loyalties, (5) connection with civilian cabals, (6) officer cliques, (7) personality conflicts, (8) intensity of attitudes, (9) political philosophy and ambition, (10) political acumen vs. puritanism, and (11) frictions with such paramilitary groups as the gendarmerie or the Garde Republicaine.

Some, perhaps most, of these causes of disunity are manageable. The contrast between Upper Volta and Dahomey indicates that a distribution of suitable government responsibilities among the officer corps is an efficient method for keeping such conflicts beneath the surface. Had Soglo yielded to demands by younger officers he might have satisfied many of them; but how long they would have remained satisfied is an open question.

Finally, the Dahomean experience suggests another major characteristic of Africa's armed forces. If the military as an institution are faced with centrifugal forces which, unchecked, could lead to the destruction of the armed forces, then protection of that institution will claim the military's first priority and take precedence over other, "national" interests. This phenomenon undoubtedly accounted for the sudden haste with which the military decided to retreat to their earlier, military role and leave the larger political system to its own devices.

More important, it raises the question whether the military's concern for the welfare of their "nation" is not just as embryonic as that of many of their civilian compatriots. Perhaps their dedication to their nation is in fact dedication to a task, like economic recovery, essentially a professional commitment to rationality much more than a web of overarching loyalties to such political entities as Upper Volta or Dahomey. Professional, rational norms were reinforced, rather than weakened, by their post-independence experience as architects of armed forces.

"Nationalism" may well be, in the eyes of African military leaders, one of their outlets for the need for a well-ordered environment. Because it has deep roots which feed on professional characteristics, it may appear more potent than do the wide nets of the civilian leaders' nationalist language. But it is also more narrow in the sense that it covers only a small area of what make up "national" loyalties.

The behavior of the Kouandété regime suggests that the military may have assimilated the concept of service to the abstraction of "nation" only imperfectly. That abstraction tended to be seen through the prism of military experience: a rational, homogeneous entity. And since the real nation bore very little resemblance to its ideal, and furthermore threatened their own rational world, the military found it most comfortable to withdraw, thus hoping to eliminate the threat.

Before considering some elements of an assessment of the military regimes from the point of view of stability, let us recall briefly the causes of instability. The most potent reasons for the downfall of civilian governments appear to have been (1) the leaders' excessive centralization which, combined with (2) economic problems, resulted in (3) general lack of confidence in their leadership and legitimacy. More specifically, these reasons were (a) in Dahomey, regional resentment at and refusal to accept political ostracism, and (b) in Upper Volta, dissipation of confidence in the leadership expressed by the only extant center of opposition, the trade unions.

It cannot be said that military rule brought about great changes in the political system of these two countries. There has been a shift in neither the power base upon which legitimate authority rests (urban elites, ethnic/regional groups, and what rural elements can be assimilated through networks of personal relationships and party structures) nor the distribution of wealth, which remains concentrated in the pocketbooks of urban elites and expatriate business groups. The one attempt to set up a "new" political system failed. The Kouandété regime could have retired and let the civilians settle the problem by themselves; but the armed forces' pride, stung by suggestions of incapacity, led the Young Turks to try their hands at a solution of their own. The Ghanaian example may also have influenced the Kouandété government: many important aspects of the Dahomean constitution and the electoral campaign are striking for their similarity with decisions by the Ankrah regime. In their haste to free themselves of the civilian problem, they overlooked either the relationship between a political and social system or the intensity of the divisions in the body politic; hence the error to pit lone dark-horses against well-entrenched regionalism.

Against the background of expectations of change over time in political attitudes discussed above, the speed used in foisting a political structure onto Dahomey precluded an alternative, middle-range solution. Ascribing the demise of successive Dahomean civilian teams to excesses committed by the leadership, we may assume that (1) one team—the triumvirate—*could* have been successful, and (2) the *existence* of pluralism is not sufficient to bring about the collapse of a political system. An alternative solution, taking into account existing regionalism as well as widespread desire for new leadership, could have been provided through a combination of three elements: first, a coalition government which allowed the politically conscious groups to participate fully in the "national" decision-making process; second, tight guarantees for the rights of individuals, and checks and balances to stabilize intragroup frictions; and third, an eminent personality as arbiter over political struggles.

Such a system could have been devised. Had the "big three" been faced with the military's determination to prepare and conduct an effective, well-prepared electoral campaign endorsing a nationally respected figure, chances are that they would have agreed to submit to the inevitable. Not counting Senegal's Léon Boissier-Palun, whose candidacy the Young Turks considered seriously before ruling against it, there was at least one man available: Dr. Emile Derlin Zinsou. Although he had served in previous governments, including that of Soglo, Zinsou possessed a capital of good will and respect at home and abroad substantial enough not to have aroused too many animosities and to have won an election as a national arbiter with a comfortable majority. Dr. Zinsou stands out among Dahomean leaders as an articulate, sophisticated, serious, and relatively moderate politician and civil servant. He was born in March, 1918, in Ouidah, received his primary and secondary education in Porto Novo, attended the William Ponty school in Senegal, and received an M.D. in Paris. He was active in politics, although not always in the topmost circles; he represented Dahomey in various French legislative bodies, edited Dahomean newspapers, and served in a number of Dahomean cabinet posts. After being his country's first ambassador to France, he became foreign minister in 1960 under Maga and again in 1966 under Soglo.

An outspoken advocate of closer inter-African economic and cultural cooperation, Dr. Zinsou opposed the dismantling of the French West African Federation, strongly favored Dahomey's adherence to the Mali Federation, and received general support from French-language states for the post of secretary-general of the Organization of African Unity. His horizons extend far beyond any Dahomean region or ethnic group, and he has cultivated a wide network of contacts in Africa and Europe. His paramount concern is the economic well-being of his country, and his contacts and integrity are well suited for securing the foreign assistance without which Dahomey cannot survive—let alone modernize. Two factors account for the Kouandété regime's failure to consider at first this type of alternative. First, its preoccupation with speed and efficiency at the expense of effectiveness. "The superior interests of a nation," declared the government, "can pass through roads whose *future efficiency* can overcome its lack of popularity."[90] Second, the Young Turks had been stung by, and resented, Dr. Zinsou's resounding refusal to serve in their government.

No political system can long survive—much less act effectively—which does not allow important, politically conscious groups to participate in common decision-making. Regional fragmentation must be considered at least a semipermanent factor, although it is not, as we have seen, responsible *per se* for the ineffectiveness of past regimes: regions follow leaders, not vice versa. The mistake made by both countries' civilian regimes, as well as by the Kouandété government, was to seek to "unitarize" an essentially pluralistic political system.

Military intervention inadvertently reinforced future demands

90. *L'Aube nouvelle,* April 14, 1968; emphasis added.

for participation in two ways. First, "liberated" political forces previously muzzled and/or isolated are not likely to accept again their being cast into the shadows. And second, the military's accent on economic recovery spread expectations of higher material rewards, as witness the unions' greater role-perceptions and increased influence in the political system.

An ideal solution should seek to conciliate all active political forces and construct a political machinery commanding the widest possible consensus. It should seek also to avoid paralysis through structural weakness; the dangers inherent in centralization are still fresh in people's minds but, though real, ought to be balanced with centrifugal realities. Perhaps the most effective way to achieve such a balance is through an arbitration mechanism—executive or judicial—which would attract an outstanding, widely respected, and politically "neutral" personality.

In view of these limitations, it is doubtful that the military, as an institution, can make long-term contributions. It should be remembered that their goals are considerably more limited than the development of politics; hence to apply to them the standards of "political development" is asking them to pass an examination for which they are not prepared, to tackle the job of a Gulliver with lilliputian weapons. Given the temporary nature of their commitment to political stewardship, they should be able at least to trace the road for future progress. Assuming that they can manage their own internal cleavages, they should be able to launch their country's economic recovery. The moratorium on open political activity —as well as their own futile efforts—may spread a consciousness of the inadequacies of past political systems as well as willingness to ask fundamental questions. There are some signs that this is precisely what is taking place. As an African editorialist recently wrote:

> Since we have had the delicate mission of managing our own affairs, it has never occurred to us, either in a delirium or in a meditation, to become conscious of what we are or what we are doing.[91]

POSTSCRIPT

In late June, 1968, Dahomey's military government announced the appointment of Dr. Zinsou as president of the republic for a five-year term. He took office on July 17, within the time limit previously set by the Alley-Kouandété regime, and was inaugurated on August 1 as the military government was dissolved.

91. *Ibid.*, December 31, 1967.

Intense activities followed the disaster of the May, 1968, presidential election. These activities underlined the depth of dissension among the leaders of the armed forces. At first, the "young cadres" sought to strengthen their position by replacing five of the ten cabinet members with paratroop officers connected with the December, 1967, *Putsch,* but the army leaders remained deeply divided. Many of them regarded staying in power as the only viable alternative, a course of action no doubt encouraged by experience in other African countries. But the unions, without whose support no government can last, were unalterably opposed to the continuation of military rule. Once the armed forces decided to return the country to civilian rule, its members disagreed sharply over the nature of future civilian leadership. One faction, led by former "strong man" Alley, favored the return of the "big three." Consequently he made a number of overtures to them and sought the advice of their rump parties during consultations with them, union leaders, and other dignitaries. But neither the party leaders in Dahomey nor those exiled in Paris could agree on a compromise formula for a viable triumvirate. Apithy and Maga immediately reconciled themselves to oppose Ahomadegbé in an almost predictable return to the pattern of earlier days. Plans to meet with the "big three," first in Niamey and then in Accra, were abandoned. Colonel Alley's support for the "big three," and perhaps his general dissatisfaction with the Kouandété regime, led him to attempt another military *Putsch* in June, 1968, although this was buried in official silence and made public only after Dr. Zinsou had agreed to head the new government.

Since reverting to the past was apparently impossible, the other faction in the armed forces, favoring a relatively neutral personality to head a new civilian regime, won the argument. Dr. Zinsou thus owed his new job to the patent bankruptcy of the previous, formal political system, and to the cleavages within the armed forces leadership who agreed on his candidacy as a last straw rather than a heavy gun in the rapidly dwindling arsenal of alternatives.

The selection of Dr. Zinsou was initially made against the combined opposition of unions and the "big three." When the nomination was made public, the former leaders in Paris—including General Soglo—declared their joint hostility and demanded free elections in which they could participate. In fact, the former "big three's" eagerness to return home probably helped the military to decide against them. Ahomadegbé, Apithy, and Maga left Paris on June 5 to return to Dahomey; their decision gave the military a few anxious moments. The crowds gathered at Cotonou airport to greet them were large and included delegations from all regions. The military believed that Dahomey's political situation could not be contained were the trio allowed to land; consequently they took firm security measures and prohibited their entry, diverting them instead to Lomé in neighboring Togo where they sought temporary refuge.

Much now depends upon President Zinsou's skills in calming restlessness and producing compromises based on respect for pluralism. Initially at least, he is not an entirely free agent since he depends to some extent on further support from the armed forces. His replacement of Colonel Alley with the "new strongman," Major Kouandété, as armed forces chief of staff, and his appointment of an army officer, Major Sinzogan, as head of the gendarmerie, testify to his concern for support from and unity in the armed forces.

At the outset, President Zinsou seems to have coped successfully with the most pressing problems he inherited. He held extensive consultations with various politically conscious groups and secured the backing of trade unions. He appealed to the former "big three" to help him, but met with resistance and unwillingness on their part. He sought next to legitimize his army mandate by calling for a popular referendum. This was held on July 28, 1968, and may be considered at least a partial hopeful success: 72 per cent of registered voters went to the polls, and 73.30 per cent of them (or 53.23 per cent of those registered) approved of their new president. More significant, at least a simple majority of registered voters cast their ballots in each of Dahomey's six departments, despite a boycott call from the "big three." (The percentages varied from a low of 53.14 in Ouémé Department to a high of 88.94 in Mono Department.) Among those who cast their ballot, the lowest percentage of approval was in Ouémé (56.89) and the highest in Mono (97.90).[92] Taking into consideration a possible saturation point in popular consultations in Dahomey, the referendum nonetheless confirms that the former "big three" are not indispensable to that country's political future. This seems to be President Zinsou's own conclusion: "Dahomeans can achieve national unity without the big three," he said after the referendum. "They exist, but they are not indispensable."[93] At the outset of his tenure, it appeared that Dr. Zinsou could manage the complex problems facing his country after the military interlude. His army mandate was legitimized by the people at large as well as by important political groups, and the French government resumed its assistance as a sign of external confidence in the new Dahomean regime.

92. For detailed figures, see *L'Aube nouvelle,* August 1, 1968, and August 4, 1968.

93. *West Africa,* October 5, 1968, p. 1163.

INTRODUCTION TO CHAPTER 3

FOUR TIMES SINCE INDEPENDENCE, Congo-Kinshasa has been shaken by military unrest or rebellion. The first event, the mutiny of the Force Publique less than a week after independence, helped plunge the country into a prolonged period of partial anarchy and uncertainty. All Belgian officers were dismissed; sergeant-majors rapidly rose to fill command positions. The Force Publique required extensive retraining to become an effective national agent. The mutiny of the Force Publique was in many ways a harbinger of the unrest that rocked East Africa three-and-a-half years later; it was the first mutiny of African troops against European officers after self-government.

The second major event in recent Congolese history installed the first caretaker regime in tropical Africa. On September 14, 1960, eleven weeks after independence, Colonel Joseph Mobutu assumed power to settle a dispute between President Joseph Kasavubu and Prime Minister Patrice Lumumba. The president relied upon his constitutional powers to dismiss the prime minister; the prime minister and members of his cabinet, in turn, accused the president of high treason and dismissed him as head of state. Confronted with rival governments, with lack of progress in ending Katangese secession, and with growing politicization of the army, Mobutu decided to take action. As ranking officer, he set up a temporary government of university students and graduates (Collège des commissaires généraux) until the end of the year.

The third Congolese crisis erupted in 1964. In simplest terms, accumulated rural grievances and loss of control by the central government helped bring major outbreaks of violence. The National

122

Congolese Army, still in the throes of major retraining, found itself ill-prepared to halt the rebellion. The reputation of the *ba-politiciens*—pettifogging politicos—fell even lower in the eyes of the Congolese officers. Although the government of Prime Minister Moise Tshombe eventually reduced the area under rebel control, parliamentary deadlock between supporters of Tshombe and Kasavubu threatened instability. "To save the country from anarchy and chaos," Mobutu intervened once again, deposing the president and forming a government of national union. This intervention, on November 25, 1965, marked the full assumption of military control. Once again, the Congo, in its fourth major crisis, pointed out a path many other tropical African states would follow in succeeding months.

What factors led to intervention? How did the government of President Mobutu develop in light of its military origins? Willame cites two major factors that resulted in Mobutu's assumption of control:

1. The first political generation in the Congo was not composed of "modernizers," able and inclined to undertake a major restructuring of Congolese society. The pattern was one, rather, of personal or patrimonial rule. When the country gained independence, national political structures (the administration, political parties) were weak and subject to easy splintering. In a brief period, groups fragmented along ethnic or regional lines; government offices were used for personal enrichment, not for national reconstruction.

2. The National Congolese Army was dramatically transformed following the collapse of the Force Publique. Once an efficient instrument of colonial repression, the Force Publique had to experience basic transformations before it could serve as an effective agent for national political development. These transformations—shifts in attitude, the rise of a military intelligentsia, greatly increased technical resources—outpaced changes in the civilian sector. In short the National Congolese Army—both its officers and its ranks—developed a relative sense of national unity.

The Mobutu government embodies the aims of a "second generation" of Congolese leaders. The patrimonialism of the first generation has been supplanted by a "Caesaristic" bureaucracy. Centralization and depoliticization mark the Congo under President Mobutu. However, the President has tried to build attachment to the Congolese political system by attachment to himself. Whether this effort to exchange the legitimacy of national political structures will succeed depends upon the imponderables of history.

C. E. W.

3.

Congo-Kinshasa:

General Mobutu
and Two Political
Generations

―――――――――――

JEAN-CLAUDE WILLAME
University of California, Berkeley
Compiled and translated by CLAUDE E. WELCH, JR.

FOR ANY OBSERVER of the Congolese political scene, significant changes seem to have taken place since General Joseph-Desiré Mobutu took over in November, 1965. A period of insecurity and uncertainty has been succeeded by a period of stability and reshaping the state apparatus; the previous institutional decentralization has been replaced by a unitary regime; after the generation of the professional politician has emerged that of the university student, the "young," and the "expert." This chapter analyzes these generational changes to illustrate continuities and discontinuities

This study was made possible by a grant from the Institute of International Affairs, University of California at Berkeley, during 1967–68. An earlier version of this paper was presented to the Conference on Generational Conflict in Africa, held at Washington University, St. Louis, Mo., in May, 1968.

between the two periods. The two political generations of the Congo epitomize the impact of military rule upon tropical Africa's largest state.

THE FIRST POLITICAL GENERATION:
A PATRIMONIAL SYSTEM OF RULE

Literature dealing with the emerging nations emphasizes the "new elites" as main agents of modernization. Whoever they may be— university graduates, military officers, achievement-oriented bureaucrats, charismatic leaders—these elites are asserted to be in a strategic position. They must create new sociopolitical institutions to mobilize the nation, link all the people into a national communications network, and provide the symbols of national integration. The overwhelming majority of scholars have taken for granted that these elites wished to "modernize," or, as Edward Shils put it, to be "devoted to the public good, critical and yet sympathetic, interested in the immediate partisanship to constitute a corps of custodians of the public good in the present and the future."[1]

Such assertions are now under attack. Aristide Zolberg, in his most recent book, asserted:

> We have now reached an impasse. . . . We realize that, in spite of the huge growth of scholarly and popular literature, our information is grossly deficient. Much has been written about the thought of various leaders in the fields of international politics, about economic development, and about the one-party itself. We know what political organizations say their structures are like and what they say concerning their operations, but we have seldom gone beyond such declaratory statements.[2]

Zolberg suggests substituting the concept of patrimonial elite for that of charismatic leadership. Although the charismatic aspects of legitimacy may have been most salient during the period of colonial rule and immediately after independence, the crucial process is similar to the one that Weber saw developing in patrimonial rule, namely, the appropriation of public offices and the establishment of relationships based on personal loyalties.[3] Guenther Roth has even suggested that the treatment of almost all political leaders in the

1. Edward Shils, "Political Development in the New States," *Comparative Studies in Society and History*, II, no. 3 (1960), 277.
2. Aristide R. Zolberg, *Creating Political Order: The Party States of West Africa* (Chicago: Rand McNally, 1966), p. 6.
3. *Ibid.*, pp. 140–41

new states as charismatic has been completely misleading on at least two counts:

> it has obscured the difference between charismatic authority and charismatic leadership, and it has taken at face value the international propaganda claims of some of the new leaders.[4]

Roth goes further than Zolberg did by proposing two ideal types of patrimonial rule: the traditional patrimonial regime, exemplified by such a country as Ethiopia; and personal rulership based on loyalties "that do not require any belief in the ruler's unique personal qualification but are inextricably linked to material incentives and rewards."[5] "In terms of traditional political theory," he concludes, "some of these new states may not be states at all but merely private governments of those powerful enough to rule."[6]

In the Congolese case, the concept of patrimonial rule or personal leadership represents a useful starting point for examining the country's first political generation. Four aspects make the Congolese political elites similar to Max Weber's patrimonial rulers.

Appropriation of Public Offices

The political bourgeoisie takes over public offices that have become a major source of wealth and prestige. Let us recall how this phenomenon occurred in the Congo. Historically, the movement for independence had its roots in the growing pressures emanating from a relatively small group of *evolués*—mostly journalists, teachers, and clerks—upon the colonial bureaucracy. The bureaucracy in turn was increasingly unable to close the gap between its prime goal—the efficiency and profitability of the colonial economy—and the aspirations that this goal had created among "its" people. In other words, rising economic levels created the demand for greater prosperity.

Thomas Hodgkin described Belgian colonial policy as Platonic:

> Platonism is implicit in the sharp distinction, social and legal, between Belgian philosopher-kings and the mass of African producers; in the conception of education as primarily concerned with the transmission of certain unquestioned and unquestionable moral values . . . in the belief that the thought and behaviour of the mass is plastic, and can be refashioned by a benevolent, wise and highly trained élite; that the prime interest of the mass is in

4. Guenther Roth, "Personal Rulership, Patrimonialism and Empire-building in the New States," *World Politics,* XX (1968), 200.
5. *Ibid.,* p. 196.
6. *Ibid.*

welfare and consumer goods . . . not liberty; and in the conviction that it is possible, by expert administration, to arrest social and political change.[7]

The term "Platonism" is unfortunate, since the relationship between the philosopher-king and his subjects envisaged by Plato took place in a *homogeneous city* and in the realm of the *political*. These two basic points were missing in Belgian policy toward the Congo. On the one hand, the colonial situation entailed radical heterogeneity, a deep psychological and structural cleavage between a dominant foreign minority and a technically backward majority based on a dogmatically asserted racial superiority.[8] On the other hand, the Belgian colonizers were willing to promote socioeconomic welfare and Christian civilization, even though they denied the colonials any share in decision-making.

The colonial situation brought an inescapable contradiction. The Belgian welfare policy produced a new type of human being—the colonized intelligentsia—whom the colonizer hated and fought. In the very beginning, this intelligentsia did not want to expel his benefactor, but to work with him. It sought, above all, to end its lack of status within the colonial structures and to solve the multiple wounds of racial discrimination. Its first grievances and demands were thus concerned with its "rights of expression," its "rights of association" . . . all demands that were expressed through such "liberal" oriented texts as the "Manifesto of African Conscience," *Congo, My Country* by Patrice Lumumba, or through cultural organizations such as the "Association pour le Maintien de l'Unité et de la Langue Kikongo," later on ABAKO, party of Joseph Kasavubu.

The seizure of power by the former *evolués* broke down the unity of the mass and the new political leadership that, at the start of independence, joined both in the expectation of general prosperity. A political bourgeoisie emerged by securing or competing for public office. Two years after independence, about 163,000 persons were employed by the state in the administration, army, police and political institutions; their salaries represented 58 per cent of national expenses.[9] As Hughes Leclercq stressed in 1961, this social stratum impoverished the whole country by inflation:

7. Thomas Hodgkin, *Nationalism in Colonial Africa* (London: Frederick Muller, 1956), p. 52.
8. Georges Balandier, *Sociologie actuelle de l'Afrique noire* (Paris: Presses Universitaires de France, 1963), pp. 34–35.
9. The figure is drawn from Benoit Verhaegen, "Traitements, grèves et politique d'austerité," *Études congolaises,* II, no. 5 (1962), 12–15.

As a result of the credit drawn by the state on the Central Bank, an increased money supply was poured into the economy through salaries, wages and other compensations to the Army and the Civil Service. Raising the monetary income of some 150,000 privileged persons, the deficit financing exercised a strong pressure on demand and led consequently to a rise in the price level.[10]

Inflated costs for manufactured goods did not further stimulate Congolese peasants to produce and sell their products to the internal or export markets but tended to drive them back to a self-subsistence level of economy. Inflation also abetted the formation of a parasitic network of foreign and native speculators with whom the political bourgeoisie closely associated in order to increase its revenue.[11] Thus, the crucial process involved in the post-independence period was the appropriation of wealth through the control over the instruments of power—legislative assemblies, administration, government—by a social stratum whose homogeneity was rooted in its narrow association with the former colonizer. This group was not oriented toward production, invention, or construction. The dynamic and pioneering dimensions that one can find in any national bourgeoisie were completely lacking. In brief, its characteristics are basically similar to those foreseen by Frantz Fanon.

> In fact, the bourgeois phase in the history of under-developed countries is a completely useless phase. When this caste has vanished, devoured by its own contradictions, it will be seen that nothing new has happened since independence was proclaimed, and that everything must be started again from scratch. The changeover will not take place at the level of the structures set up by the bourgeoisie during its reign, since that caste has done nothing more than take over unchanged the legacy of the economy, the thought and the institutions left by the colonialists.[12]

Personal Loyalties

The second central feature of patrimonialism rests, according to Weber, upon a relationship based on personal loyalties to the individual at the top. Weber describes these relations in the following way:

10. Hughes Leclercq, "Analyse générale de l'inflation congolaise," *Cahiers économiques et sociaux de l'IRES,* I (1962), 38.
11. Jean Louis Lacroix, *Industrialisation au Congo: La Transformation des structures économiques* (Paris: Mouton, 1967), pp. 206–8.
12. Frantz Fanon, *The Wretched of the Earth* (New York: Grove Press, 1966), p. 142.

The organized group exercising authority is . . . primarily based on relations of personal loyalty, cultivated through a common process of education. The person exercising authority is not a "superior" but a personal "chief." His administrative staff does not consist primarily of officials but of personal retainers. Those subject to his authority are not members of an association but are either his traditional comrades or his subjects. What determines the relations of the administrative staff to the chief is not the impersonal obligations of office but personal loyalty to the chief.[13]

In the Congo, a similar pattern of relationships has emerged from the tribalization or regionalization of the political life that has occurred since independence. A few words about tribalism are necessary. Many political scientists and African leaders have conceived of the relation between tribalism and nationalism as two ends of a continuum: "tradition–modernity." Tribalism is seen as corresponding to a state of backwardness, referring implicitly to the concept of tribe in its anthropological sense. There are, however, two basic differences between the old and the new "tribal" context. The "traditional" tribe is characterized by narrow and ill-defined ecological dimensions and by a set of kinship relations rigorously determined in terms of time and generation.[14] Modern tribalism lacks these two connotations. It has been definitively affected by colonial policy aiming at fixing populations in well-bounded and larger administrative units (the *secteur,* the district, and the province). Moreover, modern tribalism involves a set of relations much more extensive than the previous network of kinship ties. The most striking Congolese illustration of this change in the nature of tribalism may be found among the Bangala, a name arbitrarily invented by Belgian officials to identify people living in an area extending from Coquilhatville (now Mbandaka) 400 miles upstream and running inland some 100 miles on each side of the Congo River. On the eve of independence, the Bakongo of Leopoldville referred to all non-Bakongo as Bangala and the term came to be accepted by the Kasaians, Mongo, and Kwango-Kwilu people. For instance, the 1957 urban elections in Leopoldville were generally described in those terms.[15]

Thus, the contemporary form of tribalism is clearly a modern

13. Max Weber, *The Theory of Social and Economic Organization* (New York: Free Press, 1957), p. 341.
14. For an excellent explanation of the time and space dimension in traditional situation, see Lucien Lévy-Bruhl, *La Mentalité primitive* (Paris: Presses Universitaires de France, 1956).
15. See M. C. C. De Backer, *Notes pour servir à l'étude des groupements politiques à Léopoldville,* mimeo. (Brussels: Inforcongo, 1959), pp. 11–12.

phenomenon. The ethnic rivalries that have developed must be understood as urban groups and communities competing against each other for modern objects. "Tribal nationalism" was the end product of socioeconomic differentiations originated by the process of colonization itself.[16]

Decolonization in the Congo was accompanied by successive tribal awakenings, developing in a climate of intense politicization. Chronologically the first awakening came from the Bakongo, one of the most modernized ethnic groups of the country. Their political radicalism resulted from their fear of being outrun in the competition for power by the so-called Bangala, who had questioned the colonial regime by publishing their noteworthy "Manifesto of African Consciousness." Thereafter similar reactions came from the Kwilu elites. Afraid of possible Bakongo extension through their territory, they hastened to create their own political organization—the Parti Solidaire Africain (PSA).[17] Later on, the same pattern prevailed in Kasai province among the Lulua and the Basonge, both increasingly aware of the privileged treatment provided by the colonial administration to their common enemy, the Baluba.[18] On the eve of independence, the Congo was thus saturated with more than 150 parties or associations, each of them being constituted by a spontaneous reaction against "others." This phenomenon of dynamic and explosive ethnicity was eventually institutionalized by the division of the country into 21 new provinces between October, 1962, and April, 1963.

Yet the creation of these new entities was not the only result of ethnic awakening throughout the Congo. Their formation also illustrated the pre-eminence of political relations based on individual loyalties and allegiances developing not in the narrow framework of the family or household system, but in the larger context of ethnic and tribal identification defined above.

From January, 1961, onwards, the political center of gravity of the Congo did not rest on a single legitimate focus of authority.

16. "Contrary to current theories which presume that educational and economic development in the emerging nations must inevitably erode tribal loyalties, the Ibos illustrate the reverse phenomenon, i.e. that modernization may directly lead to the reinforcement of ethnic identity rather than to its deterioration" (Paul Anber, "Modernization and Political Disintegration: Nigeria and the Ibos," *Journal of Modern African Studies*, V, no. 2 [1967], 168).

17. Benoit Verhaegen and Herbert Weiss, eds., *Parti Solidaire Africain: Documents du CRISP* (Brussels: Centre de Recherche et d'Information Socio-Politique, 1963).

18. Auguste Mabika Kalanda, *Baluba et Lulua: Une ethnie à la recherche d'un nouvel équilibre* (Brussels: Editions Remarques Congolaises, 1959 [?]).

Instead, legitimacy rested upon powerful "suzerains," each of whom was influential and powerful in a specific region or within a particular tribe. Following the death of Patrice Lumumba, national political institutions either no longer functioned or survived in a comatose state. Political decisions were made by a series of "Round Tables" at which the most powerful politicians of the country gathered. These conferences legitimized the desire of these suzerains to transform their native territories into "provinces" or "states." Thus, the Round Table of Tananarive (March, 1961) formally recognized eleven new states; at the Coquilhatville conference (April–May, 1961), eighteen senators and congressmen, surrounded by their local clients, received a verbal promise that their regions would become "provinces." When the Adoula government was finally formed (August, 1961), the power of these suzerains did not diminish. The central government had no legitimacy of its own; it was, in fact, a creation of United Nation officials, backed by a loose coalition of tribal leaders who had participated in the preceding Round Tables. From the beginning of 1962 onward, the process of partition took place within the National Assembly, the Senate, and the ministry of internal affairs.

Complex relationships developed between the center and the provinces as the new provincial governments were developed. Although the overall strategy of most of the national politicians was to control their constituencies through their personal supporters, this was by no means a general rule.[19] Five types of relationship occurred: (1) Political activities in the provinces were clearly the direct consequence of those taking place in Leopoldville: Kwilu, Kwango, Lomani, Ubangi, Cuvette Centrale. (2) The national leader was chosen to act without intermediaries and to take the head of the government or the opposition in his native provinces: Lac Leopold II, Nord-Katanga, Sud-Kasai, Sankuru, Unité Kasaienne. (3) Conflicts arose between the "suzerain" and his "client," who, in turn, transferred his allegiance to another national leader: Moyen-Congo. (4) The center of political gravity was located at the provincial level, the national leader being merely a representative of regional interests of the province at Leopoldville: Nord-Kivu, Maniema. (5) Politics at the local level tended to be increasingly controlled by the central government: Maniema, Haut-Congo.

These five trends in the relationship between the national leader and his constituency clearly illustrate the instability of a patri-

19. Jean-Claude Willame, *Les Provinces du Congo: Structure et fonctionement,* Collection d'Études Politiques, IRES, vols. I–V.

monial system of rule. As Weber pointed out, two problems recur in this type of domination. First, maximum control militates against an effective government over a large territory, since the cost involved readily exceeds the personal resources of even powerful rulers. Secondly, exclusive reliance upon personal instruments of force can jeopardize the ruler's authority, since it exposes him to the possibility of united action against himself by his dependents or those excluded from the share.[20]

Role of the Military

The third structural characteristic of patrimonialism is its large use of a coercive apparatus—military or paramilitary forces—for the ruler to extend or preserve his power over territories inside or outside his immediate domain.

Weber drew special attention to the social organization of the military force that enabled a patrimonial ruler to extend or preserve his power. He distinguished five types of military organizations: (1) an army composed of personal subordinates to whom the ruler has assigned rewards in return for services or payments in kind; (2) a force composed of people who are entirely divorced from society; (3) an army based on recruitment of alien mercenaries; (4) an army composed of alien people to whom the ruler has granted some rewards for their military service; (5) a personal military force recruited among the ruler's own subjects.[21]

The National Congolese Army came from the second type, due to its roots in the former Force Publique.[22] Government policies of isolating the military from its immediate milieu and sharing conscription among the main ethnic groups helped make the Force Publique the most integrated and most efficient repressive body during the colonial era. At the time of independence, however, the unity of the Force Publique broke down. It could not avoid harassment by political leaders who attempted to find support among soldiers drawn from their own region. In other words, there was a shift from a military force of type 2 to private or tribal armies of type 5.

Six months after independence, the National Congolese Army had broken up into four fragments: (1) The so-called South-Kasai State Constabulary organized by Mulopwe ("Emperor") Albert Kalonji

20. See Reinhardt Bendix, *Max Weber: An Intellectual Portrait* (New York: Doubleday Anchor, 1962), p. 347.
21. *Ibid.*, pp. 341–44.
22. For the story of the Force Publique, see Courrier Africain du CRISP, "L'Armée Nationale Congolaise," *Travaux africain,* no. 48 (1965).

and his prime minister, Joseph Ngalula. This army was almost exclusively composed of Baluba soldiers, and was not reintegrated into the NCA until October, 1962.[23] (2) The army of the "Independent State of Katanga," created and organized by former Belgian officers and composed of three distinctive elements: a constabulary whose members were recruited among the Bayeke and Balunda tribes (the ethnic groups of Godefroid Munongo and Moise Tshombe); warriors depending on other Katangese paramount chiefs favorable to Moise Tshombe (e.g., Kasongo-Nyemlo); and a body of European mercenaries recruited among foreigners and the white population of Elisabethville.[24] (3) The "National Congolese Army" of Stanleyville, directed by Congolese officers, most of whom were members of the Batetela and Bakusu tribes and, as such, favorable to the regime of Antoine Gizenga.[25] (4) The National Congolese Army of Leopoldville, loyal to its commander-in-chief, Lieutenant Colonel Joseph Mobutu.

In addition to these four segments, numerous military units formed private bodyguards receiving their orders directly from the local ruler; this was the type (4) described by Weber. Finally, foreign mercenaries recruited in South Africa, France, Portugal, and Belgium were also used by Congolese leaders, first at the regional level during the Katangese secession, and later at the national level during the 1964 rural uprising. It is certainly not exaggerated to say that without this small band of adventurers the Congo's political fate would have been completely different.

Ideological Legitimation

Weber treated patrimonialism as a reality quite distinct from the two other variants of traditional domination: patriarchalism and feudalism. He considered patriarchalism a pure type of domination characterized by the arbitrary power of the master and the limitation of that power by sacred tradition.[26] Feudalism, on the other hand, replaced the paternal relationship by contractually fixed fealty based on knightly militarism. Patrimonial rule was distinct from both by its use of *ideological* legitimation. As Bendix pointed out,

23. See Benoit Verhaegen and Jules Gérard-Libois, *Congo 1960* (Brussels: CRISP, 1960), pp. 802 ff.

24. Jules Gérard-Libois, *Sécession au Katanga* (Brussels: CRISP, 1963), pp. 177 ff.

25. General Lundula, the commander-in-chief of this army, was the uncle of Patrice Lumumba.

26. Weber, *Theory,* p. 346.

the ideology of patrimonialism differs from that of feudalism in all these respects. Feudalism is domination by the few who are skilled in war; patrimonialism is domination by one who requires officials for the exercise of his authority. A patrimonial ruler is in some measure dependent upon the good will of his subjects . . . feudalism can dispense with such good will. Patrimonialism appeals to the masses . . . not the warrior hero but the "good king," the "father of his people" are its prevailing ideal. That the patrimonial ruler sees the welfare of his subjects is the basis on which he legitimates his rule *in his own and their eyes.* The "welfare state" is the legend of patrimonialism in contrast to the feudal image of a free camaraderie of warriors pledged in loyalty to their leader.[27]

The idea that the new rulers had to distribute wealth and welfare to their people was basic to the notion of independence. Immediate independence, slogan of Congolese nationalism in 1959–60, seemed to entail socioeconomic achievement for everybody. People expected no more taxes, no more cotton, no more census-takers, no more identity cards. The impression prevailed everywhere that the collapse of the colonial system would allow all social strata to enter the "golden age" with their rulers.[28] Political parties and their leaders systematically encouraged utopian images through which the masses perceived independence. Four years later, the promise of an "indefinite social and economic prosperity," parallel to the theme of a "second independence," led to the uprising of the deprived peasants and the *Lumpenproletariat* of the cities. The language of the rebellion was similar to that previously used by the *evolués* of 1959–60: For the image of the colonizer was simply substituted the portrait of "the corrupt politician who had sold out the Congo to the Americans." The "Simba" were the "true successors of Lumumba," who were going, like him, "to liberate the Congo from those who had stolen its wealth."

How did the politician of the first generation try to legitimize his rule and his activities? Political leaders—national as well as local—used one of two approaches, according to their positions.[29]

1. The *politician-executive*—governor, minister, head of civil service, territorial administrator, etc.—generally conceived of his role and function as being identical to those performed by former colonial administrators. His political programs remained based on the same welfare policies previously practiced by the Belgian terri-

27. Bendix, *Max Weber,* p. 365.
28. For this period, see Willy Ganshof van der Meersh, *Fin de la Souveraineté belge au Congo* (Brussels: Institut Royal des Relations Internationales 1963).
29. Willame, *Les Provinces du Congo.*

torial administrators or district commissioners. At both the provincial and central levels, there was a deep commitment to the basic colonial creed: Economic and social prosperity must be pursued through foreign corporations, external technical assistance, and Catholic missions—all backed by the political institutions. The decision-making process must go through the traditional hierarchy set up by the colonizer, from the central government down to the territorial administrator and the local chief, and back to the central government again. The government decides what is good for the people, who are occasionally referred to as "natives" (*indigènes*). Basic colonial institutions remain in operation, as well as the philanthropic organizations sponsored by the colonial government.

2. The *politician-representative*—assemblyman, senator, congressman—was a new person born with independence. More in touch with his constituents and thus more vulnerable to local pressures and criticisms, he was used to concealing inefficiency and lack of control over events behind emotive language and ritualistic activities. Members of this group called themselves "the highest authorities of the nation," the "keepers of legality." These new political "priests" closed ranks as soon as the immunity of one was threatened. The process by which representative institutions worked was, above all, formalistic. Acts, gestures, and words were thought to be significant in themselves. The act of voting or the colorful political speech was believed to have magical efficacy.

THE BREAKING POINT: THE POPULAR UPRISING OF 1964–65

The rebellion of 1964–65 represents the turning point between the first and the second political generations in the Congo.[30]

In a climate of intense socioeconomic expectations as previously described, a patrimonial type of government had a fundamental weakness. Based on a generalized system of tribal and ethnic "patronage," it tended to create enclaves of prosperity or semi-prosperity and to deepen the gap between elite and non-elite. In the Congo this cleavage was partly ecological, taking the form of growing opposition between the town and the countryside. During the colonial era a satisfactory equilibrium with respect to welfare and prosperity had been kept between the rural and urban areas.

30. For an analysis of the rebellions, see Benoit Verhaegen, "Les Rebellions populaires au Congo," *Cahiers d'études africaines,* VII, no. 26 (1967), 356.

The Congo represented one of the most industrialized countries of Africa. In 1950, about 59 per cent of the male population was employed in commercialized production, contrasted with 41 per cent living from or in a subsistence economy. The gross domestic product in 1958 revealed no major distortion between the primary and secondary sectors of the economy. At that time, agriculture, mining activities, and other industries represented, respectively, 44.6, 19.7, and 34.6 per cent of the total production of goods.[31] Although information on agricultural production does not exist after 1960, export statistics indicate that the extent of peasant participation in the economy sharply declined. Production of manioc and bananas, the most common crops produced and consumed by Congolese villagers, fell from 50,000 to 3,000 tons, and from 30,000 to 13,000 tons, respectively, between 1959 and 1964. In many respects the rural areas were thus returned to self-subsistence. Bush schools, local hospitals, and welfare institutions ceased to function or were transferred into the towns.

At the same time, political frustrations grew. Between 1961 and 1964, the Congo was in fact ruled by a loose "one-party system" at the national as well as the local level. The so-called "moderates" systematically eliminated some political factions from public life, and there was a more general tendency on the part of any majority in power to disregard the rights and demands of political minorities. As a consequence, numerous nationalist leaders and local politicians, formerly followers of Patrice Lumumba, Antoine Gizenga, or Anicet Kashamura, were constantly harassed and eventually took refuge abroad, where they formed "governments of national liberation." The coalition of this "counter-elite" (to use the expression of Jean Ziegler[32]) with some rural leaders, unemployed youth, and the *Lumpenproletariat* of the cities allowed the rebellion to start. For a short time, it seemed that Fanon's prophecy would be realized. At the beginning of 1965, two-thirds of the Congo was in the hands of the insurgents. But neither they nor the professional politicians could subsequently gain a significant victory. Leaders of the rebellion, lacking leadership capacities and any revolutionary plans and perspective, lost their strength as soon as they began to expand, while the professional politicians, unable to understand that they were not the victims but the objects of the rebellion, continued to play the "game of politics." At the same time, changes were occurring within the Congolese military of immense—though little noticed—significance.

31. Lacroix, *Industrialisation au Congo*, pp. 25 ff.
32. Jean Ziegler, *Sociologie de la nouvelle Afrique* (Paris: Gallimard, 1967).

FROM THE FORCE PUBLIQUE
TO THE NATIONAL CONGOLESE ARMY

Between the mutiny of the Force Publique and the military coup d'état of November 25, 1965, important transformations occurred within the Congolese army. The three most important were (1) the substitution of a trained army for a blind instrument of repression, (2) the birth of a military intelligentsia, and (3) the absorption of considerable technical resources by the army.

Military Retraining

In Chapter 6, Pierre van den Berghe suggests how colonial forces were transformed into national armies by the training of an African career-officer cadre to replace European officers.

In the Congo, this process of conversion began, paradoxically, with the mutiny of the Force Publique in July, 1960. This revolt against their white officers brought about an immediate Africanization of the higher ranks—a striking contrast to most tropical states. Congolese soldiers dismissed their officers without warning and democratically elected their own leaders. Recourse to an unusual procedure ran many risks, since the new officers derived authority from an unruly group of soldiers who could easily withdraw their support. In fact, only the semiautomatic reflex of obeying superior officers and the hesitation of the troops to utilize this newly acquired power prevented an era of anarchy. The soldiers chose officers according to the same criteria used by the Force Publique: training and rank. Command of the new army was taken over by former sergeants—the highest rank conferred on any Congolese during the colonial period—who succeeded in imposing authority upon the ranks without great difficulty.

As the institutional and political mechanisms under civilian control became ineffectual, the new army emerged as the sole force of relative unity. In this respect it benefited from Belgian policy which had, as a major objective, avoided introducing tribal differentiations into the Force Publique. It profited also from the excellent communications network built up by European officers which, ironically, had abetted the rapid progression of the mutiny across the country.

The unity of the army, however, was far from fully realized. Despite incessant propaganda of the army command attempting to isolate the military from politics, the Congolese national army could never escape external solicitations. From 1960 to 1962 it was cut into four rival groups, as previously noted: the Gizengist soldiers of Stanleyville, the Katangese gendarmes in Elisabethville, the pro-Kalonji militia in south Kasai, and the troops faithful to the central government stationed in Leopoldville and Equateur provinces. These divisions weighed heavily on the army's morale, particularly when the rebel troops were integrated at their former ranks when the various secessionist movements ended. To these horizontal differentiations were added vertical stratifications. Tensions resulted from the creation of an elite group within the army—the para-commandos, a sort of praetorian guard of General Mobutu. Further discontent occurred within the ranks after the massive promotion of officers and noncommissioned officers in June, 1964.

Despite these forces of disintegration, however, the Congolese national army demonstrated an *esprit de corps* that contrasted with the factionalism prevalent in politics. Among the soldiers, increased consciousness of their differences from the civilian sector grew. To quote the *Bulletin militaire,* the publication of the National Congolese Army:

> The best remedy against subversion and corruption in the army is to isolate the military, while inciting within it a positive fanaticism in favor of both the honor of its work and the nobility of its ideal, to the great contempt of human masses deprived of any notion of discipline.[33]

The military felt a profound scorn for politicians and civilians in general, who were considered directly responsible for political crises. The two groups spoke and lived a language with profound differences: the military spoke in terms of honor, discipline, sacrifice, and patriotism; the civilians propounded the concepts of justice, democracy, representation, and the rights of the population.

A New Military Elite

The second series of changes within the National Congolese Army resulted from the rise of a military intelligentsia. Immediately following the mutiny of the Force Publique, the soldiers elected as leaders a small group of sergeants who had been promoted to the rank of adjutant following a special training course in September, 1959. This group formed the nucleus of the high command of the Congolese army. In addition to this generation, who were imbued with the principles of the Force Publique, a new group of officers and noncommissioned officers progressively emerged. A large num-

33. "La Subversion, la corruption, nos deux grands fléaux," *Bulletin militaire,* IV (1964), 198.

ber of trainees was sent abroad, largely through the influence of General Mobutu and the massive assistance of international organizations and Western states. Considerable effort was devoted to training. In September, 1964, 664 officers and noncommissioned officers benefited from higher training in Belgian military schools. At the same time, 276 officers (compared with 183 in 1963) continued their training in Belgium. These figures are particularly significant when one realizes that the Congolese army included only 1308 officers and noncommissioned officers in 1964.[34]

This new generation differed markedly from the preceding one. The older generation were practitioners of armed struggle, without extensive training; the new generation received training of significantly higher level in military academies. Tensions between these two generations have simmered outside general notice, and have greatly complicated the undertakings of the Mobutu government.

Technical Capacity

Finally, the Congolese army can be distinguished from the Force Publique on the level of technical capacity. Before independence, armaments were needed for the relatively small operations undertaken by the Force Publique. After crushing mutinies in 1895, 1897, 1900, and 1941, and stamping out various peasant uprisings as late as 1931, the Force Publique (like a simple force of gendarmes) carried out only small military expeditions within a limited area.

Even though it lacked men with conflict experience, the new army was equipped with some of the most modern armaments in Africa. The Congo benefited from considerable foreign aid. The United Nations command reorganized the Congolese army. Belgium, the United States, Israel, Canada, and Italy contributed to the new operational groups created within the Congolese army, including an air force, air transport, supplies, communications, river patrols, and the like. Foreign assistance also grew as a result of the campaigns against the Congolese rebels. On June 30, 1964, the fourth anniversary of independence, there were 212 Belgian officers and about 100 American technicians in the Congo, while deliveries of American and Belgian equipment rose respectively to $6.1 million and 63.3 million Belgian francs (approximately $1.27 million).[35]

Taking account of these different factors, the army lacked only

34. Edouard Kenga, *Quelques considérations sur l'A.N.C. et ses Origines,* roneotyped (Lovanium University, 1964).

35. "L'Aide exterieure à la Republique du Congo," *Études congolaises,* IX, no. 3 (1966), 1–36; IX, no. 4 (1966), 1–20.

the temptation to intervene in the political life of the country, despite the constant desire of its leaders to make of it a "great silent force." Its growing strength included, at the time of the coup d'état, a paratroop battalion, eight infantry battalions, three battalions of gendarmes, 11 commando groups of specialized volunteers, 20 companies of former Katangese gendarmes, a company of engineers, and a mobile machine gun squadron. The National Congolese Army included 26,400 soldiers, 900 noncommissioned officers, and 400 officers. The total military budget in 1965 was 9.703 billion Congolese francs (approximately $64 million), of which 5 billion francs ($33 million) was devoted to equipment. These figures represent more than 12 per cent of the national budget, contrasted with 6 per cent in 1959.[36]

These alterations helped transform the efficient but brutal Force Publique from a colonial army into a national army. Despite the shocks of the 1960–65 period—the collapse of government authority in many areas during the rebellion, the splitting and reamalgamation of the armed forces, the international repercussions of Congolese politics—the National Congolese Army emerged a far more powerful group. At the same time, many officers were confirmed in their scorn for politicians, whose machinations, self-enrichment, and concern with ethnic loyalties seemed to make them unfit for national office. The development of the National Congolese Army thus coincided with the breakdown of patrimonialism. The stage was set for the inauguration of a new regime, a new political generation.

THE SECOND POLITICAL GENERATION: RECENT TRENDS

Clearly, the 1965 coup d'état brought basic changes in the political stratification of the Congo. Although the National Congolese Army remains the central element of permanence and continuity, new strata have emerged whose political relevance was not meaningful before.

Describing the new regime is not an easy task. One thing is certain, however: military intervention by General Mobutu has *not* led to a military regime, in terms of a government directly controlled by the army. Since November, 1965, there has been no major shift in the goals, roles, and attitudes of the military vis-à-vis the society.

36. "Les Dossiers du CRISP," *Congo 1965* (Brussels: CRISP, 1966), pp. 247–48.

Three types of relations between army and society can be envisaged:[37]

1. Army and society more or less coincide with each other. The nation is either *totally militarized* and led by a caste or a dominant ethnic group for conquest or self-defense, or *temporarily mobilized* for revolutionary and national warfare.

2. Army and society do not coincide with each other, but the Army represents one social force among others, able to influence the political process to various extents. According to this conception, which is largely shared by political scientists, the army may play a creative role, similar to that played by the Western bourgeoisie in the modernization process.

3. Army and society tend to be opposed or, more precisely, the army is opposed (or at least completely indifferent) to the transformation of the society. The army is a neutral, passive, or negative force of social change. In the Congo, this pattern has been predominant, is still present, and is likely to last.

To understand the significance of the 1965 coup d'état, we must compare it with Colonel Mobutu's first intervention in Congolese politics shortly after independence. In both cases, the army was threatened with division resulting from political and ethnic tensions; in both cases, the army had just painfully realized relative unity and stability after experiencing the 1960 mutiny and the 1964–65 rebellion. Both coups were self-protective reflexes on the part of a cohesive group.

The 1960 intervention occurred following a power struggle between President Joseph Kasavubu and Prime Minister Patrice Lumumba. The intervention must also be seen in the context of the mutiny of the former Force Publique, which had been steadily manipulated and corrupted through the interference of political factions.

On September 14, 1960, Colonel Mobutu decided to "neutralize" Lumumba and Kasavubu. Despite the interest he had shown for politics,[38] Mobutu preferred the "techniques" and "discipline" inculcated by seven years' service in the Force Publique. As a result of this preference, on September 19 he called upon university students and Congolese technicians (whether in the country or studying abroad) to aid him. This was the start of the "College des Commissaires Généraux," a transitional institution intended to fill the power vacuum before "national reconciliation" could be

37. My typology is based on an unpublished paper by Benoit Verhaegen, "Armée et régime militaire au Congo," roneotyped (1967).
38. First as a journalist, then as a friend of Lumumba.

achieved. In reality, however, the unclear functions of the new College, the lack of cohesion among its members,[39] the large number of members (39 commissioners at the end of October) and the nearly complete absence of popular support, rapidly brought about its crumbling. As time passed, the political power which temporarily had been theirs escaped completely, and was divided among factions in Leopoldville: the followers of President Kasavubu, members of the Ileo government,[40] the Sureté Nationale, the National Congolese Army, and politicians following their own leaders.

The coup d'état of November, 1965, occurred within a similar historical context: contention for control of power between the president and his prime minister, Moise Tshombe. On this occasion, however, the decision to intervene did not emanate directly from Mobutu. Although the exact circumstances surrounding the second intervention remain unclear, it seems that the source of the coup was the army itself, whose higher officers deeply distrusted the men in the government. A political shift to the "left" by President Kasavubu following his return from the meeting of the Organization of African Unity in Accra (October, 1965), the menace that Kasavubu might dismiss the mercenaries who had given valuable support in the struggle against the rebels, a belief that the army had been the "savior of the Congolese nation," and fear of seeing the army manipulated by politicians again, were among the factors disquieting the higher echelons. A top-level meeting of officers the night before the coup indicated the collective army decision to intervene.

In the beginning, General Mobutu seemed to be and to act as the direct and personal emanation of a military junta, the high command of the NCA. In its name, he declared a five-year period of military rule. The influence of the junta appeared to be substantiated by three facts: (1) the nomination of military officers at the head of regions under constant political tensions (Luluabourg, Haut-Congo); (2) the use of special military courts of justice that had been previously settled to judge special military matters (e.g., desertion) for civilian purposes, such as the fight against corruption or political agitation; (3) the utilization of the army in some spectacular and symbolic operations of popular mobilization, such as the operation called "Retroussons les Manches" (Let's Roll up our

39. Three divisions rapidly grew within the College: the technician-students, a politically neutral group; those who defended the intervention of Colonel Mobutu, a group composed of students already involved in political life (Ndele, Lihau, Mbeka, Cardoso, Mushiete); and political commissioners, such as Bomboko, Bolela, and Kazadi.

40. This "phantom" government was established by Kasavubu in the weeks preceding Colonel Mobutu's intervention. See *Congo 1960,* vol. II.

Sleeves).[41] It looked as if the military would be directly associated with the executive and judiciary processes.

After a few months, however, General Mobutu appeared to stand apart from the army, particularly the high command. The principle of military noninvolvement in civil and political matters was re-emphasized. Moreover, once the regime was firmly established, references to the high command as a "revolutionary instrument" disappeared. In October, 1966, Mobutu explicitly defined the role of the army as "an organism of execution operating in a strictly military context," not a "pressure group or a political assembly."[42] In the provinces, the military commissioners were replaced by the former civil authorities. The special military courts of justice lost their meaning once the campaign against corruption was over. Finally, after a brief period of enthusiasm, the symbolic mobilization of the people by the army ended; probably tired, the soldiers returned to their garrisons. Mobutu himself began to wear civilian dress. The coup had occurred, the first ardor for change had passed. Mobutu sought to supplant the ineffectual patrimonial system by more efficient patterns of government.

A Caesarist Bureaucracy

The current Congolese regime is best described as a "Caesarist" or "Napoleonic" bureaucracy. As such, it includes four basic features of the pure type of bureaucracy described by Weber: (1) Official business tends to be conducted more and more on a continuous basis. (2) It is conducted in relative secrecy by experts and in accordance with stipulated rational rules. (3) Officials' responsibilities and authority are part of a centralized hierarchy of authority. (4) Officials and other administrative employees do not own the resources necessary for the performance of their assigned functions.[43]

In his analysis of rational legal authority, Weber was deeply concerned with the relationship between the struggle for power and the trend toward bureaucratization. He felt it indispensable to maintain some kind of equilibrium between them. Failure to achieve a balance meant that the bureaucracy had usurped political decision-making or, as Karl Mannheim put it, had turned "all problems of politics into problems of administration."[44]

41. These operations were aimed at cleaning the dirty areas of the big cities.
42. "Les Dossiers du CRISP," *Congo 1966* (Brussels: CRISP, 1967), p. 28.
43. Weber, *Theory*, pp. 330–32.
44. Karl Mannheim, *Ideology and Utopia* (New York: Harcourt, Brace, 1949), p. 105.

This trend toward "depoliticization" and the corollary emphasis on continuity of public office, hierarchy, and centralization are basic trends of the current Congolese regime. Not only has the politician been popularly designated as the source of all evil but politics itself has become the main evil to fight. The following decisions and events between 1965 and 1967 confirm these trends.

DECLINING IMPORTANCE OF PARLIAMENT

The definition of political goals and the choice of public officials are less and less entrusted to the changing and unstable representative institutions. One of the first public acts of President Mobutu was to limit the relative autonomy within which parliamentary institutions traditionally operated. Although the president kept parliament functioning and continued to formally recognize its prerogatives, he simultaneously decreed a five-year state of emergency applicable to the parliament and other institutions. It can be called upon to collaborate—it cannot decide any more. One of its most important privileges—the nomination and removal of cabinet members, a privilege which previously produced innumerable abuses—now is in the hands of the president.

Public debate has been discouraged. Political associations have been prohibited. The CVR (Corps des Volontaires de la République, an aggregate of youth associations backing Mobutu) has refused to define itself as a "political party" but rather as "the only flag of the new regime."[45] CVR leaders do not emphasize elaboration of decisions or political education of the masses, but stress protection and surveillance. In brief, Mobutu has suspended politics—i.e., the development of regulative procedures, mechanisms and organizational patterns of communication, and setting up organs within which political struggle occurs.[46] By stressing the elements of stability and permanence, he has shelved politics. Mobutu has failed to relate "tensional forces of society" to the political order.[47]

ROLE OF "EXPERTS"

Governmental functions have increasingly been placed in the hands of "experts," acting in the shadow of the presidency and under its direct supervision. The progressive invasion of these ex-

45. *Congo 1966,* p. 62.
46. S. N. Eisenstadt, *The Political System of Empires* (New York: Free Press, 1963), pp. 94–112.
47. Sheldon S. Wolin, *Politics and Vision* (New York: Little, Brown, 1960), p. 7.

perts, most of whom are depoliticized former university students, is illustrated by the decline of professional politicians in the cabinet between 1965 and 1967. In mid-1966, practically all ministerial portfolios were in the hands of professional politicians, many of whom belonged to the second wave of politicians elected in 1965. At the end of 1966, there were nine technicians and university students and 12 politicians in the government; at the end of 1967, there were 13 university and technical school graduates in the 22-member cabinet.

In November, 1966, President Mobutu created the presidential cabinet, intended in theory to assist and advise him on administrative affairs. In fact, its role goes further than that. It has become the compulsory channel for all communications between the ministries and the presidency, thereby making it an organism of decision rather than consultation. The presidential cabinet aims at "redefining the new civil order, rationalizing the institutional structures of the state and creating better standards of living for the population by an increase of the production and a more equal redistribution of the Gross National Product."[48] It operates in complete secrecy, and is, in effect, a kind of private fortress which members of the government and parliament tried to penetrate in vain.

CENTRALIZATION OF POWER

Parallel to the increasing importance played by the experts was an accelerating centralization of power. At the end of 1966, President Mobutu concentrated the functions of chief of state and head of the government in his hands. He could directly act upon mass media through a high commissariat of information, led by his personal friend, Jean-Jacques Kande. He kept the department of defense under his aegis and controlled the national security services through Colonel Singa and his agents in the provinces. In the realm of foreign policy, he created a system of personal representatives, resident ministers, and military attachés intimately acquainted with him. Finally, the president reduced the number of provinces and reimposed the authority of the central government upon them. This process was effected in two phases. In March, 1966, the president asked the parliament to prepare a bill aiming at "a valid administrative restructuring of our country."[49] After a series of controversies among congressmen and senators, the number of provinces

48. *Congo 1966*, p. 33.
49. *Ibid.*, p. 221.

was reduced from 21 to 14, then to 12.[50] Nine months later, due to the suspected participation of four governors in the mutiny of the Katangese troops at Kisangani (July–September, 1966), President Mobutu reduced the number to 8.

ROLE OF GOVERNORS

At the same time, Mobutu took an unexpected measure. Provincial governors became state commissioners designated by the president of the republic during his term of office. No governor would work in his province of origin. This measure had the consequence of cutting the highest provincial authority from his popular and tribal basis. In Weberian terms, it meant that each governor, transferred to an alien territory, no longer owned the political resources previously necessary for maintaining himself in power; the executive office was now separated from the household and the private life of the ruler. This decision brought about one of the deepest changes in the institutional structures of the Congo. The provinces became mere administrative entities again. In the report accompanying the new law, the minister of internal affairs, Etienne Tshisekedi, concluded:

> Thus, one paradoxically comes back again to the administrative structures existing before June 30, 1960, that is, a central and strong authority basing itself on decentralized provincial administrations which realize through district commissioners and territorial administrators all the options of economic and social progress.[51]

CAESARISM

The parallel with the former Belgian bureaucracy is tempting. Centralization, hierarchy, permanence, and expertise were major structural features of the colonial bureaucracy. Yet the setting in which the colonial administration operated was substantially different, owing to racial domination by a determined minority. The setting differed as well in the importance of personal attachments. As Weber noted, one of the main consequences of bureaucratic development in a modern environment is depersonalization.

> When fully developed, bureaucracy stands in a specific sense under the principle of "sine ira ac studio." Its specific nature, which is welcomed by capitalism, develops the more completely it succeeds

50. Willame, "La Réunification des provinces congolaises," *Études congolaises*, IX, no. 4 (1966), 68–86.
51. *Congo 1966*, p. 239.

in eliminating from official business love, hatred, and all purely *personal, irrational and emotional* elements which escape calculation. This is the specific nature of bureaucracy and it is appraised as its special virtue.[52]

The Mobutu regime has not removed the personal and emotional elements cited by Weber. Although the president has made a serious effort to detribalize the society by administrative measures, his government is highly personalized. Personalization through patrimonial relationships is being transformed into personalization by attachment to the president. Mobutu has tried hard to introduce charismatic elements in his politics, especially by claiming to be the spiritual successor of Patrice Lumumba and by intimately associating his person to that of the Congolese people. "To deceive the people is to deceive me" is a favorite expression he uses in his speeches. The mass media, and especially the CVR, have echoed this policy by starting a campaign aiming at proclaiming the president "second national hero of the republic." Moreover, for the first time in the history of the Congo, the president traveled across the country many times to reinforce his popular image.

But it is primarily emotional and ideological commitments that best characterize the present regime. The dominant themes of the Mobutu government during 1966 and 1967 were highly moralizing and nationalistic. Initially, a generalized attack was launched against the professional politician whose image was associated with "corruption, treason, exploitation." When this campaign was over, the president used themes linked with the success of Lumumbism in the 1960's: complete decolonization, national dignity, and reduction of private foreign power in the Congo. From April, 1966, the theme of economic independence and Congolese control of the economy became predominant. This theme coincided with the givens of the Congolese sociopolitical setting: (1) mass expectations of a new independence; (2) pressures exercised by the upper strata of the population (middle classes, university students, bureaucrats) for full economic "congolization" to bring more rapid and deeper socioeconomic achievement; (3) the necessity for the power structure to counterattack the challenge launched by the 1964 popular uprising. Prestigious symbols, such as a new unit of currency (the "Zaire"), spectacular ceremonies, use of honorific titles, and deeper involvement in pan-Africanism, further indicated the national ends sought by the Mobutu government.

52. Max Weber, "Wirtschaft und Gesellschaft," in *From Max Weber, Essays in Sociology,* trans. and ed. H. H. Geerth and C. Wright Mills (London: Routledge and Kegan Paul, 1964), pp. 215–16.

Sociopolitical Forces Backing the Regime

Any political system—traditional, transitional, or modern—must secure some degree of internal support among several strata of the population in order to survive, let alone achieve political stability. In the Mobutu government, as in previous Congolese regimes, the army remains the central element of coercion. A second continuity appears in the ideological realm where, as previously mentioned, the shadow of Patrice Lumumba continues to determine the identifications of the ruling elite. Discontinuities appear in the diminished role played by a large segment of the political bourgeoisie and in the emergence of urban strata—the youth and the university students— who previously had not fully shared the benefits of independence.

THE ARMY

The Congolese regime, as previously mentioned, is not an out-and-out military government. Relations between President Mobutu and the NCA remain confused. Two examples demonstrate the ambiguous character of these relations: the "Pentecost plot" shows the Army as the most zealous watchdog of its unity and security; the "Mulamba affair" illustrates how President Mobutu is at times the prisoner of internal rivalries among the military rank and file.

On May 30, 1966, President Mobutu sent a personal message to the population:

> Tonight, a plot against me and the new regime has been hatched by some irresponsible politicians. They have been arrested and will be indicted for high treason. This plot has been thwarted thanks to the vigilance and loyalty of the National Congolese Army.[53]

Four persons were arrested: Evariste Kimba, who had been prime minister for three months in 1965; Jerome Anany, former minister of defense in 1964; Alexandre Mahamba, former minister of land from 1960 to 1961; and Emmanuel Bamba, former minister of finance and leader of a well-known Kimbanguist church. The "Pentecost plot," as it was later called, remains unreal for many observers. The four politicians allegedly involved had no popularity even in their regions of origin; no weapons or significant documents were ever seized; apparently the purported conspirators held very few meetings. On the other hand, the plotters reportedly came into con-

53. *Le Courrier d'Afrique,* May 31, 1966.

tact with many military officers. According to official statements, one of them, Major Efomi, revealed the plot to both Colonel Bangala, governor of Kinshasa, and General Mobutu. A meeting of Colonel Bangala, other high-ranking officers, and the conspirators was arranged, at the end of which the four politicians were arrested. Although all the circumstances are not completely clear, the best explanation is that the plot was organized and dramatized by army officers to crush a very limited opposition coming from some politicians who had complained about the government's lack of regional representativeness. From a single political discontent, the army conjured up a conspiracy against the regime and its head.

The role of Mobutu as a prisoner of his army was made particularly clear when he dismissed Prime Minister Colonel Leonard Mulamba in October, 1966. During the rebellion, Mulamba had gained a reputation of bravery, even invincibility, among his troops. He stood in the front ranks to defend Bukavu against a heavy attack by the insurgents, while most of the NCA was in full flight. This was the first real battle won by the army without the help of white mercenaries. Mulamba naturally became one of the most popular figures in the Congo and was designated prime minister in November, 1965. The army was reluctant to support the rapid rise of this relatively young officer, however. Specific grievances openly expressed by the military high command concerned his attitude toward the Katangese mutiny. Mulamba was accused explicitly by Lieutenant Colonel Malila, chief of staff of the NCA, of having supported the rebels, or at least of having prevented the army from eliminating the mutineers by force.[54] Mobutu tried to save his prime minister in vain. Even the ministry of defense was denied Mulamba by the military high command.

THE YOUTH AND THE CVR

Since the military coup, Mobutu has received impressive support from youth organizations. In January, 1966, these groups joined to form the CVR. This movement has never tried to rally political support. Rather, it has served primarily as an organization of detection, parallel to the national security services controlled by military officers. During 1966 and 1967, the CVR served as a subsidiary instrument for the city police or as a primitive intelligence service to spy on foreigners and politicians suspected by the regime.

The spontaneous growth of the CVR and the eruption of youth into the political stage are rooted in the sociological role of youth

54. *Congo 1966,* p. 30.

and in the changing role of politicians. Both the frustrations and political awareness of youth have been rising. Nearly half of the population is less than 15 years old. Before independence, opportunities—education, employment—existed for them. After 1960, however, the situation deteriorated rapidly. The youngest found fewer schools waiting for them; the older ones found fewer jobs. Many of them found the only possible outlet in politics.

Since independence, local and national parties and, in some instances, the politicians themselves have recruited bodyguards among the urban youth. These young people, most of whom left school after primary education, played a limited role as a pressure group. They lived under the shadow of patrons, parties, or other political associations, and formed, in a sense, manpower available for electoral purposes. When parties were declared illegal, when the image of the politician became equated with corruption and dishonesty, and when it became clear that Mobutu would rule without permitting civil opposition, these unemployed young people spontaneously gathered together. Two examples seemed to have inspired them. In Congo-Brazzaville, youth movements, especially the National Movement for the Revolution, became a powerful instrument of rule for the revolutionary regime of Massamba-Debat. The second example came from the 1964 rebellion, the prime mover of which had been unemployed rural young people. In a sense, we can consider the CVR as the peaceful and nonrevolutionary continuation, in the privileged urban setting, of the attack previously made by the "Simba" and rural recruits of the Popular Army of Liberation against ineffectual and degenerate political institutions.

TENTATIVE CONCLUSIONS

To conclude, I will rephrase the Congolese political process in terms of four concepts: power, authority, force, and influence.[55] Power is a relation involving both a conflict of interests or values and the threat of sanctions, i.e., any promised reward or penalty by which a structure can maintain effective control over policy. Authority refers to both the source and the restraint upon the exercise of power or, in other words, to the legitimacy of political structures. Force, contrary to power, radically reduces the scope of decision-making since the subject has no choice as to course of action. Finally, influence like power has both rational and relational at-

55. Peter Bachrach and Morton S. Baratz, "Decisions and Non-Decisions: An Analytical Framework." *American Political Science Review,* LVII (1963), 632–42.

tributes; influence differs in that potential sanctions are not utilized.

The picture of Congolese politics drawn in this chapter shows that no autonomous structures of either power or authority have emerged. Instead, under the two political generations, decision-making has been carried out by force, violence, and influence. The patrimonial rulers initially monopolized public offices; contrary to traditional patrimonialism, however, they lacked authoritarian and centralized power of command. This group, torn by internal struggles, could not control events through meaningful sanctions. It failed to transfer the previous agreement on the need for independence to new, legitimized goals. Since the arrival of the second political generation, dominated by a Caesarist bureaucracy, the Congolese political process has shown increasing rationality and coherence. However, the legitimacy of the regime has been based on short-lived elements of emotions and personalization—in short, upon influence. Outside economic and political agencies, particularly major mining and financial interests, the United Nations, and powerful states linked to the Congo by bilateral treaties continue to act in the periphery of the sociopolitical realm; since they have no direct access to sanctions and legitimacy, they rely upon influence and informal pressures. Finally, the National Congolese Army has remained an instrument of coercion. The 1964–65 rebellion failed to rationalize its tremendous appeal among the rural masses, to create a new revolutionary leadership, and to develop an ideology of political and socioeconomic development; as a result, its initial strength degenerated into sheer violence.

The Congo under President Mobutu thus continues to seek for a political process based upon power and authority. Until the legitimacy of national political structures is assured, instability and uncertainty will continue to plague the country.

INTRODUCTION TO CHAPTER 4

"IT IS NOT THE DUTY of the army to rule or govern, because it has no political mandate and its duty is not to seek a political mandate," President Kwame Nkrumah told the National Assembly of Ghana on February 1, 1966. Within the same month, while Nkrumah was en route to Peking, members of the 2d Brigade seized control and ousted the long-standing civilian government. The establishment of the National Liberation Council, a coalition of senior army and police officers, made Ghana the eighth tropical African state to gain military leadership.

As president, Nkrumah sought to maintain close control over the armed forces. Through his direct intervention, as in forced retirements of officers, establishment of a presidential regiment, and apparent undercutting of military professionalism, he antagonized senior officers of both the police and the army. However, as Kraus points out, the institutional grievances of the armed forces must be viewed as part of the declining legitimacy of the Nkrumah government. Unresolved regional and ethnic tensions; a worsening economic situation; the absence of effective political choice: these were among the background factors that undercut the government's position. Inattentive to Ghanaian problems, Nkrumah sought to project his vision of pan-African unity without a fully secure domestic base. The fall of his regime was assuredly not inevitable—perhaps more than any other deposed African leader, Nkrumah sought to ensure military loyalty—but was made more likely by his policies.

The members of the NLC justified its intervention in terms of the absence of meaningful political choice without mentioning the

152

military's institutional interests which Krause indicates precipitated the coup action. To quote General Ankrah's broadcast of February 28, 1966:

> This grave step was taken because no other means was available to restore to the people of Ghana the blessings of liberty, justice, happiness, and prosperity for which we all have struggled for so long. In taking bold steps, the Ghana armed forces and the Ghana police service acted in accord with the oldest and most treasured tradition of the people of Ghana, the tradition that a leader who loses the confidence and support of his people and resorts to the arbitrary use of power should be deposed.
>
> No one can doubt that Kwame Nkrumah had completely lost the respect and confidence of the people of this country through his capricious use of power and the Draconian measures he resorted to at the expense of our national institutions.[1]

Jubilation greeted the NLC's seizure of power. Remaining remnants of the Convention People's Party, once a powerful mass-movement, were swept away. The NLC pledged to restore civilian rule as quickly as possible, eventually setting a target date of September 30, 1969. Kraus notes that the NLC necessarily depended heavily upon civil servants to carry out policy objectives; open political activities, particularly the establishment of parties, were prohibited until the closing months of the NLC's announced rule.

The simple restoration of civilian rule will not by itself bring tranquillity to Ghana, however. The art of politics, as de Tocqueville commented, is the art of associating together—and this, in turn, requires a belief that conflict can be managed. Kraus sets forth the serious unresolved problems—legitimacy, participation, nation-building and state-building—that will confront the successors of the National Liberation Council. Military rule brought back a measure of stability, but it did not necessarily establish solid foundations for civilian rule. The effective management of conflict in Ghana in coming years will continue to pose major challenges.

C.E.W.

1. *Africa Research Bulletin,* III, no. 2 (1966), cols. 467AB.

4.

Arms
and Politics
in Ghana

Jon Kraus
University of South Carolina

The coup d'état of February 24, 1966, toppled the Nkrumah regime in Ghana and brought to power an army-police coalition, the National Liberation Council (NLC). The coup may be ascribed to a variety of causes common to the many coups which have occurred in African countries in the last several years. Coup leaders in Ghana justified their intervention by the flagrant abuse of their powers by ex-President Kwame Nkrumah and Convention People's Party (CPP) leaders, widespread political repression, a sharp economic decline, and rampant corruption. An observer would also have to cite as precipitating factors the distinct grievances of the institutional groups, elements of the army and police, which undertook the coup, though the new leadership has alluded to this cause only slightly.

Much of the material and the analysis in this chapter is drawn from the writer's Ph.D. thesis on the single-party system in Ghana.

There are important problems involved in trying to determine the sources of the coup in Ghana, a small state of 7.6 million people (in 1960). While some of the manifest sources of discontent with African governments which appear to give rise to military intervention are broadly similar, it is evident that the salient factors which have precipitated intervention in the political systems in different African countries have varied. However, even when one focuses on a particular case, as with Ghana, it is difficult to isolate the significant factors involved, to estimate degrees of discontent among the population and the crucial support groups, and to distinguish which factors and degrees of discontent constitute a threshold beyond which a coup d'état or some form of military intervention in political life is highly probable.

Almost every African country has been subjected to various attempts at military intervention and civil violence since independence. Aristide Zolberg has noted that among African states "the incidence of conflict and disorder appears unrelated to such variables as type of colonial experience, size, number of parties, absolute level or rate of economic and social development, as well as to the overall characteristics of regimes."[1] This directs one's attention to more fundamental factors of political life. Is the fragility of authority endemic to the new political systems of Africa, particularly since they have experienced simultaneous crises concerning the legitimacy of authority, the nature and extent of political participation, and state-building and national integration? Is it possible for a new African government to bargain successfully with—i.e., reasonably satisfy—most of the numerous significant claimants to power, status, and material allocations, given the limited resources and new political systems in which actual and potential political actors have little vested interest? Is it possible in these states to avoid the advent to power of those with the arms to make decisive their claim to power or belief in their ability to organize the system more effectively?

The specific factors which are the immediate precipitating causes of coups and other military and civil violence in the new African states are themselves a consequence of more generic circumstances of politics. Thus, one can most usefully account for the coup in Ghana and examine the politics and prospects of the National Liberation Council and its successor civilian regime (see the postscript on page 218) by studying the configuration of immediate factors within the context of an examination of the political system.

1. Aristide Zolberg, "The Structure of Political Conflict in the New States of Tropical Africa," *American Political Science Review* LXII (1968), 70.

Socioeconomic and Political Background

Within the Gold Coast there were a large number of distinct traditional states which, partly helped by the British policy of indirect rule, maintained a sense of their separate identities through-out the colonial period. Although the Akan-speaking states of the Colony and Ashanti shared a common cultural heritage, there were 62 separate traditional states in the Colony area (the first colonized, southern region) in 1931, varying greatly in size and importance. There were several dozen states in Ashanti, many of whom were constantly engaged in a struggle to assert their autonomy from the Ashanti Confederacy. And in the Northern Territories the colonial government recognized some two dozen political units when the "protectorate" was established—which, Fage notes, fails to take into account the autonomous tendencies of many of the subunits.[2] Although social, economic, and political change helped to erode certain aspects of the traditional social and political systems as interrelated sets of norms, values, and structures, these systems survived colonial rule. Territorially, the four parts of the Gold Coast were administered separately during the colonial period; no interregional political links developed.

There were important economic advances in the Gold Coast between 1900 and 1945, particularly in terms of the significant percentage of farmers who had been drawn conclusively within a cash economy (most notably but not exclusively the many peasant cocoa farmers), a growing wage labor force, and large increases in education, urbanization, communications, governmental revenue, and external trade. However, this social and economic growth was sharply skewed regionally and ethnically within the country, with the southern Colony area being most favored in all aspects (including cocoa production almost until World War II), the south-central Ashanti region second, and the British Togoland trusteeship territory to the east (a strip running the length of the country) and the vast Northern Territories coming last in almost all aspects. Modern distinctions in terms of education, wealth, and secularization—all providing access to wage employment, material benefits, and high modern status—helped to compound and exacerbate older distinctions based on language, customs, social and political structures, and historical enmities.

2. Gold Coast, *1931 Census: Appendices,* Table xx, p. 21; J. D. Fage, *Ghana: A Historical Interpretation* (Madison: University of Wisconsin Press, 1959), p. 26.

The social and economic modernization and the subordination of the traditional African states to colonial authority brought about some radical changes in social values, the structures and norms of authority, and patterns of participation. The colonial structure rested in significant measure on the traditional authorities, whom it utilized as local agents. It sought to protect both the office of chieftaincy and its occupants from challenge. By removing ultimate power from the hands of the traditional authorities and then sustaining them in the face of community disfavor, the colonial administration helped to bring both traditional leaders and chieftaincy itself in many areas into disrepute. Among the Akan-speaking traditional states in south and central Ghana, chieftaincy was an elective (from royal lineages) and limited majesty, hedged by the councils of lineage elders or other, higher chiefs in council and, to a lesser extent, by the traditional prerogatives of the commoners (nonroyal lineage and nonslave) with regard to the enstoolment (election) or destoolment of their chiefs. With modernization and access to new social roles and values, the essentially religious norms which regulated and sanctified social roles, behavior, and structures were significantly undermined. Thus, the chiefly office, its occupants, and the traditional and colonial prerogatives and abuses associated with both attracted a high level of antagonism from those modernized and transitional men who saw both the colonial and traditional authorities as restricting their drive for social mobility and political power.

An anticolonial nationalism erupted at the end of World War II. Prior to then, a small, bourgeois, merchant-professional class with aristocratic proclivities (partly comprising old coastal trading families) had emerged and promoted African advancement by constitutional reform, in political competition with the chiefs. The post–World War II nationalism was precipitated by imminent expectations of change and the felt grievances of many groups: the merchant-professional class, denied commercial opportunity, social status, and political power (by the chiefs); the anguished cocoa farmers, whose trees, stricken by a contagious disease, were being cut; rural youth (commoner) associations, constrained by colonially supported traditional power; ex-servicemen, petty traders, and frustrated, alienated primary- and middle-school leavers (both graduates and dropouts), educated to the opportunity but bereft of the possibility of social mobility and modern status within the confines of a colonially and traditionally structured society. The diffuse grievances of many groups were animated by expectations and events and were aggregated in the sentiment that things could only be put right under African rule. Throughout much of the Colony and Ashanti the legitimacy of colonial authority and its agents—the chiefs—was discredited and spurned, and legitimacy passed to those who recognized, demanded, and incarnated the right of African rule.

Political Demands, Participation, and Structures

As the anticolonial nationalism moved to militance (1948–52), as well as during an interim period (1951–57) of internal self-government, certain social cleavages became highly politicized and were manifested in different political structures. During both these periods of significant social stress, there was a widely manifest *class-community conflict* in the Colony and Ashanti,[3] which was initially a conflict between modern secular and traditional authority, the latter represented by chiefs and councils. With the great expansion of political participation in the 1950's through the extension of the franchise, there was a wide-scale politicization of primordial ties, resulting in the rise of confessional, ethnic, and regional parties. Participation in these political groups was animated not only by primordial ties but by socioeconomic grievances, since, as noted, the extension of modernization was skewed regionally and ethnically and thus did not result in cross-cutting but in reinforcing ties and identities among traditional groups. Salient during the early period (1948–52) was a *class conflict*. This ranged the older, reformist merchant-professional class, mostly in the Colony, against a post–World War II generation whose leadership was predominantly petty-bourgeois—teachers, small traders, a few larger businessmen, and journalists—and whose support included the relatively small but growing number of semi-industrial workers, an urban and rural lower-middle, transitional class of the partially educated, and a large number of peasant farmers attached to the capitalist-export economy.

These class-community and class conflicts of the 1940's and 1950's—which may well reoccur in the late 1960's and 1970's—reflected some fundamental social and political cleavages which shaped the structure of political conflict in Ghana during the 1950's and 1960's. Politics occurred in the context of an unintegrated society, in which the host of traditional societies—with their values, norms, and structures (not just political)—overlapped with the emergent, modernizing society. Traditional structures competed

---

3. The non-Akan states of the Northern Territories and the Ewe states in British Togoland did not experience this class-community conflict, in the case of the Northern Territories largely because there was insufficient modernization to sponsor an emergent class.

with new, weak political structures for political authority, and an increase in the authority of the latter did not necessarily mean a decrease in that of the former.[4] Traditional structures and norms helped to animate the politicization of primordial loyalties and, with the anticolonial movement itself and then the imminent prospects of self-government, nurtured the vast inflation of political demands to which the new government was subjected. The nature of the society along with the relative scarcity of economic resources severely limited the range of political choice.

The political structures which arose in the postwar period to aggregate and represent the diffuse interests articulated were proto-parties and, more importantly, party-movements. The latter combined characteristics of a broad social and political (national or subnational) movement with those of a party and maintained elements of each at all times. As movements, they functioned (or believed they were functioning) in an extraconstitutional environment, tended to subordinate specific interests to an overriding interest (often rendering those specific interests illegitimate), attempted to integrate or align intimately to their cause all associational groups, and worked toward a moral community (whether village, traditional state, ethnic group, or country) above the divisiveness of partisan politics, united in common abhorrence of a "stranger" (e.g., colonialist or other ethnic groups). As parties, they recognized (from time to time) and worked within a constitutional framework, competed in elections, recognized the legitimacy or at least the necessity of satisfying specific interests for electoral support, and more or less tolerated opposing political groups.

The first important postwar political party was the United Gold Coast Convention (UGCC), led by the intelligentsia of the small merchant-professional class, which began as a proto-party or faction to aggregate both its class grievances (vis-à-vis the chiefs and colonial structure) and nationalist sentiment. Its leadership was almost wholly composed of lawyers; it was basically elitist and reformist in nature. Animated by events (chiefly, an anti-inflation campaign, the February, 1948, riot, and the cocoa crisis) and a young secretary-general (Nkrumah) brought home from England to organize it, the UGCC quickly became a very loosely structured social and political movement, to which a large number of smaller associational, youth, and political groups attached themselves. Out-

4. On the unintegrated, or syncretic, nature of African society and on a conceptualization of diverse political systems attempting to authoritatively allocate values within a single state, see Zolberg, "Political Conflict," and *Creating Political Order: The Party-States of West Africa* (Chicago: Rand McNally, 1966), pp. 128–34.

standing and influential among these were farmers' groups, the Ex-Servicemen's Union, trade unions, and youth groups in the Colony and Ashanti. Aware that colonial authority had been gravely undermined, the British government (as distinct from the parochial colonial administration) prepared to give way to constitutional change and award the UGCC leadership a power position. With their leadership and tactics challenged from within by younger, better organized, and more militant elements, some of them close to Nkrumah, the UGCC elite, cautioning patience, refused to submit its leadership to popular, "uneducated" opinion. A final schism occurred in mid-1949, bringing the birth of the CPP and leaving the UGCC with many disputatious leaders and few followers.

There has been a contentious debate over the nature of the CPP.[5] It has been referred to as a party, a movement, and a political machine, the latter designation being used quite differently by various observers. It had characteristics of all three, and changed in both structure and function over time.

In the pre-independence period it was a relatively loosely structured party/movement (as characterized above), a fragile national coalition which the leadership persisted in trying to integrate and render coherent and responsive to its aims, an attempt which was hardly altogether successful. It began as a populist, anti-traditional-authority, anticolonial, antiprofessional, "common man's" movement, extraparliamentary in inception and spirit, populist in ideology, and chiliastic in vocabulary. It derived its legitimacy from its militant nationalism (which grew tactical during 1951–57), from its identification as the party of the commoners, in whose behalf it facilitated and legitimated a social and political revolution which was already occurring at the grassroots in the Colony and Ashanti, and from Nkrumah's charismatic appeal, which was sharply limited in range and over time but was initially crucial to securing the CPP as a reasonably coherent political structure. Explicit in all three sources of legitimacy was the CPP's decidedly secular dedication to rapid social and economic change.

As the first organized national movement, it had an initially powerful impetus, drawing to it nationalist aspirations, many specific interest groups, the educated and semieducated commoners

5. See David Apter, "Ghana," in *Political Parties and National Integration in Tropical Africa*, ed. James S. Coleman and Carl G. Rosberg, Jr. (Berkeley and Los Angeles: University of California Press, 1964), pp. 259–315; Dennis Austin, *Politics in Ghana: 1946–1960* (London: Oxford University Press, 1964); Henry Bretton, *The Rise and Fall of Kwame Nkrumah* (New York: Praeger, 1966); Zolberg, *Creating Political Order;* and Jon Kraus, "On the Politics of Nationalism and Social Change in Ghana," *Journal of Modern African Studies,* VII, no. 1 (1969), 107–30.

seeking rapid social mobility, and all those who sought to gain advantage from a winner. Its organizing impetus was strong, but membership itself was often a casual thing. Sweeping to power in the 1951 elections, the CPP utilized its powers and resources to organize and attempt to win the support of the farmers (in the United Ghana Farmers' Council, through the para-statal Cocoa Purchasing Company), the trade unions, the ex-servicemen, youth associations (which it tried with difficulty to absorb, even when its leaders were CPP), Muslims, chiefs, and various ethnic groups. Basically, the party was organized around the local councils established in 1951 (providing local control and patronage) and the parliamentary constituencies.

The CPP leadership sought to maintain a national focus, a predominantly secular appeal, and a fairly broad ethnic/regional representation in government.[6] Its local partisans recruited politically on the basis of ethnic and other parochial ties but sought to orient and integrate parochial solidarities and interests into the larger, nationalist organization.

There was a small, national leadership, with an undivided national orientation, and strong, demanding, and parochial constituency party leaders, whose interests frequently differed from those of the national leadership. The national leadership, in which Nkrumah was pre-eminent, and the constituency leadership both lent to and derived strength from each other.[7] To the extent that the CPP

6. The following table compares: (1) the regional distribution of all seats in the National Assembly (regardless of party); to (2) the percentage of Ministers and Ministerial Secretaries (MS), from each region represented in the CPP government after the 1954 and 1956 elections (all CPP). The CPP held a larger percentage of the total number of seats in the Colony than it did in the other regions.

	Colony	TVT*	Ashanti	Northern Territories
Percentage of Assembly seats	42.5	12.5	20	25
1954: Percentage of Ministers	54.5	9.1	18.2	18.2
Percentage of MS	45.5	18.2	18.2	18.2
1956: Percentage of Ministers	61.6	7.7	15.4	15.4
Percentage of MS	54.9	15.4	15.4	15.4

* Trans-Volta Togoland, later Volta, region.

7. In 1954 Apter noted that "observers often remark at the accessibility of Nkrumah in the party. Rather than accessibility, it is evidence of direct control, and direct and constant need by the member to receive his mandate from Nkrumah for role activity and support. Support, instead of stemming primarily from local units, comes from above; it is endowed as grace" (David Apter, *Ghana in Transition* [New York: Athenaeum, 1963], p. 208). This overstates Nkrumah's authority, charismatic and/or legal-rational (as prime minister and dispenser of patronage); the support relationship was more mutual, and when some of the local leadership shifted into opposition in Ashanti in 1954–55, it drew away much of the CPP's local support.

can be likened to a "political machine," organizationally and in terms of the dispensation of resources and favors to party faithful as a means of control, it comprised one primary machine directed from the national level and a large number of lesser machines. The local machines were attached, but not always responsive, to the top leadership, having their own interests, pressures, and constituencies to take into account.[8] The national leadership often made accommodations to the local leadership—in order not to create disturbances and impair party unity—as the local leadership made accommodations within its own fief.

In the CPP Nkrumah was *the* leader from the beginning, the magical, popular nationalist hero, Osagyefo,[9] and he successfully turned back challenges to his tactics (vis-à-vis the British) and authority in the early 1950's. His increasingly secure grasp of leadership prerogatives was enhanced by his position of formal authority within the government. In the early 1950's CPP propagandists started to turn the spontaneous, often evangelically phrased, glorification of Nkrumah's qualities into a cult. None of this, however, secured Nkrumah and the CPP from local political demands nor reduced the fragility of the CPP structure.

The parochial, heterogeneous nature of the societies in the Gold Coast and conflicts in values and interests rendered the CPP subject to fragmentation as, with the expansion of political participation and the imminence of full African self-government, many stepped forward to claim their communities' share in the status, material, and power benefits of self-rule. With independence near, the nationalist orientation which the CPP had given particularistic demands was weakened. Specific interests, and parochial and ethnic susceptibilities, perspectives, and jealousies reasserted themselves. The CPP found that its local roots were not only its strength but its weakness. There were many specific (e.g., economic), local, or ethnic interests which were dissatisfied with the distribution of amenities,

8. Apter referred to the CPP in the mid-1950's as "the most effective mass political organization in Africa . . . a Tammany-type machine with a nationalist ideology . . . a militant elect who dominate and spearhead the nationalist movement," referring to the machine in organizational terms (*Ghana in Transition*, p. 202). Zolberg supports this analysis in terms of organization but also regards the CPP as a political machine in terms of its maintenance in power through the allocations of resources and favors to the party faithful: patronage (*Creating Political Order*, pp. 23, 160). Henry Bretton, regarding only the late 1950's and 1960's, and then not too closely, conceives the CPP as Nkrumah's "personal political machine" (*The Rise and Fall of Kwame Nkrumah*).

9. The most acute analysis of Nkrumah as a political leader is by David Apter, "Nkrumah, Charisma, and the Coup," *Daedalus*, XCVII (1968), 773–75.

162

power and status. Equally important, there were significant social groups which disputed the legitimacy of CPP leadership, the secular state, the criteria of political participation and authority, and the limits of state and nation. Neither the political demands which were made nor the political conflicts which arose were clear-cut. Value and interest demands were interwoven and compounded by parochial channels of articulation and aggregation. Such was the diffuseness, quantity, and intensity of demands based on interest, ethnicity, and values that it was difficult if not impossible for the national CPP to represent all satisfactorily. The CPP quickly came to regard demands based upon ethnicity as being both illegitimate and as destructive to itself as assertive traditional authority. Although the CPP leadership engaged in considerable political bargaining with interest and ethnic claims, it was prone to regard this process as anathema to the party as a *national* movement and inconvenient in reducing its own options. Virtually unopposed by any *organized* political groups from 1951 to 1954, CPP leaders regarded the CPP as the incarnation of the nation, a view that rendered them inhospitable to the claims of new groups.

A number of political groups arose in the early and mid-1950's to contest the CPP. Available as an ally to all of these political groups were many of the traditional authorities. Their power and status were reduced in 1951 by a local government act which replaced the chiefs and their councils as organs of local government with two-thirds-elected local councils; the elections were all but swept by the CPP in 1952. The opposition of some chiefs was intense and grounded in values as well as interest, for they regarded the CPP as destructive of the moral universe which sustained their society and their office.

It is important to note that, with a single exception, all the significant political groups which arose to oppose the CPP did so not as *parties* but specifically as *movements,* cursing the social divisiveness allegedly introduced by party politics. Both the CPP and opposition political leaders, for diverse reasons, entertained beliefs concerning the sanctity of social solidarity and the evil of social and political conflict, which inspired each to view the other in particularly abhorrent terms.

After their electoral defeat in 1951, the UGCC leaders continued to oppose the CPP and amalgamated with several small urban factions in 1952 to form the Ghana Congress Party (GCP). It constantly sought, but could not find, a constituency outside of the several chieftaincies whose rulers were directly related to its two primary leaders, Dr. Kofi Busia, a university professor, and J. B.

163

Danquah, a lawyer. They demanded government by the "best men" available, not the CPP riffraff and malcontents.

The Togoland Congress (TC), established in 1951 by the Ewe in southern British Togoland, battled for the separation of British Togoland from the Gold Coast and a union with French Togoland. Insistent upon polarizing sentiments between the CPP and TC among the Ewe, the TC was sustained by an acute feeling of social and economic neglect under the British, a strong Ewe subnationalism (whose form and direction were greatly disputed among the Ewe themselves), and a fear that the Ewe would forfeit both a distinctive historical identity and their prerogatives if British Togoland was "swallowed up" by Ghana. The Muslim Association Party (MAP) was formed in 1953, drawing off CPP Muslim support, to rectify the social and economic neglect of the Muslims (about 12 per cent of the population). It drew most of its support from the Muslim *Lumpenproletariat* in southern towns, where Muslims, many of them immigrants from surrounding territories, lived in the *zongo* ("stranger") wards and held low economic positions. It recruited militantly on the basis of common religious ties and neglect.

The Members of the Legislative Assembly (MLA's) from the Northern Territories established the Northern People's Party (NPP) in early 1954 in order to represent distinctly and for electoral purposes the social and economic demands of their seriously underdeveloped region. It was primarily organized around the still-powerful traditional state councils of important northern chiefs. It was extremely loosely structured and ethnically diverse, though in each area it recruited on a parochial (often subethnic) basis. Its leaders included teachers, educated subchiefs, and important state council employees and were often of a royal lineage. Politically inexperienced in national politics and fearful of manipulation by the south, NPP leaders demanded a distinct status for the North in the government and a huge socioeconomic development program.

In the 1954 general election the GCP, MAP, and NPP together won 20 out of 104 seats and almost 21 per cent of the total vote, though most of this was due to the NPP's 15 seats and 9.7 per cent. In contrast, the CPP won 72 seats, with 56.4 per cent of the vote, and was strong in all regions. A large "Independent" vote was primarily a CPP "rebel" vote; it was indicative of the CPP's inability to maintain the loyalty of the communities of those men who had been denied a CPP candidacy.[10]

10. Derived from Gold Coast, *The 1954 General Elections* (mimeographed). Eight of eleven elected independents were CPP rebels, six of whom quickly returned to the CPP.

The rise of the National Liberation Movement (NLM) in Ashanti posed the most serious threat to the CPP because it undermined a strong area of CPP strength, raised divisive issues, and polarized political action. The emergence of the NLM was occasioned by two specific grievances: cocoa farmers furiously demanded that the government cocoa price be raised;[11] and the many unsuccessful CPP "rebels" and their supporters in Ashanti (25 per cent of the Ashanti vote in 1954) angrily charged that the national CPP had dictated the nominations to the Ashanti constituencies and that the southern CPP leaders—"strangers"—were dominating Ashanti. These two groups provided an incendiary spark, igniting a range of diffuse interest and value demands which many among the Ashanti had articulated but which had until then found no group to adequately aggregate. The Ashanti harbored a strong sense of historical significance as a people.[12] There was a pervasive suspicion that the Ashanti, with a powerful military heritage of dominance over the states to the south and north, were now being dominated by southern peoples. The CPP "rebels" and Ashanti Youth Association leaders turned to the chiefs for support, and the threat to Ashanti helped to heal commoner-chieftaincy antagonisms in many areas. As a rich region, producing 50 per cent of the cocoa, it felt it was being shortchanged to subsidize poorer regions.

Ashanti identified itself as a nation and the NLM as a national movement (explicitly not a party), dedicated to restoring a responsive indigenous leadership in Ashanti. It quickly became in many respects a mass party/movement, captained by many ex-CPP commoners, strongly supported by many chiefs, and organized broadly—if often from the chiefs' state councils, which were the only available political structures not controlled by the CPP. It recruited less in terms of secular demands than of Ashanti nationhood and drew under its wing many associational groups which

11. The government-controlled Cocoa Marketing Board price was set at the same price in 1954 as it had been in 1953, far below a rapidly rising world market price, in order to prevent inflation and to create funds available for development investments; it accomplished both goals. Cf. Tony Killick, "The Economies of Cocoa," in *A Study of Contemporary Ghana: Vol. I, The Economy of Ghana,* ed. W. Birmingham, I. Neustadt, and E. N. Omaboe (Evanston: Northwestern University Press, 1966), pp. 365–69.

12. One refers here to the core states of the old Ashanti Confederacy, immediately surrounding Kumasi, the Ashanti capital. Many of the outer states, especially the Brong states, who were former members of the Confederacy, were CPP stalwarts. The party conflict was in some areas a restaging of historic conflicts between the Kumasi-centered Confederacy and states desiring autonomy. There was anything but unanimity among the Ashanti in the NLM-CPP conflict, even in the core states. It split families, villages, and chieftaincies.

severed their ties to the CPP. It proposed a federal rather than a centralized state, in which federal powers were weak and residual powers went to the regions, a new constitution, and a new election. All of these demands it supported with a furious, patriotic fervor. Intimidation and violence became rife in Ashanti as the NLM and CPP battled for support.

One may, with good reason, hypothesize that the CPP leadership looked askance upon the proliferation of political demands and competing groups and was basically intent upon preserving political prerogatives for itself. Nonetheless, the meaning of some of these demands and the intent of some opposing political parties were such as to reduce Ghana's viability as a state, impair its capacity for development, and appear to the CPP leadership to represent challenges to its authority as government by illegitimate means for illegitimate ends. This does not mean that the CPP regarded all these groups as illegitimate or their expressions of interest unjustified or beyond its capacities or convenience to honor.

The CPP was intolerant in ideological or value terms to political participation and recruitment primarily on the basis of ethnicity (the NLM and TC) and communal ties (the MAP and Islam). It regarded this as basically divisive to the nation-state. It could readily be seen how political recruitment by parochial appeals impaired the tenuous sentiment of loyalty to national institutions and perspectives; the CPP recognized this both in terms of NLM, TC, and MAP utter defiance of the government, and in the large defections from CPP ranks to the NLM, TC, and MAP. The TC advocated territorial fragmentation, and the NLM's demand for federation could have been equally destructive of the sinews of the state.

The 1956 general election did not settle matters, from which CPP leaders undoubtedly drew lessons. The CPP again won 72 of 104 seats in the National Assembly, with 57 per cent of the vote. However, the opposition parties had won popular pluralities in Ashanti and the Northern Territories and refused to accept a constitution which failed to meet their demands. Amidst threats of secession and defiance from the TC and NLM, the CPP was compelled to accept British mediation, in order to attain independence and, consequently, a constitution with which it was far from satisfied and prepared to alter after independence.[13]

13. Cf. Geoffrey Bing, *Reap the Whirlwind: An Account of Kwame Nkrumah's Ghana from 1950 to 1966* (London: Macgibbon & Kee, 1968), pp. 185–94. Bing was an adviser to the CPP government during the frustrating constitutional negotiations with the British. The 1957 Constitution represented a compromise settlement, with the NLM and its allies attempting to limit as

The difficulties in finding acceptable limits to conflict between the CPP and the opposition derived from: the high level of distrust with which each political leadership perceived the intentions and behavior of the other; the nature of the politicized social cleavages, featuring commoner-chieftaincy, national-parochial, and class-community conflicts; Nkrumah's and his lieutenants' desire to maintain themselves in power and to pursue in an unfettered manner their own valued political, social, and economic designs, which were personal, local, national, and international; and the often needlessly provocative behavior of many opposition leaders, predicated on a profound distaste for CPP leadership, CPP power, and the consequences of a social revolution they were incapable of reversing. This animated among some a willingness to sustain almost any cause and course which would embarrass, disrupt, or bring down the government.

It is conceivable that a level of political tolerance adequate to the maintenance of relatively democratic procedures might have developed if the political crises had eased off; there was certainly wide distress at the level of social and political conflict. However, a range of demands arose simultaneously on the morrow of independence, which again gave Nkrumah and his lieutenants a sharp sense of unease. The more significant included: a minor but alarming Ewe rebellion in former British Togoland; the rapid rise of an angry, aggressive political movement among the Ga in Accra; a long, economically troublesome strike by the Motor Drivers' Union, as well as defiance and threats of strikes from large public service employees' unions; economic demands forcefully thrown up to the government by the irate, pro-CPP Ex-Servicemen's Union, which threatened to march on Nkrumah's residence; and, capping this, an incipient revolt by angry, backbench CPP parliament members, who threatened to go over to the opposition side if they were not accorded more influence.[14] The nature, extent, and intensity of these demands and conflicts as well as the CPP leadership's perception of them set the stage for the post-independence order.

---

far as possible the prerogatives of the central government. Under "entrenched" clauses, however, there were to be popularly elected regional assemblies with a variety of secondary functions (to be determined later), the maintenance of the present number of regions, which violated the CPP's commitment to the Brong and other dissident states in Ashanti who wanted to escape Ashanti control, and measures to protect the "traditional functions or privileges of a chief."

14. Austin, *Politics in Ghana*, pp. 373–76, notes these immediate post-independence crises, except for the important incipient backbench revolt, which in the person of two MP's was linked up with the threatening rallies and protests of the Ex-Servicemen's Union.

The Post-Independence Order

The behavior of Nkrumah, the government, and party in the post-independence period must be viewed from a number of perspectives intertwined in the thoughts and behavior of the political actors. Nkrumah and those who were and who became his lieutenants sought to establish a national society and political system, which would surmount all political cleavages and sustain CPP power, the latter both a personal concern and a belief in the rightness and necessity of a strong national and secular leadership. They also sought to fashion a new institutional framework, though this was undertaken gradually, on an *ad hoc* basis. And they sought to develop the Ghanaian economy as rapidly and dramatically as possible. Nkrumah, in particular, entertained as a fundamental aim a large role for Ghana and himself in Africa's liberation, unification, and international presence. Through these goals Nkrumah and his lieutenants sought to legitimize their power and roles.

At independence, Nkrumah, the CPP, and the government cannot be said to have enjoyed a high degree of legitimacy in many areas of the country.[15] The unwillingness to accord legitimate authority to the government and Nkrumah was a function not only of political opposition and distrust but also of the primacy of attachment to traditional and local structures and values.

The central problem of the political system was that there was no legitimized authority structure or institution, one which was, or was perceived to be, broadly acceptable to the Ghanaian people. Whatever the contribution of Nkrumah's charismatic authority to legitimizing the CPP had been, many Ghanaians in Ashanti, British Togoland, and the Northern Territories clearly refused to recognize it. The legitimacy of the new secular structure of authority, the National Assembly, was, like Nkrumah's charisma, a victim of the 1954–56 political conflict when the opposition deemed it wholly unrepresentative and spurned it; in the post–1956 period it was regarded as too manipulable an instrument of the CPP regime, which was regarded as fundamentally dictatorial even before it became so.

The responses of Nkrumah, the party (with varying responses at national and local levels), and government to problems of power,

---

15. Dennis Austin disagrees, arguing in a post-coup article, "Opposition in Ghana: 1947–67," *Government and Opposition*, II (1967), 541, that only among the Ewe in the British Togoland trusteeship, later part of the Volta region, was there a refusal to accept governmental authority as legitimate.

legitimacy, state-building, and national integration were heavily influenced by the bitterness and distrust in the 1954–56 conflict and by the wealth of ethnic (Ga, Ewe, and Ashanti), interest (labor, ex-servicemen, business), and power (opposition, internal CPP) demands forced upon them in the months following independence. The immediate post-independence measures were designed not only to assert and sustain CPP and government power but also central government strength and legitimacy, national integration, and the secularity of modern structures (e.g., banning parties based on ethnicity, religion, and region, which forced the opposition to amalgamate into the United Party).

In the years following independence in 1957, the CPP, party and government, moved to employ measures to control the demand side of the political system: to control, restrict, or suppress groups or institutions concerned with the articulation, aggregation, and communication of interests. This did not occur at once, but was the consequence of a series of political and economic crises, in each of which the CPP felt threatened and applied restrictive measures. These regulative efforts featured the use of both the carrot and the stick: the politically and/or administratively accomplished destoolment of important opposition chiefs (except the Asantehene, who in 1958 pledged to uphold the government) and the attempted depoliticization and limiting of their authority and functions; the centralization of constitutional authority, through the legal removal of the Constitution's "entrenched" clauses, which was hardly evil in itself;[16] abolition of regional assemblies and the appointment of CPP leaders to the political/administrative positions of Regional Commissioner (1957), filled by members of Parliament, and District Commissioner, beginning in 1958, filled by local leaders, who were in theory directly responsible to the head of government, Nkrumah; suppressive political tactics and election fraud against the opposition, often on local initiative,[17] which went hand in hand with party and government inducements to opposition leaders and areas to partake in government largess; a host of increasingly repressive statutes, some with unduly severe sanctions, which served to delimit

16. Austin tends to see this centralization of authority solely as repressive (*Politics in Ghana*, pp. 377–80), which is not the view of Bing, then attorney general, who had a hand in the constitutional changes (*Reap the Whirlwind*, pp. 191–98).

17. Although Bing's apologetics with regard to government behavior in the 1964 referendum are nonsense, it is clear that some of the suppressive electoral tactics were initiated locally in the period 1957–60, as in the parliamentary by-election in Anlo South, where the central government voided the local CPP efforts and the opposition won (*ibid.*, pp. 296–97).

personal and civil liberties, the best known of which was the earliest, the Preventive Detention Act.

New problems involved in state- and nation-building required a ritualization and rationalization of authority. Ritualization involved nonpartisan measures like establishing and making familiar a national flag and anthem, replacing British with African regalia in Parliament in 1960, and more partisan measures like placing Nkrumah's face on new coins and stamps, Nkrumah's move to Christianburg Castle (the residence of British governors) to symbolize the transfer of authority, and the building-up of Nkrumah as the father of the nation, beyond reproach and criticism (which received legal sanction). At a later stage, an adulatory, effusive cult of the Nkrumah personality was diffused through press, radio, party and government channels, and schools.[18] In the 1960's there were some ambitious plans to undertake the socialization of youth—for example, through the Young Pioneers (whose appeal varied with the availability of uniforms), to inculcate deference to Nkrumah, the party, and the state.

The extension of government authority was closely linked with the expansion of CPP authority, though in a manner which tied it inextricably to the government and state. The result in structure was what Zolberg has aptly called the "party-state," in practice an increasing monopolization of "legitimate" political prerogatives by the CPP government leadership, Nkrumah above all. State and party were linked, providing ample demonstration of party power, through the replacement of colonial servants by CPP Regional Commissioners and District Commissioners. In its efforts to control groups making demands, the government "recognized" (a colonial precedent) the CPP-controlled United Ghana Farmers' Council (UGFC) as the official farmers' organization in 1957. The ambitious head of the Trades Union Congress (TUC), John Tettegah, drew upon government power (the 1958 Industrial Relations Act and amendments) to centralize the TUC in CPP hands, in exchange for bringing organized labor under government sanction. In 1959 the government created the Central Cooperative Council in order to replace the nonpartisan Cooperative Alliance and the Ghana Cooperative Marketing Association (cocoa) and to develop industrial and commercial cooperatives (which never got off the ground).

18. The Nkrumah cult was nothing compared to the Mao cult in China but was an undeniably stifling presence nonetheless. The cult was also manipulated within the CPP by the new militants of 1960–62, e.g., Tawia Adamafio, against the "old guard," and in 1964–65 by the "old guard" against the "scientific socialists."

The CPP leadership of these and other associational groups meant in practice that they were not accountable to their own constituencies but to Nkrumah and the government. Although some of these leaders, such as the UGFC's Appiah-Danquah, represented the interests of their followers to the government more forcefully than others, they were often interested in bringing their organizations to support government policies, with little or no consultation with their groups: for example, the UGFC in contributions of 16 per cent of earnings for development and in price reductions in cocoa; the TUC in the 5 per cent forced savings in 1961, against which rank-and-file unionists revolted in the politicized Sekondi-Takoradi strike of 1961.[19] Unable to articulate discontent with specific policies and leaders, the discontent of workers and farmers was increasingly aimed at the system as a whole. Although the party-state enveloped these groups, it frequently could not control them beyond the national leadership level (and often not even there) due to their size, the responsiveness of subordinate leaders to membership pressures, and their bargaining power as strategic (and therefore politically worrisome) economic and solidarity groups; they could and did readily frustrate government policies.

Opposition strength declined steadily from 1957 to 1960, due to a swing back to the CPP, a desire for an end to social conflict, government repression, and the attraction of greater power. Opposition chiefs were destooled, the UP lost local elections, and the number of UP members in the assembly dwindled from 32 in 1957 to 13 in mid-1960, when Ghana became a republic (6 were detained, many more "crossed the carpet" to the CPP). At a relatively early point, some opposition leaders considered violence. The arrest of two UP MP's in December, 1958, for involvement in a plot to kill Nkrumah and others worsened the position of the UP and was a major source of CPP apprehensions and the readiness of the government to increasingly resort to preventive detention.[20] In the 1960 presidential election, the UP received only 11 per cent of the votes. Violence increased in 1962 with the attempted assassination of Nkrumah in August and random bombing of crowds later in the

19. See the excellent study by St. Clair Drake and Leslie A. Lacy, "Government Versus the Unions: The Sekondi-Takoradi Strike, 1961," in *Politics in Africa: Seven Cases,* ed. Gwendolen Carter (New York: Harcourt, Brace & World, 1966), pp. 67–118, on the breakdown in communications between CPP associational group leadership and the rank and file; and Ghana, *Statement by the Government on the Recent Conspiracy,* December, 1961.

20. For varying accounts of this case, involving the UP and an army officer, see Austin, *Politics in Ghana,* pp. 381–82, 424–29, and Bing, *Reap the Whirlwind,* pp. 239–77.

year, which brought the government to a heavier reliance on repressive measures and instruments of force, the military and police.

The CPP leadership's attempts to control interest articulation and aggregation and to ignore political demands when communicated not unnaturally resulted in a decline in political participation. Success in reducing opposition strength left the CPP without the stimulus of political conflict. The tendency of the CPP leadership to identify the CPP with the nation, as in its early years, became again explicit as Nkrumah's 1959 assertion that "the CPP is Ghana and Ghana is the CPP" was voiced on all occasions. This claim to represent the nation was practiced locally by inducing people, even former opposition members, to join the CPP. Membership became more widespread, more nominal; relaxation in local political conflicts and ever-present pressures and demands of local societies rendered the CPP an increasingly diffuse, socially conservative, and parochial organization. Since its inception its roots had been indigenous, not alien. With a decline in social stress, these roots—kinship and clan ties, local and ethnic solidarity, local interests both traditional and modern—exerted themselves.[21] The CPP remained a distinct organization but one with only a limited responsiveness to national direction.[22] This was not much altered by the reorganization of institutions, when in the 1960's the district became the major local unit of government (councils), administration (district commissioners), party, and parliamentary representation (1965). One reason for the lack of discipline in the local-national link was that District Commissioners were assigned to their own home areas.

The radicalization of the CPP party-state starting in 1959–60 derived from a number of interrelated sources: realization of the atrophy of the CPP and of the sloth, corruption, and pursuit of self-interest by many local and national leaders; the drive of new CPP elites for status and power; the search for a coherent ideology, as a guide and as an instrument of socialization and CPP legitimation; the emergence of vast economic ambitions and problems; and challenges to Nkrumah's pan-African leadership with the appearance of

21. Cf. David W. Brokensha, *Social Change at Larteh, Ghana* (Oxford: Clarendon Press, 1966), who, though discussing an area where political and normative conflict were not intense, stresses the strength of local institutions and concludes that "even the powerful CPP has to contend with the strong localism, emerging as almost a Larteh institution" (p. 266).

22. Zolberg observed in 1965 that the CPP "has almost ceased to be a tangible separate organization"; however, it had long reflected "all the cleavages, components, norms, and structures that prevail in an underdeveloped country" (*Creating Political Order*, p. 98).

many new states in 1960 and an anti-Western animus fueled in part by the Congo crisis and African dependency.

Nkrumah's realization of the need to revitalize the CPP in order to mobilize certain strata for economic development and to recapture the CPP's early drive demanded new orientations, functions, and power for some party structures—the TUC, UGFC, and party press—and the creation of new structures—the Central Cooperative Council, Young Pioneers, Young Farmers League, and ideological cadres.[23] The "old guard" petty-bourgeois CPP leadership included among others some capitalist entrepreneurs, large and petty traders, and others who had acquired economic interests and enriched themselves during their years in power. They represented the drive for social mobility and status of a new, acquisitive, lower-middle and middle class of educated commoners: they were not the socialists Nkrumah sought for Ghana's development. Both TUC and UGFC leaders and the few militants in the press were seeking new roles and power, and Nkrumah gave them status, money, and power to challenge the "old guard," who were readily attacked as corrupt "self-seekers." The CPP was reorganized for the umpteenth time (on paper), and a Ga CPP militant, Tawia Adamafio, a latecomer to the CPP (1953), was made secretary-general. Tettegah and Adamafio, in close partnership and with the support of the press militants, sought to re-energize the party through party organs, new but short-lived TUC units, and through Party Study Groups which vigorously attacked the incompetence and conservatism of the CPP government leadership. While Adamafio (with Nkrumah's support) proclaimed as the official slogan "The Party Is Supreme," his quick acquisition of a government post, as minister of presidential affairs, was recognition of the overwhelming preponderance of government as distinct from CPP power.

Major political alterations were started between 1960 and 1962 which were continued after Adamafio fell from power in August, 1962. Nkrumah and the militants began to intervene more directly

23. While many observers agree that the CPP leadership tactically defused its radical elements in the 1950's in order to attain independence, Bob Fitch and Mary Oppenheimer in *Ghana: End of An Illusion* (New York: Monthly Review Press, 1966) argue that the CPP failed to organize the revolutionary potential of the oppressed classes (urban and rural proletariat), temporized in breaking its colonial ties, and thus fundamentally undermined its own revolutionary impulses in 1961–66. Their assessment of the possibility of revolutionary change is "petty bourgeois romanticism" and "adventurism," quite unrealistic, as a segment of the British left agrees. See Roger Murray, "Second Thoughts on Ghana," *New Left Review*, XLII (1967), 37–39.

in the bureaucracy, stimulating change by bringing some departments directly under the president's office.[24] The UGFC became enormously powerful, acquiring in 1961 a monopoly on cocoa buying (eliminating independent marketing cooperatives) and later important roles in developing producer cooperatives and agricultural mechanization. The CPP MP's, under siege of the militants, suffered some, but became a more critical and institutional group. Nkrumah, urged on by the militants, determined that the state should play the central role in economic development, established institutions for serious planning, whose plans he and his ministers generally disregarded, launched many new state industries, received the US-UK-IBRD loan for the vast Volta dam–alumina complex and then turned to the Communist countries for aid and export markets for cocoa during his summer, 1961, three-month tour. Bitter factional, power struggles broke out within the CPP, chiefly between the old and new elites, sometimes over programs. Ideology was used as a weapon by the new socialist militants against the insufficiently socialist "old guard"; Nkrumah's top lieutenants and most senior ministers, Finance Minister Komla Gbedemah and Minister of State and Agriculture Kojo Botsio, were driven from the party and government—Gbedemah into exile and opposition, to return after the coup, Botsio and the old guard to be recalled within a year when Nkrumah found the militants incompetent. The militants were aggressive, not too bright, subject to ideological corruption, and divided among themselves by ambition, ethnicity, and ideology.

There also began the search for a usable ideology, a tortuous journey, in part serious, grievously marred by indecisiveness over its use, and thus its shape—whether it should be an integrative myth (Nkrumahism, African socialism, "Consciencism"—a chronological progression marked by increasing popular incomprehension and withdrawal) or a vanguard ideology ("scientific socialism").[25]

24. The reasons for bringing departments under the president's office varied: the Budget Department was there for a year, to facilitate the establishment of a slush fund for Nkrumah, for internal and pan-African purposes, the Labor Department for less than a year at Tettegah's behest, the Chieftaincy Secretariat to reduce conflicts and corruption, some departments to facilitate coordination and reduce political interference (e.g., Planning, Volta River Secretariat), while others were there due to Nkrumah's particular interest (e.g., African Affairs Secretariat, handling relations with all African states) or his concern with security (e.g., intelligence, taken from the police after the assassination attempt).

25. See Colin Legum, "Socialism in Ghana: A Political Interpretation," in *African Socialism,* ed. Wm. Friedland and Carl Rosberg, Jr. (Stanford: Stanford University Press, 1964), pp. 131–59.

The vanguardists, who were wholly dependent on Nkrumah for support, were ahead when the coup occurred, but only within the confines of an increasing Nkrumah cult and at the expense to the regime of the increasing alienation of the rest of the party—local, regional, and national—whose leadership ignored or merely mouthed the revolutionary rhetoric.

The advent of ideology as a weapon brought new repressive measures, arbitrarily rather than massively applied, and new attacks against social and political institutions—the civil service, universities, and judiciary. These measures in turn spawned plotting and violence, such as the attempted assassination of Nkrumah by a policeman in January, 1964.

The January, 1964, constitutional referendum, marked by massive intimidation and fraud and making Ghana by law a one-party state, brought home to many their loss of political participation, as did the 1965 parliamentary election, a non-event, in which the candidates were selected by Nkrumah and his lieutenants and returned unopposed (though almost all former MP's kept their seats, itself a recognition of their local ties).[26]

Nearly successful assassination attempts induced Nkrumah to withdraw from public view and eye all suspiciously. A network of informers was established, anti-rumor-mongering laws passed.[27] Nkrumah governed by manipulating among contending factions and interests (party and nonparty), playing one group off against another in order to maintain his leverage and autonomy, thrusting for change but obsessed with the need for order. Decision-making was unstructured, a function of Nkrumah's inattention, his varying advisers, his desire for haste in implementation of an idea before it was closely examined (e.g., economic projects), his vacillation, and his failure to discipline his ministers. Much of Nkrumah's time was devoted to pursuing his pan-African and international politics; his responsiveness to political demands, internal and external, was conditioned by his perception of himself as a national and international revolutionary leader, for example, his failure to appreciate the articulate opposition to the financial costs of his pan-African ambi-

---

26. See Jon Kraus, "Ghana's New 'Corporate' Parliament," *Africa Report,* August 1965, pp. 6–11.

27. A high civil servant who asked his superior about the rumor that Nkrumah had shot a soldier at the castle after the January, 1964, assassination attempt was arrested and convicted under a "publication of false news" law, which made the civil service extremely apprehensive, even though the conviction was later quashed.

tions and the dislike and distrust of Ghana's increasingly intimate ties with the Communist countries.[28]

The restriction of claims on the political system did not lessen the demands but assured the rise of subterranean politics—pursuit of interests through kinship, personal, and bureaucratic links—and anomic dissidence, few instances of which were reported by the controlled press. The choking-off of channels of interest articulation and communication lessened the flow of information to party and government leaders; thus, they were uninformed about popular demands and grievances or doubted their creditability, and when expressions of discontent broke out they were surprised and occasionally panicked, often responding initially with repression and by suspecting malign if not subversive intentions.

A political system had developed in Ghana under conditions noted earlier as being generic to politics, in particular, the inflation of demands, the politicization of traditional cleavages, and, thus, the limited legitimation of national political authority. The national system which developed over time in Ghana, and elsewhere in much of Africa with variations in emphases, had the following characteristics: an increasing centralization of decision-making power in the hands of the leader and a strong tendency to personal rule; an increasing reliance in this rule upon personal loyalties (whence, return of the "old guard," increase in the number of Nzimas—Nkrumah's ethnic group—in the cabinet and security service), partly secured by material rewards, including the allocation (appropriation) of offices and direct benefits (money, housing); in response to the rapid increase in participation and demands, the creation of oligarchic controls and manipulation of interests and groups; despite attempted centralization and curtailment of subsystem autonomy, relative degrees of autonomy for subordinate political leaders outside the national center and in certain structurally differentiated groups.

Some observers have noted how closely these new political systems resemble the patrimonial system described by Weber, stressing the above features as well as increasingly salient traditional sources of ideological legitimation, with a shift from a future to a past-orientation, and reliance upon a personally controlled coercive apparatus.[29] However, as Zolberg points out, authority in these states

28. On the context of the development of these ties, see Jon Kraus, "A Marxist in Ghana," *Problems of Communism* XVI, no. 3 (1967), 42–49.

29. See Zolberg, *Creating Political Order*, pp. 134–35; Guenther Roth, "Personal Rule, Patrimonialism, and Empire-Building in the New States," *World Politics*, XX (1968), 194–206; Bretton's *The Rise and Fall of Kwame Nkrumah* focuses simply on Nkrumah's personal rule.

tends to rest upon a clustering of charismatic, traditional, and bureaucratic traits. It is important to note that in Ghana the bureaucracy, even though manipulated, was more differentiated, specialized, and institutionalized (particularly in terms of behavioral norms) than elsewhere in Africa and, therefore, with the exception of certain presidential secretariats, operated much less as personal instruments of rule than on a legal-rational basis. Also, even allowing for the large element of mystification in Ghana's political cultures (including Nkrumah's cult), there was increasing secularization, and the main thrust of ideological legitimation and of leadership goals was oriented to the future, not the past.

The regime entertained a certain range of permissiveness, the limits of which, while not clear, were frequently probed. The acceptance of CPP goals provided a basis for criticism between the ideal and the practice, which left a lot of room for complaint, such as in the National Assembly, which spent much time in the regime's last years criticizing the government's economic performance. R. O. Amuako-Atta, after having been dismissed as minister for opposing the UGFC cocoa-buying monopoly in 1961, had pursued his opposition in the Assembly and sounded an early warning: "What I am saying is in the interest of us all, politically. Because if there are irregularities and they are not pointed out now and are brooded upon, the next thing we shall see is some sort of revolution."[30]

Basic to the regime's loss of critical support groups were its economic policies and the disastrous economic conditions in the last several years. The development potential of the economy was fundamentally limited by its basic colonial character and by the structure of the world market demand for its most important export, cocoa, which provided 65 per cent of its foreign exchange earnings.[31] Nkrumah and his ministers felt that the most rapid possible economic development was imperative, and development for them was synonymous with industrialization and increasing expenditures and jobs. Up to 1959, the development emphasis had been on infrastructure and social services (especially education). By 1961–62 the government had decided on a structural change in the economy by means of a preponderant role for the state sector and a push for industrialization and the mechanization of agriculture

30. Ghana *Parliamentary Debates: Official Report,* XXIII (May 17, 1961), 682.
31. Tony Killick, "The Possibilities of Economic Control," in *Economy of Ghana,* ed. Birmingham, Neustadt, and Omaboe, pp. 411–38; Douglas Rimmer, "The Crisis in the Ghana Economy," *Journal of Modern African Studies,* IV (1966), 17–32.

through producer cooperatives and the state farms.[32] In 1961 the government also tardily imposed economic controls in response to a sharp decline in the cocoa price and a balance of payments deficit.

In the next five years the government encountered steadily worsening economic conditions, due to factors both within and beyond its control. An increased cocoa crop brought a rise in local demand and inflation but not more foreign exchange because of the decline in the world price (from $603 per long ton in 1958 to $241 in 1965). Severe balance of payments deficits, only sporadically reduced by import controls, depleted foreign currency reserves. The regime, and Nkrumah directly, refused in the face of increasing inflation to curtail its huge budget deficits (expenditures exceeded revenue by 60 per cent in 1962–63, 27 per cent in 1965), which the government financed by dramatic increases in internal and external borrowing.[33] This heavy external borrowing, much of it for hastily and ill-considered agricultural and industrial development projects and extravaganzas, quickly resulted in an intolerable debt burden, since 82 per cent of this external debt consisted of medium-term supplier's credits. The malfunctioning of import controls, due to administrative incompetence and corruption, political corruption, and hoarding,[34] resulted in frequent scarcities of consumer goods and drastic shortages of spare parts, which caused a decline in productivity in the private sector and the laying off of workers. The GNP increased between 1955 and 1962 at an average annual rate of 4.8 per cent, but by 1964 it dropped to 2.8 per cent and in 1965 to 0.2 per cent, practically nil; Ghana's estimated rate of population growth was 2.6 per cent.[35]

Government inattention to problems, lack of discipline, and self-indulgence exacerbated development problems unduly. Commitments were made for development projects without serious study, outside existing plans, with medium-term financing for long-term projects; there was little attempt until the last year to compel the

32. Attempts to increase agricultural productivity were not accompanied by any alteration in land tenure except for some acquisitions of land by the state. Ghanaian political leaders, including Nkrumah, were economic innocents.

33. The precise size of Ghana's external debt at the time of the coup was simply not known; initially estimated as high as $800 million, provisional government figures indicated $600 million (Ghana, *Economic Survey*, 1965, pp. 28–29).

34. See Ghana, *Report of the Commission of Enquiry into Alleged Irregularities in Connection with the Issue of Import Licenses*, 1964 (Akainyah Commission); Ghana, *Report of the Commission of Enquiry into Trade Malpractices in Ghana*, 1966 (pre-coup, Abraham Commission); Ghana, *Summary of the Report of the Commission of Enquiry into Irregularities and Malpractices in the Grant of Import Licenses*, 1967 (Ollennu Commission).

35. *Economic Survey, 1965*, pp. 13–14.

proliferating state industries to be profitable or even accountable.[36]

Economic conditions served to discredit the regime and stood in articulate mockery of the party-state's boasts of progress. The vast increases in revenue required to finance rising government expenditures were extracted from wage and salary earners, cocoa farmers (by "voluntary" development contributions, special taxes, and, finally, hesitantly, reductions in the cocoa price), and foreign businesses. A painfully high rate of inflation reached a high in 1965, when the consumer price index (base: March, 1963 = 100) rose from 128 to 165, with the largest increase in local food costs.[37] Statistically, the standard of living declined, though, in fact, there were vast compensatory increases in social services, in health, water supplies, education, and village development. (In fact, basic to Ghana's dilemma was the regime's attempt to provide high levels of social services without the productivity to finance them.) Employment stood still or declined in 1965, with more school leavers seeking jobs.[38]

Popular support for the regime eroded with the decline in economic conditions, creating the opportunity for the military to intervene with the anticipation of widespread public approbation. The military and police might well have intervened in any case in behalf of their own institutional interests. But despite the regime's authoritarianism, the probability of a coup would have been reduced if economic life had been more buoyant, discontent less animate, and the military and police thus unarmed with this crucial public issue to legitimize their seizure of power.

THE ARMED FORCES IN THE POLITICAL KINGDOM

Changing Character and Roles of the Military and Police

The erosion of political choice, the failure of the opposition assassination attempts on Nkrumah, and their inability to organize re-

36. For the minister of finance's scathing criticisms of the conduct and performance of state industries, see "The Financial Position of State Corporations" in Ghana, *The Budget, 1965,* 1965. At the end of 1963, £G13.6 million of the total of £G15.1 million in losses by state corporations was made by 3 of the then 35 enterprises: State Mining Corporation, Ghana Airways, and State Farms—all three deliberately subsidized.

37. *Economic Survey, 1965,* p. 148.

38. Provisional 1965 estimates showed a drop of 4.8 per cent in wage and salary employment, a large decrease in the private sector and a slight increase in the public sector, which was disguised, subsidized unemployment (*ibid.,* p. 97), while later figures show a small overall increase in 1965 (Ghana, *Economic Survey,* 1967, p. 96). Official statistics underestimate unemployment.

sistance left the military and the police as the only institutional or other groups capable of challenging the Nkrumah regime. As Zolberg has noted, the shift from power to force in the face of declining legitimacy by weak governments is likely to have severe, counterproductive consequences, among them: "a shift in the relative market value of existing structures," where parties and administrative structures decline in value and any structures capable of using force acquire increased value; the involvement of instruments of force in political life exposes them to its problems and possibilities and makes the political leaders directly dependent upon them; force excludes other options and thus induces counterforce.[39]

The army-police coalition that seized power in early 1966 represented an armed establishment which had grown enormously since independence and had become increasingly involved directly in the regime's security during the 1960's. The army and police had played no positive role in the independence struggle, but had served as instruments of colonial order, British-officered, and with low social status.[40] With independence the army retained the functions of internal security and border protection and acquired the additional one of being a symbol of national independence and prestige. The rapid expansion of the army after 1960 was undertaken by Nkrumah to provide for internal security and an African army which could be available to maintain a Pax Africana, to free African states of dependence on external military power. This desire was stimulated by Nkrumah's frustrating experience with the Congo crisis and the growing awareness that change in Rhodesia, Portuguese Africa, and South Africa could only be accomplished through armed force.

Ghana's army was thus expanded and given public recognition, and the officer corps was given pay and fringe benefits to approximate parity with the civil service (e.g., in 1961 a newly commissioned 2d lieutenant received £663 per annum, a college graduate entering the civil service £680). In 1961 the basic pay of a private was about double that of the national minimum wage. The army increased from about 4,000 in 1957 to about 6,000 to 7,000 in 1960–61,[41] and then doubled to 14,600 at the time of the coup in February, 1966. A navy and air force were established in the late 1950's and had 970 and 650 men, respectively, by 1966. Between

39. Zolberg, "The Structure of Political Conflict in the New States of Tropical Africa," p. 77.
40. William Gutteridge, *Armed Forces in New States* (London: Oxford University Press, 1962), pp. 26–29.
41. *West Africa,* December 30, 1961, p. 1449.

180

independence (March, 1957) and April, 1961 the Africans in the officer corps increased from 25 to 154 (British officers increasing from 220 to 230).[42] The Ghanaian Military Academy was established in 1960, initially with 60 students per class, then 120. By the time the officer corps was totally Africanized in September, 1961, there were over 200 African officers; by the time of the coup there were between 550 and 650 in all three services. In 1960 Ghana's army was poorly equipped and trained.[43] Nkrumah's ambitions for the simultaneous modernization and expansion of the army were both difficult to accomplish and expensive. Military expenditures, which had risen from 1.3 per cent of the total budget in 1954–55 to 4–5 per cent between 1957 and 1960, rose further to 7.5 per cent in 1962–63, 6 per cent in 1963–64, and 8.4 per cent (estimated) in 1965.[44]

The police, involved more intimately at an earlier point in internal security (the Special Branch), were given less public recognition but equal professional opportunities (through earlier Africanization, a police college, and advanced training in Britain), pay, and benefits. Police strength was greatly increased, growing slowly from about 6,000 in 1957 to 7,500 in mid-1961, and then rapidly to 12,500 by early 1966.[45]

The senior army officers had been drawn from the senior noncommissioned officers in the colonial Gold Coast regiment and sent for training to Britain, to Mons and Eaton Hall Officer Cadet Schools or the Royal Military Academy, Sandhurst; there were estimated to be 47 Sandhurst graduates in the officer corps in 1962.[46] Although some cadets were sent to other Commonwealth countries for training, Britain remained the chief source of external training; it also continued to be the principal adviser of Ghana's army, even after Africanization (when 120 of the 200 British officers were retained as advisers) and the commencement of Russian training of the presidential guard in 1963.

The secondary school education requirement for officer candidates

42. *West Africa*, December 22, 1956, p. 1034; Ghana, *Parliamentary Debates: Official Record*, XXIII (May 23, 1961), 822–23.
43. Major-General H. T. Alexander, *African Tightrope* (New York: Praeger, 1965), pp. 11–13 (British former Chief of Staff, Ghana Army, 1960–61).
44. *Ghana Annual Estimates, 1963–64, Part I, The Consolidated Fund*, Vol. XVI; *Ghana Annual Estimates, 1965, Part I, The Consolidated Fund*, Vol. XVII.
45. See detailed report on police, *Parliamentary Debates: Official Record*, XXIII (May 18, 1961), 708–30. Both CPP and opposition were genuinely highly congratulatory to the minister of interior on his handling of the police.
46. Gutteridge, *Armed Forces in the New States*, p. 43.

meant that the military had to compete for personnel who had access to greater economic and social status possibilities. As importantly, it meant that the officer corps was overwhelmingly drawn from the areas of highest education, i.e., southern Ghana, from which 26 of the 28 African officers were drawn in 1956. Estimates of the ethnic breakdown of the officer corps are not available. However, although efforts have been made to rectify this ethnic/regional imbalance, it is evident that the overwhelming proportion of officers is still from southern Ghana. There is a similar skewing in the regional recruitment of police officers, while the majority of the other ranks in both services were drawn from the economically backward Northern Territories (except in technical services).[47]

The single most important factor determining the military subculture has been the exposure to British military professionalism, procedures, organization, and personnel. Most Ghanaian officers appear to have had great respect for and worked readily under their British officers; they were not pushing for the sudden, total Africanization which occurred in 1961. Their common educational background, economic status, and sense of military professionalism rendered them a rather conservative social group, identifying not only with British military norms but British beliefs and life styles generally as well as with their counterparts in the Ghanaian police, civil service, and professions. Particularly, those who received training in Britain were in part Anglicized.[48] But this can be overstressed, for they cannot be characterized as a caste remote from their own social roots; indeed, there were ethnic/regional cleavages within the officer corps. Their identifications and shared professionalism did not induce a respect but more often a disdain for the CPP. The CPP politicians were regarded as self-serving and in good measure corrupt, Nkrumah and the regime as repressive and dictatorial.

The rapid expansion of the army and officer corps after 1961 may well have created a new officer generation, one which has experienced much less direct British influence in training as well as less rapid promotion. In addition, the military and police became agencies of social mobility, and frustration with the rate of promotion is likely to have a direct impact on future officer behavior.

47. *Ibid.*, p. 35.
48. For example, see A. A. Afrifa (one of the coup leaders), *The Ghana Coup* (London: Frank Cass, 1966), for his nearly ecstatic comments on British institutions, including the British constitution and Sandhurst ("best part of my life," "independent thinking, tolerance," "one of the greatest institutions in the world," pp. 49–51) as well as the evident effect of British opinion upon his attitude toward his own government (pp. 72, 108).

Civil-military relations were harmonious in the first years following independence. The military had no influence within the government, but Nkrumah expressed great personal interest in the military's development, serving as his own defense minister until early 1960; he assigned the portfolio to his most trusted lieutenant, Kofi Baako, in September, 1961, following Africanization. Norms of apolitical professionalism were stressed, but the main civilian control on the military was the British buffer of officers commanding the Ghanaian army.

An enormous breech in civil-military relations was occasioned by the service of Ghanaian military (and police) units in the Congo in 1960–61 under UN command. If Nkrumah's support of Lumumba was accepted as a political decision outside the military sphere, the political role played by Nkrumah's emissaries during the Kasavubu-Lumumba struggle and after the Mobutu coup rendered the neutrality of Ghanaian units suspect and made them victims of physical abuse and murder by the Congolese. The erratic conduct of Congolese politicians and the political designs of Nkrumah and his CPP ambassadors lowered the respect of many officers for politicians in general and aroused resentments at political interference.[49] Some returned to Ghana bearing ideas of a coup.

The years of radicalization, 1960 and 1961, were also characterized by a heavier imposition of party-state power and an insistence upon identification of party with state, the corollary to which was that the military owed loyalty not only to Ghana but to the CPP and Nkrumah personally. This, of course, violated the doctrine of the British officers which was to "keep the army out of politics and politics out of the army," a view argued often to Nkrumah by his British chief of defense staff.[50] In this context came CPP demands for more rapid Africanization of the military, both from parliament members and party militants, although there were also criticisms of the increasingly high expenditures on the military. In the context of the Congo crisis and the involvement of Western powers on behalf of secessionist Katanga, the September Belgrade Conference of

49. While Afrifa's *The Ghana Coup* cannot be accepted uncritically, his view on this matter appears to be representative: "The fault was that of our politicians at home who had placed us under the command of the United Nations, and at the same time taken active and sinister roles in the whole Congo affair. . . . Kwame Nkrumah had placed us in a terrible dilemma through an unbridled political adventure. . . . I began to feel the rashness of Kwame Nkrumah's politics . . . what had gone wrong. We had lost lives in a struggle which was not ours, in a cause that was not ours" (pp. 66, 70). On the army in the Congo, see Alexander, *African Tightrope*, pp. 50–74.
50. Alexander, *African Tightrope*, p. 20.

nonaligned states, and Nkrumah's Communist-country tour came a reassertion of Ghana's nonalignment. The most important manifestation was the sudden Africanization of the officer corps in September, 1961, which meant a double promotion for Ghanaian officers and, more significantly, an end to the neutral British buffer between the politicians and the military. They now confronted one another directly, for example, on such matters as Nkrumah's order that the military send 400 cadets to the Soviet Union to balance training in the West (they weren't available; 68 were sent)[51] and his suggestions that the military seek free arms from the Communist countries, both of which notions were strongly resisted by Ghanaian officers.

In the increasingly repressive Ghanaian environment, the military as well as the police became more involved in internal security. At the same time Nkrumah sought means to control these instruments of force upon which he was more and more dependent. Not only Nkrumah but many lesser CPP leaders were apprehensive as to the new military arrangements and the possibility of a coup d'état.[52] After the August, 1962, assassination attempt upon Nkrumah and the bombing which followed in Accra, the army was virtually placed in charge, at one point cordoning off Accra and conducting a complete house-to-house search for weapons (which damaged the sensibilities of some politicos) and manning a blockade of Accra until 1964. The army and police senior officers in each region, with the CPP regional commissioner, constituted an internal security committee. Military intelligence and the police Special Branch looked for subversion, not least an attempt by opposition elements to entice military personnel into violence, as had been attempted unsuccessfully in 1958 and successfully in the 1962 bombings.[53]

Nkrumah devised a number of means to control and balance the military and police, many of which were counterproductive, in part because of the lack of a tradition governing boundaries between civil and military spheres, in part due to the heaviness of some controls. This gave rise to and increased antagonism toward the regime. However, it appears that the notion of professionalism held by

51. At insistence of his new Chief of Defense, Gen. S. J. A. Otu, the cadets were brought back to Ghana after a year, interrogated, and sent through the whole course at the military academy.

52. See *Parliamentary Debates: Official Record*, XXVI, 30, 42; XXVII, 691–92, 700.

53. On the 1958 Awhaitey affair, see Austin, *Politics in Ghana*, pp. 381–82, 424–29, for a skeptical account of its significance, and Bing, *Reap the Whirlwind*, pp. 239–77, who was then attorney general and persuasively argues the significance of the case.

some officers included the proposition that only the army should make decisions about army matters, and that all decisions about the use of the armed forces were best decided by the military.[54]

Attempts to bind the military more closely to the regime included: the establishment of an Armed Forces Bureau in 1962, which sporadically sponsored lectures; a June, 1964, order by Nkrumah that the military enlist all personnel in the CPP, which most resisted successfully; and the demand for periodic affirmations of fealty to Nkrumah, the last of which came right before the coup. Rivalry was encouraged between the police and the military, and among the services, over equipment and budgetary allocations. A military counterintelligence unit was established to mount surveillance on the military, which caused particular resentment among officers. After the January, 1964, assassination attempt on Nkrumah by a policeman, he rendered the police a less effective counterweight to the army by disarming it, detaining eight of the most senior police officers, and then transferring the Special Branch from police to presidential control, an accusation of incompetence which angered the police.

The only effective counterpoise to the military and police was Nkrumah's development of the President's Own Guard Regiment (POGR); and, based on the coup leaders' comments, it is difficult to resist the thought that the most important reason for the coup was the army's fear that it was being gradually opposed and replaced by the POGR. The POGR was set up by Nkrumah's British defense chief as a ceremonial guard for unfit soldiers and Congo relief tours. It was only in 1963, following the 1962 assassination attempt, that Nkrumah decided to build it up into a security guard, drawing on soldiers from the regular army to expand it into two regiments. One of these was formed by 1966, with 50 officers and 1,142 men, while another was in training. The POGR was itself a part of the presidential detail department, which included small civilian security units. In August, 1965, Nkrumah detached the presidential guard from Army command and made it directly responsible to himself. Chief of Defense Staff S. J. A. Otu and Army Chief J. A. Ankrah were "retired" from their positions when they protested this action. Among many officers the abrupt dismissal of their senior officers, particularly Ankrah, who was popular and highly respected for his Congo duty, was greatly resented as a humiliating, illegitimate

---

54. An observation made by Bing, *Reap the Whirlwind*, pp. 415–26, and supported by many military grievances cited by Afrifa, *The Ghana Coup*, and other officers in the press.

political intrusion into the military.[55] Additionally, officers felt that the army was in tatters and being deprived of badly needed resources such as uniforms, housing, and weapons that were going to the presidential guard, which was armed and trained in part by Soviet security specialists and headed by a northerner, Colonel Zanlerigu. Relations between the army and the POGR were quite poor.

The army could have pulled the coup alone, not the police, and it seems possible if not probable that the army elements involved were primarily moved to action by institutional grievances.[56] It is conceivable that the coup might not have occurred, at least not then, if it had not been for these grievances. However, there is no doubt that both army and police leaders were also fundamentally affronted by the Nkrumah regime's arbitrary rule, repressive behavior, and corruption, as well as by the declining economic situation. They had no doubt that they would receive popular support.

Several existing accounts of the coup make it unnecessary to review the coup itself, save to indicate a few factors which bear on the successor regime and the military and police forces.[57] First, while there had been previous coup plots by different officers, in this successful coup attempt there were very few people in on the planning until the end (considerations of security undoubtedly played a role in this), and these were Ewe: Colonel E. K. Kotoka, 2d Brigade commander in Kumasi; John W. K. Harlley, police commissioner since January, 1964, previously head of the Special Branch and, thus, quite familiar with the regime's security apparatus; and his former deputy in the Special Branch, A. K. Deku, deputy commissioner of police. The circle of coup plotters was widened to include others—such as Kotoka's brigade major, A. A. Afrifa (Ashanti), and then other 2d Brigade officers in Kumasi; the commander of the 1st Brigade in Accra, Colonel A. K. Ocran (Fanti), only a day-and-a-half before the coup; and other deputy police commissioners (a

---

55. Afrifa says "the dismissal of our Generals by Kwame Nkrumah was one of the major factors that led to the coup." He adds that "I anticipated he [General Ankrah] would take some military action to extricate himself from this humiliation and all it implied for the freedom of Ghana" (*The Ghana Coup*, pp. 100–101). On Kotoka's attitude, see *West Africa*, April 22, 1967, p. 517.

56. Although cited by coup leaders as a grievance, the people's militia was never formed (though many signed up for it), and it is extremely unlikely that Nkrumah would have ever armed such a body.

57. See Afrifa, *The Ghana Coup*, pp. 31–42; Kwame Nkrumah, *Dark Days in Ghana* (London: Lawrence & Wishart, 1968), pp. 20–42; and Major-General A. K. Ocran, *A Myth Is Broken* (Harlow, Essex: Longmans, Green; New York: Humanities Press, 1968), pp. 40–84, which is very detailed.

Ga and a northerner). But the important role played by the Ewe in the coup and on the NLC has animated criticism against the NLC for favoring the Ewe and has also caused envy and antagonism within the army, giving rise to ethnic factions.[58]

Second, it was a relatively small sector of the army that launched the coup action, 600 men drawn from companies in the 2d Brigade in Tamale. The coup plotters anticipated a possible division within the army. It is clear that certain elements of the military (and police) had a stake in the Nkrumah regime, e.g., the most senior officers, none of whom were included in the coup—including the army chief, General Barwah, who was killed resisting arrest—and all of whom were arrested, the presidential regiment, which resisted the coup from the triple-walled Flagstaff House for half a day, and other officers and units which were directly benefiting from the Nkrumah regime. The significance of this division was multiple. There have been some purges of "undesirable" or potentially undesirable officers from both the army and police. Despite immediate post-coup promises that the POGR would be reintegrated into the regular army, some of its officers have definitely been purged, as have senior officers, some of whom have been sent abroad to join or head diplomatic missions. The appointment of General Ankrah to head the NLC was devised to unify the army, but invariably the coup rewarded some and delivered sanctions or relative disadvantages upon others: coup leaders received several rapid promotions (the most extreme being that of Afrifa, who went from a pre-coup major to a post-coup brigadier) and positions of power in the NLC, the reorganized army, or the regional administration; some of those high in Nkrumah's army were purged, while some others who had been favored by Nkrumah apparently suffered reductions in rank, while those not involved simply retained their former rank. There has been resentment and jealousy at this variable distribution of benefits of the coup within the army and police.

Third, and perhaps most significant, was the coup itself, a seizure of power which established a precedent, one which involved an initiative by junior officers in the military (two colonels and a major) and a relatively small force that dashed 405 miles from Tamale to Accra. The result has been a willingness by many officers to discuss the possibility of a coup against the NLC and several

58. Afrifa remarks that "in the course of his career, Colonel Kotoka was accused many times, particularly by the late Major-General Barwah, of tribalism and of being pro-Ewe. I do not think this is a correct assessment," though he also thinks it pertinent to note, with reference to his involvement that "the Ashantis and Ewes . . . are . . . traditional allies" (*The Ghana Coup,* pp. 33, 40).

plots, one of which was launched on April 17, 1967, by junior officers with a 120-man reconnaissance squadron. The main grievance animating this *Putsch* was lack of promotions. The coup leader, 27-year-old Lieutenant Arthur, who duped other junior officers and his men into following both his orders and his apparently-not-improbable tale that the whole army was rising against the NLC, planned to kill all senior officers, from colonels up, though, in fact, the only officers killed were Ewe, including General Kotoka. In addition to this junior officer initiative, the previous coup precedent may account for the failure of officers in Accra to resist the coup attempt, which was not so much put down as petered out.[59] The most recent plot (November, 1968) involved the alleged participation of Air Marshall Otu in a plot with Nkrumah and other ousted CPP leaders to overthrow the NLC. He was cleared of this charge in October, 1969.

Political Structures, Demands, and Participation

On February 24, 1966, the NLC was established as the ruling body in Ghana. It was composed of four army and four police officers (a fourth police officer being appointed several days after the coup to achieve parity between the army and police). The first priority of the NLC was to systematically dismantle CPP political structures. The relative ease with which the regime was toppled (while Nkrumah was out of the country) indicated not only that the soldiers had the guns but that the CPP's political structures had decayed and were incapable of responding to their own demise. The CPP, parliament, constitution, and all auxiliary party organizations were dissolved. The gates of Ussher Fort Prison in Accra at once expelled the Nkrumah's regime detainees (political and criminal) and gathered in the detainees of the new regime, which included hundreds of CPP leaders, right down to the district level. In order to reduce any remaining support attitudes, expose the old regime, in particular break "the myth surrounding Nkrumah," prepare for legal prosecution of CPP leaders, primarily for corruption, and, thereby, firmly legitimize its seizure of power, the NLC immediately authorized a large number of judicial commissions of enquiry into the old regime. By 1968 more than forty commissions had been appointed; the proceedings of some were heavily attended and given prime place in the news media. The extent of the corruption and

59. See *West Africa*, April 22, 1967, p. 541; April 29, 1967, p. 570; May 6, 1967, p. 605; May 13, 1967, p. 615.

arbitrary rule disclosed by the Commission proceedings and reports astounded even the more jaundiced, thoroughly discredited the old regime, and undoubtedly cooled the public's desire for a rapid return to party politics.[60]

The political structures established by the NLC took into account its immediate need for support in ruling the country (being unable to do so by itself), explicit and implicit demands of the public and strategic groups, and demands for participation by certain key groups and strata. The NLC was, thus, able to establish a coalition of support and undercut the probability of open opposition.

The NLC was overwhelmingly and jubilantly endowed with legitimate authority by Ghanaians, whose relief at the overthrow of the regime was far greater than the coup leaders had anticipated. The NLC immediately justified its assumption of power by its promise to restore democratic, civilian rule under a new constitution which would provide a separation of powers and thus prevent another such concentration of power in the hands of a single man. It promised to remain in power only until pressing economic problems were relieved, the people readied for their responsibilities, and a constitution prepared. Though the NLC declined to assign a specific period of rule (estimating two years), there was little doubt of the coup leaders' fundamental commitment to a restoration of civilian rule at an early period. Indeed, several NLC leaders, Afrifa in particular, were eager to restore civilian rule as soon as possible and were worried at the effect of prolonged NLC rule upon their soldiers, whom they regarded as too interested in politics.

The NLC was directly dependent upon the civil service, and especially the advice of senior civil servants. In the beginning, all NLC members except General Ankrah, who was NLC chairman, retained their army and police positions and met at least weekly to make decisions. Thus, the senior civil servants were thrust into an enormously powerful position on matters, such as economic problems, of which the NLC had little knowledge. The NLC immediately established a range of committees composed of senior civil servants to provide specialized advice. The most important of these

60. Three aimed directly at Nkrumah were Ghana, *Report of the Commission to Enquire into the Kwame Nkrumah Properties* (1966), a judicious account of the financing of political manipulation; Ghana, *Report of the Commission to Enquire into the Affairs of NADECO Limited* (1966); *Report of the Commission of Enquiry on the Commercial Activities of the Erstwhile Publicity Secretariat* (1967). Others included one of irregularities in import licenses, the Housing Corporation, and the local purchase of cocoa by the UGFC, plus nonjudicial exposés on *Nkrumah's Subversion* and *Nkrumah's Deception of Africa*.

189

was the economic committee, which was chaired by E. N. Omaboe, the young, energetic, and capable government statistician whose advice Nkrumah had ignored. The civil servants were soon playing a visibly prominent role and took to their new capacity and power with eagerness. Though he had badgered, altered in structure, and too frequently ignored the civil service, Nkrumah had greatly strengthened its skills and capacity, facilitating its functional differentiation and specialization, though not its effectiveness. The military-police bureaucratic structure was the fundamental instrument of NLC rule. Regional administration was assigned to a committee of a senior police and military officer, assisted by the regional secretary (a civil servant), whose importance was demonstrated when he was formally made a member. Local administration was assigned to representatives of important ministries with local offices, including the police, until mid-1968 when civilian participation was extended to the local level by the appointment of prominent, often professional, people to office.

The NLC gave immediate attention to the depressing economic situation, which called for crucial decisions based on NLC preferences and technical advice provided by the economic committee. Six days after the coup the NLC responded to the public's explicit demands for economic relief by reducing taxes on a host of basic consumer goods. It also sought to restore economic stability and balance the budget through the reduction of expenditures rather than increased taxation, and by the recognition of the leading role of the private sector.[61] The NLC and its advisers felt that an austerity program was necessary, which would hardly be popular. And the public was already besieging the NLC with demands, expecting it, as Ankrah put it, "to drop manna from heaven for them."[62]

Soon after the coup the NLC sought and was quickly offered the counsel of Ghana's, especially Accra's, significant professional and middle class, including the former leading opposition UP politicians, some of whom emerged from detention or, like Professor Busia, returned from exile. The NLC looked to the professional class for support and help and tended to regard its members as representative of the public good and its political heir apparents. Jurists, many lawyers, civil servants, and other professional class members were appointed to prominent positions—as members of the commis-

61. Broadcast by NLC Chairman Ankrah, March 2, 1966, in Ghana, *The Rebirth of Ghana* (1966), pp. 33–39.
62. "Broadcast by Lt.-Gen. Ankrah, NLC Chairman, 25th May, 1966," *Press Release No. 6/66* (Washington, D.C.: Embassy of Ghana, May 27, 1966), p. 3.

sions of enquiry, delegations to the African countries (to restore decent relations with the many countries which Nkrumah had denounced or intervened in), boards of the 50 state corporations, and editorial boards of the government-owned newspapers; the first editors were former UP members.

Although the NLC banned all political organizations upon seizing power and specifically proscribed some which sprang up (e.g., an ex-detainees organization), demands made upon the NLC with regard to the formation of policies and programs, the allocation of material resources, and the shaping of the political future were demands for participation which the NLC found it partly necessary to respect. It lacked many skills which were needed, justified the coup in terms of democratic values, required the support of strategic groups, and genuinely wished to be popular. For these reasons, the NLC was susceptible to the demands by the professional class and UP politicians for direct participation, which were immediately offered to the NLC. Strong suggestions that the NLC give civilians a role in the government were made soon after the coup, partly in response to the prominent role played by senior civil servants. Former UP politicians, in particular, as well as other professional class members were mistrustful of the large role being assigned to civil servants. They felt that the civil servants were not providing the NLC with policy alternatives and that they were neither responsible to the people nor equipped by their training and outlook to make essentially political decisions. It was alleged that some senior civil servants had cooperated too closely with the Nkrumah regime, become his pawns and collaborated in the abuse of power and corruption, and been the recipients of appointments and promotions on the basis of their political orientation. The latter assertion was only marginally true, but former UP politicians were particularly suspicious of the past conduct of civil servants. Opinion at the University of Ghana, where a Legon Committee on National Reconstruction emerged as a significant voice, also opposed civil servants' wielding great power.

Former UP and professional-class leaders believed that their participation should be structured in official roles in order to relate the NLC to the public and the public to the NLC, offer policy alternatives, and advise on the political consequences of NLC measures.[63] It was suggested that civilian advisers should replace civil servants as heads of ministries. Reluctant to surrender its

---

63. This was Busia's proposal to the NLC, which he addressed as a body when he returned to Ghana. He and others, including Akufo-Addo, also suggested this kind of proposal to NLC members separately.

ministerial prerogatives, the NLC distributed ministerial portfolios among its members in mid-June, 1966 (which they held while continuing in their professional positions). Then, on June 23, the NLC appointed a 23-man Political Committee to offer policy proposals and advise it on its past decisions.

The Political Committee's composition could not be called a "balanced ticket," though the NLC paid some attention to regional and ethnic representation. It was a mixed ticket, overwhelmingly professional-class in representation, including six professors, four jurists or lawyers, only one chief, and one trade unionist, the new TUC secretary-general. Its chief characteristic was its domination by the old opposition. The chairman, Akufo-Addo, was a former opposition leader, appointed to and removed from the Supreme Court by Nkrumah, an important NLC adviser, currently Supreme Court chief justice. Vice-chairman, later chairman, was Professor Kofi Busia, former UP leader. No less than 14 of the 23 members had actively opposed the CPP, 10 as UP leaders, including Joe Appiah, Wm. Ofori-Atta, Reginald Amponsah, and Northern leaders such as S. D. Dombo, J. A. Braimah (later CPP), and A. Karboe; at least another 3 had been known UP supporters. While not, perhaps, an unnatural selection, it was too heavily weighted to the UP to avoid some criticism, particularly from those that believed that Ghana required new political leaders and admired neither the UP nor CPP. It is relevant to recall that the public had rejected in substantial measure the opposition parties (which later formed the UP) in the 1950's at the polls, and four Political Committee members specifically. In response to this, the NLC enlarged and broadened the committee in December, 1966.

The NLC, former UP leaders, and the merchant-professional class shared a common interest in restructuring political life in Ghana, but the latter two were not altogether uncritical of the NLC concerning certain policies and its pace of return to civilian rule. Some continued to push for more civilian participation in government while some, especially the politicians, wished not to be too closely identified with the NLC, especially since, as Afrifa pointedly reminded UP leaders and Political Committee members, "this is not their government." In March, 1967, Busia, who is close to Afrifa, distinguished the UP from the committee, recognizing the danger of the UP becoming the scapegoats; he observed that military regimes are "notoriously and inherently unstable" and "by nature authoritarian," and urged that the NLC set a date for elections.[64] Al-

64. "One Year After the Coup," speech given at Legion Hall, Accra, March 3, 1967, mimeo.

though an NLC member then inspired a newspaper campaign against Busia, the attempted coup in April informed NLC members that they were giving insufficient attention to security because of their other work.

By July the NLC decided to enlarge civilian participation. It formed an Executive Council, composed of fourteen civilian commissioners, all prominent nonpoliticians (save one), who were assigned ministerial portfolios; Ankrah, Harlley, and Afrifa retained the posts of defense, external affairs and interior, and finance, respectively. A week later the Political Committee was abolished and replaced by a National Advisory Committee of 31 members, including the 14 commissioners and only 4 UP politicians. Its functions were reduced, and Busia retained the chairmanship.[65]

In November, 1968, the NLC decided to dissolve the National Advisory Committee in order to let members prepare themselves for a political role. It is difficult to evaluate the role of the Advisory Committee and the Political Committee; their sessions and decisions were secret. However, they did serve as visible evidence of civilian political participation, an indication of the NLC's caretaker role. They also afforded the NLC a range of opinions on public questions and perhaps capped the more vocal advocates of a rapid return to civilian rule while benefiting from their support and judgments.

A common interest of the NLC and former UP and professional-class leaders was to raise the level of political responsibility and morality. To this end a nonpartisan Center for Civic Education was inaugurated in June, 1967, initially government-subsidized and headed by Busia. Branches were set up all over the country, though fewer in the north than elsewhere. Although it sponsored far more exhortation than explanation, its platforms served as a nonpolitical stage for raising critical issues about the NLC and for the appearance of Busia and a raft of young lawyers while the political ban was still in force. It was often attacked on the basis that it was being used as a political and organizing vehicle for Busia and others.[66]

On its assumption of power the NLC promised to guarantee chieftaincy and sought chiefly support. The chiefs gave this and, in turn, sought to reclaim prerogatives and authority locally, where they moved into the vacuum left by the demise of the CPP. In late 1966 and early 1967 the NLC responded to the demands of many

65. See *West Africa*, July 8, 1967, pp. 883, 903; July 15, 1967, p. 934; July 22, 1967, p. 961.
66. See *West Africa*, July 6, 1967, p. 791; *Legon Observer*, October 25–November 11, 1968, pp. 24–26.

destooled during Nkrumah's regime and of aggrieved chiefdoms whose subunits had acquired autonomy and increased traditional status: the NLC removed from office 172 chiefs alleged to have been elected or appointed in a noncustomary manner, demoted 194 chiefs of subchiefdoms who had been elevated to paramount chiefs, and restored another 35 uncustomarily destooled.[67] Unfortunately, it has for some time been no longer clear what constitutes the "customary" way, and local chieftaincy conflicts have abounded. Even where the alterations in the status and officeholder of chieftaincy under the Nkrumah regime appear to have been simply a matter of partisan politics, the intermingling of traditional, local, and modern political structures and conflicts make it probable that recent changes will not go unchallenged.[68]

As important is the political role which the chiefs have sought. Through their traditional councils, Regional Houses of Chiefs, and a post-coup periodic Joint Meeting of Houses of Chiefs, the chiefs had the advantage of working through political structures when most others were banned. Though they were not successful in their recommendations for a "no-party" system of government (which would, of course, leave them more powerful),[69] the draft constitution drawn up by the constitutional committee and published in early 1968 awarded the chiefs a significant role in local politics. The draft recommended new local councils which are a fusion of local and traditional councils in which traditional leaders will have two-thirds of the seats by appointment, with one-third elective; on district councils, which have the more significant functions and assign others to local councils, two-thirds of the seats are to be elective, for commoners, and one-third appointive, for traditional members.[70] The Constituent Assembly passed this provision; it is likely that there will be widespread commoner-chieftaincy con-

---

67. Ghana, *NLC Decree 112* and *136* (*Chieftaincy [Amendment] Decree[s]*); *West Africa*, December 12, 1966, p. 1434; December 17, 1966, p. 1467; February 25, 1967, p. 286.

68. For example, one of the leading anti-CPP chiefs, the *okyenhene* of Akim Abuakwa, has been re-enstooled, though the CPP and anti-chief sentiment were overwhelmingly powerful in this area, with similar sentiment, based on traditional and modern animosities, likely to reappear. Many of the chiefs destooled since the coup in Brong-Ahafo represented their own communities, with both chiefs and people pro-CPP because they were anti-Ashanti dominance; this sentiment will certainly persevere. In the north, the larger but formerly subject Frafra and Kusasi communities, which achieved autonomy under the Nkrumah regime, have been again brought under the Mamprussi Paramount.

69. See *West Africa*, July 15, 1967, p. 924.

70. Ghana, *The Proposals of the Constitutional Commission for a Constitution for Ghana*, 1968, pp. 174–183.

flicts, which could conceivably fuel another populist movement, and antagonism between commoner-controlled district and traditionally controlled local councils.

In accord with chiefly elitism and a distaste for social conflict, this provision represents an attempt to depoliticize local government by establishing a close correlation between authority in local government and traditional communities. In seeking to institutionalize certain traditional divisions in society, it probably underrates the levels of secularization and social change; intending to obstruct both, it would in many areas increase conflict. Having exercised power for fifteen years locally, commoners will be reluctant to restore it to the chiefs, with "their interminable litigation, dispute, and intrigue."[71]

The chiefs have also been awarded an important role in the electoral college which selects the powerful, nonexecutive president in the dual executive recommended by the draft constitution: the Regional Houses of Chiefs elect 24 chiefs, or 11 per cent of the electors, and another 48 nonchiefs, or 23 per cent which gives them a strong bloc influence. In addition, the Constituent Assembly created a National Assembly of Chiefs with appellate jurisdiction in chieftaincy disputes, and chiefs will sit on the president's advisory Council of State.

The NLC has been responsive in varying degrees to the interest groups which have reorganized or been created since the coup. With the dissolution of the UGFC (i.e., its integration with the Cocoa Marketing Board), the old cooperative organization, the Ghana Cooperative Marketing Association, and some new private groups have entered the cocoa purchasing field. The cocoa farmers constitute a powerful influence, although they are presently not a cohesive force. The farmers were immensely dissatisfied with the operation of the UGFC.[72] For both political and economic reasons, the NLC has attempted to rectify conditions, placing farmers' representatives on the Cocoa Marketing Board (the same old trusted pre-CPP men), making farmers' tools available at lower subsidized rates again, and raising the cocoa price to farmers as the world price has risen: after

---

71. Irritation with the demands of chiefs manifested itself quickly. One writer noted the chiefs' desires for "prestige, personal power, and economic advantage," the lack of "even the semblance of a stable tradition of sound rule in any of our chiefdoms," and their current clamoring for a role: "The beaches have been over-crowded: there is hardly any room for commoners to do their somersaults!" (Joe de Graft, "Chiefs and National Politics," *Legon Observer*, October 28, 1966, pp. 3–4).

72. See Ghana, *Report of the Committee on Enquiry on the Local Purchasing of Cocoa*, 1966, pp. 3–26.

several small increases, the price went up by 30 per cent in mid-1967 and another 8 per cent in mid-1968; this price was guaranteed for three years. The importance of cocoa farmer support can be seen from the arguments offered by former UP leaders that the price should be further increased.

The TUC is one of the few associational groups linked to the CPP which survived the demise of the Nkrumah regime. As a relatively coherent, large organization,[73] it has been regarded, and seen itself, as an important economic force and a potentially significant political one. Union behavior is thus important to the NLC and aspiring politicians.

Four days after the coup and the arrest of central TUC leaders, the NLC appointed as acting TUC secretary-general Benjamin Bentum, an intelligent, critical-minded unionist who had been chairman of the TUC Executive Board in 1964 and was dismissed for feeding information on TUC corruption to the police; although he was made a low-ranking minister in Nkrumah's 1965 government, his contacts with Police Inspector General Harlley secured his TUC appointment, which has since been confirmed in several elections.

The TUC has undergone a reorganization since the coup, establishing a new constitution with regular elections. It has faced severe organizational problems: the desire of unions for more autonomy in reaction to the TUC's centralization under the Nkrumah regime; the tendency of the rank and file to opt for wildcat strikes in defiance of union leaders; and the departure of certain groups, including teachers. Bentum has shown a willingness to cooperate closely with the NLC's efforts to restore economic development, even when this has meant, as it has, a very high level of unemployment stemming from cuts in government expenditures and the rationalization and closing of state enterprises, including numerous state farms. The position of Bentum and other union leaders who have attempted to dampen the numerous strikes has been made difficult by the reactions of the NLC, which has refused to legalize strikes. By mid-1968 the number of strikes in the two years since the coup, all economic rather than political in inspiration, was 40 per cent greater than in the five years preceding it. Since then there have been several large strikes of several thousand workers, some involving sabotage (e.g., in Takoradi by a railway union), and violence (e.g., police shot several miners in early 1969); the NLC has arrested strikers and sanctioned the firing of workers who

73. It *claimed* 386,750 members in 1965, or about 75 per cent of the 512,000 wage and salary workers noted by the 1960 census. The actual number is now much less.

refused to return to work.[74] Union dissidence has been closely watched by the police as a likely basis for Nkrumah-inspired disruptions of NLC rule; NLC members have frequently denounced strikes as the work of "subversives," "saboteurs," and "agitators"; Police Inspector General Harlley linked a disorderly railway strike in September, 1968, to a Nkrumaist plot. Bentum, in not opposing NLC actions but instead pleading for the rehiring of fired workers, has lamented that "I do not want to be a secretary-general who only breaks strikes."[75] The decision by Bentum in early 1969 to take a case of 2,000 fired workers to the ILO illustrated both the relative freedom in Ghana and the growing alienation of the unions from NLC rule.

In response to TUC demands, the NLC has given trade union leaders places on more governmental commissions than did the Nkrumah regime, and there were nine unionists among the 150 members of the Constituent Assembly. There have been wage raises, including a 15 per cent raise in the minimum wage in mid-1968, with further increments to follow; however, this was unsatisfactory to the TUC, for the wage worker was hurt by the devaluation in mid-1967, and the TUC sees a growing gap between lower and upper income groups. While the consumption-oriented TUC is extremely wary of being controlled again by a political party, Bentum announced in August, 1968, that a TUC conference would be convened after the ban on political activities was lifted to determine if the unions should form a party, back one, or remain aloof. With its internal union, ethnic, and regional rivalries, the TUC is not a monolith, but it is likely to be a powerful factor in post-coup politics.

Ghanaian merchants and entrepreneurs benefited considerably from the NLC's emphasis upon the private sector and pressed demands for a larger economic role. A large and varied number of businessmen's organizations represent a growing and ambitious private sector, which includes a good number of large-scale entrepreneurs (not a few of them businessmen who were formerly CPP leaders). The NLC has been responsive. Although it has sought foreign private capital, in order to promote indigenous businessmen the NLC in January, 1969, restricted the business activities of foreigners (especially Indians and Lebanese) and reserved to Ghanaians certain sectors: taxi operations; small scale businesses with under 30 employees; retail trade with a sales volume of less than about $500,000; wholesale trade with sales of less than $1 million;

74. *West Africa*, December 24, 1966, p. 1495, June 8, 1968, p. 676, November 30, 1968, p. 1423, March 8, 1969, p. 282; *Evening News*, May 27, 1968, p. 3.
75. *West Africa*, September 14 and 21, 1968, pp. 1082, 1115.

and representation of overseas manufacturers.[76] The government has actively supported the extension of credit facilities, long a complaint, made available technical expertise, encouraged links between domestic and private capital, and considered the establishment of a stock market to provide financing for growth. Business associations continue to beseech the government to make other economic sectors exclusively Ghanaian.

NLC as a Political Broker

The NLC's performance has been circumscribed by Ghana's economic conditions, the priority it has given to the economy, and the tools it has used in restoring economic health. Advised by its technocrats and foreign economists, the NLC has sought to end Ghana's drastic balance of payments problems through renegotiating its external debts, a continuing task, cutting drastically Ghana's imports and rationalizing the import license system, successfully securing foreign aid, devaluing the cedi by 30 per cent in mid-1967, and severely cutting the budget (which required a relearning of budgetary discipline in government departments). In 1966 the investment budget was cut by 17 per cent, in 1967 by 20 per cent, budget surpluses achieved; by the end of 1968 Ghana also had a surplus on visible trade.[77] The basically sound rationale behind this severe retrenchment was that Ghana must and could utilize more productively the investments it was making, but the immediate economic and social costs have been high and the political costs cannot yet be measured.

There has been a low real rate of growth in GNP, 0.6 per cent in 1966, 2.4 per cent in 1967, which, with an estimated population growth of 2.6 to 2.7 per cent, meant that there was a decline in per-capita GNP.[78] Perhaps most critical, at least in the short run, was an enormously high rate of unemployment. As a result of the rationalization and curtailment of state enterprises, and the cuts in government investment, unemployment soared; by mid-1968 at least 64,000 workers had been fired, and there were estimates that fully 25 per cent of the wage labor force was unemployed; this probably underestimated the situation, and by early 1969 unem-

76. *West Africa,* July 13, 1968, p. 819.

77. In new cedis (I NC = $.98), Ghana had a deficit on current account (excluding debt servicing) of NC 200 million in 1965, NC 134 million in 1966, less than NC 20 million in 1967, and a surplus of NC 29 million in 1968, when there was an increase in exports from NC 244.9 million in 1967 to NC 341 million (*West Africa,* March 1, 1969, p. 249).

78. Ghana, *Economic Survey, 1967,* p. 104.

ployment was still growing, despite real efforts by the NLC to redeploy the unemployed.[79] As noted above, trade unions were becoming more restless and aggressive. There was a business recession, despite the fact that government encouraged both foreign and domestic private capital, showing a decided preference for private over state enterprise (it sold several small state enterprises to Ghanaian entrepreneurs and successfully solicited foreign private participation in eight state corporations). And there was considerable dissension with the return of charges for previously free social services, e.g., school and book fees, which produced some anomic disturbances. These latter measures were not unfeeling but reflected an indication of self-discipline which distinguished the NLC from the Nkrumah regime; whether or not a successor civilian regime can or will also discipline popular desires remains to be seen.

The NLC was greatly aided in its efforts by a surging cocoa price, though cocoa had been neglected and the crop was damaged by rains in 1968, reducing it from the previous year by over 20 per cent in volume. Inflation was reduced on local food prices but not imported goods (Accra retail price index—June, $1954 = 100$: 1966 average, 204.5; 1967, 190). Some regressive taxes were lowered, and private consumption expenditure increased. Although the NLC announced a new development plan in mid-1968, which allowed for slightly increased development investments, the combination of heavy external debt repayments, government restraint, continued skilled labor shortages, and dependence on private capital does not create an encouraging economic prospect.

It is within this context that the NLC's performance as a caretaker regime and political broker must be judged. In practice, the NLC's rule has been a holding operation, marked by a low level of intensity but the arranging of an important restructuring of political roles.

The NLC was most anxious to "cleanse" the body politic of the CPP but at the same time create a climate of national reconciliation and avoid wide-scale witch-hunting, particularly by the former UP against the civil service, which has escaped close examination but not criticism. NLC leader Ankrah frequently exhorted the public to bury past differences and accept penitent CPP members back to the fold, but the antagonism towards former CPP leaders remains quite high. A chief means advocated for purifying the

79. *West Africa*, July 6, 1968, p. 791; August 17, 1968, p. 951. The Workers Brigade, reduced from 25,000 to 8,000 in January, 1969, announced a further reduction of 5,000 members and a 50 per cent slash in salary for 2,000 others (*Sunday Mirror* [Accra], January 26, 1969, p. 16).

system and preventing future contamination was the banning of former CPP leadership at all levels from holding public office. There was considerable debate on this, within the NLC, Political Committee, and the press; some newspapers advocated no ban on the basis of a citizen's ability to choose within a democracy (e.g., the *Ghanaian Times*, though it had earlier suggested, after Harlley revealed a plot in early 1967, that the NLC "bundle the whole caboodle of creeping, corroding, and dangerous communist vermin from the country"[80]) while the *Pioneer* rationalized CPP disqualification on traditional grounds, and the *Daily Graphic* editor said "all the nabobs, activists and ideologues" should be "effectively and finally removed from the political scene."[81]

In January, 1968, the NLC decreed that leaders of the CPP and affiliated organizations (UGFC, TUC, National Council of Ghana Women, Young Pioneers, National Association of Socialist Students Organization, and others) right down to the district level were banned from holding public office for 10 years.[82] By mid-1968 NLC lists included more than 5,000 banned members; though they were allowed to appeal to an exemptions committee, it surveyed applications extremely critically, refusing to exempt from the ban well-known if belated CPP dissidents. There was public reaction to the lack of discrimination in this ban, and in late August the leaders of affiliated organizations were removed from the ban. The exemption of Komla Gbedemah, Nkrumah's former top lieutenant, famed CPP organizer, and former minister of finance who fled the country in October, 1961, caused another crisis, owing to suspicions that Gbedemah was shown special favors as an Ewe and confidant of Police Inspector General Harlley, with whom he enjoys close relations. This was part of a more diffuse suspicion of Ewe designs upon public offices, present and future. Brigadier Afrifa immediately denounced the whole ban, as did the *Pioneer*. Then in February, 1969, the NLC removed the ban on all but 152 major CPP leaders.

Evidently, there was a high level of disagreement within the NLC concerning the banning of former CPP leaders, and, thus, at the end of April, some days before political party activity was again to be permitted, the NLC changed its mind again, and then again two days later. On April 28, it banned from being a founding member or from holding office in a new party (and, on April 30, entering Parliament) all those who had held any of the following positions on or

---

80. February 23, 1967, p. 8.
81. *Pioneer* (Kumasi), March 4, 1968, p. 2; *West Africa*, October 14, 1967, p. 1344.
82. *NLC Decree 223* (*Election and Public Offices Disqualification*) (January 10, 1968).

after July 1, 1960: minister, regional commissioner, district commissioner, member of Parliament, chairman of city or municipal councils, member of governing board of statutory corporations or other government-appointed boards (with a few exceptions), member of the Presidential Detail Department (a bodyguard), special adviser to the president, CPP Central Committee member, general secretary, CPP regional secretary or regional propaganda secretary, or member of the national or regional executive committees. Then on April 30, this was altered by changing the effective date to the day before the coup, February 23, 1966, and by removing MP's and board members of statutory corporations and other boards from the list entirely.

In part, this kind of policy alteration on a touchy subject is indicative of the relative flexibility of NLC rule, which has derived, in proportions impossible to measure, from a relative openness to public opinion and pressures (it wanted to do right and be liked), an open-ended pragmatism and dependence upon the advice and expertise of others, and divisions within the NLC itself. Police Inspector General Harlley—and, before his death in 1967, General Kotoka as well—is reputed to be the strong man on the NLC. However, until his forced resignation in late March, 1969, General Ankrah had played a central and authoritative role in the NLC. Brigadier Afrifa, the youngest member but one of the coup insiders, has been the gadfly of the NLC, taking outspoken public stands which he has not infrequently first posed publicly and sometimes in sharp disagreement with current NLC policy (e.g., on CPP disqualification). He has constantly prodded others for a rapid return to civilian rule, pushing even the Political Committee as early as August, 1966, to take up the issue, and encouraging civilians, particularly the press, to be critical of the NLC.

However, the military/police composition of the NLC, its concern with security in terms of Nkrumaist plots, continued government ownership of the main newspapers (except the *Pioneer*), and the maintenance of certain repressive laws and the decreeing of others has certainly inhibited the redevelopment of an independent and critical press and thus reduced the levels of information available to the regime. Thus, on the one hand, Brigadier Afrifa has asked intellectuals to criticize the regime, the press to warn it "when we go wrong," and complained, with some accuracy, that the Ghana press is merely "a catalogue of activities of members of the NLC" and that the only change has been that "NLC has been substituted for CPP."[83] On the other hand, there have been veiled warnings to the

83. Afrifa speech, March 20, 1967, quoted in Busia, "One Year After the Coup"; *West Africa*, March 18, 1967, p. 388.

press by other NLC members to be "responsible," detention and prosecution of several members of the press for publishing "false news," under the October, 1966, prohibition of rumor-mongering decree (which was repealed finally in late 1968),[84] and the surreptitious firing of two editors and two editors-in-chief of government-owned newspapers in mid-December, 1967, for their editorial opposition to the Ghana-Abbott pharmaceutical company agreement, under which, it was felt, Abbott was unduly favored.[85] In response, the commissioner of information, Osei-Bonsu, resigned—an act of integrity which has made him popular. While the NLC has established an autonomous public corporation for government radio and television, it has, for its own purposes, kept direct control of the newspapers and, at police insistence, kept certain repressive laws on the books, e.g., NLC Decree No. 93, a law, equal to one first sponsored by the Nkrumah regime, which permits the detention of people for 28 days or *more*, i.e., as long as the police want. During 1967, the police and Harlley were gaining a reputation for being heavy-handed.

The exhortations both to support and to criticize the NLC have resulted in some uncertainty about the proper limits of political behavior. The political environment has been fairly leisurely, but the NLC has armed itself with enough restrictive decrees and used them just often enough to disabuse politically articulate Ghanaians of any inherent faith in the benevolence of prolonged military rule.

The legitimacy of NLC authority rests not only upon its overthrow of Nkrumah but on its promise to restore democratic civilian rule, and in this area criticism has been legitimate. For instance, after the draft constitution was published in 1968, a high level of criticism was focused on certain provisions, which in turn provided the NLC with information. In fact, in comparison with other African countries, Ghana has a rather highly structured communications system, both formal and informal, which conveys attitudes and demands to those in power. The NLC's inability to fulfill demands has forced it to respond, like the Nkrumah regime, with a high level of exhortation.

However, the NLC could afford to pace slowly the restoration of

---

84. *NLC Decree 92 (Prohibition of Rumours)* was passed on October 1, 1966, after only six months of NLC rule; it forbade the publication or reproduction of any statement "likely to cause fear or alarm or despondency to the public or to disturb the public peace or to cause disaffection against the National Liberation Council," evidence of which was the conveying by one person to another of any such statement or rumor, which made one liable to a fine not to exceed about $1,000 or a prison term not to exceed three years or both.

85. See *West Africa,* January 6, 20, 27, 1968, pp. 22, 79, 110, respectively.

civilian rule since there were not great demands for a rapid return. This was borne out by an extensive public opinion poll completed in February, 1968, which indicated that 91.8 per cent of people liked the NLC, only 55.35 per cent wanted a civilian government (a majority of those interviewed in the Northern and Volta regions were against civilian rule, and just under a majority in Brong/ Ahafo and the Central regions), and, of those wanting civilian rule, 20 per cent were uncertain when, 13.6 per cent wanted it in 1968, 9.65 per cent in 1969, 44.75 per cent in 1970, 3.3 per cent in 1971, and 8.7 per cent in 1972 and after.[86] Insofar as it is accurate, this poll probably reflects not only a distaste for the Nkrumah regime, extended to politicians in general, and traditional sentiment against political parties, which are regarded as divisive, but also the ability of NLC leaders to play politics, to wield symbols of authority with some facility, to palaver with both traditional leaders and modern interests, to move with public opinion, and to learn from experiences (e.g., in foreign policy, where the NLC's initially exaggerated Anglophilism has been altered, in light of both experience in power and the reaction in public opinion to the shift back to reliance on Western countries).

The symbolic output of the NLC is sharply different than that of the Nkrumah regime. The public's apparent acceptance of these symbols reflects both some basic social values and a sharp shift in the social location of power and influence. The old and new merchant-professional bourgeoisie and middle class are making quite explicit their values in matters relating not only to politics and economics but to marriage, inheritance, and family life, where their middle class values differ from those of the more populist CPP. The regime propounds a middle-class morality, and there has been a wide-scale religious revival since the coup, which appears to encompass all sectors of society. There is a renewed emphasis on "quality," the salience of the British cultural referent (to the middle class), traditional status and concerns, and capitalist development, the latter highly favored by a country with many petty traders, merchants, and incipient entrepreneurs. The tone of the NLC can perhaps most readily be compared to that of the Nkrumah regime by noting to whom national awards have been given: Nkrumah gave "Black Star" medals to CPP, TUC, and UGFC militants, while the last NLC Independence Day awards were given to senior public servants in health (two), agriculture, prison

86. A poll carried out by Jeafan Ltd., Accra, with a sample of 8,100 people, 900 in each region, and distributed within many districts. See *Daily Graphic* (Accra) February 10, 1968, pp. 8–9, and previous Saturdays for results by district.

service, and police, and to a Catholic sister and bishop for educational work.[87] There is, of course, strong emphasis on the "glorious February Revolution" and the redeeming mission and continuing duty of the military and police.

One effect of NLC rule and the ban on parties has meant that political participation in terms of the expression of demands has often been articulated and aggregated by non-national, traditional structures. There has been much comment and complaint about the role of tribal or ethnic ties. NLC leaders have often condemned tribalism in economic and political life. It is difficult to measure the significance of ethnic and other particularistic orientations for the political future, but Brigadier Afrifa reflected a strong concern when he noted in October, 1967, that "our society is tending towards disintegration and the unity of Ghana as one nation is facing its greatest challenge. The reason for this, as I see it, is that we are becoming too tribalistic in our outlook. Herein lies dangers," which, he added, suggested a quick end to NLC rule.[88] In late 1968, Kofi Busia, not noted for this emphasis, indicated that tribal groups were springing up all over Ghana and would have to be united into a national entity.[89] The proliferation of ethnic organizations with local or regional orientations is to be expected in the absence of national political structures. They have been reinforced in their behavior patterns by NLC attempts to respond to their representations (e.g., the NLC has launched a separate development plan for the Upper Region and numerous projects for the Northern Region in response to politically salient complaints of backwardness and neglect by leaders from these areas). Strong jealousies and enmities based on the perception of ethnic discrimination and the use of traditional structures for interest articulation and aggregation may not result in separatist groups when the ban on politics is lifted, but it is unlikely that NLC has strengthened national unity.

Building Political Structures

The NLC has moved slowly and purposefully, if somewhat uncertainly, towards the restoration of civilian rule and the creation of new political structures. In the process, it has had to face up to

87. *Daily Graphic,* March 6, 1969, p. 1. The previous year's recipients of awards included the Chief Justice, Harlley and two other NLC police members, two leading chiefs, plus 68 others who received lesser awards, among whom were prominent judges, civil servants, and professors.
88. *West Africa,* October 28, 1967, p. 1407.
89. *Ibid.,* November 9, 1968, p. 1330.

problems of legitimate authority, political participation, and national integration, problems which are likely to become more acute when politics revives. It has changed its plans several times, in response to public pressure for the setting of a date for civilian rule and the shortage of time in which to accomplish necessary tasks.

With instructions to prepare a draft constitution which specifically provided for a separation of power, a Constitutional Commission was set up in November, 1966. Of its original 18 members, 11 were former opposition members, 8 of these formerly UP. The commission, headed by Chief Justice Akufo-Addo, held hearings in all regions, received 721 memoranda, heard evidence from 567 individuals or organizational representatives, and published the draft constitution of 161 pages in early 1968.

The draft constitution is so armed with checks on possible abuses of authority as to make conflict likely and the work of government quite difficult. It provides for a dual executive, with a prime minister chosen from the majority party and responsible to Parliament and a one term (eight years) nonexecutive president, chosen by an electoral college composed of the 140 MP's, 24 chiefs, and 48 regional representatives and provided with important powers: in consultation with a prescribed advisory Council of State, he appoints the most important state officers, including the chief justice and military commanders, can withhold his consent from bills approved by parliament (with a two-thirds majority needed to command his assent, or, after six months, a majority), and has exclusive authority within the government on matters relating to election and destoolment of chiefs. There is a 140 member unicameral, nonsovereign National Assembly, whose powers are checked by both the president and Supreme Court. The constitution is supreme, again protected by the president and Supreme Court, whose proposed functions are large and quite political, including jurisdictions in chieftaincy, labor, administrative, and constitutional issues, where on anyone's request it may pass on the constitutionality of a proposed bill or law. There are a variety of independent state officers to check government practices, including an ombudsman and an electoral commissioner.[90]

Only after the draft constitution's publication did the NLC set up an electoral commissioner to devise registration and voting procedures and adopt new voting registration lists; this started in September and made slow progress. In May the NLC announced its

90. See *The Proposals of the Constitutional Commission for a Constitution for Ghana.*

schedule for a return to civilian rule. Constitutional legitimacy was to be provided by an elected but non-party Constituent Assembly which would meet in May, 1969; three months were allowed for its deliberations. Political parties would be permitted after the Assembly finished its business, which allowed a hectic month or two for organization and the election campaign before the restoration of civilian rule by September 30, 1969.[91]

Both the draft constitution and the schedule for civilian rule came under heavy criticism in the press and at public meetings. A chief target was the large role assigned to the judiciary and chief justice (the draft's chief architect), which was opposed by, among others, NLC Deputy Chairman Harlley, Kofi Busia, and the Attorney-General Victor Owusu.[92] In the Constituent Assembly itself Kwesi Lamptey warned that Ghanaians might end up with a constitution providing for government of the people by lawyers for the future chief justice.[93] Other objections were the difficulty of amending the constitution (especially relating to chieftaincy), the age (at least 50) and extensive prerogatives of the president, the likelihood that this nonpolitical office would be inevitably entangled in and reflective of political divisions, the Council of State, and the lack of salaries for MP's (since affirmed by the Constituent Assembly) which was intended to, and will, make it likely that only rich men ("of quality") could afford to be MP's. Reflected in the constitution and resented, also, is the decided sense of elitism of its chief framers, e.g., inducing the "best men" to participate in government by allowing non-MP's in the Cabinet (rejected by the Constituent Assembly: "nobody is better than anybody in Ghana") and the idea of the Council of State as composed of "a small body of prominent citizens of proven character and ability." The Ghana Youth Council declared the Constitution a conspiracy against youth.

Criticisms of the schedule for civilian rule focused particularly upon the extremely short period for the organization of political parties before the elections. In response to this and the slowness of voter registration, the NLC decided in late October, 1968, against an elected Constituent Assembly. It announced an indirectly elective 150-member Constituent Assembly which would be composed of 49 representatives of administrative districts (elected by the NLC-appointed local council members), and 91 representatives of 37 organizations, including houses of chiefs, city and municipal

91. *West Africa,* June 1, 1968, p. 646.
92. Akua Asaabea Ayisi, "The Limits of Power in the Draft Constitution," *Ghanaian Times* (Accra), August 19, 1968, pp. 6–7.
93. *Ibid.,* January 25, 1969, p. 1.

councils, universities, farmers' and market women's associations, TUC, and a large number of professional bodies including the bar and journalists' associations. The military and police were to elect 2 members each and the NLC to nominate 10 members (eventually 14, as the military and police did not choose theirs).[94]

The representativeness, and by inference the legitimacy, of this indirectly elected Constituent Assembly was soon questioned, not least by those stalwart upholders of legitimacy, the Bar Association and individual lawyers, who quickly disputed the number of seats assigned to various groups (e.g., the Bar Association *vs.* market women).[95] Then, one of the first substantive issues to which the Constituent Assembly turned in January, 1969, was a resolution to seek full powers for itself in promulgating the constitution, rather than submitting it to the NLC or holding a referendum to confirm it.[96] The legitimacy of the Constituent Assembly and the NLC banning from public office (i.e., from effective political participation) of 152 former CPP leaders has been questioned by Komla Gbedemah.[97] The NLC obviously entertains notions that party politics has a distorting effect and has thus, by not lifting the ban on political groups, attempted to shield the Constituent Assembly in its work from partisan divisions. Until Afrifa became NLC chairman in April, 1969, it vacillated continuously on when the ban would be lifted, with one NLC member saying "soon" and another saying "later."

Tribes, Classes, and Generals

The probability of future military and/or police intervention, direct or indirect, in the political system once the NLC has relinquished power to a civilian regime will depend upon: (1) the nature and level of political conflict within the new system; (2) the nature and orientations of the successor political system and governments; and (3) the beliefs, interests, and coherence of the military and police as institutional groups.

The discussion of politics during 1951–57 above noted that there was a high level of political conflict revolving around the legitimacy of authority, the nature and forms of political participation, and national integration, and was based upon traditional, ethnic, regional, and religious cleavages in what was essentially an uninte-

94. *West Africa,* November 2, 1968, p. 1298.
95. *Ibid.,* November 23, 1968, p. 1389.
96. *Ibid.,* February 1, 1969, p. 134.
97. *Ibid.,* March 29, 1969, p. 367.

grated, plural society. Neither the CPP nor opposition leaders trusted one another or could predict, except with trepidation, the behavioral limits of one another. While a power struggle was certainly involved at one level, at another level a more fundamental set of conflicts basic to social change involved sharp shifts in the social location of power, notions of legitimacy, behavioral limits, and the proper structure, nature, and limits of political authority. These were exacerbated by a singular distaste for and fear of the consequences of sociopolitical conflicts upon the social and political orders by both sides. In order for the NLC successor system to maintain itself, it will somehow have to institutionalize at the level of cultural belief the idea that conflict is potentially manageable.[98] The continuing salience of traditional, primordial, and local orientations, and thus the identity of friends, enemies, and interests in particularistic terms, breeds enmity and distrust rather than a confidence in widely shared behavioral limits and the manageability of conflict, which can be achieved only over a period of time.

The significance of this tendency to avoid or eliminate conflict will be affected by the nature of successor politics. Ethnic and local ties, sentiments, and loyalties, and the enhancing of the expression of local secular interest, by playing upon these particularistic links, will continue to be politically salient, in terms of political organization and recruitment at the local level, political socialization, and interest articulation. However, particularistic sentiments and loyalties will be only one of the factors shaping party politics and are likely to play a contributive rather than decisive role in shaping the major variations in the configuration of successor politics. There is considerable sentiment against purely ethnic or regional parties, a valued (but nonattributed) remnant of the Nkrumah regime. This sentiment was expressed in late April, 1969, by an NLC decree which forbade political parties formed on a tribal or religious basis, or those whose "structure or mode of operation are not national in character." As soon as parties were re-established it was clear that specific regulations requiring a skeleton national basis for the establishment of a party will not prevent parties from having explicit ethnic or regional orientations, but this law may contribute to reducing the fervor of explicit ethnic politics.

One of two political patterns is likely to emerge, with considerable tension between the two patterns and with variations in the support of ethnic and other particularistic groups playing an important role. First, it is possible that the merchant-professional-led

98. See Zolberg, "Political Conflict in the New States of Tropical Africa," pp. 86–87.

middle class will dominate politics and control power through the agency of one more or less major party, which will bring other more particularistic or localized parties into a national coalition. Fundamental to this pattern are alliances between merchant-professional and traditional leaders or (more rarely, with a couple of exceptions) ethnic groups or traditional states in certain areas. In contrast to the lower-middle- and middle-class CPP leadership, the professional and middle class pose relatively few dangers to the renewed authority and status of traditional leaders (who are, often, no longer so traditional), or at least the dangers are more latent; both share a strong inclination to moderation, order, and slowly paced change.

A number of factors will facilitate the political domination of a merchant-professional led coalition, assuming either a reasonably open political system in which elections are regularly held or the return to a more restricted system (either at the local or national levels). First, Ghanaian professionals, especially lawyers but other highly educated persons as well, and large businessmen receive a high level of deference, though certainly not as great as in the pre-CPP period, when after World War II it was simply assumed that they would be the heirs to British power. Professionals constituted the overwhelming majority of the 1969 Constituent Assembly and were chosen even by market women and farmers' associations. Second, in some respects the new institutional structure prescribed by the draft constitution, whose major provisions have been accepted, will facilitate their political domination. Designed by the professional class to inhibit the accumulation of power at the center, it grants a high level of autonomy and power to certain political roles which are filled by professionals, e.g., the lawyers in the judiciary, or traditional leaders. The NLC gave these professionals (lawyers primarily, also doctors, professors, economists, and other fairly highly educated specialists) important public and political roles and high visibility during its rule, grooming them for successor leadership. The decision of the professional-class dominated Constituent Assembly that members of parliament would receive no salaries was deliberately intended to make it economically difficult for other than professionals to seek parliamentary office, to prevent the propertyless (meaning effective property, including professional skills) lower-middle class, from which the bulk of the CPP leaders were drawn, from being able to afford the cost of political leadership. Third, the existence of minor parties fragmented along particularistic lines and confined in their range of appeal and organization will greatly facilitate recognition and acceptance of the ascriptive right to political leadership (based on education, wealth, and moral worth) put forward by the merchant-professional class. Fourth, the explicit and implicit support of the NLC and important military leaders has helped and may continue to help, within certain limits, this class secure and maintain its leadership.

The merchant-professional bourgeoisie and new middle class have a very definite sense of their distinct status and shared economic interests which gives them a coherence in their political beliefs and behavior and induces them to distinguish themselves and their interests sharply from those of the petty-bourgeois, lower-middle class, the growing number of skilled and unskilled workers, and the transitionals, among them the young unemployed and underemployed school leavers (graduates and dropouts). The CPP leadership, national and local, was in large measure a propertyless petty-bourgeois and lower-middle class, though among CPP leaders at both levels there were some large and middle-sized merchants and entrepreneurs, most of whom became divorced from the party in the 1960's. The lower-middle class became a politically coherent class in viewing and using the state as its effective property and source of power and control. As the dominant class under the Nkrumah regime it came eventually, particularly in the 1960's, to have little regard for the interests of the (effectively) propertied middle and merchant-professional class. The professional class as a whole was disdained and credit facilities for merchants and entrepreneurs were cut back. The pursuit of rapid economic development through structural change, an increasingly primary role for state enterprises, and industrialization forced the Nkrumah regime to extract a high level of the savings of cash-crop farmers and workers through high rates of taxation and control of wages, salaries, and agricultural prices. This brought the regime into conflicts, which could not be readily articulated under prevailing political conditions, with not only the merchants, professionals, and middle class, but also the cash-crop farmers and the workers.

The merchant-professional class is loath to let this reoccur. Its members distrust immensely the political qualities and tendencies of the unpropertied, their tendency to tax highly, and their use of political instruments to bring about social and economic leveling. The merchant-professional class is seeking and will probably find political allies among the cash-crop (especially cocoa) farmers and many chiefs; they share with the latter the common interest of keeping the lower-middle class and transitionals in a political netherland. The chiefs will want and need support in repressing commoner challenges to their renewed local authority.

In nonindustrial, transitional societies, once access to political power has been assured to a small indigenous bourgeoisie and middle class, there is often no longer the impetus to extend political participation and, hence, in a poorly integrated country, the political system itself. Rather there is the emergence of the tendency within the new class to make alliances with traditional structures and leaders in order to consolidate its power at the national center. Much of Ghana's officer corps identifies itself and the protection of its institutional interests with the merchant-professional class leaders, has clearly and explicitly demonstrated its support for them, and may be expected to support them in various ways and in certain exigencies.[99] The degree to which this tendency manifests itself depends on a number of factors, among the most important of which are cultural values concerning equality and the structure of the economy. For example, is there a rapidly expanding economy which can supply jobs, offer opportunities, and respond to the economic and social demands of the lower strata (which will be expressed politically), or is economic growth slow, the economy lopsided, and the political system faced with a high level of demands? In the case of Ghana, even leaving aside its current problems, the structure of the economy is such that it cannot readily fulfill the demands made for jobs by the school leavers at various levels or the multitude of economic demands made by workers, farmers, civil servants, and various communities. Social strata in Ghana are not closed, though the merchant-professional bourgeois and middle class have a fairly high level of class consciousness, nurtured in part by a distinct sense of elitism which one suspects is partially a British inheritance. On the other hand, social mobility, at this point but at a diminishing rate, is largely a function of an increasingly accessible higher education. In addition, persisting and sociopolitically salient kinship ties and ethnic orientations do link people across class divisions and militate against the institutionalization of class ranks or anti-equalitarian beliefs.

Competition among professional and middle-class political leaders could conceivably prevent merchant-professional class domination.

99. On the relationship of the middle classes to coups in Latin America, see Jose Nun, "A Latin America Phenomenon: The Middle Class Military Coup," in *Latin America: Reform or Revolution*, ed. J. Petras and M. Zeitlin (New York: Fawcett, 1968), pp. 145–85. Nun suggests that the middle class, of which one representative group is the military officer corps, is in many cases threatened by the working classes as well as the old oligarchy; the vote is the principal instrument of the former. The army comes to the defense of the middle class "and allows for political instability in the defense of a premature process of democratization" which threatens the middle class (p. 147).

A large number of political parties proclaimed their existence after the NLC permitted the return of political activities as of May 1, 1969. It is too early to analyze these parties, but many are unlikely to last. Almost all are headed by professionals, mostly lawyers or businessmen. Building on old UP ties, Kofi Busia is the head of the new Progress Party, and many of the old UP leaders have joined him, though its leadership includes a very large percentage of Ashanti; the leadership of the Ashanti farmers' organization also supports Busia. Joe Appiah, also an Ashanti, an ambitious and popular attorney and politician, formerly a CPP and then, after 1954, an NLM and later still a UP leader, has split with Busia and formed the Nationalist Party. By mid-1969 it appeared to have less ex-UP leadership support but was making explicit overtures for northern and cocoa farmer backing. A much heralded "Third Force" had been organizing among leaders since mid-1966 in order to provide a new leadership without the old divisions between CPP and UP played out under different names in a new arena; it emerged, with less leading supporters than it had hoped for, as the All-People's Congress (APC), under the leadership of Dr. John Bilson, a medical doctor. The major competitor to Kofi Busia for political leadership has been Nkrumah's ex-lieutenant, Komla Gbedemah, who announced the formation of a National Alliance of Liberals party, drawing some of his major supporters from the right wing of the CPP. Among other parties which had announced themselves by mid-1969 were: the All People's Party, led by Dr. E. V. C. de Graft Johnson, a barrister; the People's Popular Party, with which a number of smaller groups quickly amalgamated, slated to be led by ex-CPP Minister Imoru Egala, from the Upper Region, who was banned from politics at the last moment and whose interim leader is Dr. William Lutterodt, a medical doctor; the Republican Party, led by P. K. K. Quaidoo, a businessman and former CPP minister who was dropped from Nkrumah's government in 1961 and later detained briefly; the Ghana Labour Party, without the support of the TUC and led by a trade unionist, Frank Wudu, which amalgamated itself with Quaidoo's Republican Party; a planned National Youth Party, led by a Takoradi businessman, J. K. Boison, which merged with the Ghana Democratic Party, led by John Alex Hamah, an ex-unionist and CPP dissident who has challenged with no success Bentum's leadership of the TUC; and four or five other parties, including a Black Power Party. The most important parties will probably be Busia's Progress Party and Gbedemah's National Alliance of Liberals, but the unwillingness of other parties to join any of the major ones may help to splinter professional-class leadership, whose tendency to factionalism was notable in the 1950's.

The second possible pattern would be the re-emergence of a populist party seeking to establish itself on a national basis, led by middle class and lower-middle class leaders. Like other parties, it would draw support from various traditional areas but would also seek to find common ground among farmers, wage laborers, petty-bourgeois elements (especially traders and primary school teachers), the unemployed and underemployed transitionals, and certain sectors of the middle class. Such a party would provide a dynamic impulse to extending political participation on a secular basis, a national basis for linking up parochial ties, and a populist developmental orientation to government policy.

On the basis of his CPP background, it was assumed that Komla Gbedemah was interested in building such a party. On the right wing of the CPP, a CPP opponent in exile after 1961, an economic moderate, and an entrepreneur, Gbedemah has support within the NLC, particularly from Police Inspector General Harlley, a fellow Ewe who is politically sensitive. Gbedemah appears to have retained popularity with the public; public opinion polls held in late 1968 and early 1969 showed Gbedemah the most favored to be the next head of government.[100] On the other hand, in mid-1969 there was no indication that Gbedemah had retained his populist orientation; his closest supporters were businessmen like himself, and the announced program of the National Alliance of Liberals, not to mention the name itself, did not reflect an interest in raising populist issues. In March, 1969, he indicated that he would consider joining forces with Busia. A grand coalition, in which political divisiveness was held to a minimum, would please many who dislike intense political competition and would certainly help to secure merchant-professional class political domination.[101]

None of the parties which had emerged by mid-1969 advocated socialism, though most spoke of a welfare state; this may be responsive to the current distaste for state enterprises but may also be indicative of the lack of interest in appealing to the propertyless

100. See polls appearing bimonthly in the *Weekly Spectator* (Accra), summary in *Ibid.*, March 8, 1969, p. 12; the latter figures, unlike the bimonthly polls, are not in percentages but in an unexplained "national total in points." Gbedemah received 214 "national points" out of a well-scattered 1300, with Busia second, and M. K. Apaloo and Joe Appiah third. The involvement of the Nigerian head of the polling agency, Jeafan, as the middle man in the Ankrah scandal may cast some doubt on the neutrality of the poll results.

101. Polls showed more than a majority desiring a coalition government of all parties.

and the dispossessed. Given the lack of a central overall issue to which people can respond over and above particularistic links and sentiments, such as the independence struggle, it will be difficult to form one or more genuinely national parties in Ghana. It will probably be even more difficult, at this time, to provide a single focus of discontent around which to rally the lower-middle class and transitionals in a powerful populist party.

The tendency of the military and police to intervene in the political arena once the NLC retires depends in part upon the levels of competence and conflict in the new political system and in part upon the orientations, interests, and coherence of these institutional groups. Since the police do not have the capability to intervene unilaterally, as does the military, comment will be devoted primarily to the military.

There is, at one level, a strong orientation against arbitrary government and authority and for democracy, an orientation held by part of the military and police which instills them with a sense of mission. An awareness of this sentiment could help set limits to political behavior by new political elites. But the orientation itself could also serve as a pretext for future intervention. Speaking to cadets at a passing-out parade at the Ghana Military Academy in late 1966, Ankrah exhorted that "as professional soldiers we are not interested in politics," but that "our pre-occupation . . . is to ensure that the people of this country . . . will no longer be subject to the caprice and domination of a single political party or individual." This concern imposes "additional responsibility" on the soldiers as "guardians of the freedom and liberty of the people."[102] A semipurist strain animated some NLC leaders in the early period of NLC rule, especially General Kotoka, which is not surprising given the manifest corruption in public life. The NLC indicated that economic recovery, an end to public corruption, and citizen education were necessary before civilian government could be restored.[103] An increasing appreciation of the dimensions and long-term nature of the problems involved as well as demands for an end to NLC rule induced the NLC to drop these conditions. But its sense of being a guardian of public life has remained.

To suggest that this is hardly the NLC's only orientation is not to underestimate its sense of mission. The NLC's investigation of accusations of corruption against General Ankrah and its decision to accept his resignation and elect Brigadier Afrifa as the new NLC

102. *Ghana News,* IV, no. 10 (Washington, D.C.: Embassy of Ghana, October, 1966), 7–8.
103. *West Africa,* April 1, 1967, p. 446.

chairman in late March, 1969, indicate its willingness to apply its strictures to itself, even to its great embarrassment.

Another primary military orientation is to order and stability. Should coercion and violence attend political competition in the future, the military may well feel far more disposed to intervene than it did in the past, and with less excuse. Respect for politicians among the military and police is not high. The promises of politicians are suspect, their inability to fulfill them and their self-enrichment anticipated. General Kotoka, before his death, thought that politicians talked too much and that the people required a strong guiding direction; he would have banned CPP leaders from public life for twenty years and was not sure when political parties should return, if at all.[104] It is likely that this view is representative among the military. As before, one of the military's primary roles will be to assist the police in maintaining internal security and order; its previous direct assumption of control has further habituated it to order rather than political competition and conflict, with all its attendant posturing, corruption, compromises, and social disorders.

Lastly, since military leaders assumed political authority, some have developed a taste for it. Though he often denied an interest in politics, General Ankrah's downfall stemmed from his ambition to be president and his acceptance of funds from foreign companies which he passed on to politicians to organize support for his candidacy; he was, in any case, the leading contender for the presidency. At various times it has been felt that Brigadier Afrifa was interested in a political future; his future plans have varied, and it would be surprising if he did not feel that he has something to contribute. It is equally clear that he has pushed hardest for a rapid return to civilian rule. However, the now-established precedent of a military route to political power in Ghana has already enticed some military men and will undoubtedly excite others.

Military belief that its professional autonomy and interests are being violated by politicians, the major source of the 1966 coup, is a possible source of future intervention. There may well be early conflicts in civil-military relations, to begin with over the military's proportion of the total budget, which has grown significantly, from a new high in 1965 of 8.4 per cent (estimated) to 9.4 per cent (estimated) in 1967–68 to 10.3 per cent (estimated) in 1968–69. Supporting this budget, Brigadier Afrifa, finance commissioner, said that "owing to the neglect suffered by our Armed Forces in the past,

104. Apter, "Nkrumah, Charisma, and the Coup," p. 789, n. 10; *West Africa,* April 22, 1967, p. 577.

it has become imperative to re-equip the entire army *to make it justify its existence.*"[105] Afrifa offered the hope that the military budget could be reduced in the future; a new civilian government might well wish this to be in the near future. This would threaten the expansion of the military and various of its building programs, which are proceeding apace. A new government might also wish to diversify Ghana's military dependence, as did Nkrumah, initially in a manner not objectionable to the military (i.e., ties with Common-wealth countries and Israel). Since the coup the Ghana military has renewed intimate ties with the British military.

The constitution provides protection to the military's sense of professional autonomy and interests; instead of a divided military, as Nkrumah attempted, civilian control will be divided. An Armed Forces Council under the control of the prime minister and government will guide policy, but the General Officer Commanding the Armed Forces (GOC), responsible for military administration and control, will be chosen by the president with the advice of his Council of State; the service chiefs will be chosen by the president on the advice of the Armed Forces Council. If General Ankrah had been elected president, the military would probably have felt that its fundamental interests were safe; with a civilian as president, there is less assurance.

A lack of coherence within the military itself lessens constraint upon military adventurism in the political sphere. The military's internal command and control capability was damaged, and ambitions and further plotting nurtured, by the break in the chain of command and the arrest of senior officers at the time of the 1966 coup and during later attempts, and by the gradual elimination of many senior officers: Defense Chief General S. J. A. Otu was left in retirement after the coup. General Barwah was killed and General Aferi retired; General Kotoka was killed in the April, 1967, *Putsch*, and General C. C. Bruce, then GOC, and Rear-Admiral Hansen were both sent abroad as military advisers to Ghanaian embassies due to their ineffective response to the *Putsch* attempt; Air Marshall Otu was arrested in late 1968 for allegedly plotting the overthrow of the NLC. The most popular and well-known officer, General Ankrah, was disgraced by involvement in a scandal. Sixteen officers placed in "protective detention" after the April, 1967, coup were not restored to their units, and some of the officers in the two battalions of Nkrumah's POGR were not reintegrated into the army. The head of the NLC is currently a 33-year-old brigadier, Afrifa. As in the

105. *West Africa,* July 27, 1968, p. 868, emphasis added.

Middle East and Latin America, internal dissidence and factionalism can lead to military intervention, particularly if dissident
political leaders seek support from the military, as occurred under
the Nkrumah regime and already under the NLC, with Nkrumah's
agents tempting some officers.

A fundamental problem of future civil-military relations concerns
how a civilian government can handle and maintain in a subordinate status a military and police which have been ruling directly
and retired willingly (with the country's thanks and blessing) when
the government is in part dependent upon the latter which possess
the instruments of coercion. The *Legon Observer* suggested in late
1968 that the "one remaining and historic moral duty" of NLC
members was their immediate retirement from their military and
police positions; it offered that the new parliament should immediately pass a bill retiring NLC members, not a measure designed to
win the affections of either service. This was discussed in the Constituent Assembly but is unlikely to occur.[106] Removing experienced
leaders who have known the frustrations as well as pleasures of
political authority would not solve the problem and might well
exacerbate it. In the same way, a civilian government cannot avoid
but will have to seek to contain the military and police as strong
institutional interest groups with a high level of access to decision-
makers.

There are no certain guarantees against military intervention.
The best assurance of civilian supremacy is a government that can
demonstrate that it has both popular and elective legitimacy and a
high level of capability. To say that Ghana, even with its present
debilitating economic problems, has as good a possibility of meeting
these criteria as any state in Africa is hardly a sanguine prognosis.
Its growing educational institutions, with a broad primary and
restricted secondary school base, are likely to spew forth far more
school leavers on the labor market than can be absorbed, and current estimates of unemployment—25 per cent among wage laborers
and 10 per cent of the total labor force—are without any doubt
understated. Ghana's enormously high population increase, currently estimated at 3 per cent, will only exacerbate this problem.
The political system can attempt to slow down the rate of social
change or to cope with the anticipations and expectations for jobs
and enhanced life chances which are the product of this social
change by finding new means of accelerating economic growth.
Political leaders will probably be compelled to opt for the second

106. *Legon Observer,* December 6, 1968, pp. 1–2.

alternative because they are unable to stem the tide of demands, but they currently appear indisposed to make vigorous use of governmental machinery to this end, given the disastrous economic experiences of the Nkrumah regime and the strong indigenous interests in behalf of private capital. All this only makes more difficult the basic problem that, in a developing country where the capabilities of the economic and political systems are quite limited and encounter serious structural problems, there is a high probability of conflict between constitutional legitimacy and stability, on the one hand, and democratization of political processes, i.e., the extension of active political participation, on the other. The economic, social, and political demands stemming from democratization and the political conflicts they generate are likely to have a destabilizing impact upon Ghana's fragile new institutions.

POSTSCRIPT

On October 1, 1969, the NLC handed over power to a civilian successor government, formed by the Progress Party (PP) under the leadership of Prime Minister Kofi Busia.

The overwhelming victory in the late August, 1969, election of the PP, whose leadership is almost wholly merchant-professional middle class in composition, confirms in part one of the two political patterns noted above as likely to emerge with the restoration of civilian rule. The ban against tribal-ethnic-regional parties as well as the large amount of support the PP leadership gathered at an early stage undoubtedly helped it to aggregate under its umbrella local and particularistic leaders and groups that would otherwise have supported other parties. Among the new PP leaders in Busia's cabinet are eight prominent former UP leaders, three former high-ranking civil servants (in finance, trade and industries, and as attorney-general), and among the newcomers are lawyers, a doctor, and a university professor. A large number of the PP assembly members have higher education and are members of the merchant-professional middle class.

The PP won the election by a wide margin, gaining 105 of the 140 Assembly seats and 59 per cent of the total vote, as compared to 29 seats and 30 per cent of the vote for Gbedemah's National Alliance of Liberals (NAL).

Three main factors can be adduced to explain the PP's overwhelming victory and the voting pattern. First, and probably most important, the PP leaders started with high post-coup public visi-

218

1969 GENERAL ELECTION: SEATS AND VOTES BY REGION

Region		PP		NAL		UNP[a]		APRP[b]		PAP[c]		Independents	
		Number of Seats	Percentage of Votes	Number of Seats	Percentage of Votes	Number of Seats	Percentage of Votes	Number of Seats	Percentage of Votes	Number of Seats	Percentage of Votes	Number of Seats	Percentage of Votes
Ashanti	22	22	77	—	17	—	2	—	—	—	1	—	2
Brong/Ahafo	13	13	85	—	14	—	1	—	—	—	—	—	—
Central	15	15	71	—	19	—	3	—	6	—	2	—	—
Eastern	22	18	59	4	33	—	2	1	1	—	1	—	2
Western	13	10	53	—	16	—	1	—	7	2	21	—	2
Greater Accra	9	3	36	3	32	2	23	—	—	—	4	1	5
Volta	16	2	18	14	77	—	3	—	—	—	1	—	1
Upper	16	13	56	3	34	—	2	—	2	—	3	—	21
Northern	14	9	48	5	43	—	2	—	3	—	3	—	2
Total Seats	140	105		29		2		1		2		1	
Total Percentage of Votes			59		30		4		2		3		2

a United Nationalist Party, led by Joe Appiah, won two seats in Accra.
b All People's Republican Party, led by P. K. K. Quaidoo, APRP's only winner.
c People's Action Party, led by Ayarna Imoru (from the North), won two seats in Nzima areas.

SOURCE: *The Legon Observer*, September 5, 1969.

bility in important roles under the NLC, were regarded as rightful heirs to the Nkrumah regime and NLC, looked like they would win, and thus benefited from a bandwagon effect from all those individuals and communities who wished to participate in the power, material, and status rewards of being on the winning side: a very secular cluster of reasons. Local candidates and conflicts played an important role in some constituencies, but in increasing or decreasing the PP plurality; the party designation appears to have been decisive in much of southern and central Ghana. Second, and related, the election results were in part a repudiation of the CPP: the PP was identified with Busia and opposition, the NAL with Gbedemah, and Gbedemah with the CPP. At least eight NAL candidates were former CPP leaders, and many former CPP local leaders were active in NAL election organizing. Third, the voting pattern in south and central Ghana showed a marked ethnic/cultural cleavage, with the Akan areas voting overwhelmingly for the PP (in Brong/Ahafo, Ashanti, and Central regions, to a lesser degree in the Western and Eastern regions), and the Ewe and some adjacent non-Akan areas voting strongly for the NAL (Volta region). The Akan, a linguistic/cultural rather than traditional state or ethnic grouping, were apparently responding to the diffuse fears of Ewe domination of national government (widely fanned by local PP leaders), noted above in terms of the predominant role of Ewes in the coup, the NLC, and, allegedly, top government positions under the NLC. As these fears and rumors multiplied and circulated, they contributed to the high anti-NAL sentiment and, in turn, provoked a previously unknown solidarity among the Ewe.

In the more parochial Northern and Upper regions, local factors and candidates were more important than the party label or anti-Ewe sentiment, and the vote was divided more evenly between the PP and NAL. The UNP, APRP, and PAP all fared poorly, contesting for only one-third to one-half of the seats and finding only local pockets of strength.

The PP is a large, loosely organized party, based largely upon the leadership support of local notables (including traditional leaders), the merchant-professional middle class, and, in some areas, ethnic youth associations. With the great power and patronage advantages that now accrue to it as government, it is possible that in the near future the PP will continue to enjoy the bandwagon effect, drawing in more support. It is, however, more liable to be subject to fragmentation, as different associational groups, interests, and communities become dissatisfied with their share of government allocations or with the depressed economic conditions. In 1968 GNP grew by only 0.8 per cent, while population increased by 3 per cent; investment declined by 3.5 per cent, largely because of continued decreases in government spending; about 25 per cent of the wage-labor force of 600,000 is unemployed, with employment in the non-wage-labor sector down also and over 300,000 people actively seeking wage employment.[107] The NAL has sufficient strength in several regions to look like a creditable alternative and thereby reap advantages from the PP government's distress.

A funny thing happened on the way to civilian rule. At the last moment, the NLC asked the Constituent Assembly to reconsider a motion to substitute for the presidency for five years a Presidential Commission composed of the chairman (Afrifa) and deputy chairman (Harlley) of the NLC and the Chief of Defense Staff (Ocran). The Assembly agreed to do so for a period not to exceed three years and at the next Parliament's discretion. Thus, a core of the NLC stays in office, though Brig. Afrifa has said that he will not go back to the army after his term of office and both Police Inspector-General Harlley and Police Commissioner A. K. Deku (both Ewe) have resigned their police positions. The NLC's reasons for pushing for this change are unknown, but this transitional arrangement may have some advantages for stability, in reassuring the military about its institutional interests and, perhaps, in keeping political activities within legitimate bounds. Leading members of the PP have made clear their determination that this will not become a permanent feature.

107. *West Africa,* November 1, 1969, p. 1318.

INTRODUCTION TO CHAPTER 5

FEW AFRICAN STATES have experienced revolution—sudden, violent reorganization of the political system and its leadership. Algeria, alone among the countries examined in this volume, experienced years of guerrilla warfare before independence. The struggle against France helped shape a revolutionary ideology, which has been explored by Frantz Fanon and other writers.

Rebellion broke out against the French government on November 1, 1954. The struggle escalated: French authorities arranged the kidnapping of Algerian leaders, including ben Bella; the Army of National Liberation (ALN) was created in 1956; a provisional government was established by the Algerians in 1958 to seek international recognition; intensified military operations led to regrouping the population and fortifying the Moroccan and Tunisian borders against raids by the external ALN; discontent among the French citizen population of Algeria led to the uprising of May 13, 1958, which toppled the Fourth Republic; United Nations debates became increasingly more heated. Finally, following protracted negotiations, the de Gaulle regime and the provisional Algerian government reached agreement on independence, granted July 3, 1962.

Born in unrest, Algeria has continued to suffer from violence and uncertainty. As Professor Zartman notes, the dismissal of leading ALN members less than a week before independence catalyzed a struggle for power. The ALN, its roots deep in the social context, shared in the mystique of revolutionary legitimacy with the FLN, the dominant political movement; indeed, the two were difficult to disentangle. However, the legitimacy born of revolution is unstable,

222

and the interpretations of its precise objectives diverse. Revolutionary ideology, with its emphasis upon national unity and popular identity, has both eased and complicated the building of support for the Algerian government.

During the first six years of independence, segments of the Algerian armed forces have been involved in abortive rebellions every year except 1966. The complex, intramilitary maneuvering that has characterized recent Algerian history grew, in large measure, from the clandestine organization of the ALN—a secrecy necessary for its success when it was under attack by the French. The conversion of the ALN into a technologically efficient, professional army has proved difficult; the splits between the interior and exterior ALN, the continuation of regional (*wilaya*) loyalties, and uncertainty about "the Revolution" have plagued reorganization efforts.

The overthrow of President ben Bella by Houari Boumedienne in mid-1965 apparently occurred to protect the "professional" interests of the army, to keep it from total domination by ben Bella and the FLN. Ben Bella was the consummate politician. Incarcerated by the French during most of the revolution, he had quickly moved into command after independence by rising above the battles among the provisional government, the ALN and its *wilaya* commanders, and similar groups. Collaboration between Boumedienne and ben Bella withstood many strains, until ben Bella offended both the "professional" army, by encouraging formation of a militia, and Boumedienne, by moving against the "Oudja" group with whom Boumedienne was closely associated. Boumedienne now faces the task of building legitimacy for his government on a more stable foundation than "the Revolution" and the demands for consumption which it helped to inspire.

C.E.W.

5.

The
Algerian Army
in Politics

I. William Zartman

New York University

PRINCIPLES

Politics in Algeria is revolutionary. This means essentially five things:

1. There is no *legitimacy* outside of revolutionary symbols, groups, and policies.[1] "The Revolution" is invoked by any govern-

This chapter is a completely revised version of a paper originally presented at the Princeton University Conference on the Middle East, 1965. This study is based on interviews with Algerian political and military personnel and French and American diplomatic and military personnel in Algeria, and also on research in current sources, notably *Le Monde* (Paris), *el-Moudjahid* (Algiers), *al-Djeich* (Algiers), *Jeune afrique* (Tunis), *Maghreb* (Paris), *Annuaire de l'Afrique du nord* (Aix-en-Provence), and other sources. Specific attribution is not given when so requested by the source or in establishing the general train of events. This study is part of a project directed by the author at the Center for International Studies of New York University, on Revolution in Developing Countries.

1. See, particularly, Jean Leca, "Le Nationalisme algérien depuis l'indépendance," in *Les Nationalismes maghrebins,* ed. Louis-Jean Duclos, Fondation

ment seeking to legitimize its incumbency, to which the opposition responds by decrying the betrayal of the Revolution and by promising a return to it. Contenders for power come from among those who have participated in the revolutionary war, in combat or in prison, and who have thus established a mystical bond between themselves and the people, through which the needs and desires of the mass are "known" and represented. Any political criteria for policies are couched in terms of bringing the fruits of the Revolution to the parts of the population most closely identified with it and represented by their spokesmen; although any precise definition of revolutionary expectations will probably be absent, they do include political positions as well as economic improvements, thus completing the circle.

Since legitimacy of this sort is basically unstable, and does not derive from more durable sources such as institutions or a history of satisfactions, governments so legitimized are continually in need of proving their right to rule and are inherently beleaguered and defensive.

2. The revolutionary war gave rise to a strong millennialist feeling, including immediate *expectations* for the fruits of the Revolution.[2] Those who participated in the war expected things to be better after it was over: in a typically ambiguous set of feelings, they expected to be rid of the disruptive and humiliating foreigner in order to return to their life undisturbed, but also in order to benefit from social change and economic improvement. In addition, they expected an immediate inheritance of the visible goods of modern life in Algeria, and accession to the newly vacated positions of power, prestige, and employment. The latter set of expectations was easier to achieve than the former, and in time conflicted with it. Visible goods were immediately inherited through the peasant land seizure that began in late 1962, was legalized by the March, 1963, decrees, and was gradually transformed into broad nationalization of agriculture and industry. Participants in the war occupied vacant positions, only to find—after a suitable period of enjoyment—that their

---

nationale des sciences politiques, Etude maghrébine no. 7 (Paris: 1966), pp. 61–82; Hisham B. Sharabi, *Nationalism and Revolution in the Arab World* (New York: Van Nostrand, 1966) esp. pp. 82–92; Leonard Binder, *The Ideological Revolution in the Middle East* (New York: Wiley, 1964), esp. pp. 179–82; and Donald E. Weatherbee, *Ideology in Indonesia,* Yale University Southeast Asia Studies, Monograph series no. 8 (New Haven: 1966), esp. pp. 1–19. See also speech of Mohammed Cherif Messaadia to the 1964 party congress on the ideologues' and the technocrats' views.

2. There has been much less attention devoted to this aspect of revolution, unfortunately. See, however, Herbert Feith, *The Decline of Constitutional Democracy in Indonesia* (Ithaca: Cornell University Press, 1962).

deprivation under colonial rule and their experience in fighting the revolutionary war were not always useful in running farms and factories (particularly in commercializing their products and maintaining their equipment) or in improving the lot of the people from positions of government and party leadership. Worse, other Algerians—urban ideologues and technocrats—told those who participated in the war of their incompetence. The ideologues sought an immediate stopgap in ideological explanations of current shortages and doctrinaire assurances of a clear road to future prosperity; divided between government and opposition, they were chased out by, then with, ben Bella. The technocrats are more pragmatic and more useful to the effective running of a state mechanism, but their effectiveness is based on stable government and sufficient time, a point on which they are weaker than the ideologues.

The dilemma then remains: expectations are both high and immediate, two characteristics that are not propitious for their satisfaction; impatient reactions growing out of dissatisfaction create instability that retards effective government even more and reemphasizes the importance of the army.

3. If *power in* such a situation does not grow directly out of the barrel of a gun, it does grow out of possession of a gun.[3] Politics has been escalated closer to violence as a result of war and political change. The military, by its structure as a disciplined body, by its command and presumed monopoly of force, by its composition as a national organization, and by its position as successor to the nationalist guerrillas, plays a predominant role in determining who rules and who revolts.

The National Peoples Army (ANP) is in a poor position to rule by itself; its aims are limited, its numbers small, and the more emphasis it places on its nature as a professional army, the more its own legitimacy is contestable. However, it does feel it has a mission as watchdog on the Revolution, a role that is minimal in "good times," that leads to intervention in the political process when the Revolution is not being carried out, and that is ambiguous in between. Because of this situation, factional splits within the ANP are of primary significance, and there is no question of a civilian-controlled, apolitical army existing in Algeria for some time.

At the same time, the raw and ultimate nature of power in revolutionary Algeria means that no governmental change can take place against the army, or without the army being involved. Its military

3. See Chalmers Johnson, *Revolutionary Change* (Boston: Little Brown, 1966), esp. pp. 7–14; Frantz Fanon, *Les Damnés de la terre* (Paris: Maspero, 1961), esp. pp. 29–79.

nature makes the army the best organized and only truly national (i.e., drawing from the entire population) group in the country; its organization gives it special interests to watch over and defend; its successor relation to the ALN makes it the strongest political institution to grow out of the Revolution; and its past performance and beliefs (viz., Fanonism) shows it unafraid to use its power to defend the Revolution or its own interests. No other organization has these strengths; the only current competitor to the army is one of its parts.

4. The *political system* is being redefined.[4] This poses dual, and also somewhat incompatible, needs. On one hand, there is pressure for institutionalizing or state-building. New bodies and procedures must be established to carry out governmental and political processes, that is, to make decisions on the allocation of goods and services in society and to establish channels for the integration of the population through political participation and identification. On the other hand, there is pressure for socializing or nation-building. The war and the Revolution excluded collaborators, Messalistes, bourgeois, and profiteers from the political system. The war and the Revolution also consecrated the downtrodden, exploited mass as the reference point of the new political system. Since this mass is not a class, ethnic group, or region, but is largely undifferentiated in political thought, and since the revolutionary situation creates pressures for rapid, assertive definition of the political system (there is not time to build consensus on precedent or demonstrative bases), concepts such as national unity and general will become important. Thus every leader has to show that he represents all the people; plurality and divisions must be overcome or destroyed; opposition is treasonous and the work of enemies. The fact that the politicization of Algerian society in a clandestine situation during the revolutionary war tended to focus action and identification on organizational, regional, functional, and personal fragments of the nationalist movement only increased the need to think in terms of national unity.

5. Criteria for entry into the *political class* are changing from wartime experience to technical competence. By far most numerous in the political class of the 1960's are the *mujahidin;* and since they joined the fight when young, they die off only slowly. *Mujahidin* are simply "those who fought" in the *wilayas*, the external army, France, etc., with any more precise identification difficult and per-

4. See Samuel Huntington, "Political Development and Political Decay," *World Politics* XVII (1965), 386–430; James Heaphey, "The Organization of Egypt," *World Politics* XVIII (1966), 177–93.

haps unrewarding. More important is the fact that they know who they are, which reinforces localistic politics and personal loyalties. The *mujahidin* form a sort of inchoate party, or a political society-within-society, and they attempt to occupy all possible positions of power, both as their reward for their exertions (*jihad*) and as a base from which to enact programs to continue these rewards. The background of this group is generally rural, as is the focus of many of its demands; this point is also a basic source of alienation from the urban proletariat and the technicians. The *mujahidin,* however, have the legitimacy but not the skills—political or technical—to govern alone.

The technicians are far fewer, less coherent as an interest group, less clear in their leadership, and devoid of any mass organization behind them. They are better armed with skills, and their training and view of the needs of the state give them a sense of mission (but also sometimes a sense of right and personal enrichment as strong as those of the *mujahidin*). But they do not have the support or the legitimacy to govern by themselves.

Governing over this sort of dichotomized political class requires mediating leaders, or brokers,[5] who can combine skills and legitimacy to meet expectations. The brokers are more a role than a group, open to be filled by those who can reconcile the other two elements. *Mujahidin* or technicians may be political brokers, but in so acting they lose some of their former character as they seek to work with both elements. The brokers' base of power has none of the narrow, fraternal character of the two other elements; it is necessarily broader and more "national," but also necessarily less direct. Their power derives from their ability to use and satisfy the political class and expectant mass in Algerian revolutionary society. Hence, the brokers are both necessary and vulnerable. They are dependent on the satisfaction of the other elements of the political class, neither of whom can themselves govern alone but who can remove the incumbent brokers indirectly by withdrawing their support or directly by overthrowing them.

both mujahidin & technicians

The army spans this class. Officers from the interior National Liberation Army (ALN) who fought the guerrilla war often see the peacetime ANP as a means of watching over the Revolution and over the interests of them who fought for it. Another group of officers, however, came from the external ALN, which organized and trained

5. The term is used differently from the "horizontal" concept, as for example in Lucian Pye, "The Non-Western Political Process," in *International Politics and Foreign Policy,* ed. James N. Rosenau (New York: Free Press, 1961), pp. 293–94, originally appearing in *Journal of Politics.*

in bases in Tunisia and Morocco during the war; their experience is
in forming a regular army, not in guerrilla warfare, and some of
them had French military experience. Their numbers are slowly
swelled by newly trained junior officers, many of whom share the
same training experiences and a feeling of solidarity with technicians in the civil service. This group also considers itself to be a
watchdog over the Revolution—but a Revolution whose continual
progress is assured by competent management; in addition, it is
interested in developing a technically competent army, and in
watching over the interests of this army, as necessary, with the
government.

Leaving aside the Provisional Executive and Provisional Government (GPRA) of 1962, Algeria has known two bodies of brokers:
the ben Bella group and the Boumedienne (Oujda) group. The
second, closer to both the *mujahidin* and the technicians (but
especially to the technicians) than was the first, came to power
because the ben Bella group was unable to satisfy—and in fact
threatened—the two basic elements of the Algerian political class.
If there is a single line that can be discerned through the actions of
Colonel Houari Boumedienne[6] since March, 1962, it is interest in
the specific task of running the army with like-minded members of
the external ALN, through the encouragement of young professional
officers (technicians) and the training of older officers (*mujahidin*)
into professionals, and dedication to the general task of defending
the Revolution. To accomplish this, Boumedienne and his political
associates must be among the brokers, and the other (non-army)
brokers must admit the same aims. Army officers need be placed in
the civilian administration only to the extent necessary to protect
these aims. When the professional control and development of the
army are threatened by the government, however, the army must
intervene actively to protect its interests, and secondarily, the
interest of the Revolution, for the army is the microcosm of the
political class (and hence of the Revolution) and has the means of

6. Boumedienne: born 1925 at Guelma (between Annaba and Constan-
tine), studied Arabic literature at the Zitouna (Tunis) and al-Azhar
(Cairo), MTLD of Messali Hajj, schoolteacher in Guelma, joined FLN in
Cairo 1954, entered *wilaya* V (Oranie) from Morocco 1955, *wilaya* V com-
mander 1957, commanded western Algeria from Morocco 1958, ALN General
Staff and then chief of staff 1960, created external ALN, CNRA, fired by
GPRA 1962, defense minister 1962, FLN Central Committee and Political
Bureau 1964, chairman of Revolutionary Council 1965. On Boumediennne's
views, skilfully expressed, see his speech before the 1964 party congress. On the
guardian role or supermission of armies, see Samuel Huntington, *Political
Order in Changing Societies* (New Haven: Yale University Press, 1968), pp.
225–27, 232.

deciding revolutionary politics. With the government in "sure" hands, the army officers can then return to the task of building up their own organization. Under this line of thought, the political and military roles of the army can be understood, even if not easily separated. Twice the army has installed a regime that is essentially civilian (although involving *mujahidin*); in both cases it acted to preserve its own group interests.

HISTORY

The Army of National Liberation[7] was created by the Soummam Congress of the National Council of the Algerian Revolution (CNRA) on August 20, 1956.[8] Over the preceding two years, small terrorist bands had grown into an extended guerrilla force requiring internal organization and external coordination. Categories of soldiers, partisans, guerrillas, supporters, and sympathizers existed on paper but were not separated in reality (producing wide variance in estimates of size). The Soummam Congress fixed ranks (to colonel), established units, created 6 territorial divisions (*wilayas* or provinces, and their subdivisions) and devised new categories (*mujahidin*, or combatants; *musabilin*, or partisans; *fidayin*, or terrorists). It also established a command structure, placing the ALN under the military department of the Executive Coordinating Committee through an East and West Committee for Military

7. The following is not a political history of independent Algeria, but an explanation of the military role in that history. For various treatments of independent Algerian politics, see Davis C. Gordon, *The Passing of French Algeria* (New York: Oxford University Press, 1966); Arslan Humbaraci, *Algeria: The Revolution that Failed* (New York: Praeger, 1966); William H. Lewis, "Algeria Changes Course," *Africa Report*, November 1965, p. 8; and "Algeria Against Herself," *Africa Report*, December 1967, p. 9; Gerard Chaliand, *L'Algérie est-elle socialiste?* (Paris: Maspero, 1965); Hervé Bourges, *L'Algérie à l'épreuve du pouvoir* (Paris: Grasset, 1967). The best articles on the Algerian army are by Jean Lecouture, "Anatomie d'une armée," *Le Monde*, July 14, 1965, and by Gerard Viratelle, "Le Régime militaire algérien," *Révue française d'études politiques africaines* XXXVIII (1969), 63–78. See also *Le Monde*, June 20, 1965; David Wood, *The Armed Forces of African States*, Institute for Strategic Studies, Adelphi Papers, no. 27 (London: 1966), p. 5; Daniel Guerin, "Un état dans un état: l'Armée," *Combat*, January 25, 1964.

8. Greater details can be found in Jacques Duchemin, *Histoire du FLN* (Paris: Table Ronde, 1962); Paul A. Jureidini, *Case Studies in Insurgency and Revolutionary Warfare: Algeria, 1954–1962* (Washington: Special Operations Research Office, 1963); Mohammed Bedjaoui, *Law and the Algerian Revolution* (Brussels: International Association of Democratic Lawyers, 1961), among others.

Operations (East covering *wilayas* 1–3, and West covering *wilayas* 4–6). With the establishment of a Provisional Government (GPRA), the military department became a ministry under Belqasim Krim in September, 1958, and then an Interministerial War Committee composed of Krim, Abdelhafid Boussouf, and Lakhdar Bentobbal in January, 1960. At the same time (CNRA Tripoli Congress of December, 1959), the Committees for Military Operations East and West, with their bases of operations in Morocco (Oujda) and Tunisia (Ghardimaou), were combined into a single General Staff, headed in March, 1960 (after what appears to have been a period of organization), by Boumedienne, the former head of *wilaya* V and then of one of the Committees for Military Operations. Throughout the war, *wilaya* commanders were formally appointed by the Executive Coordinating Committee or its successor upon proposal by the *wilayas*, but again this formal rule often covered some exceptional tensions and negotiations.

The Soummam Congress had affirmed the basic primacy of the interior over the exterior and the military over the political, but these two principles were both unrealistic and contradictory. At best the *wilayas* tended toward autonomy (from each other as well as from the exterior), but dependence on the outside for armaments and worsening military fortunes produced strains. After the *quadrillage* tactics of the French army, combined with the fortified barriers at either end of the country, had become effective in 1958, ALN heavy units were broken down into light, mobile commando groups, and the main force of the army moved outside the country to the Tunisian and Moroccan sanctuary, where after 1960 the General Staff began in earnest to build up a conventional army. During the last two years of the war, the military had effectively ceded its primacy to the political: the ALN drilled, the *wilayas* sniped, but the GPRA negotiated. Thus, even before independence, contrary practices and expectations were created among the military.

If *mujahidin*, *musabilin*, and *fidayin* are counted as ALN, there was little rank and file to the FLN outside army. Already by 1958, the FLN in Algeria had come to be the GPRA (and its subordinate organs) plus the ALN. Thus, at independence, Algeria had an army and its supporters-sympathizers, but no civilian mass organization or party. During the war, the army had been recruited on a volunteer basis by the unit commanders; although highly motivated by patriotism or adventure, its feelings of allegiance and loyalty (or rivalry and rebellion) were focused on the local, *wilaya* level, and were heightened by the clandestine nature of internal operations and the difficulty of maintaining a balanced relation between interior and exterior. This gives a very different type of identification and motivation than a nationally conscripted and organized army. By the end of the war, the figures generally accepted (with the usual reservations) were 35,000 members of the external army in Tunisia (25,000) and Morocco (10,000), and 15,000 *mujahidin* and between 50,000 and 100,000 *musabilin* and *fidayin* inside Algeria. The immediate postwar figure of 130,000 (out of a total population of 11 million) is therefore not a very surprising inflation, if at all, although it was clearly too large a military population for the polity to use or the economy to support

Thus, the political position of the army at the end of the war involved two major issues: "reconversion" (including reduction) to a single conventional military force, and the relation of that force to a civilian government. The latter was merely a continuation of the wartime internal-external and political-military problems, and it broke out into the open at the moment of Algerian independence when, on June 30, 1962, the GPRA sacked the three leading members of the ALN general staff—Boumedienne, Ahmed Qaid ("Sliman"),[9] and Ali Menjli[10]—and another ALN colonel. The incident, which turned catalyst in the struggle for power over the new state, was followed by a period of several weeks during which all sides lined up their forces (while others sought to mediate). Acting to defend its interests, the external ALN joined Ahmed ben Bella, who from headquarters in Tlemcen proceeded to win over the *wilayas.*

Two border *wilayas* joined the Tlemcen forces, through Boumedienne's close contact with *wilayas* I (Colonel Tahar Zbiri)[11]

9. Qaid: born 1921 at Tiaret (between Oran and Algiers), studied in the military school (Hussein-Dey) and normal school (Algiers), municipal councilor in Tiaret, joined UDMA of Ferhat Abbas 1951, joined FLN 1956, commanded southern sector in *wilaya* V 1958, western Algeria command 1959, General Staff 1960, CNRA, negotiated Evian Accords 1962, fired by GPRA 1962 and arrested by Krim, elected to assembly from Tiaret 1962 and 1964, Minister of Tourism 1963, resigned 1964, Central Committee and Political Bureau FLN 1964, Revolutionary Council 1965, finance minister 1965, FLN party executive 1967.

10. Menjli: ALN General Staff 1960, negotiated Evian Accords 1962, fired by GPRA 1962, elected to assembly from Constantine 1962 and 1964, vice-president of assembly FLN Central Committee and Political Bureau 1964, Revolutionary Council, 1965.

11. Zbiri: born 1930 at Souq Ahras (near Tunisia), worked in Ouenza iron mines 1964, MTLD of Messali Hajj, battalion commander in Tunisia 1958, CNRA, commander *wilaya* I (Aures) 1958, supported ben Bella and led drive against *wilaya* IV 1962, FLN Central Committee and Political Bureau 1964, ANP chief of staff, 1964, Revolutionary Council 1965, revolted and fled to Tunisia 1967–68.

and V (Major Ahmed Boujenan ["Abbas"])[12] and ben Bella's with *wilaya* V (Colonel Bouhajar ben Haddou ["Othman"]).[13] Similarly, ben Bella established a close personal relationship with the commander of *wilaya* VI (Colonel Mohammed Chaabani).[14] The remaining *wilayas* were truer to both their nature as warlord fiefs and to general *wilayist* views: because both formed cohesive power centers in their own right, *wilayas* III (Colonel Akli ["ou al-Hajj"])[15] and IV (Colonel Yussef Khatib ["Hassan"])[16] stood out against both reconversion and the dominant power coalition.

At the same time, the ALN of all persuasions, under the pretext of combating the diehard colonials' Secret Armed Organization (OAS), spread over the countryside into areas where it had never before operated, some of which had been occupied by the French army (now withdrawn to its barracks) and some of which were the bailiwick of other *wilaya* units. In late July, the external ALN took over part of *wilaya* II, leading to a split in the allegiance and territory of the *wilaya* for two weeks until an agreement could be signed separating military from political affairs within the *wilaya* and handing over the former to the external ALN ally (Major Larbi ben Rejem ["Larbi"]).[17]

12. Boujenan: born 1934?, joined FLN 1954, deputy commander *wilaya* V 1957, commander military region II (*wilaya* V) 1963, commander Cherchell Military Academy 1964, General Staff 1964, FLN Central Committee 1964, Revolutionary Council 1965, died in auto accident 1968.

13. ben Haddou: born 1927, tailor, joined FLN-CRUA 1954, CNRA, commander *wilaya* V 1962, commander military region II (*wilaya* V) 1962, FLN Coordinator Oran 1963, arrested by Boumedienne and released by ben Bella 1963, FLN Central Committee 1964, elected to the assembly from Oran 1964, president Veterans Association 1965, Revolutionary Council 1965.

14. Chaabani: born 1930, commander *wilaya* VI (Sahara), supported ben Bella in drive against *wilaya* IV 1962, commander military region IV (*wilaya* VI) 1963, ANP General Staff 1964, FLN Central Committee and Political Bureau 1964, revolted and executed 1964.

15. Ou al-Hajj: born 1911 in Kabylia, elementary education, soldier in French Army, deputy commander *wilaya* III (Kabylia) 1958, commander *wilaya* III 1959, commander military region VII (*wilaya* III) 1962, joined Ait Ahmed's FFS in dissidence but returned during Moroccan border war 1963, FLN Central Committee and Political Bureau 1964, elected to assembly from Kabylia 1964, Revolutionary Council 1965, FLN Executive Committee 1965, sided with Zbiri 1967, retired.

16. Khatib: born 1933 in al-Asnam (Orleansville), son of office clerk, attended medical school (Algiers), led students' strike 1956, entered ALN medical service *wilaya* IV (Algerois), commander *wilaya* IV 1962, elected to assembly from al-Asnam 1962, FLN Central Committee and Political Bureau 1964, Revolutionary Council 1965, FLN Executive Committee and medical studies 1965, sided with Zbiri 1967, physician in Algiers 1968.

17. Ben Rejem: born 1924, deputy to Boubnider in *wilaya* II (Constantinois) 1962, took over *wilaya* II for ben Bella 1962, commander VI military region (*wilaya* II) 1962, relieved 1963, imprisoned 1964–65, military attache to Moscow 1965. On the problems of *wilaya* II, see Bourges, *L'Algérie*, p. 67.

The *wilayas'* alliance with the politicians of the Tlemcen group, however, was only tactical. In line with their ideas of who should hold power, they sought at the same time to set up their own political group in order to dominate the political scene and mediate between the contending groups. The *wilayas'* conference, in Tlemcen and Orleansville (al-Asnam), 16–21 July, broke down over the choice of a representative for *wilaya* III on the brokers' group (Political Bureau), thus undoing the *wilayas'* claim to power. The *wilayists* were too busy trying to defend their individual fiefs to unite against the centralized coalition around ben Bella.[18] When the Tlemcen group was able to cut the same knot in its favor (replacing Krim by Said Mohammedi ["Nasser"][19] as *wilaya* III representative on the Political Bureau), the Bureau was set up and on 3 August was installed in Algiers. The agreement was reached by compromise, against the wishes of Boumedienne's army group who wished to enter Algiers by force and who had already sought to solve the crises by kidnapping opposing leaders.

A show of force by the external ALN and allied *wilayas*, and popular fatigue with the month of crisis, led the politicians to unite to hold power, and then to consolidate their position by announcing the rapid reconversion of the ALN as one of the Political Bureau's priority tasks. To Boumedienne, reconversion meant consolidation of a military establishment. To the *wilayas*, however, reconversion meant exclusion from power, and so *wilayas* III and IV again entered into dissidence. The spokesman for *wilaya* IV was clearly opposed to Boumedienne's views when he announced, "We are against a classic type army, in other words a professional army, an unproductive army, a drain on the country's budget."[20] Nevertheless, the Political Bureau was able to call upon the *wilayas* committed to it (I, II, V, and VI), under the control of the external ALN, to restore its authority, and, on September 9, ALN forces entered Algiers. In the two months that the army had been fighting itself, it was not the external ALN but the *wilaya* forces rallying to

18. An excellent portrayal and analysis of the 1962 events is Jean-Claude Douence, *La Mis en place des institutions algériennes*, Fondation nationale des sciences politiques, Étude maghrébine, no. 2 (Paris: 1964), esp. pp. 51–59. Cf. Regis Debray, *Revolution in the Revolution?* (New York: Grove Press, 1967), pp. 78, 95, 106.
19. Mohammedi: joined Axis French Volunteers Legion in World War II, commander *wilaya* III 1958, CNRA, General Staff for western Algeria 1958, GPRA 1960, Political Bureau 1962, elected to the assembly from the Kabylia 1962 and 1964, Veterans Minister 1962, vice-president 1963, FLN Central Committee and Political Bureau 1964, Revolutionary Council 1965.
20. Lieutenant Allouache in *Le Monde*, August 13, 1962.

ben Bella and Boumedienne that swung the decisive weight for the Political Bureau against the holdouts in *wilayas* III and IV.

Re-establishment of the Political Bureau was again a result of compromise, if also of military action. While the troops of Boumedienne fought against *wilaya* IV, the emissaries of ben Bella negotiated. The Political Bureau was thus able to bring in *wilaya* support under the protection of the external ALN, while the latter's pro-regime activities only increased the antimilitary feelings of the interior forces; as a result, the Political Bureau increased its options of allies and the military increased its dependence on the Political Bureau. It was not until September 23 that the Political Bureau allowed Boumedienne to occupy large areas of *wilaya* IV and seclude its forces; fighting continued as late as December. Not until over a year later, under more rigorous circumstances, did the ANP finally move into *wilaya* III.

The same maneuvering for positions and settling of accounts by the bureau and the army was evident within the new institutions. On the list of candidates for the National Assembly, drawn up during the August truce, ALN members received 72 of the 196 seats, allocated by the General Staff and the *wilayas*. The list included two *wilaya* commanders and five other colonels, 25 majors, 25 captains, 12 lieutenants, one officer-candidate, and 2 soldiers. On the second list, revised early in the month when the elections were postponed to 20 September, the ALN list was pared to 59. *Wilaya* members were replaced by officers of the external ALN, many of them little known. Not only *wilayas* II and IV, which had (in whole or in part) opposed the Political Bureau, but also *wilaya* V, were reduced by the General Staff; yet *wilaya* III remained in a favorable position. When the assembly opened, ALN deputies tried to gain dominant positions in the new institutions. An alternate slate of candidates for the assembly's bureau, made up largely (in its final form) of external ALN officers, was defeated in a sharp debate. Former ALN members also sought to obtain preferential treatment for former *mujahidin*. A majority of the assembly's defense commission was made up of ALN officers (although few of them remained in uniform as ANP officers). No sooner was the new assembly in its chambers than differences began to appear between the civilian politicians and the military-*mujahidin* group.

To this point, it is difficult to speak of "the military" or "an army," just as it would be inaccurate to designate Washington, Hamilton, and Monroe as the "military in politics." It is possible only to speak of inchoate groups, and then with care. Several hundred officers about Boumedienne began to emerge as the nucleus of the "new army," designated the National Peoples Army (ANP) in late 1962. This nucleus was built around the general staff and officers of the external ALN but even this was not a homogeneous group. Some 250 of the ANP had been commissioned or noncommissioned officers in the French army. Others had had interior careers before reaching Ghardimaou or had temporary interior assignments from the exterior. To this external nucleus were added leaders and lesser officers from the interior. There is no single thread that ties together all these forces, unless it be their own political estimate of (1) who would win in the power struggle, and (2) whose victory would most advance their aims. Obviously, unity built on a common conclusion in these terms is unstable.

Furthermore, those considered "military" up to this point, while remaining in the political class, frequently moved out of uniform and into "civilian" politics and administration, although in politics they retained their regional base, dominating local and influencing national affairs through their *wilayas*. This was accomplished by their taking over the local FLN and administrative organization and the police, rather than through the army, since the ANP was being organized to minimize *wilayist* influence and particularism. Of the 59 ALN deputies in the Constituent Assembly, only 7 are identifiable in later military roles. Thus, even if the sympathies of ex-ALN members for the ANP point of view is recognized, the professional ANP—as distinguished from the *mujahidin* in and out of uniform—was poorly represented in state organs.

The *wilayas'* paramilitary threat to the army and particularist threat to the central government remained, and it was in the interests of both the ANP and the brokers to bring the *mujahidin* under central control. Yet the position of the *mujahidin* was maintained in November, 1962, in the creation of seven new military regions, a potentially important aspect of reconversion. The regions coincided largely with the old *wilayas, wilaya* VI suffering most by being cut up into two military regions (III and IV). *Wilayism* was not restricted to those who had opposed the Political Bureau and/or the external ALN. Generally, the defense ministry was unable to control its military regions, and—whether for political or military purposes—unable to exert its authority over their commanders. Major ben Rejem, who had come from *wilaya* I to capture Constantine in July in collusion with the external ALN and had been rewarded with the military leadership of *wilaya* II and then the command of the military region VI, was recalled and finally ousted in February, 1963, for insubordination; his demands had included, above all, more spoils for the *mujahidin*. If ben Rejem was difficult to dislodge,

Colonels Zbiri and Chaabani were worse; their contacts with the central government went directly to ben Bella without passing through defense channels, and Boumedienne's efforts to move them were unavailing. It was not until the appointment of Majors Abdelghani[21] and Boujenan in late 1962 and 1963 to head military regions I and II (*wilayas* IV and V), respectively, that these two regions were brought under the defense ministry's control, and then only because their predecessors—Colonels Khatib and ben Haddou—were removed for insubordination. However, ben Haddou did not remain removed, and between 1963 and 1965 was an object of contest between Boumedienne, who obtained his removal, and ben Bella, who had him restored to Oran. Defense control over the remaining military regions was tenuous. A meeting in Constantine in June, 1963, protested not only pay arrears but also favoritism and promotions bestowed on ex-*wilaya* troops at the expense of former external ALN soldiers.

When Boumedienne was able to crack down on dissidence, he seized the occasion. In early August, 1963, in the absence of ben Bella, he ordered a rapid military operation against insurgents at Dra al-Mizan, and later in the month the ANP struck against remnants of *wilaya* IV. When the dissidence of the Kabylia broke out in September, 1963, it was merely an extreme case on the local level of the same *wilayism* (reinforced by Berber ethnic separatism and by government inattention to a poor region), combined on the national level with an opposition movement to the Political Bureau. Dissidents mingled indistinguishably with the local population, and military operations were restrained on both sides. Although Zbiri and Said Abid[22] were appointed chief of staff and new head of military region VII (*wilaya* III) by ben Bella on 1 October, the day after Boumedienne had left for Moscow, Zbiri did not send the troops into action, and the ANP started fighting only on 10 October, four days after Boumedienne's return. The army moved gingerly into the

21. Abdelghani: born 1932?, served in French army, *wilaya* V, commander military region I (*wilaya* IV) 1962, division commander 1964, commander military region IV (*wilaya* VI) 1965, Revolutionary Council 1965, commander military region V (*wilayas* I and II), 1968. (Note that because his first names are Mohammed ben Hamed, Abdelghani is universally confused in Revolutionary Council listings with Major "Moussa" [Mohammed ben Hamed], who never was a member of the council but rather remained in jail until 1966).

22. Abid: born 1933 in Kenchela (Aures), son of a poor bus-driver, attended secondary school in Constantine, joined FLN at Batna (Aures) 1954, fought in *wilaya* I (Aures), deputy of Zbiri in *wilaya* I 1962, commander military region V (*wilaya* I) 1963, commander military region VII 1963, commander military region I (*wilayas* IV and III) 1964, judge military court 1964, Revolutionary Council 1965, captor of ben Bella 1965, suicide ? 1967.

dissident regions of *wilayas* III and IV, under orders to fire only in self-defense, while the central government organized meetings for political "re-education" and made dramatic gestures (nationalization of all colonial lands on October 1).

Two events permitted the liquidation of the Kabyle dissidence. One was the outbreak of hostilities with Morocco on October 8, 1963. The military action on the Algerian side was run, as far as possible, as a professional military campaign, with little coordination with Algiers. Boumedienne established his headquarters in Colomb-Bechar after taking the last strategic point in the Kabylia; he ordered the attack on Figuig after the cease-fire independently of political plans in the capital; and he returned to Algiers a week after the cease-fire went into effect. The national emergency provided ben Bella an appeal for national unity which allowed a reconciliation with ou al-Hajj, and the *mujahidin*—including those in the assembly, which had been suspended for the purpose—flocked to fight the Moroccans. The lessons of the result were not lost to the professional army leadership, including Boumedienne; the poor results—surrenders in the field, inadequate logistics, poor training, inability to make significant advances on the ground, failure to cut off the Moroccan encirclement of Tindouf—showed that a professional army had not yet been created and that even enthusiastic patriots with guerrilla experience could not provide an instant army. Boumedienne opposed both the admission of volunteers to the army and the negotiated cease-fire that ended the inconclusive war.

The other event was ben Bella's agreement of November 12 with ou al-Hajj, which again ended the *wilayists'* dissidence by compromise, erasing their defeat. When the Kabyles found that their nationwide support had not increased over the previous year, they sought a compromise and received a widespread amnesty with promises of increased attention and participation in the political processes. The agreement provided for the establishment of an FLN congress within five months, an element basic to the *mujahidin's* position since their demand for the recalling of the CNRA during the struggle for power in 1962. To Boumedienne, becoming more and more aware of the depth of the needs posed by his commitment to a professional army, this development was not encouraging. Nor was ben Bella's recurring tactic of making peace with the opposition encouraging to a group whose successful defense of its interests depended on its remaining the major support of the regime.

Indeed, until the outbreak of the Kabyle dissidence and the Moroccan war, Boumedienne's political position had been strengthened as he proceeded to build up a professional army. Mohammed Khider, who had pressed not only for reconversion of the ALN but also for its civilian control, resigned from the Political Bureau in April 1963 after failing to rally a majority to his plan for a mass party. It was the ANP (not the workers) that occupied important French land holdings in March to render them vacant, and it was the ANP (not the FLN) that distributed pamphlets when Nasser visited Algiers in May. The same month, the balance of forces was consecrated by the promotion of Boumedienne to the first vice-presidency. In the first presidential government, formed in September, Boumedienne's position was buttressed by the "Oujda Group," of seven ALN associates—Bouteflika ("Abdulqader"), Boumaza, Nekkache, Medeghri, Qaid ("Sliman"), and Cherif ("Jamal"). Although none of the seven was "military" in any sense, their past political and continuing personal relations with Boumedienne made them part of his group of political brokers, sharing his political views. The resignation of Ferhat Abbas from the presidency of the assembly in mid-August left Boumedienne's group the major support of ben Bella.

As in September, 1962, however, this dominant position was weakened by the Kabyle compromise and ben Bella's subsequent maneuvering. The 53-man preparatory commission picked by ben Bella to begin work on the party congress contained only two junior ANP members plus Boumedienne (and his five ALN associates). The ANP as such was being moved out of political councils. After a time, Boumedienne refused to sit on the commission as it moved to impose civilian control over the ANP. The image of the military was further weakened by its suppression of the Oran unemployment riots in January, 1964; again it had been pushed into the dilemma of using its force to support the regime, or not using its force and permitting the further crumbling of the state mechanism on which the formation of a professional army depended. As before, it acted to support the coalition of *mujahidin* in local administration and brokers in Algiers while at the same time bitterly criticizing that coalition.

Although there had been rumors of a Boumedienne coup since November, 1963, after the ou al-Hajj agreement, the face-off did not take place until March, 1964, before the party congress, when Boumedienne and his group of ministers threatened to resign unless collegial government—including, for the ANP, military control of the reconverted army—were restored. The immediate victory[23] that

---

23. Probably the most important nonmilitary result was the elimination of Mohammed Harbi from the editorship of *Révolution africaine* in September, 1964, and the reduction of his Trotskyite group's influence over government policies. For Harbi's views on the militia, see "Les Fusils de la colère," *Révolution africaine*, June 13, 1964.

appeared was the territorial reorganization of the army, through the establishment of five new military regions that did away with the two main centers of warlordism, the Kabylia and the Aures (*wilayas* III and I). At the same time, the general staff was enlarged by the appointment of Colonel Chaabani, restive commander of former military region IV, and Majors Boujenan and ben Salem, Boumedienne's allies. Furthermore, to avoid having any center of power rival to the defense ministry, Boumedienne had the functions of the general staff reduced to organization, planning, and recruitment, with command functions eliminated. Quite naturally, ben Bella noted the army's strength and agreed to its demands, but alerted of the danger, proceeded to rearrange his alliances.

It was therefore a defensive and beleaguered ANP that organized to protect its interests when the party congress opened on April 16. Of the 1700 delegates, over 200 were ANP officers, sitting together in uniform, generally neither smiling nor applauding. Their position was negative, since the "theses" of the preparatory commission included subordination of the army to the party, concentration on a social role for the military, and training by the ANP for the party's "counter-army"—the militia. Their results were equivocal: the ANP was to have a "special relation" to the party directly under the control of the Political Bureau, which contained 9 former ALN officers among its 17 members (but only 5 members were Boumedienne's allies and none of these 5 were ANP officers), and a militia was to be created. The party's larger governing body, the central committee, which included the Political Bureau and 65 other members, had about 10 ANP senior officers, most of them not allies of Boumedienne in his views of a professional army. Control of the congress had fallen into the hands of that old coalition inimical to the professional army, an alliance of ben Bella's brokers and the *wilayists.*

In June the important question of the militia was discussed heatedly by party organs. It was decided to place the militia under the party except in "military situations" (suggesting that its primary function lay elsewhere), and *Révolution africaine* wrote of the urgency of its establishment in view of "the confrontation which awaits us."[24] The appointment of Major Mahmoud Guennez,[25] a former Ghardimaou captain and chairman of the assembly's defense

24. *Ibid.*, June 11, 1964.
25. Guennez: member of ALN General Staff 1961, elected to assembly from Batna 1962 and 1964, chairman of assembly interior and defense committee 1962, commander of militia 1964, president of the Association of Algerians in Europe 1965, FLN deputy executive 1968.

commission, to head the militia was a partial victory for the ANP, but his deputies do not appear to have been army men. In the assembly elections of September, 1964, there were no ANP candidates.

Once the congress was over, new elements of dissidence broke out, giving the army more work to do in support of the regime it disapproved, and, paradoxically, giving ben Bella new occasions to mend his fences. Ben Bella's attempt to encourage Chaabani's ambitions against the defense ministry rebounded, for his promotion from his fief in Biskra to the confines of Algiers led him to open revolt in July, to capture a week later, and to execution within two months. In the event, the incident provided the occasion for a victory for Boumedienne's point of view; it showed the real dangers of continuing warlordism—carried to such a point in Chaabani's case that he lost the popular support of his own region because of his autocratic exactions—and it presented a situation where compromise was finally impossible and capital punishment became necessary, for the first time since the war.

The Kabyle dissidence was revived throughout mid-1964 and met increased pressure from ALN units. The four major leaders—including Ait Ahmed and Azzedine[26]—were captured during the latter half of the year, and another historic leader—Rabah Bitat—returned to the fold. While leaning on the ANP, ben Bella took over the major police functions of the interior ministry in July (leading to the resignation of Medeghri and then of Qaid), won over another of Boumedienne's former allies (Nekkache), declared exceptional powers to himself on July 6 after an assassination attempt, and then proceeded to broaden his alliances among the groups that the ANP had defeated and to reduce further the strength of the Boumedienne group.

In this situation, both ben Bella and Boumedienne appeared to be chafing more and more under the alliance which held them together. Since, of course, neither was willing (or able) to retire from power, the problem for both came to be to find a new partner. Ben Bella, already strongly committed to the left-wing coterie in his palace, sought to strengthen his ties with what was on many points his closest brotherhood—the left opposition. In January, 1965, he negotiated the surrender of Moussa Hassani, and with him the collapse of the National Council for the Defense of the Revolution (CNDR), although Boudiaf remained outside his grasp. In June he

26. Azzedine: fought in *wilaya* IV (captured by Massu and played double agent 1959), ALN General Staff 1961, commanded Algiers Autonomous Zone 1962, brother-in-law of Tayebi.

pardoned Ait Ahmed and reached an agreement with the largely Kabyle Socialist Forces Front (FFS), as well as liberating Abderrahman Fares and Ferhat Abbas. At the same time he sought to remove some of the Boumedienne group from the Council of Ministers. The shift of alliances threatened both the army's watchdog role over the Revolution and the military control of military affairs, made more and more necessary by the increasing success in the reconversion of the army. The military coup to replace the political brokers, therefore, merely awaited a propitious moment to take place.

The morning of June 19, 1965, was not only propitious:[27] it was necessary, for if ben Bella were to be removed, it would have to be before he was legitimized by the impending Afro-Asian Conference at Algiers. It was clearly the army, too, that did the removing, not only in that tanks and troops were used, but in that the leading officers were the direct agents.

It is in the logic of the preceding discussion that the army be able to return to its barracks following a change it imposes on government. Military control of the military was preserved, as was the unity of command. Acceptable brokers were in power. But it is also within the logic of the situation that the splits within the military be thus transferred onto the level of the political brokers. The new 26-man Revolutionary Council represented two groups in alliance: the *mujahidin* and the professionals, joined by other scattered personalities.[28] Although it is clearly too much to claim that a revolt by one of the army factions was inevitable or predictable, it was possible to say from the beginning that this split between the two natures of the military would pose problems that would have to be dealt with if a revolt were to be avoided.

27. An interesting detailed account is found in Bourges, *L'Algérie,* pp. 121–42. The specific trigger incident was ben Bella's dismissal of Bouteflika on the eve of the Afro-Asian Conference. Junior officers were not informed of the plot but received sealed orders to act soon after midnight, which they obeyed (*Le Monde,* July 6, 1965).

28. The Council comprised Boumedienne and his directeur de cabinet (Abdelqader Chabou), the five commanders of military regions (Abid,* Chadli Benjedid, Salah Soufi, Abdelghani, and Abdallah Belhouchet), the chief of staff and two General Staff officers (Zbiri,* Boujenan,* Abderrahman Bensalem), the five *wilaya* commanders at the time of independence (Zbiri [already counted],* Nsalah Boublider ["Saout al-Arab"],* ou al-Hajj,* Khatib,* ben Haddou), two gendarmerie and national security company commanders (Ahmed Bencherif, Ahmed Draia), eight ex-ALN political figures (Bouteflika, Qaid, Cherif, Medeghri, Menjli, Mohammedi, Mohammed Tayebi, Mohammed Salah Yahyaoui), and two civilian political figures (Boumaza,* Ali Mahsas*). Starred (*) members were eliminated by the end of 1967 and the council met thereafter along with the Council of Ministers as the highest policy-making body.

The Revolutionary Council was little suited to governing, and was more a facade of institutionalized collegial leadership and a symbolic head of state than a governing body.[29] It appears to have met three times in the latter half of 1965, three times in 1966, and once in 1967. After March, 1967, it did not meet at all, and Boumedienne clearly became head of government rather than simply the procedural chairman of a board. Yet it was because of serious differences which broke out among the brokers that the council deadlocked and Boumedienne was obliged to rule. *Grosso modo,* these rivalries pitted left-wingers and *mujahidin* against technicians and the "Oujda Group." But the most important rivalry was that which opposed Zbiri to Boumedienne, for only the ANP chief of staff had the hardware and personnel at his disposal to challenge the top incumbent effectively.

Yet by his very position, Zbiri disarmed himself. Unlike Boumedienne as ben Bella's number two man, Zbiri could not represent the professional army—principally because Boumedienne did.[30] Boumedienne had overthrown ben Bella to safeguard certain military values; Zbiri could only (and also naturally, in view of his background) seek to represent *mujahidin,* and defend their values. These latter included above all collegial leadership, coupled with the replacement of certain ministers and council members (notably Bouteflika, Abdessalem, and Cherif), all of them part of Boumedienne's entourage accused in some way of undermining the Revolution. Boumedienne was able neither to resolve the disputes himself, however, nor bring himself to call a meeting of the Revolutionary Council for the same purpose; the longer he waited for the latter course (in the absence of the former), the more he increased the potential allies of Zbiri, many of whom were not interested in overthrowing the regime but simply reshaping or clarifying its decisions.

The Six-Day War of 1967 temporarily delayed the growing split among the brokers and their military supporters, although the details of the crisis' effects on Algerian politics are not known. ANP units were sent to the UAR, but there is no indication of their number, length of stay, command, or experiences. ANP units were also involved in training 5,000 students for a 45-day period beginning on 15 July, although again the details of this army venture into parapolitical as well as paramilitary mobilization are not

29. An interesting comparison could be made with the role of the Supreme Council in Sudan. For another subject of revealing comparisons, see note 36.
30. An otherwise good analysis in *Le Monde,* December 17, 1967, misses this point.

available. Reports in *al-Djeich* are written in the "the-tough-life-is-good-for-you" vein, colored with revolutionary ideology;[31] had the experiment continued, it would indicate that the ANP was taking on the mobilization role of a party.[32]

Whatever the effects of the summer war, it did not eliminate the growing split centering on Boumedienne and Zbiri and involving their military followers more closely. Beginning with the November 1 festivities, Zbiri stopped functioning as army chief of staff, refusing to preside over the military review in protest against the lack of consultation over Boumedienne's speech for the occasion. When Zbiri took refuge in the armored camp of his cousin and brother-in-law and Boumedienne ordered the camp surrounded, an act of political pouting was turned into a putative coup.

Yet Boumedienne appears to have been struck by the soundness of some of Zbiri's criticisms, and in fact each of them actually operated against the chief of staff. Thus, collective leadership involving *mujahidin* had worked out neither for the army nor the party, and both Zbiri and Boumedienne came to agree that a change was necessary. However, the only change possible involved increased power for technicians and less for *mujahidin*. After consulting party organs, Boumedienne decided to prepare a working single-party regime with an early party congress. To do this, he removed the entire FLN executive, including not only its head, Cherif of the "Oujda Group," but also his four *mujahidin* associates (notably ou al-Hajj, Khatib, and Boublider,[33] all close to Zbiri), and replaced them with Finance Minister Qaid, also of the "Oujda Group." Boumedienne also announced that changes in the FLN would soon affect other sectors as well. On the army side, he also saw that the general staff was not functioning and that the high-ranking *mujahidin* who headed the military establishment were—for all their qualities—incapable of handling an army that was and should be becoming more and more professionalized. During the latter months of the year, young technicians were promoted over the heads of *mujahidin* and put in charge of armored and other units, and changes in the general staff—including its chief—were discussed in government circles. Both reforms revealed a strengthened resolve by

---

31. See particularly *al-Djeich*, September, 1967.

32. A two-year draft for 19-year-olds was announced in March, 1968, and put into effect in June, 1969, under the direction of the ANP.

33. Boublider ("Saout al-Arab"): born 1927 at Oued Zenati, worked as a peddler, CNRA, commander of *wilaya* II (Constantine) 1962, captured with ben Tobbal by ALN and supported ben Bella 1962, military attaché in Cairo 1963, arrested and released 1963, FLN Central Committee 1964, Revolutionary Council 1965, FLN executive 1965, sided with Zbiri 1967, retired 1968.

Boumedienne to make his own policy, pass over the Revolutionary Council, and ignore the efforts of ANP colonels and majors and council members who had been trying for months to reconcile him with Zbiri. Thus, Zbiri's dissidence, which broke out on December 14, 1967, resembled previous army moves in many ways. Like the 1965 coup, it was precipitated by personnel changes threatening the participants. Like the 1962 takeover, it began with a march on Algiers from the surrounding area. Like neither, however, it failed, for Zbiri did not have command of his army.

The two years following the Zbiri revolt have been marked by a silence and stability on the military front that expresses both the ANP's satisfaction with the regime and its control by the government. Zbiri and some associates fled abroad, others melted away into civilian life. The military has become decidedly less conspicuous in Algerian public life, as Qaid has tried to revive and control the party. Over the newly installed structure of local and departmental assemblies,[34] the commanders of the five military regions—Belhouchet (Algiers, I), Chadli (Oran, II), Mohammed Zerguini[35] (Saoura, III), Mohammed Atteila[35] (Oasis, IV), and Abdelghani (Constantine, V)—function essentially as governors, maintaining a balance among the three other forces of the country—assemblies, party, administration. As the army returns to its barracks to continue its watchdog role, it is among the other three forces that the active politics is waged.

SOCIAL ORIGINS AND ORGANIZATIONAL VIEWS

ANP officers constitute an inchoate, heterogeneous group, coming from the *wilayas*, external ALN, and postwar recruitment, with backgrounds in urban or rural employment (or unemployment), maquis, French army, student life, and so on. Using a figure of 60,000 for ANP strength and an officer:troop ratio of 1:15 (a low ratio that seems realistic in view of ANP antecedents and recruiting), about 3,750 are officers. Since there seem to be not over 25

34. No ANP members ran for communal assemblies (APC's) in February, 1967, but one *meharist* ran—and won—for the departmental assembly (APW) of the Oasis, in the Sahara, in May, 1969.

35. Zerguini: former French officer, took over *wilaya* II 1962, deputy commander military region VII (*wilaya* III) 1963, deputy commander military region I (*wilaya* IV) 1963, training in Russia 1964, diplomatic mission to Moscow 1965, deputy chief of staff 1966, commander military region IV (*wilaya* VI) 1968 and acting chief of staff. Atteila: *wilaya* I, deputy commander military region V (*wilaya* II).

colonels, no lieutenant colonels, and not over 150 majors, the vast majority are junior officers, a higher proportion than in a classical army. There is no telling how many of these belong in the *mujahidin* category and how many are professionals (technicians), although it is safe to assume that those who have been "professionalized" through successful assimilation of modern training in military techniques and values will make up the largest group of subsequent promotions. Static, this dichotomy between *mujahidin* and professionals would already give rise to friction; since it is dynamic—in that the professionals are increasing and are trying to convert the *mujahidin* to their skills and views, and in that power will follow these shifts in the long run—friction is heightened. Such a view suggests that previous origins, ties, and experiences are of secondary importance.[36]

The ANP has a popular base, drawing largely from the lower social strata: "sons of *fellahin* and sons of workers." But social origins are less important for the ANP than social change; the army is composed not of workers and *fellahin* but of their sons, whose present situation differs from their origins by their training, profession and status.[37]

No *single* tie, experience, or origin is the key to the army's political action, and no constant *hierarchy* of ties can be established as a source of motivations. Moreover, no *combination* of past ties, experiences, and origins is sure to produce the same action, reaction,

---

36. There are no comparable works on Algeria to refer to. Valuable insights are found among the hostile criticisms of Daniel Guerin, *L'Algérie caporalisée?* (Paris: Centre des Études Socialistes, 1965), pp. 1–25. Some basis for comparison is found in the analysis of social classes in André Michel, "Les Classes sociales en Algérie," *Cahiers Internationaux de Sociologie,* XII (1965), 207–20. The most interesting bases for comparison are with the colonial and Liberation Army components of the Moroccan Royal Armed Forces; see I. William Zartman, *Morocco: Problems of New Power* (New York: Atherton, 1964), pp. 62–116; B . . ., "Le Maroc," in *Le Rôle extra-militaire de l'armée dans le tiers monde,* ed. Leon Hamon (Paris: Presses Universitaires de France, 1966), pp. 31–67; and Phillippe Schneyder, "Les Armées africaines," *Esprit,* XXXV (1967), 300–318.

37. A good, if unsympathetic, commentary is presented by Daniel Guerin: "60,000 men, nearly all sons of *fellahs.* They are neither volunteers nor conscripts, but mercenaries, earning 150F [$30] a month, a rather comfortable sum in such a poor country. These *junud,* most of them illiterate, undergo a totalitarian type of psychological and political conditioning. The troops are commanded by well-paid young officers who form a sort of medieval knighthood, narrow-minded, deformed by the military point of view, haughty. Socialists they are indeed, and it is thanks to their pressure that European holdings could be nationalized, the veterans could be given jobs, the orphans aided. But the socialism with which they have been inculcated and which they favor is Maoist, tough, and authoritarian" (*L'Algérie caporalisée?,* p. 20).

allegiance, or alliance in any two individuals. Any search for such simple motivations seems quite vain. By the same token, such restrictions are also applicable to the *mujahidin*-technician dichotomy. Useful and valid though it may be as an interpretive generalization, this dichotomy is not going to cover all cases, nor, by the same token, will it be invalidated by the professional who allies with the *mujahidin* or vice versa. Finally, it may also be said that, all things being equal, similarities in ethnic or geographic origins, in war experiences, or in educational "promotions," are all causes of friendships, debts, and solidarity feelings, and they can be the basis for lasting ties, lasting enmities, or later appeals for alliances. These reflections may seem banal, but it is important to state them because they are often forgotten and often exceeded, and are about the maximum that can be posited on the political importance of social origins.

A major principle of the professional's military doctrine is to keep the army–people identity on the broad, abstract level of the "general will," and through military organization to minimize the detailed or particularist effects of social origins. "Part of the logic of military organization is to cut off the troops from civilian interests so that they will accept their officers' orders unquestioningly."[38] Experience with the *wilayas* has clearly brought home the importance of this principle. ANP units are not organized on a regional basis. In times of crisis (after *wilayist* dissidence, after the 1965 coup), army units are shifted about the countryside; the expansion of the external ALN throughout the country in late 1962 was an early application of this idea. Officers from the same *wilaya* are scattered about, and mingled with professional officers who keep an eye on them. Training activities serve not only to professionalize the *mujahidin* but also to turn their loyalties from a region to a professional military establishment. The activities of the Political Commissariat—the publication of *al-Djeich*, the political and civic action training and indoctrination programs, the placing of political commissaires in military units, and training draftees—aim at filling the same function.

All of these activities serve not only to strengthen the army as a national organization, but also to increase the importance of the professional military against *wilayist* tendencies. Soldiers and

38. Chalmers Johnson, *Revolution and the Political System* (Stanford: The Hoover Institution, 1964), p. 19. The next two paragraphs (and scattered other material throughout the study) include information gathered through interviews inside and outside the ANP in Algeria in July, 1966, and February–June, 1969.

officers are not "delegates" from their home regions, ethnic groups, or social classes to the army. When they go home, on leave for example, they return to their *former* origins but as delegates of the army, in a new social status. Fraternization between the military and the population in areas where army units are stationed varies with geography. In the Sahara, the army is active in a civil affairs program and invites local elements to barracks visits, to mess dinners, to local projects. But here the army's relations are strikingly similar to those of the special French Army officers assigned to the interior regions before independence (although, of course, now both the military and the populations are Algerian). Around urban areas, the military are usually seen together; they are billeted apart from civilians; their activities are separate from civilian activities; and when the bridge is made (mess dinners in Algiers, visits to army farms and industries), it is done by permission and invitation. Even the criticism heard in Algeria of the well-off military helps to reinforce the army's separateness; part of the military's nature of an interest group is to remain a thing apart, to keep the privileges and maintain the *esprit* that are important to a modern, professional army.

This divorce between social origins and military status has been remarkably successful considering the time passed since independence. In none of the prime instances of army dissidence (ou al-Hajj, Ait Ahmed, Chaabani, ben Rejem, Azzedine, Zbiri) were the breakaway army leaders able to count on even a large percentage of their junior officers and troops. In each case, the government made a great point of announcing the junior officers who remained loyal to the ANP, and in each case, when the dissidence ended, the leader was surrounded by only a small group of followers. In the final showdown, in June, 1965, there were no known defections from the army to the former government, and army solidarity held during the military takeover. In 1967, there were no notable defections to the revolt from any military region (including Zbiri's old *wilaya*) except around Algiers, and it was the military cadets who stopped Zbiri's columns.[39]

There is an evident identity of military views between Boumedienne and the Oujda group, on one hand, and the professionals or military technicians, on the other.[40] At the same time, as there is

39. Boumedienne's speech, in *Maghreb,* January–February, 1968.
40. For an analysis of Boumedienne's views, see I. William Zartman, "The Role of the Army in the Algerian Polity," in *Man, State and Society,* ed. Zartman, originally presented at the Princeton University Conference. For a comparative note on the role of "technicians," see Herbert S. Dinerstein,

a need for the Boumedienne associates, as a brokerage group, to work with the *mujahidin* on the political level, there is also a need for Boumedienne and the professionals to work with the *mujahidin* in the army. To the extent that the *mujahidin* recognize the professionals' technical skills and the brokers' political skills, this working relationship is accepted. Thus the three categories or elements, in the army as in the political class, are all kept in place by each other, by the need for each others' skills, and by a partial overlap of views and values. For all this interdependence among the three categories, the major present and potential split is based on the degree of social change or professionalization within the military leadership, buttressed by but not dependent on previous ties and backgrounds. The major factors that keep this split from reaching political proportions are the effectiveness of the brokerage groups and the success of organizational and training measures to create a coherent, reconverted, modern army—in other words, the way in which the two original problems of control and reconversion will be handled. If it were not "professionalized," the army would fall prey to social and socially based political divisions that already exist within Algerian society. "Professionalized," it forms an important part of the new class of the nation, a means of personal modernization and rapid social advancement of its members.

It is therefore in the interest of the army to maintain myths of national unity and popular identity, while seeking to implement programs of modernization and social change among the military. In such a way, the army can become in reality what it is in theory: the spearhead of the Revolution. By the same token, its nature (and cohesion) as an interest group in politics is reinforced. However, in the process, "Revolution" becomes identified in technicians' terms of construction rather than in *mujahidin*'s terms of consumption. Since construction is a slower, less immediately satisfying process than consumption, the army's role as an agent of control holding down dissatisfaction (including the dissatisfaction of *mujahidin* leaders in its midst) and hence as an active element in politics is enhanced.

"Soviet Policy in Latin America," *American Political Science Review* LXI (1967), 83; and E. P. W. da Costa, "Soviet Industrialization and the Underdeveloped Areas," in *The Strategy of Deception,* ed. Jeane Kirkpatrick (New York: Farrar, Straus, 1963), pp. 72, 82 ff.

INTRODUCTION TO CHAPTER 6

FEW ANALYSTS of contemporary African politics draw parallels with the politics of fifteenth-century Italy. The classic description of the politics of Italy in this period came from Niccolo Machiavelli. The peninsula, ripped by warfare among its petty principalities, lacked unity, peace, and cohesion. Mercenary armies vied for control—and often turned against those who had hired them. These armies remained divorced from day-to-day life; they attracted the penurious, the disadvantaged, the ill-educated. Loyalty was purchased; it did not arise from deep-seated patriotism. In *The Prince* and *The Discourses*, Machiavelli pleaded for Italian unity and armies of responsible citizens; political instability, mercenary forces, and the absence of *virtù* went hand-in-hand.

Such conditions, it can be argued, plague much of contemporary Africa. Almost without exception, current standing forces developed from nuclei of colonial armies that had been responsive to the governing powers, not inspired by positive, post-independence, national goals. Professor van den Berghe notes, in the following chapter, that the men in the ranks were viewed as "hated and despicable tools of the white conqueror." The armies of Africa thus originated as symbols of colonial domination, not symbols of national liberation. Their conversion into efficient, respected, and legitimate agents of government poses particular difficulties.

Professor van den Berghe comments that "national" armies presuppose the existence of a nation. In its absence, armies become prey to factionalism along many lines of cleavage, such as ethnicity or regionalism. The sociology of armed forces in contemporary Africa thus is intertwined with the complex sociology of individual African states. The seven types of armed forces distinguished in the

250

following chapter thus are derived from the social setting—and where this setting suffers from the deficiencies noted centuries ago by Machiavelli, political instability and military involvement are two sides of the same, debased coin.

C. E. W.

6.

The Military
and Political
Change in Africa

Pierre L. van den Berghe
University of Washington

A CLOSELY RELATED PAPER written in 1964 and published in 1965 began with the sentence: "Probably more than any other continent at any time in world history, Africa is led by pen-wielding intellectuals, rather than by the modern equivalent of saber-rattling men on horseback."[1] The rapidity with which this statement lost its validity is an indication of the pace of change in Africa today. Three important sets of military events have taken place since then on the African continent:

1. A wave of military coups swept aside civilian regimes, including some that seemed as solidly entrenched as any in Africa. Most surprising to many outside observers was the facility with which

---

1. Pierre L. van den Berghe, "The Role of the Army in Contemporary Africa," *Africa Report*, March 1965, p. 12. This article is the basis for the present chapter.

Nkrumah's regime was overthrown. The moral of these events is that almost all African states have precarious political institutions, even those which seemed to have developed monolithic one-party systems.

The fundamental error of judgment in ascribing great solidity to those militant one-party regimes probably lies in not taking into account the vast difference in technological development between the Eastern European communist states and militant African socialist countries. Again, with the partial exception of South Africa, no African state can even approximate the solidity of modern technocratic centralism such as characterizes the Soviet Union, Poland, Czechoslovakia, or even Yugoslavia or Red China. African states do not have the financial, technological, and personnel resources to be totalitarian. Their degree of penetration at the local level remains in most cases rather tenuous. A high degree of ideological and practical mobilization is only possible in countries which have broken away from their agrarian traditions, and such conditions exist only in South Africa. The resemblance between Guinea, Mali, Tanzania, Algeria, and Ghana under Nkrumah on the one hand, and "people's democracies" on the other hand, is almost purely confined to ideological rhetoric, as indeed was the similarity between the French and the American Revolutions nearly two centuries ago.

2. Africa's largest army, that of the United Arab Republic, met the most thorough and rapid defeat dealt to any military force in the world since the German *Blitzkrieg* of 1940, and that at the hands of a nation only one-tenth the size of Egypt. The obvious "lesson" from this episode is the obverse of that which can be learned from guerrilla warfare. In the latter, small and poorly equipped forces can indefinitely engage large modern armies, as African liberation movements have done in Kenya, Algeria, Angola, Mozambique, and Portuguese Guinea. In conventional warfare, however, large numbers and ideological fervor are no substitutes for a sophisticated technology of destruction. Thus, no African army, with the possible exception of that of South Africa, could hold its own in a conventional contest with a "developed" country.

3. The Nigerian civil war not only confirmed the fragility and artificiality of most African states, but it cast armed forces in a novel military role. The Katanga affair, with which the Ibo secessionist movement has been compared, is, of course, quite different. Tshombe's secession, and the succession of foreign interventions which followed, were in good part exogenous, while the Biafran case represents an independence movement by the Ibo nation. For the first time, a section of a state's armed forces was used in an attempt

to establish the principle of ethnic sovereignty. This contrasts sharply with the internal role of most African armies which has been to maintain the integrity of the artificial, multinational polities inherited from colonialism.

This new source of insecurity from the military is quite different from the post-independence mutinies of the Congo, Kenya, Uganda, and Tanzania. The mutinies were a transitory phenomenon of units that were still essentially colonial mercenaries under expatriate officers. These old colonial armies still lacked any kind of integration either with the state as a whole, or with any ethnic segment thereof. The Nigerian case, on the other hand, is one where the armed forces themselves are drawn into the centrifugal turmoil of competing ethnic nationalisms.

Clearly, a comprehensive analysis of the role of the army must include a study of both the internal organization and leadership of the armed forces themselves, and the place of the army in the society at large.[2] As a preliminary way of classifying the African material, we may distinguish seven types of armed forces.

1. *The Raiding Citizen-Army* is characterized by nonprofessionalism and egalitarianism. Many cattle-herding, stateless societies of East Africa, such as the Nuer, the Masai, the Dinka, and many others, had military organizations of this type. All ablebodied men fought together in periodic raids against their neighbors under the informal, nonprofessional, spontaneous leadership of warriors who did not have permanent, full-time military offices. The Boer commandos of South Africa, up to the Anglo-Boer War, could also be classified under this type of military force. Often, but not always, these armies were organized into age-regiments composed of all men who had been initiated within a certain time period. Most importantly perhaps, and unlike the other types, raiding citizenarmies are monoethnic. They are the military arm of an ethnic group, and are frequently coterminous with all the able-bodied men in that given group. Today, the significance of this type of army is largely ethnographic, although ethnic conflicts between pastoralist groups within modern states occasionally still erupt along those

2. Among the fairly recent contributions on the topic are William Gutteridge, *Armed Forces in the New States* (London: Oxford University Press, 1962); Morris Janowitz, *The Military in the Political Development of New Nations* (Chicago: University of Chicago Press, 1964); James S. Coleman and Belmont Brice, "The Role of the Military in Sub-Saharan Africa," in *The Role of the Military in Underdeveloped Countries,* ed. John J. Johnson (Princeton: Princeton University Press, 1962); *Africa Report,* January 1964; and Leo Hamon, ed., *Le Rôle extra-militaire de l'armée dans le tiers monde* (Paris: Presses Universitaires de France, 1966).

lines, and, of course, the border hostilities between Somalia, Kenya, and Ethiopia assume, in part, that character. With the rise of centralized monarchies, the raiding citizen-army became more permanently organized, more rigidly structured, more professionalized and hierarchized, as exemplified by the Zulu, Swazi and Ndebele armies which were in a transition phase between types one and two.

2. *The Palace Army* is characteristic of traditional monarchies, and is led by a corps of professional officers. Often there is a relatively small permanent force, a palace guard, composed of professional soldiers. In times of war, this regular army is supplemented by large levies of peasants led by their feudal lords. Typically, high-ranking officers are aristocrats, and the soldiers, at least of the elite corps, are low-status retainers or mercenaries (often slaves or foreigners). Such an army constitutes the major instrument of power for the "establishment" (the king, the nobility, the clergy of the official state religion, etc.). The palace army is apolitical in that, while being a tool used for the preservation of the *status quo*, it is not in itself an independent source of power or policy.

In succession crises, however, such as commonly occurred in traditional African monarchies, sections of the palace army and military retainers of large feudal lords may side with one pretender or another, but not on behalf of candidates of their own. (When this happens, the palace army falls into what may be called the Praetorian Guard pattern, one which is alien to Africa.)

Palace armies were common in pre-colonial African states, notably in the great Sudanic Empires of Ghana, Mali, Songhai, Kanem, and Bornu; in the Hausa, Nupe, and Fulani states; in Oyo, Ashanti, Dahomey, Benin, Ruanda, Urundi, Buganda, and numerous other monarchies. Dahomey in the eighteenth century probably represents the most extreme form of this type of army. The whole society became transformed into a despotically ruled, slave-raiding war machine where even women did active military service. Unlike the first type of army which has lost much of its practical significance in contemporary Africa, modernized versions of Palace Armies still exist in Morocco, Libya, and, even more clearly so, in Ethiopia. However, in the very process of modernizing the technology of the means of violence, and opening up the officer corps to commoners, the Palace Army can transform itself into a *Putsch* army.

3. *The* Putsch *Army* is characterized by the fact that its officer corps is both highly professionalized and politicized. This leads to the familiar pattern of military dictatorship, either of the unstable

junta form or of the stabler, one-man *caudillo* type. From a sheer instrument of power in the hands of a ruling class external to it, the army becomes synonymous with the government, and the army general staff with the ruling clique. Typically, military coups are led by younger senior officers (often of colonel rank) from privileged military units such as armored cavalry, paratroops, or commandos. The political ideology of military dictatorships is usually poorly formulated, and may range from rigid conservatism to "authoritarianism of the left." However, conservative military dictatorships tend to ally themselves more with the moneyed bourgeoisie than with the feudal aristocracy whom they often supplanted. Being parvenu technocrats of violence, putschists are typically "modernist" and antitraditional in outlook.

This type of army which has been so prominent in several Latin American countries has recently grown in importance in Africa. The United Arab Republic represents the oldest African army of this type. Egypt has by far the largest standing army of any independent African state in absolute terms, and the second largest relative to population size. Its military budget accounts for approximately one fourth of the continental total, and is second only to South Africa's. The Sudan had returned to civilian rule in 1964, but, since 1966, Nigeria, Ghana, Congo-Kinshasa, and several smaller states have been taken over by military regimes. Historically, *Putsch* armies can arise out of modernized palace armies, or out of national armies.

4. *The Revolutionary Citizen-Army,* which traces its ancestry back to the eighteenth-century armies of the First French Republic, is represented in Africa by the Algerian, Angolan, Mozambique, and Kenyan armies of liberation. This fourth type of army is similar to the first in that it is nonprofessional and relatively egalitarian. Its distinctive elements are, of course, the high degree of political fervor, not only among leaders, but also in the ranks, and the revolutionary aims of the army which is not so much an organization of specialists in violence, as the militant vanguard of the masses in the overthrow of the *status quo*. Both democratic ideology and the demands of guerrilla warfare, calling for small-scale and relatively autonomous units, maintain the egalitarian character of this kind of army. After victory, such revolutionary armies sometimes become the national armies of the newly independent country; this is particularly easy if the army is led by a highly articulate and modernist intelligentsia as was the case in Algeria. In Kenya, however, where the leadership was less educated (in the Western sense), and where the revolution was crushed militarily before

independence was granted, the Mau Mau leaders were robbed of their political victory by more Westernized and conservative elements.

5. *The Herrenvolk Army* is represented by South Africa, and, on a smaller scale, by the settler army of Rhodesia. Alone among the European colonists in Africa, the Boers consistently pursued a policy of not arming the indigenous population, and of monopolizing the use of firearms. Nonwhites were enlisted in the South African army during the two world wars, but only as auxiliary, unarmed, noncombatant troops. During the Anglo-Boer War, Britain used some African troops against the Boers, but, generally, the conflict remained a "white man's war." To all intents and purposes, then, the South African army is a lily-white force, dedicated to the maintenance of white supremacy. Aside from lack of pigmentation as a necessary criterion of membership, the Herrenvolk army is characterized by a relatively low degree of professionalism and a rather high degree of "Herrenvolk democracy," traceable to its origins in the Boer commandos of the seventeenth, eighteenth, and nineteenth centuries. From the viewpoint of the dominant white group, the army constitutes a relatively egalitarian national vigilante system for the perpetuation of a racial caste society. In addition to regular army units, there are numerous "shooting commandos" of reservists whose main function is intimidation of the African population.

The Herrenvolk army includes, of course, career officers, but the latter do not play a significant political role *qua* army officers. The army is apolitical in the sense that it does not constitute an important autonomous source of power, or a threat to whatever white government is in power. Nor is the Herrenvolk army purely and simply a tool of the governmental power clique. The South African army has thus a dual nature: it is both an instrument of minority rule and an internally democratic citizen-army representing the ruling white minority. With the rapid modernization and expansion of the army in recent years, Herrenvolk egalitarianism is on the wane, but, nevertheless, the South African (and the Rhodesian) armies are distinctly different from any of the other types represented on the continent. In a sense, the Herrenvolk army is a modernized and stabilized version of a raiding citizen-army whose members have become a ruling caste in a wider society. This Herrenvolk or vigilante army is now being strengthened to meet the growing menace of an African revolutionary citizen-army. Between 1961 and 1964, the South African military budget increased from $112 to $291 million, and is now the largest on the continent,

257

thereby making the Herrenvolk army the best-equipped in Africa.[3]

6. *The Colonial Army* was, until recently, the most common kind of African military organization, and also the most uniquely African. Its instability in the immediate post-independence period and its highly peculiar characteristics make it a fascinating and much neglected object of study. As the name implies, the colonial army is constituted by the "native troops" of the various European powers: French *tirailleurs sénégalais*, German *Askaris*, Belgian Force Publique, British King's African Rifles, etc. With the exception of the white South Africans, who were numerous enough to make up their own repressive army, all the other colonial powers have found that the cheapest and most convenient way of keeping their overseas empires was to use "native" troops under European officers. France and Portugal technically distinguished between "civilized" and "uncivilized" people rather than, strictly speaking, between whites and blacks, but in practice there prevailed much the same segregation of military units, and virtually the same exclusion of black Africans from the ranks of commissioned officers, until quite late in the colonial period.

Unlike the "palace" variety, colonial armies have been the power instrument of a "modernist" foreign conqueror instead of a traditional native aristocracy. The term "mercenary" does not apply very well to colonial soldiers, because the latter have often been coerced into service rather than attracted to it by monetary incentives, and because these incentives were often quite small.[4] Nor are colonial soldiers comparable to conscripts in a citizen army. They are in reality, armed and somewhat privileged helots, more or less compelled by circumstances to serve their foreign masters in conquering and subjugating fellow Africans, usually from other ethnic groups.

Several consequences derived from these conditions. "Native" troops, though cheap, were not always reliable. Mutinies were not uncommon, but they were fairly easily repressed with the help of other troops from rival ethnic groups; resistance often quickly evaporated as the mutineers lacked leadership and scattered into small undisciplined bands of marauders. As a means of maximizing the reliability of colonial troops, garrisons were often stationed far from home, among traditional enemies or, at least, among people with whom they shared little in common. Consequently, colonial

3. *Africa Today,* March 1964, p. 6.
4. Britain relied mostly on volunteers for its colonial forces, except during wartime, but the other colonial powers generally exacted quotas of men from various chiefs, or used one form or another of involuntary conscription.

armies were often regarded by the local civilian population as hated and despicable tools of the white conqueror.[5] Within colonial armies, white officers came, in time, to be regarded as symbols of colonial domination, thereby reducing further the loyalty of African units in the latter years of colonialism. Nevertheless, largely because of the general lack of schooling, and, hence, the lack of modern leadership among African soldiers, colonial troops remained largely apolitical and did not play a leading role in the struggle for independence. The latter was mostly achieved through the agitation of the trade unions and political parties led by the intelligentsia, organized by the white-collar class, and supported by the urban proletariat. In some cases, of course, independence resulted from the guerrilla activities of armies of the fourth type, but these were rarely recruited from colonial troops. Demobilized soldiers who had fought in World War II did contribute somewhat to the development of anticolonialism, especially in West Africa, and some Algerian soldiers defected to the FLN, but seldom were colonial soldiers found on the forefront of independence movements. African liberation never had its cruiser Aurora or its Petrograd garrison.

The numerous problems which beset many African countries upon independence were further complicated by the fact that they inherited, along with the whole administrative apparatus of the former colonies, these colonial armies. Alienated from the civilian population and from their own officers who, typically, were not Africanized in time for independence, these troops often became a danger for the new states. After independence, the white officers, as hated symbols of colonialism, were quickly deposed by means of mutinies, as in Congo-Kinshasa, Uganda, Kenya, and Tanganyika. The lack of African commissioned officers, and, hence, of effective leadership beyond small groups led by sergeants and corporals, led to the disintegration of military units which often turned against the local civilian population, and in the case of the Congo, contributed to plunging the entire country into disorder.

Thus, a number of African states, in the immediate post-independence period were in the rather unusual situation of having armies which could quickly become worse than useless. Many former colonial armies were unreliable as an instrument of policy, disliked by the general population, and yet also incapable of providing an effective alternative to civilian government. So long as they lacked a cadre of African career officers, colonial armies could not be used for a *Putsch*, or indeed for any concerted social pur-

5. Gutteridge, *Armed Forces*, pp. 4, 28, 30.

poses. Their very existence posed a constant threat of disorder to the government they were supposed to serve. With the crash program of training for African commissioned officers and the purge of mutineering elements in the former colonial armies, this volatile phase proved transitory,[6] and many of these troops have been converted into either *Putsch* or national armies.

Two crucial factors are at work in influencing the cohesion and discipline of former colonial forces in African states. One is, of course, the extent to which the officer corps had been Africanized before independence. Here the case of the Sudan is instructive. Between 1953 and 1956, some 400 junior officers were trained at the military academy in Khartoum, so that at the time of independence the Sudanese Defence Force was entirely commanded by Africans.[7] The former colonial army had developed such a highly professionalized officer corps that it quickly converted itself into a *Putsch* army by taking over the government, an example which has been frequently emulated since. Thus, ill-disciplined armies led by expatriates are a threat to civilian governments in that they easily turn to mutiny, plunder, and illegal violence; but cohesive armies with African officers can also topple weak civilian regimes by staging successful coups.

The second important factor in determining the behavior of former colonial armies after independence is the extent to which these armies acquired legitimacy and prestige among the population and the ruling group. In most parts of the continent, the mass of Africans have regarded the army with fear or hostility. In some traditional African societies (mostly in West Africa) the military profession was linked with low social status, and this attitude was carried over to colonial armies. But, more importantly, colonial armies became symbols of white domination. Unless the colonial army was given legitimacy by the political leaders of liberatory movements in anticipation of independence, its instrumental value was jeopardized, and its role in the process of nation-building was destined to be marginal. The former Belgian Congo represents an extreme case in which both factors basic to military reliability were entirely unfavorable: there was not a single African commissioned

6. However, it takes some time to establish professional norms in the officer corps. For example, in the Congolese National Army, after nearly four years of independence, a battalion commander was reported as having been absent without leave from his unit for a period of five weeks; and another battalion commander has been arrested for selling his unit's vehicles on the open market. Cf. *The Times* (London), June 2, 1964.

7. Coleman and Brice, "The Role of the Military," p. 366.

officer at the time of independence, and the Force Publique was generally hated among the civilian population.[8]

7. *The National Army* is that which most people would regard as the most desirable, i.e., a modern, apolitical army under civilian control and performing limited technical functions in international defense and internal security. (Actually, the term "national" is somewhat misleading in the African context, because most African states are not nations but rather multinational conglomerates of ethnic groups. I am thus using the term for lack of a better one.) To be "national" an army must be led by local officers, be regarded by the citizenry as using violence for legitimate ends, and be integrated with the other political institutions of the country.

There are at least two possible models for national armies. One is that of the draftee army led by a professional cadre of apolitical commissioned and noncommissioned officers, and supplemented by specialized, elite units of volunteers. This model, however, seems most amenable to a multiparty, Western type of democracy, and is unusual among the new states of Africa. Another possibility, which is more in keeping with the one-party structure of many African states, is the conception of the army as a party militia, highly politicized but under firm civilian control. This alternative is suggested by Nyerere, for example when he defines the role of the reorganized Tanzanian army: "I do not want it to be an elite force, but an army integrated with the national life and attuned to our own political system. . . . The task is to insure that the officers and men are integrated into the government and party so that they become no more of a risk than, say, the civil service."[9] Such an army is more a logical outgrowth of a revolutionary citizen-army than of a colonial army, but with proper reorganization, indoctrination, and infiltration of the officer corps by party cadres, the transition is conceivable.

It was not only the colonial past of African armed forces which made their transformation into national armies so difficult. The fragility and artificiality of most African states, and the lack of institutionalization of politics made in fact for the fairly rapid metamorphosis of colonial armies into *Putsch* armies rather than national ones. Indeed, one should not expect a national army to arise before the nation itself has become a reality.

When the colonial powers withdrew there were two ways in which

8. Even in colonial times, the Force Publique had proved unreliable, and various units thereof mutinied on a number of occasions.

9. *Africa Report,* October 1964, p. 16.

the power vacuum could be filled (aside from neocolonialism and outside influences). The one-party or dominant-party structure with a charismatic leader and a bureaucratic mandarinate of Western-educated intellectuals seemed for a while to become characteristic of most African states. But the second alternative, the no-party military regime, now seems clearly in the ascendancy.

In retrospect, it seems that the apparent solidity of some of the one-party civilian regimes, such as that of the CPP in Ghana, was more a function of the weakness of the military (and hence of the lack of any alternative source of power) than of any inherent strength in the one-party structure. There was some delay between independence and the wave of coups because it took some time for the newly trained African officers to develop *esprit de corps* and political consciousness. Once these had arisen, and once the former colonial troops had become disciplined instruments, the still weakly institutionalized civilian governments often proved easy to topple. African officers learned the necessary skills to grab power before civilian government had the time to become firmly established. In addition, lowly urbanized societies with a low level of technological development can be controlled (at least in the minimal sense of suppressing disorder and policing the capital city) with a relatively small military establishment. A company-sized army took over power in Togo, for example.

In one important respect, African military regimes are different from many of their Latin American counterparts. African officers are not representatives of a traditional landowning aristocracy or an urban bourgeoisie. These classes are weak, indeed almost nonexistent, in most African countries. Rather, officers are, for the most part, recently made-good technocrats of violence who, much like African politicians, achieved their position through Western education in mission schools and European post-secondary training. Like the civilian rulers of Africa, they are a foreign-trained educational elite. Their outlook is more pragmatic and less ideological, but they are as modern and antitraditional as the politicians whom they replace. African army officers are "progressives" in the technological if not in the ideological sense. The main differences with their civilian counterparts is that their training and ability seem to be of lower quality on the average. This they tend to make up by a greater degree of financial puritanism, at least in the early phases of their takeover.

There are many other special facets to the role of the army which make African military sociology peculiarly interesting. One of them is the ethnic composition of former colonial armies and now of

national or *Putsch* armies. Generally, the colonial powers have recruited their troops from illiterates, who made more pliable soldiers,
and from groups which had strong military traditions and were
reputed for their fierceness. Often the ethnic groups from which the
Western-educated elite were recruited were poorly represented in
the colonial troops, and vice versa. Thus, in Kenya the intelligentsia
was predominantly Kikuyu and Luo, and the units of the King's
African Rifles were almost entirely drawn from other ethnic
groups. Similarly, in Ghana and Nigeria, the army was recruited
mostly from illiterate non-Christian northerners, whereas the Western-educated elite was predominantly Christian and southern. This
differential ethnic recruitment of soldiers and scholars accounts for
much of the antipathy of the intelligentsia for the military.

Ethnic composition of the armed forces also constitutes an important political issue in African countries which are almost all
ethnically pluralistic. This is particularly true of large states such
as Congo-Kinshasa and Nigeria. In the latter country, for example,
the fear of northern troops in the south was one of the factors
leading to the civil war. Here, the role of the national or *Putsch*
armies is antithetical to that of the old colonial troops. Under
colonialism, the army was essentially an instrument of internal
repression, and that aim was best secured by fostering ethnic
rivalries, and by recruiting troops from bellicose groups feared by
the general population. Since independence, African armies, to be of
any use, must be converted into instruments of national unity
against outside threats. This very antithesis of aims, in which ethnic
composition is but one factor, constitutes an additional difficulty in
the reconversion of colonial armies into effective and politically
reliable tools of national policy.

One of the ways in which African armies can become a factor of
national unity is to combine short-time military conscription with
basic education and political indoctrination. While colonial policy
had preferred lowly educated and apolitical troops, independent
states seek to create literate citizen-soldiers propagandized into the
national ideology. Another way of integrating the army into the
general population and of creating goodwill toward the military is
to use the armed forces for constructive purposes such as sanitation,
rescue, transportation, public works, and the like, as is done in a
number of states. Thus the army becomes a powerful force for the
education and modernization of new states.

Another point of interest in studying colonial armies is the role
they played in supporting or undermining the colonial system as a
whole. Generally, there is no question that "native troops" served

European imperialism well. They conquered much of Europe's empire, "pacified" African peoples into outward submission, and fought in colonial and world wars as far as Asia and Europe. Yet, at the same time, through the use of African troops in the two world wars, colonial armies contributed significantly, albeit indirectly, to the demise of colonialism. For the first time, tens of thousands of men came in contact with the outside world, associated with white men and women on terms of equality and intimacy, became exposed to quite different racial and political attitudes from the ones held by Europeans in the colonies, and witnessed the military defeat of their colonial masters. In short, war experience unveiled a new world where whites could not keep up their pretense of being a master race. Many returning African servicemen, disgruntled at being demobilized and unable to readjust to civilian life, often became inarticulate but nevertheless effective agents of discontent and unrest against the colonial regime. Though lack of education often prevented Europe's black mercenaries from becoming prominent in the nationalist movements, the demobilized soldiery was undoubtedly an appreciable element of malaise in the post–World War II era, especially in West Africa.

The above remarks barely scratch the surface of the topic. I should simply like to suggest that the systematic analysis of the very special role of colonial-type armies in the transition phase from dependency to sovereignty, such as in preceding chapters of this book, will greatly contribute to political sociology.

We must also stress that the present typology is suggestive rather than definitive, and that reality is more complex than we implied. For example, several types of armies can coexist and, indeed, have often done so, in the same territories. Colonial armies have frequently been used to fight against armies of the first and second types. The Herrenvolk army of South Africa is being developed in anticipation of guerrilla warfare by a revolutionary citizen-army. Sometimes there is an inverse relationship between the development of several types of armies: for example, since the outbreak of the Angolan war of independence, the Portuguese have practically disarmed their colonial troops in their "overseas provinces."

In addition, there is an eighth type of army which fought *in* Africa, but has not been *of* Africa—namely the white armies of the various European powers, when they fought with each other over the control of Africa as in World War II, when they endeavored to put down independence movements as in Algeria and Angola, or when they carried out acts of aggression against African states as did Mussolini against Ethiopia, and France and Britain against Egypt in 1956. The racist mercenaries who have roamed in the Congo in the last few years are also an interesting case, though they belong as much in the annals of banditry and psychopathology as in the study of the military. Because of the transient and expatriate character of these European forces we have excluded them from this study.

Predictions about Africa are much more risky than average. The rapid pace of change and the great diversity between African states combine to invalidate generalizations and projections almost as soon as they are made. It seems reasonably certain, however, that the continent will continue to become more rather than less militarized. At present, Africa still devotes an absolutely, as well as proportionately, lower amount of resources to its armed forces than any other inhabited continent. Only the UAR and South Africa can be described as fairly highly militarized societies. At most a dozen independent states have more than 5000 soldiers under arms, though often quasi-military police forces inflate these numbers. Yet, with only half-a-dozen exceptions, annual military expenditures are still below $5 per capita, and well below the educational budget. Half of the African states still have over 500 civilians per soldier and policeman.

The role of the military in Africa will continue to increase in several ways. The impending racial confrontation in southern Africa will almost certainly take a military form. Civil wars along Nigerian or Congolese lines may develop elsewhere. There is little prospect of a lasting peace in the northeastern corner of Africa, and other international wars, involving African states such as Morocco and Algeria or Ethiopia and Somalia, can be expected to erupt occasionally, at least to the extent of undeclared border flare-ups. More civilian regimes will probably be toppled by coups as they tend to become more tyrannical, elitist, and corrupt.

African armed forces will also continue to emancipate themselves from foreign control, or at least they will continue to multilateralize their dependence by drawing from different foreign countries for military aid, technicians, and weapons. The Africanization of the officer corps, still far from finished in some states, will soon be complete, at least for line officers.

Finally, we may expect that most independent states will pursue a policy of integrating the armed forces into civilian society. Civilian regimes will, of course, attempt to neutralize the political role of their armies, and military regimes, conversely, will sometimes seek legitimacy by coopting civilians, advocating a return to constitutional rule, or staging plebiscites.

In any case, the rather special nature of African armed forces and their growing prominence make their study imperative. African armies are clearly becoming one of the key elements in the political and social change of the continent.

Appendix A

Armed Strength and Defense Expenditures of African States in 1966

Country	Armed forces (regular, excluding gendarmerie and police)	Defense budgets (US $ thousand)	As percentage of total government expenditure	As percentage of estimated GNP
WEST AFRICA				
Chad	900	$ 5,835	13.5	1.8
Dahomey	1,800	4,070	12.0	2.0
Gambia	—	nil	—	—
Ghana	17,000	42,000	7.4	2.5
Guinea	5,000	5,870	8.1	3.1
Ivory Coast	4,000	8,825	6.9	2.4
Liberia	7,000	3,100	6.7	1.8
Mali	3,500	8,825	21.2	3.2
Mauritania	1,000	4,060	17.9	5.1
Niger	1,200	3,650	10.8	1.2
Nigeria	11,500	54,000	9.9	0.9
Senegal	5,500	21,050	11.6	7.6
Sierra Leone	1,360	2,585	4.9	1.3
Togo	1,450	2,757	13.5	4.1
Upper Volta	1,500	2,819	14.1	6.1
Total, West Africa	62,710	$169,446		
NORTH AFRICA AND THE HORN				
Algeria	48,000	$101,000	11.1	4.2
Ethiopia	35,000	31,175	17.0	2.3
Libya	7,000	14,000	5.8	3.5
Morocco	44,800	62,000	10.5	4.7
Somali Republic	9,500	6,670	18.1	4.8
Sudan	18,500	40,000	17.7	4.4
Tunisia	17,000	8,180	4.1	1.5
UAR	180,000	480,000	17.4	8.6
Total, North Africa	359,800	$743,025		
CENTRAL AFRICA				
Burundi	950	$ 970	6.9	0.7
Cameroon	3,500	15,800	19.5	4.2
Central African Republic	600	2,325	7.9	0.6
Congo-Brazzaville	1,800	3,785	8.9	10.9
Congo-Kinshasa	32,000	22,500	14.5	1.7
Gabon	750	2,540	7.6	5.1
Malawi	850	1,500	3.3	1.1
Rwanda	1,500	1,300	9.7	0.7
Zambia	3,000	13,525	5.7	2.5
Total, Central Africa	44,950	$64,245		

Country	Armed forces (regular, excluding gendarmerie and police)	Defense budgets (US $ thousand)	As percentage of total government expenditure	As percentage of esti- mated GNP
EAST AFRICA				
Kenya	4,775	$10,200	6.9	9.8
Malagasy Republic	4,000	9,130	8.8	1.0
Tanzania	1,800	7,225	3.8	0.3
Uganda	5,960	17,025	10.2	1.5
Total, East Africa	16,535	$43,580		
SOUTHERN AFRICA				
Rhodesia		$ 16,900	6.6	1.9
South Africa		322,000	19.9	3.5
Total, Southern Africa		$338,900		

SOURCE: David Wood, *The Armed Forces of African States,* Institute for Strategic Studies, Adelphi Papers, no. 27 (London: 1966), pp. 28–29.

Appendix B

Violence and Military Involvement in African Politics from Independence through 1968

THE FOLLOWING PAGES summarize recent (i.e., post-independence) political events in black-ruled African countries in which violence and/or military involvement has occurred. Events have been drawn from published sources, and include the following categories:

1. Coups d'état and other direct military intervention.
2. Overt threats of military intervention.
3. Mutinies, barracks uprisings, and other intramilitary unrest.
4. Riots, strikes, demonstrations, bombings, sabotage, assassinations, and other forms of civil disorders.
5. Arrests of significant political figures.
6. Border clashes.
7. Involvement of foreign powers in military affairs, such as training programs, and dispatch or removal of non-African troops.

ALGERIA (Independent July 3, 1962)

1962　On June 30, shortly before independence, the provisional government stripped three major FLN leaders—Chief of Staff Colonel Houari Boumedienne, Major Sliman, and Major Menjli—of their ranks. FLN members said they would recognize only Boumedienne, not the new ben Khedda government, an action followed by Colonel Tahar Zbiri. Only one of the six *wilaya* commanders supported ben Khedda at independence. Clashes between Muslims and Europeans during independence celebrations, July 4–6, resulted in over 100 killed and hundreds injured. French Army units assumed control of the European section of Oran with the cooperation of the Algerian government July 8. The conflict between "internal" and "external" ALN continued during July and August, was finally resolved August 3 when ben Bella proclaimed the formation of a seven-man political bureau to supplant the provisional government of ben Khedda. Ben Bella was elected premier by the National Assembly on September 28.

1963　Minister Khemisti was shot by a Muslim in Algiers on April 12.

On June 16 the last French troops left Algiers after 137 years of military presence.

Berber revolt occurred in the Kabylia area with Colonel ou al-Hajj implicated. Army units were sent to put down the rebellion. On October 8, however, intense fighting broke out on the Moroccan border and continued for several weeks. Following an appeal for national unity, ou al-Hajj agreed on November 12 to end the Kabyle dissidence.

1964　Over 1,000 political prisoners were reported to be in jail as counter-revolutionaries. The group included Colonel Mohammed Chaabani, removed from command of *wilaya* IV June 30, arrested July 8, and executed September 3.

1965　President ben Bella was ousted on June 19 in a bloodless coup by army forces led by the minister of defense, Boumedienne.

1967　The government reported crushing an attempted coup by dissident army units led by ex-Chief of Staff Colonel Zbiri on December 14. Ten were killed and one hundred wounded in the clash.

BOTSWANA (Independent September 30, 1966)

1967   Ten armed guerrillas were found near Seronga swamp on March 17. The last British troops left the country in September. An attempt to sabotage the President's plane was discovered in November.

BURUNDI (Independent July 1, 1962)

1962   Five were sentenced to death on November 29 for their roles in the 1961 assassination of Crown Prince Rwangasore.

1964   The Burundi embassy in Leopoldville was sacked by students protesting alleged Burundi aid to Congolese rebels. An aide was hurt, and protests were sent to the Congo government on August 11.

1965   Premier Pierre Ngendandumwe was assassinated in Bujumbura on January 16. Seven Burundi politicians were held, while the assassin was reported to be still at large on January 17.

An unsuccessful coup was reported October 19, with Premier Leopold Biha wounded and the palace attacked. King Mwambutsa was reported safe, but Defense Secretary Captain Michael Micombero reported missing. Martial law was declared the next day, and 34 soldiers and policemen convicted of roles in the coup were executed (2 others escaped) on October 23. Bahutu mobs attacked Watusi villages following the arrest of scores of Bahutu politicians in connection with the attempted coup. Many Watusi were reported slain. After a nationwide search for suspected leaders of the coup, many dissidents were rounded up and nine more were executed. Micombero was given dictatorial powers on October 25. Twenty-four more executions were reported on December 21 after mass trials.

1966   Premier Micombero staged a military coup, overthrew King Ntare V, and declared the country a republic with himself as President on November 28. Provincial governors were replaced by army officers and a nationwide curfew was set. Two large bands of Watusi warriors were believed to have crossed into Rwanda before the coup, and one group of about 1,000 was reportedly routed by the Rwanda army—the Burundi army was not involved. Hutu-Tutsi tensions continued. On December 7, Micombero was raised from the rank of Captain to Colonel.

CAMEROON (Independent January 1, 1960)

1960   Terrorists associated with the banned Union des Populations du Cameroun attacked Douala and Yaoundé from December 30, 1959 to January 2, 1960. Thirty-five were killed. Violence spread, and French troops arrived to put down riots on January 13. Unrest in the Bamileke area was particularly severe: terrorists killed 62 in raids on border towns on February 20; 72 more were killed in Dschang and Banon on February 24; 31 were killed in Bafang on March 4; 30 were killed in Douala on April 9. Security forces killed 213 rebels on June 5.

Opposition leader Felix Moumié was poisoned in Switzerland on November 4.

1962   Ex-Premier Andre Mbida, ex-Minister Charles Okala, and two others were accused of subversion on July 1. Ex-opposition leader Prince Akwa Dika was jailed for acts against the state on August 3.

1964   Ex-Minister Pierre Kandem Ninyim was executed for the murder of an MP on January 4.

The armed forces nearly ended, by August 23, the civil war that began before independence and in which possibly 100,000 died.

1966   236 villagers were killed by terrorists who opposed the government December 12. 17 were sentenced to death on May 14, 1967, for the 1966 murders.

CENTRAL AFRICAN REPUBLIC (Independent August 13, 1960)

1966   Army head Colonel Jean-Bedel Bokassa seized power and ousted President David Dacko January 1. All Communist Chinese nationals were ordered to leave the country on January 3. Five days later, a number of officers were dismissed for alleged collaboration with the "Peoples Army of the Central African Republic."

1967   France airlifted troops to Bangui in early November upon the request of President Bokassa, who maintained he was faced with hostility over his austerity program, which was intended to curb corruption and cut large civil service salaries.

REPUBLIC OF CHAD (Independent August 11, 1960)

1961   Speaker A. Kotoka was held, stripped of office, and expelled for his alleged attempt to kill President François Tombalbaye, on October 4.

1963   On September 1, President Tombalbaye declared an emergency following clashes of demonstrators and security forces. Opposition leaders were held, and the state of emergency was lifted on September 22.

1964   President Tombalbaye charged that adventurers were planning a Sudanese plot against Chad, and threatened expulsion and repatriation of Sudanese on June 14.

Three ministers and two assembly members were arrested in connection with Mangalme district disturbances in which one assembly member and others were killed.

1966   The government closed the border with Sudan and imposed curbs on Sudanese in Chad as President Tombalbaye's 14-day time limit for Sudan to give proof of goodwill expired. It was reported that 390 had been killed in the past 10 months in this border dispute. The border was closed on August 25.

1967   56 were reported killed in battle of "bandits" and government forces February 22 in Salamat.

1968   President Tombalbaye asked France for troops to put down rebellion in the north on August 29.

REPUBLIC OF CONGO (Independent August 15, 1960) Brazzaville

1963   Workers, striking for higher pay and protesting the Youlou government, marched on Brazzaville prison and released all the inmates. Five were killed, twelve hurt, in the rioting. Curfew was imposed on August 13. 1,000 French troops were dispatched to help put down the riots on August 14, but President Fulbert Youlou resigned in the wake of the riots. A new government, headed by Alphonse Massamba-Débat, took control after a period of confusion.

The chief of staff was briefly imprisoned December 3 by men in the ranks, protesting their lack of pay in November; he was released on the basis of government promises.

1964   Pro-Youlou, anti-government riots broke out in Brazzaville on August 15.

1965   Grenade and bomb attacks against the government were reported in Brazzaville. Eighteen were arrested as supporters of Youlou between July 18 and July 27.

1966   On January 10, an attempted coup by members of the governing National Revolutionary Movement collapsed.

Disturbances broke out in Brazzaville June 27, following dismissal of paratroop commander Captain Marien Ngouabi. Chief of Staff Moutsaka and other officers were arrested after forces loyal to Massamba-Débat regained control.

1968   Coup attempt alleged by mercenaries "inspired by high finance and internal reaction" occurred during trip abroad by President Massamba-Débat, on May 13–14.

The National Assembly was dissolved, and activities of Political Bureau of the National Revolutionary Movement (NMR) suspended by the president; a new committee for the defense of the revolution was set up August 1 following an abortive coup attempt by members of the paramilitary Civil Guard and radical members of NMR July 31. Confusion continued, with the arrest of paratroop Captain Ngouabi leading to the occupation of Brazzaville by men loyal to him and the release from jail of former army commander-in-chief Mouzabakani and two captains August 2. In the president's absence, Lieutenant Poignet, the secretary of state for national defense, took over as head of state August 3. Ngouabi was named army commander-in-chief August 4; the president returned to Brazzaville to announce cabinet resignation. On the following day, a National Revolutionary Committee (CNR) was established. Ngouabi stated August 10 that the army believed intervention necessary "to prevent the country from falling into chaos and dismemberment." The constitution was annulled August 16. Captain Raoul was appointed prime minister August 21, taking over several powers previously held by the president; Mouzabakani was named minister of interior, Poignet minister of defense. A state of siege was proclaimed August 30, with arrest warrants issued for two former ministers charged with distributing arms. On September 17, Massamba-Débat was removed from the presidency. Ngouabi, now president of the CNR, announced October 2 that the armed forces had taken power for a "temporary period" until new political institutions were established. He formally took office as president of the country January 2, 1969.

DEMOCRATIC REPUBLIC OF THE CONGO (Independent June 30, 1960) Kinshasa

1960   There was some fighting in Leopoldville and Luluabourg during independence celebrations; 100 were arrested and curfews were imposed on July 3. The key event, however, was the mutiny of the Force Publique on July 5, which added to the growing chaos in the country. Prime Minister Patrice Lumumba dismissed all European officers, imposed martial law, and claimed an assassination attempt by a group of Belgian officers on July 9.

Foreign governments became involved when 1,000 Northern Rhodesian troops arrived at the Congo border, claiming to be ready to protect Europeans on July 11. Rebel troops met the challenge by attacking Elisabethville, fighting loyalist troops and Europeans; five were killed and many hurt. Europeans were advised to leave the country, still on July 11. Belgian troops arrived and fought in Elisabethville; Premier Moise Tshombe declared Katanga independent from the Congo and asked for Belgian troops on July 12. Belgian troops recaptured Jadotville in Katanga, killing 50 mutineers on July 13. The United Nations authorized UN troops to replace Belgian troops; Congo asked Belgium to withdraw its troops; Belgium refused on July 17.

Tshombe refused to allow UN troops into Katanga. The USSR threatened to intervene if Belgian and NATO troops did not leave. Belgian troops finally left Leopoldville on July 24. UN troops entered Katanga on August 12, after anti-government riots in Leopoldville since the departure of the Belgian troops. Lumumba declared martial law for six months on August 17. Government troops were sent to Kasai to check another secessionist movement on August 20. The last Belgian troops left Katanga on August 31.

Civil war broke out between government troops and Baluba tribesmen; in Kasai, Bakwanga fell to the rebels with 300 killed on September 2. Political confusion worsened when President Joseph Kasavubu ousted Lumumba as premier, replacing him with Ileo; Lumumba defied the order on September 5, and ousted Kasavubu as president; however, the deputies canceled both ousters on September 8. Lumumba was arrested by the Congo army, but released after three hours on September 13. The Congo army intervened in a coup led by Colonel Joseph Mobutu, which led to widespread violence September 15. Lumumba was arrested by Mobutu and held for trial, on December 3.

1961 The forces of Mobutu and Lumumba clashed in many areas of the country during January and February. Lumumba escaped from the Leopoldville jail, and he was murdered by "villagers" in Katanga on February 13. Political confusion continued, as the Gizenga regime was set up in Stanleyville as the purported legal heir to the Lumumba regime.

Tshombe was arrested and freed many times during May and June. At his final release he announced an accord with Prime Minister Joseph Ileo to end the secession of Katanga, on June 23. The Gizenga regime was dissolved in favor of the new government headed by Cyrille Adoula on August 7.

UN and Katanga troops clashed, with many killed, during September and October. A cease-fire was arranged and took effect in October, but fighting broke out again in November. Tshombe agreed to end the secession of Katanga and to put the army under Kasavubu on December 14.

1962 Fighting broke out between Gizenga and Lundula forces in Stanleyville on January 14. Tshombe continued his secession after agreeing many times to end it, but he accepted the UN plan to end secession in principle. Throughout the entire year fighting continued in Elisabethville between UN and Katanga troops.

1963 UN troops controlled Katanga by May, thus ending the secession of the province.

On October 3, the National Revolutionary Council (CNR) was formed to overthrow the Adoula government.

1964 Army unrest continued. A Lumumbist attempted coup in August led to the arrest of 2,000, including five officers. On January 29, 1964, rioting broke out among supporters of Lumumba in Stanleyville; a battalion was disarmed. UN troops were removed. Adoula resigned, and Kasavubu named Tshombe to head the government on July 7. CNR groups made advances in several parts of the country, seizing Stanleyville on August 5. Almost 1,000 Belgian troops were landed in Stanleyville by US planes to rescue Europeans in November. Widespread fighting occurred, particularly in Maniema, North Katanga, Stanleyville, and Kwilu.

1965   It was estimated that over 1,000 rebels or suspects had been executed in Stanleyville as government forces liberated the city from them. Approximately 12,000 Congolese had been killed in the Stanleyville area between October and January.

Kasavubu ousted Tshombe as premier and named Evariste Kimba to replace him on October 14. But Major-General Mobutu deposed Kasavubu in a bloodless coup on November 25, making himself president and Colonel Leonard Mulamba premier.

1966   Kimba and three associates were convicted of a plot to kill Mobutu and were executed on June 3.

1967   Tshombe was tried *in absentia*, found guilty of treason, and sentenced to death on March 13.

Mobutu claimed that foreign paratroopers had landed in Kisangani, and that foreign settlers had attacked the Congolese army in Bukavu. Many foreign observers believed the paratroopers were dissident elements of the Congolese army led by white mercenaries. The "government of public safety" set up by Colonel Leonard Monga (an associate of Tshombe) finally collapsed in November, as the rebels fled into Rwanda.

DAHOMEY (Independent August 1, 1960)

1960   Two were killed and eighteen wounded in riots following the first general elections on December 12.

1961   The government uncovered a plot to assassinate President Hubert Maga and a number of ministers on May 30.

1963   A coup led by Colonel Christophe Soglo October 20 ousted the government after four days of rioting and strikes; Maga was placed under arrest on October 29.

1964   Government troops clashed with supporters of ex-President Maga; 193 were arrested.

1965   Army chief, General Soglo, staged a second coup on November 17, overthrowing President Sourou Migan Apithy and Prime Minister Justin Ahomadegbé. Tahirou Congacou was named president October 29, then replaced by a full-fledged military government under Soglo, December 22.

1966   Widespread strikes over the national security program
       October 3–6 led to police and army occupation of key
       points in Cotonou.

       A group of young army officers staged a coup December 17
       against General (now President) Soglo. The new regime
       was headed by Major Maurice Kouandété.

1968   Former leaders called for a boycott of presidential elec-
       tions in May; only 27 per cent of those eligible voted. The
       army decided to continue to rule, but confronted growing
       unrest and abruptly withdrew in favor of a civilian gov-
       ernment in mid-July.

ETHIOPIA (not under colonial rule)

1960   Crown Prince Asfa-Wossen was involved in an abortive
       coup by the Imperial Household Guard while Emperor
       Haile Selassie was in Brazil; the outcome was in doubt
       from December 15 to 17. The Emperor resumed control in
       Addis Ababa, reporting that nineteen government leaders
       were thought to have been executed by the rebels, on
       December 18. Lieutenant Colonel Geheneyo, leader of the
       revolt, was hung on December 20; General Mangistou
       Newaye and another leader were hung December 26. Am-
       nesty was granted to the other rebels and the prince was
       exonerated on December 27.

1961   Two more hangings resulted from the December coup, one
       in March and one in September.

1962   Twelve were held for conspiracy endangering the security
       of the state on October 14.

1963   Somalia charged the Ethiopian army with massive re-
       prisals against Somalis in the Ogaden area with many re-
       ported dead and wounded, on August 18 and 19. The
       border dispute with Somalia flared in the wake of Somali
       acceptance of USSR military aid; Selassie charged on
       November 15 that Somalia provoked the border incidents.

1965   The premier of Sudan reported that a shipment of Czech
       arms had been sent to Sudan for Eritrean rebels seeking
       independence from Ethiopia on June 9.

1966   Several "dissidents," reportedly including Brigadier Gen-
       eral Taddasse Biru, were arrested for alleged conspiracy
       November 26. They were tried and sentenced in February,
       1967.

1967   Reports spread that Cuba and Communist China had agreed to train guerrillas for the Eritrean secessionist movement, which was waging a terrorist campaign against Ethiopia. Army raids halted Eritrean Liberation Front terrorism on April 30, but another large scale drive was opened against the Eritrean rebels from August 27–31.

GABON (Independent August 17, 1960)

1960   Premier Leon Mba proclaimed a six-month state of emergency to deal with post-independence difficulties, on November 18.

1962   A Gabon-Congo soccer game in Libreville led to such bitterness that nine Gabonese were reported killed in Libreville and one in Brazzaville; in return, the Gabon government expelled 3,000 Congolese on September 23. President Youlou declared a state of emergency after retaliatory attacks on Gabonese in Brazzaville and Pointe-Noire in which at least 7 Gabonese were killed and 40 hurt. 1,000 Gabonese were given refuge in an army base near Brazzaville on September 25.

1964   An army committee took over the government in a bloodless coup, forcing Mba to resign and arresting him and high government executives on February 19. President de Gaulle sent troops in response to a diplomatic request based on a French treaty of 1961 which successfully restored the M'ba government; the French reported eighteen Gabonese and one French trooper killed on February 21. Street riots in Libreville were quelled on March 3, but demonstrations continued until French troops intervened on March 6. 1,000 opposition backers were reported kidnapped and released in the jungle far from Libreville on April 13. The opposition protested the elections, but the French troops made a show of force to keep order on April 16. Seventeen were convicted for their roles in the coup attempt on September 10; Lieutenant Daniel Mbene, purported leader of the coup, received a 20-year sentence.

GAMBIA (Independent February 18, 1965)

1965–68   There have been no military or paramilitary incidents.

GHANA (Independent March 6, 1957)

1957   Various subversives were deported during September and October. Twelve government supporters were jailed for kidnapping four opposition members on November 6. The government proclaimed an emergency in Kumasi over tensions and clashes between rival Moslem factions.

1958 36 were held in an attack on the Ashanti regional commissioner's home on February 2. Six, including two MP's, were jailed for conspiracy to prepare an armed attack against Ghana, in order to prevent the amalgamation of British Togoland on March 13. Nine leaders of the opposition United Party were exiled on April 6. Opposition member Reginald Amponsah of the United Party was charged with sedition and jailed on September 21. Police seized Chief Nana Ofori Atta II on September 25. 43 were arrested for plotting to assassinate Prime Minister Kwame Nkrumah and two cabinet ministers on November 11.

Members of the Convention People's Party and the United Party clashed in Kofiase, killing one and injuring three on November 21. The government held two opposition leaders for a plot to assassinate Nkrumah on December 21.

1959 Opposition party supporters were jailed for their role in an alleged plot to assassinate Nkrumah on September 20. Riots in various parts of the country accompanied the elections in October. 70 United Party members were jailed for the role they allegedly played in the election riots, in November; 16 were sentenced the following March.

1960 Ghana strengthened her security forces to forestall a possible attack from French Togoland, and demanded assurances from France on March 16. Twelve opposition leaders were arrested for allegedly having plotted to use French Togoland as a base. Nkrumah continued to threaten to integrate French Togoland into Ghana during February, March, and April.

1961 Canada began the training of the Ghanaian Army on July 4.

Workers struck and demonstrated in Takoradi and Kumasi against the austerity budget and the national compulsory savings plan from September 6–23. The government declared a state of emergency due to the strike on September 8, and imposed curfews on September 12. 48 labor and opposition leaders were arrested for subversion on October 4.

400 Ghanaian cadets were to be trained in the USSR, it was announced in September. On September 22, General

H. T. Alexander, expatriate chief of staff, was dismissed by Nkrumah.

Explosions damaged the statue of Nkrumah in Accra on November 7. 1,000 government opponents were arrested under the preventive detention law during November and December.

1962 Between August and November, there were many bombing attempts against Nkrumah. The first occurred in Kulun-gugu, in the northern region, on August 2; 1 person was killed and 56 injured, but Nkrumah was unharmed. Two more were killed and 63 injured when a bomb exploded in a crowd outside the presidential palace on September 10. 100 were hurt in two bomb blasts during a birthday rally for Nkrumah in Accra on September 21. Twelve more were killed and 256 injured in bombings in Accra and Tema, leading to declaration of a state of emergency in the two cities on September 23. The next day there were three more bombings, and 230 were arrested for breaking curfew. The final bombings in Accra injured two children on November 8.

A large crowd marched on the Accra jail, demanding the execution of former ministers Ako Adjei and Tawia Ada-mafio on September 13. (They were sentenced to death for treason on December 10, 1963; the sentences were not carried out.)

1964 An assassination attempt against Nkrumah, in which a police guard was killed on January 3, led to the closing of the border with Togo on January 4. The police were blamed for the attempt, and ten senior officers were arrested on January 8. Anti-US demonstrations in Accra also followed the attempt. The purge of the police began on February 7. President Nkrumah forced the retirement of Generals S. A. Otu and Ankrah in July.

1965 Ghana mobilized her military forces because of the Rhodesian crisis, and broke her ties with Great Britain over the crisis in December.

1966 Nkrumah was ousted in an army-police coup while on a visit to Hanoi on February 24. The Presidential Guard (POGR) remained loyal and defended the presidential palace but were defeated by the army; General Barwah, head of the POGR, died in the attack. All cabinet ministers were jailed on February 24.

1967   The government reported a plot by Nkrumah's backers, and four were arrested on January 24. An attempted coup on April 17 was quickly crushed, the leaders jailed, and 120 mutineers disarmed. General E. K. Kotoka was killed by the insurgents; Lieutenant Samuel Arthur and Lieutenant Moses Yeboah, leaders of the abortive coup, were publicly executed May 9.

1968   Marshal M. A. Otu, commander of the armed forces, was arrested for suspected complicity in subversive activities on November 20. Major General O. K. Ocran was named acting commander of the armed forces, and Brigadier E. C. K. Amenu was named commander of the army.

GUINEA (Independent October 2, 1958)

1959   Guinean policemen reportedly invaded a French military camp and evicted civilian personnel on January 12.

1961   President Sekou Touré stated that an attempted coup was staged at the Democratic Party convention, and that the French embassy was involved, on December 27. He ordered a purge of all "doubtful officials" from the administration and the arrest of persons attacking the Democratic Party on December 30.

1965   On November 11, the Guinean government reported that a plot to overthrow Touré had failed. Radio Conakry charged that President Felix Houphouet-Boigny of Ivory Coast was implicated.

1966   Ivory Coast moved troops to her border after President Touré announced plans to send troops to Ghana to reinstate Nkrumah on March 18. Ghana seized Guinea's foreign minister and eighteen members of Guinea's delegation aboard a US airplane on their way to a meeting of the OAU in retaliation for Guinea's support of Nkrumah on October 30. Guinea placed the US ambassador and the Pan American traffic manager under house arrest in Conakry. The ambassador was freed, but a mob attacked his home, and the aides at the US embassy were held in "office arrest."

IVORY COAST (Independent August 7, 1960)

1961   Ghana reported that many Sanwi tribesmen fled to Ghana to avoid arrest for refusing to disavow their allegiance to the banished tribal chief on January 20.

1962 Thirteen people were convicted in a plot against President Felix Houphouet-Boigny uncovered in January, and were sentenced to death April 11. The sentences were not carried out.

1963 President Houphouet-Boigny announced that an "ideological" plot had been uncovered. More than 100 were arrested, including six cabinet members, four members of the National Assembly, and the former president of the Supreme Court. Verdicts included 6 sentences of death, 2 life sentences, and 19 jail terms.

KENYA (Independent December 12, 1963)

1963 Somali raiders ambushed a Kenyan police patrol, wounding two, on December 16. A state of emergency was declared in the Northern Frontier District as local Somalis reported terrorism by raiders, December 26–27.

1964 26 were killed and 15 wounded in a tribal battle near the Ethiopian border on January 13. Many were reported dead in tribal clashes in the Northern Frontier District, on August 7.

African soldiers mutinied over pay at the campus near Nairobi and Nakuru January 23. British troops were called in on January 25, and put down the mutiny on the 27th. Sixteen junior noncommissioned officers and men in the ranks were convicted of mutiny in April, receiving terms of five to 14 years.

The government put the nation on emergency alert because of the visit by Zanzibar's field marshal, John Okello, on March 1.

1965 An alleged Mau Mau leader and his top aides were killed in a police raid on January 27.

Three days of sporadic anti-Asian rioting in Kisumu stemmed from a strike by African mechanics in Asian-owned garages, March 27.

USSR training of Kenyan fighter pilots without government knowledge was revealed in Parliament by Defense Minister Mungai March 31.

Students from the Lumumba Institute raided the KANU (Kenya African National Union) headquarters in vain attempts to take over the party on July 7. 27 were charged with an abortive coup and pleaded not guilty.

1966 Mass demonstrations occurred in Nakuru April 28 and May 30. Police seized five leaders of the opposition Kenya People's Union (KPU) on August 5. Opposition leader Oginga Odinga called these arrests the culmination of long-running oppression and intimidation. On November 5, the KPU secretary general, G. Makakha was jailed. New security laws were put into effect on November 5.

1967 The defense minister reported that 40 Somali *shifta* (bandits) and 3 soldiers had been killed in a fierce battle on August 19.

Somalia agreed to resume diplomatic ties with Kenya and to curb the border wars that had caused the death or disappearance of nearly 3,000, after charging that Kenyan troops had killed 63 Somalis in the disputed Northern District, September 13 and October 29.

LESOTHO (Independent September 30, 1966)

1966 King Moshoeshoe was placed under house arrest by the prime minister following anti-government demonstrations. The government threatened to replace the chief on grounds of misconduct December 27. King Moshoeshoe asked Great Britain to send troops to support him in his dispute with the government; the British government refused December 28. Basotho tribesmen attacked police headquarters at Butha on December 30, wounding a few tribesmen and one policeman.

1967 Dr. Makotoko and Mtsu Mokhehle, leaders of opposition parties, were arrested on charges of inciting public violence in January. They later received suspended sentences.

LIBERIA (Independent from 1847, events recorded from 1955)

1955 An unsuccessful assassination attempt on President William V. S. Tubman occurred during the celebration of his re-election. The assassin was seized and linked with the opposition party on June 24. 30 were charged with treason on September 17 for their roles in the June plot. Seven of these, including two ex-ministers, were subsequently sentenced to death.

1958 President Tubman's emergency powers were extended four months after the discovery of "wholesale smuggling" of explosives into the nation on August 27.

1961 President Tubman asked for emergency powers to deal

with subversion by "foreign agencies"; his request was linked to labor agitation and a general strike, September 13. The government restricted foreign missions as a result of plots against Tubman, and asked for the recall of a UAR diplomat on October 4.

1963 A plot to assassinate President Tubman was uncovered. Five men were arrested February 5, including the commander of the National Guard, Colonel David Thompson.

1965 Two Ghanaians were held for subversion, May 7.

1966 On October 10, President Tubman announced, after returning from Europe, that an attempted overthrow of his government had been foiled.

LIBYA (Independent January 2, 1952)

1952 During the February elections, eight were killed and 63 hurt in scattered violence. The government deported the opposition leader, Besher Bey Sadawi, and his close followers because of threats of violence.

1954 Minister Shalhi was assassinated by S. M. Sanussi, the Queen's nephew, on October 6, and a state of emergency was proclaimed on October 12. Several members of the royal family were ordered exiled to the desert, reportedly to avoid further unrest following the Shalhi assassination, on October 19. S. M. Sanussi was sentenced to death on December 12 and hanged February 7, 1955.

1958 Great Britain was reported to have reinforced her troops after warning King Idris of another plot to overthrow him on July 20.

1959 Police broke up riots in Tripoli, March 21.

1964 Students demonstrated to protest the conservatism of the Idris regime, on January 26–28.

1965 Sabotage was blamed in the bombing of four British Petroleum Company oil wells; the wells were afire May 16. The fires continued to burn in two of the three wells through June, and three more oil tanks and a water pipeline were blown up on July 23.

Demonstrators in Tripoli charged that the government had illegally declared progressive candidates in Parliamentary election defeated, May 9. Business and public services were paralyzed on May 11 and a general strike called, May 13.

MALAGASY REPUBLIC (Independent March 26, 1960)

No events of military significance reported.

MALAWI (Independent July 6, 1964)

1964 There was a widespread strike among civil servants to protest Prime Minister Kamuzu Banda's policies on September 30.

Eight critics of the government were killed in a clash between Banda's League of Malawi Youth and the opposition group lead by Henry Chipembere. Banda was given emergency powers to respond to the clash.

1965 Two were killed in a riot in St. Johnston, the center of opposition to Prime Minister Banda, on February 13. The prime minister claimed on March 1 to have crushed the Chipembere uprising.

1966 A Portuguese military patrol crossed the border from Mozambique, killing four, wounding seven, and taking many prisoners on October 30.

MALI (Independent June 20, 1960)

1960 The secession of Senegal from the Mali Federation brought the arrest of leading Soudanese (Malian) politicians and their repatriation in August.

1962 Three ex-ministers were sentenced to death in a mass trial of those charged with a plot to overthrow the government, October 2.

1963 President Modibo Keita reported that nomads were rebelling in the border area and threatened to use force to prevent rebellion, December 8.

1968 The National Assembly resigned and handed over all its powers to President Keita because of the "revolutionary situation" January 18. A Committee for the Defense of the Revolution was set up. Political purges, giving President Keita greater powers and increasing Chinese influence, were reported starting in February.

A November 19 coup deposed President Keita while the President was returning from a national tour. Lieutenant Moussa Traoré and a 14-member National Liberation Committee (CMLN) took command. No senior officer was named to the Committee. The Army commander-in-chief, Colonel Sekou Traoré, and all members of the government and the Committee for Defense of the Revolution, were arrested. The following day, Captain Yoro Diakité set up a provisional government, including several civilians. The militia and various organizations linked to the Union Soudanaise were dissolved.

MAURITANIA (Independent November 28, 1960)

1962　24 Mauritanians were tried on charges of murder (3 Frenchmen had been killed in a grenade attack on an army post March 29) and treason. Three were executed and the others jailed May 3.

1963　Four were held for plotting with Morocco to overthrow the government August 15.

1966　Riots over the linguistic commission report took place in February and March, apparently pitting Negroid inhabitants of the south against Arabic-speaking northerners.

MOROCCO (Independent March 2, 1956, France; April 7, 1956, Spain)

1958　The government sent troops to the Rabat area to combat local anti-government guerrillas in October. During the celebration of the anniversary of the King's reign, riots took place in many areas resulting in 48 killed, 200 wounded in November.

1959　Government troops clashed with supporters of Berber chief Lyonssi in the Fez area. The rebels numbered about 5,000; clashes continued on and off throughout the year.

1961　Clashes between Moroccan and Spanish troops in Spanish Sahara continued throughout the year.

1962　14 Baha'ists were tried in Nador for rebellion; 3 were sentenced to death, the rest to life imprisonment, in a drive to outlaw the sect, during December.

1963　Five members of the opposition party (Istiqlal), including three military police, were arrested for anti-government activities in June. 10 per cent of the National Popular Forces Union members were arrested and charged with a plot against King Hassan's regime in July.

1965　Twenty-five were killed, and dozens hurt in Casablanca riots about government cut-backs in education. Workers struck in support of the students. Riots continued throughout the month of March; 724 rioters were sentenced to prison in April.

1967   Jews were harassed throughout the country after June 6, the day the Six-Day War began. About six were killed; the government deplored the killings.

NIGER (Independent August 3, 1960)

1963   On December 2, 63 were ousted, including former Foreign Minister Zodi Ikhia, for involvement in an alleged plot to overthrow the government of President Hamani Diori. Sentences imposed in May, 1965, included acquittal for 18, death sentences for five, and varying terms of imprisonment.

1964   The government crushed an attempted revolt by political exiles under ex-Premier Djibo Bakary—four were executed, two jailed, and others captured, October 15.

1965   An attempted assassination of President Diori in a grenade attack was foiled April 14.

NIGERIA (Independent October 1, 1960)

1962   Tension grew in the Western Region as a result of a split in the dominant Action Group. A minority faction led by S. L. Akintola disrupted parliamentary proceedings twice, leading to a proclamation in May of a state of emergency by the federal government. The opposition leader, Chief Obafemi Awolowo, was put under house arrest on September 23 and charged, along with 26 others, with treason. Crowds in Western Nigeria demonstrated against the federal government in September and October.

1963   Chief Anthony Enahoro, an Action Group leader, was deported from Great Britain and sentenced to fifteen years for plotting against the government; Chief Awolowo was sentenced to ten years for treason.

1964   Twenty were killed in riots in Benue Province on February 21 over the murder of a clan head.

A nationwide strike over low pay paralysed many activities June 5–10. Sixty were killed in scattered political clashes and rioting on July 19. Over 1200 were estimated to have been killed during July and August in tribal clashes in the northeast.

2,000 United Progressive Grand Alliance (UPGA) members demonstrated against the government in Lagos. The army patrolled the streets for a full week in December. The UPGA boycott of the polls led to victory for the Nigerian

National Alliance (NNA), with tremendous intra-governmental tensions focused on President Nnamdi Azikiwe, who finally named NPC leader Abubakar Tafawa Balewa Prime Minister.

1965 The Eastern Region refused to accept the election results; and demanded an end to federation, January 5. Elections subsequently were held peacefully. However, a regional election in the west resulted in thousands of injuries and several hundred deaths in rioting, during October and November.

1966 In a swift, bloody coup, the federal prime minister and minister of finance, as well as the prime ministers of the Western and Northern Regions were assassinated the night of January 15-16. The uprising, led by a group of young officers (largely Ibo), appeared to portend revolutionary changes, but by January 16, commanding officer Aguiyi-Ironsi, who was not involved in the planning or execution of the coup, asserted his control.

Many Ibos were killed in the north during the first half of the year. The dead were estimated at 500; 3,000 were injured.

In a second coup staged by northern troops, General Aguiyi-Ironsi was seized and killed July 29. Lieutenant Colonel Yakubu Gowon assumed command. Hundreds of Ibos in the north were killed in June and July, and an estimated 300,000 Ibos from the Northern Region fled to the Eastern Region.

1967 The Eastern Region seceded May 31, declaring itself the independent republic of Biafra. The central government mobilized military action against Biafra; federal troops invaded the Eastern Region on July 8. Eastern troops seized the Mid-Western Region on August 9. This successful and unexpected seizure, the result of a coup by midwestern Ibo officers, brought an immediate statement from General Gowon that "total war" would be waged. As federal troops pressed toward Enugu, Biafran forces withdrew from the mid-west September 21; Enugu was taken by federal forces October 4, Calabar October 18.

1968 Peace efforts remained at a standstill as federal forces continued to tighten a noose around Biafra, with the capture of Onitsha March 22 and Port Harcourt May 20.

By late in the year, with the concentration of Biafran forces into a tight area, and with arms shipments still being flown in, the war reached an apparent stalemate.

RWANDA (Independent July 1, 1962)

1962   The country gained independence under fear of reprisals from Watusi refugees based in neighboring Burundi. Clashes occurred early in July.

1963   14 were executed for terrorism in raids from bases at the Uganda border, January 12. A rumor circulated in the United Nations that armed refugees would return from their base in Burundi, November 28.

1964   8,000 Watusis were killed in reprisal for December raids; it was alleged that about 130,000 Watusis had fled since the Bahutu took over government control, January 22. Burundi Premier Ngendandumwe said that the Organization for African Unity should assume responsibility. New clashes were reported on February 6. UN Secretary General Thant offered maximum help and sent an aide, Max Dorsinville, on February 8 to mediate. The exiled Mwami urged the world to end the "carnage." However, UN commissioner Dorsinville reported on March 5 that tribal warfare casualties were greatly exaggerated and that neither Rwanda nor Burundi saw the need for the UN presence. Minister Mudenge blamed foreign agitators for instigating tribal troubles and the UN reported March 6 that from 870 to 1,000 Watusis were dead.

Burundi Vice Premier Masumbuko put the Watusi toll at 20,000–25,000 and reported that 15,000 refugees were in Burundi, March 8. The United Nations airlifted 3,000 Watusi refugees from Congo to Tanzania November 9, and 1,000 more to Tanzania, December 23.

SENEGAL (Independent June 20, 1960)

1961   Arrests followed the discovery of a secret arms dump at Ziguinchor, October 24.

Foreign Minister Doudou Thiam charged "provocative" acts by Portuguese Guinea in a message to the UN Security Council, such as territorial incursions and airspace violations by low-flying craft, December 29.

1962   The government charged that plotters in Mali, led by Doudou Gueye, planned the overthrow of Senegalese government, March 4. Four were convicted and sentenced for plotting against the government in cooperation with the exiles in Mali, April 15.

Premier Mamadou Dia was ousted after a clash with President Leopold Sedar Senghor, in which the president capitalized upon army and paratroop loyalties. Dia and two ex-ministers were arrested and Senghor assumed full control December 18 and 19.

1963   Demonstrators sought the release of ex-Ambassador Tidjane Sy, held on charges of incitement to revolt; two policemen and some demonstrators were hurt September 28.

Election clashes killed 22 and injured 60, December 1–3.

1967   National Assembly leader D. Diop was slain February 4. An attempt to assassinate Senghor at Dakar was unsuccessful. M. Lo and E. M. Drame, backers of ex-Premier Dia, were accused of the assassination plot March 23 and 24; Lo was executed June 30.

SIERRA LEONE (Independent April 27, 1961)

1961   Prime Minister Milton Margai ordered the arrest of 29 opposition party members for planning to disrupt the independence festivities April 24, and five days later the Parliament declared a state of emergency and approved special detention laws. Opposition leader Siaka Stevens was jailed for conspiracy and libel against the prime minister June 27.

1963   A short general strike was waged to protest government fiscal policies on September 10.

1967   Prime Minister Albert Margai (brother of Milton) reported crushing a coup by army officers, and declared a three-month state of emergency on February 8. Following a hotly disputed election, opposition leader Stevens was sworn in as prime minister but was immediately arrested by an army group headed by Brigadier David Lansana; martial law was declared. Demonstrations took place in Freetown in support of Stevens March 21. Lansana himself was deposed March 24 in a bloodless coup. Both Margai and Stevens were held in "protective custody," and the army suspended the House of Representatives and the constitution. A "National Reformation Council" was set up by the ruling junta.

1968   Disgruntled by the lack of progress toward restoring civilian rule, a group of warrant officers grouped in the Anti-Corruption Revolutionary Movement seized control, imprisoned almost all army and police officers, and invited Stevens to return from exile in Guinea. A civilian government under Stevens was installed.

Unrest in Bo and Kenema districts led to the postponement of by-elections in November. Ethnic tensions mounted among Mende supporters of the SLPP, and a state of emergency was declared November 19. Clashes between demonstrators and army and police units occurred in Bo, Kenema, and Tongo.

SOMALIA (Independent July 1, 1960)

1960   Following the National Assembly election of President Osman, demonstrators of three opposition parties attempted to march on the Assembly, one was killed and 32 hurt, July 2; 80 demonstrators were arrested.

1961   Somalia charged that Ethiopian planes and troops had killed over 100 Somali nomads along the border in the Damat region, January 2. Crowds in Mogadishu demonstrated against Ethiopia and US military aid to Ethiopia the following day. 400 Ethiopians were wounded in clashes in Harar province, January 3. Further clashes were reported in April and August.

An abortive army coup in Hargeisa (capital of the former British-ruled Somaliland Protectorate) brought numerous arrests December 10.

1962   Chiefs of five tribes in the northern region of Somali asked Emperor Haile Selassie of Ethiopia for aid in liberating them from oppression and degradation under Somali rule, October 18. 50 were hurt and 33 killed in clashes in Geldeget and Burtele, October 28.

1963   21 army officers accused of plotting against the government after the abortive 1961 military coup were acquitted, March 9.

Four were killed in clashes at Hargeisa, an emergency was declared and curfew imposed, May 3.

1964   Somali raiders attacked a police post in Kenya January 2 (see Kenya, 1963). Ethiopian planes destroyed two Somali border police posts January 17. Ethiopia reported that her security forces had killed 26 Somali raiders and captured ammunition, a supply truck, and 26 men on January 18. Somali and Ethiopian forces clashed at the border February 8. Ethiopia reported that 2,000 Somali troops had invaded but been dispersed after clashes, killing 100 Somalis and injuring 220. 9 Ethiopians were killed and 44 hurt in the fray February 9. President Osman declared a state of emergency throughout Somalia as the border fighting continued through May. Despite peace talks in the Sudan during March, the tensions could not be eased. Fighting also erupted on the Kenya border, with Somalia charging April 24 that 574 Somalis had been killed, 210 wounded in Northern Frontier District of Kenya in the past 15 months. Other border conflicts were reported. In late August it was reported 70,000 fled to Ethiopia, charging that the government discriminated against those in former British Somaliland; Somalia claimed the flight to be normal nomad migration.

1966 Ethiopia reported a border clash with Somalia in the Ogaden area April 1. However, relative calm appears to have returned as the three governments undertook to reduce tensions.

Sudan (Independent January 1, 1956)

1957 Nine officers were arrested June 12 for conspiring to overthrow the government; they were subsequently convicted and sentenced.

1958 Sudan reported a "huge infiltration" of Egyptians into a disputed area north of the 22nd parallel February 21. On July 24, an attempt by pro-Nasser forces to seize the government was reported.

Political gatherings and demonstrations were banned in Khartoum and Omdurman October 28, as tensions mounted as a result of government instability. On November 17, Lieutenant General Ibrahim Abboud seized the government, charging that political wrangling, corruption, and instability were the cause of the seizure. He invoked a state of emergency, suspended the constitution, and dismissed parliament. The Supreme Council of the Armed Forces assumed power.

1959 On May 22, units of the eastern and northern army commands attempted to enter Khartoum, the result of tensions that had, in March, led to dismissal of Major General Abdel Wahab. Two ministers, 15 army officers, and several other political figures were arrested. On November 10, Omdurman radio reported an attempted mutiny at the army infantry school led by officers who had been dismissed following the abortive May revolt. General Abboud reported that the revolt had been crushed. Following a court martial, five plotters were executed December 3.

1960   Demonstrations against the military government were reported in Khartoum on November 26.

1961   Two ex-ministers and a dozen other top officials were arrested for "rumor-mongering" July 12. Most were released in January, 1962.

1963   The southern secessionist movement continued to grow in strength during 1963. Groups of terrorists joined in the Anya'nya sought to gain independence for the three southern provinces.

1964   Three were sentenced to death for trying to seize the town of Wau in the southern province of Bahr-el-Ghezal on February 22. 300 Christian missionaries were deported for their links with alleged southern rebels on February 28. On March 4, 29 were sentenced, 34 acquitted, in trials in the south.

The failures of government policy in the south dramatically increased tensions in Khartoum late in October. Anti-government student demonstrators attacked and tried to burn the US Embassy in Khartoum, October 25–26. Several were killed and hundreds arrested despite the curfew and patrolling tanks and army units. Forced to capitulate as government authority collapsed in the face of a general strike, General Abboud dissolved the ruling Armed Forces Supreme Council and the cabinet preparatory to the drafting of a constitution and election in response to the "collective wishes" of the people. Seven army officers, including the former labor commissioner, Lieutenant Colonel Abdehalem, were arrested on November 9. As pressure continued to mount, Abboud resigned as president and army commander on November 15. A civilian government under Premier al-Khalifa was established. At least 10 were officially reported killed and 400 hurt in racial rioting between Arabs and Africans in Khartoum December 8; the following day, 38 were reported killed and more than 500 hurt in racial outbreaks, but the toll in riots was believed to be far above official reports.

1965   Major demonstrations occurred in Khartoum on February 7 and February 27. To calm the situation, elections were scheduled for a constituent assembly April 21. 14 were killed at Khashm-el-Gikba as policemen resisted the efforts of People's Democratic Party supporters to prevent voting in the election; 300 were arrested throughout the country, April 22. Four ex-army officers were held for plotting June 5. On June 9, fifteen men, including two ministers, were held in connection with the probe of a shipment of Czech arms. Police used tear gas in Khartoum to break up a student demonstration for the immediate trial of members of ex-President Abboud's military junta, July 6.

Fighting in the south intensified in the latter part of 1965, particularly with the capture or purchase of arms destined for the Congo by southern rebels. In October, 60 army officers reportedly mutinied and refused to receive orders until higher officers heard their grievances about the war in the south.

1966   On December 28, Premier al-Mahdi reported loyal troops crushed a revolt by troops at the Gordon training school, near Khartoum. More than 300 military officials and leftist and communist politicians were arrested for alleged complicity; most were shortly released.

1968   Southern political leader William Deng was murdered May 5, reportedly in ambush.

SWAZILAND (Independent September 6, 1968)
No events of military significance reported.

TANZANIA (Independent April 26, 1961)
1964   The first battalion of the Tanganyika Rifles seized key points in Dar-es-Salaam January 19–20 in a dispute over pay and the continuation of British officers. The mutiny subsequently spread to Tabora. With President Nyerere in hiding, British commandos landed January 25 and rapidly crushed the mutiny. Members of the two battalions were disarmed and dismissed; Nyerere called for reconstituting the army on the basis of the TANU Youth League.

Numerous opponents of merger between Zanzibar and Tanganyika were arrested in Zanzibar due to fear of a coup against Vice-President Karume on November 6. 62 more were arrested for subversion and charged with aiding a plot by "Western Powers" to overthrow government on November 11. Two days later, five plotters were sentenced to death.

1965 200 university students demonstrated at the British embassy in Dar-es-Salaam to protest lack of British force against Rhodesia after the November unilateral declaration of independence.

Togo (Independent April 27, 1960)

1961 Eighteen men were arrested in a plot to assassinate President Sylvanus Olympio and cabinet members December 14.

1962 In an unsuccessful attempt to assassinate President Olympio, an unidentified man was killed January 22.

1963 A few days after rebuffing veterans' demands for higher pensions, President Olympio was assassinated by military insurgents January 13. Five cabinet ministers were arrested and, after a period of indecision, the military junta appointed former Premier Nicolas Grunitzky as president. The purported pro-north bias of the new government and steps taken against the southern Ewe helped prompt an abortive overthrow effort April 10, led by ex-Minister Kutukuli.

1966 The army halted an attempted coup against President Grunitzky on November 20; once again, Ewe supporters associated with former President Olympio were blamed.

1967 On the fourth anniversary of the assassination of Olympio, a second military coup ousted the Grunitzky regime. Lieutenant Colonel Etienne Eyadema assumed the presidency. On April 24, he was slightly wounded in an assassination attempt by a member of the palace guard.

Tunisia (Independent March 20, 1957)

1957 After independence, a series of clashes occurred between Tunisian mobs or troops and French troops still stationed in the country.

1958 French planes attacked the village of Sakiet-Sidi-Youssef in reprisal for Tunisian downing of a French plane; 72 were killed, 80 wounded, in February. Tunisia increased pressure on France to remove its troops; clashes between

Tunisian and French troops continued throughout 1958. Total mobilization of Tunisian forces was ordered May 25.

1961   France and Tunisian troops clashed at the French base of Bizerte. The French launched massive air attacks to break the siege. By August the fighting stopped, with 670 Tunisians and 30 French killed, and 1,205 on both sides wounded. A negotiated settlement brought rapid French withdrawal from the base.

1962   The government reported crushing a plot against the Bourguiba regime, with over 100 arrested, on December 24. The following month, seven officers were sentenced to death for their roles in the alleged plot.

1966   A student demonstration in Tunis during December was broken up by police and the national guard; 40 were arrested.

UGANDA (Independent October 9, 1962)

1963   Ethnic violence flared in April between Dodoth and Turkana, and in October as hill tribes launched a campaign for autonomy from Toro rule.

1964   Army troops in Jinja mutinied January 23, reportedly over pay. British officers and noncommissioned officers and a government minister were held. Following an appeal from Prime Minister Milton Obote, Great Britain sent troops that put down the mutiny January 26. Four mutineers were sentenced in May.

Border tensions became acute in March, leading to a declaration by the prime minister March 28 that areas bordering on Congo and Sudan were disturbed.

A long-standing dispute between Buganda and Bunyoro, the "lost counties" issue, was resolved by a referendum November 6, in which voters favored rejoining the area to Bunyoro. Riots broke out in Buganda shortly thereafter.

1965   On May 17, the government of Kenya seized eleven truckloads of weapons on the Tanzania-Uganda road for which no license had been obtained.

1966   In a rapid move February 23, Prime Minister Obote seized all power, stripping the president (the Kabaka of Buganda) of his power by suspending the constitution. Tension mounted in Buganda, and a state of emergency was proclaimed. Direct military action was undertaken May 25 against Buganda following riots over demand by the Kabaka that President Obote remove the government from Kampala and the rest of Buganda by the end of the month. The Kabaka's palace was occupied May 25–26 following heavy fighting, during which the Kabaka escaped. Obote insisted that "the oneness of Uganda must be assured" and that the Baganda had been planning armed insurrection to control the entire country.

1967 On November 3, the National Assembly extended, for a further six months, the state of emergency in Buganda; it was continued April 25, 1968, for an additional six months.

UNITED ARAB REPUBLIC (events recorded from 1952)

1952 In a rapid coup July 23, officers led by Mohammed Naguib and Gamal Abdel Nasser deposed King Farouk.

1953 Hundreds were arrested, including 25 military officers, and all political parties were dissolved January 16 with the discovery of a plot to overthrow the government. The military governor of the Western Desert was subsequently imprisoned for attempting to incite rebellion in the armed forces. Many other sentences were also imposed. On June 18, a republic was proclaimed, with Naguib both president and premier.

1954 Intramilitary disputes led on February 25 to the resignation of Naguib as president, premier, and revolutionary Command Council leader after the Council rejected his request for autocratic powers; Vice-President Nasser became premier and Council leader. On April 28, 16 officers and 40 civilians were arrested for plotting against Nasser; 13 of the officers were convicted and imprisoned. In October, more than 500 members of the banned Muslim Brotherhood were arrested for anti-government activities; the following month, several Brotherhood leaders were tried, found guilty, and executed.

1956 On July 27, President Nasser nationalized the Suez Canal. In October, the Sinai peninsula was invaded by Israel; Great Britain and France sent troops to occupy the canal area. Heavy fighting occurred, until a UN-imposed cease-fire ended the conflict and brought the withdrawal of invading forces.

1957 A purge of military officers resulted during July and August in 32 arrests. Eleven were sentenced to prison in October.

1965 In September, an attempt by the Muslim Brotherhood to assassinate Nasser was discovered; 4,000 were reported arrested. In December, 6 former army officers and 19 others were charged with plotting to overthrow the government and were given life imprisonment.

1966 In April, 162 Muslim Brotherhood members and 20 army officers were arrested for complicity in alleged plots; apparently, dissatisfaction centered on Nasser's handling of the conflict in Yemen.

1967 In the wake of the war with Israel June 5–11, President Nasser tendered his resignation but then returned to the presidency. During August, 150 senior army officers were arrested; Field Marshal Abdel Hakim Amer, a close associate of Nasser, committed suicide after his arrest.

UPPER VOLTA (Independent August 5, 1960)

1966 A coup lead by army chief Sangoulé Lamizana toppled the government of President Maurice Yaméogo January 3, following strikes and demonstrations in Ouagadougou. In September, 20 people were injured in Kedougou in clashes between backers of ex-President Yaméogo and Lamizana.

1967 35 arrested following discovery of August 5 plot intended to restore Yaméogo. 24 were sentenced, including the wife and the son of the former president, and 11 were acquitted June 5 of complicity.

ZAMBIA (Independent October 24, 1964)

1965 Following the Rhodesian unilateral declaration of independence, the British Cabinet decided to send a token force to Zambia to help defend the Kariba hydroelectric complex; because of succeeding events, the troops were not sent.

1966 150 university students and Rhodesian nationals staged an anti-British riot at Lusaka to protest killing of seven African guerrillas in Rhodesia on May 1.

1967 On October 30, Zambian and Congo troops and police captured Lumpa sect leader Alice Lenshina, who led rebellion in 1964 prior to independence.

1968   On April 7, the Zambian Government reported Portuguese
        planes bombed 3 villages on the border with Angola,
        killing 6 and wounding 20. Following riots and violence in
        the Copperbelt, Lusaka, and rural areas in August, the
        government banned the opposition United Party and ar-
        rested its leader, N. Mundea.

Bibliography

BOOKS

AFRIFA, COLONEL A. A. *The Ghana Coup, 24th February, 1966.* New York: Humanities Press, 1966.

ALEXANDER, H. T. *African Tightrope: My Two Years as Nkrumah's Chief of Staff.* London: Pall Mall, 1965.

ANDRESKI, STANISLAW. *Military Organization and Society.* Second edition. Berkeley and Los Angeles: University of California Press, 1968.

APTER, DAVID. *The Politics of Modernization.* Chicago: University of Chicago Press, 1965.

AUSTIN, DENNIS. *Politics in Ghana 1946–1960.* London: Oxford University Press, 1964.

BELL, M. J. V. *Army and Nation in Sub-Saharan Africa.* Adelphi Papers, no. 21. London: Institute for Strategic Studies, 1965.

BIENEN, HENRY. *The Military Intervenes: Case Studies in Political Development.* New York: Russell Sage Foundation, 1968.

BRINTON, CRANE. *The Anatomy of Revolution.* New York: Vintage, 1965.

CHORLEY, KATHARINE. *Armies and the Art of Revolution.* London: Faber and Faber, 1943.

COLEMAN, JAMES S., and ROSSBERG, CARL G., eds. *Political Parties and National Integration in Tropical Africa.* Berkeley and Los Angeles: University of California Press, 1965.

COWARD, H. R. *Military Technology in Developing Countries.* Cambridge, Mass.: Center for International Studies, 1964.

DAALDER, H. *The Role of the Military in the Emerging Countries.* The Hague: Mouton, 1962.

ECKSTEIN, HARRY, ed. *Internal War: Problems and Approaches.* New York: Free Press, 1964.

EMERSON, RUPERT. *From Empire to Nation: The Rise to Self-Assertion of Asian and African Peoples.* Cambridge: Harvard University Press, 1960.

EWING, LAWRENCE L., and SELLERS, ROBERT C., eds. *Reference Handbook of the Armed Forces of the World.* Washington: Robert C. Sellers Associates, 1966.

FINER, SAMUEL. *The Man on Horseback: The Role of the Military in Politics.* London: Pall Mall, 1962.

FISHER, SYDNEY NETTLETON, ed. *The Military in the Middle East.* Columbus: Ohio State University Press, 1963.

GOODSPEED, D. J. *The Conspirators: A Study of the Coup d'Etat.* London: MacMillan, 1962.

GLICKMAN, HARVEY. *Some Observations on the Army and Political Unrest in Tanganyika.* Pittsburgh: Duquesne University Press, 1964.

GREENFIELD, RICHARD. *Ethiopia: A New Political History.* London: Pall Mall, 1965.

GUTTERIDGE, WILLIAM. *Armed Forces in New States.* New York: Oxford University Press, 1962.

_____. *Military Institutions and Power in the New States.* New York: Praeger, 1965.

HADDAD, GEORGE M. *Revolutions and Military Rule in the Middle East: The Northern Tier.* New York: Speller, 1965.

HAMON, LEO, ed. *Le Rôle extra-militaire de l'armée dans le tiers monde.* Paris: Presses Universitaires de France, 1966.

HANNING, HUGH. *The Peaceful Uses of Military Forces.* New York: Praeger, 1967.

HENDERSON, K. D. D. *The Sudan Republic.* New York: Praeger, 1965.

HOSKYNS, CATHERINE. *The Congo Since Independence, January*

1960–December 1961. London: Oxford University Press, for the Royal Institute of International Affairs, 1965.

HOWARD M., ed. *Soldiers and Governments: Nine Case Studies in Civil-Military Relations*. London: Eyre and Spottiswoode, 1957.

HUNTINGTON, SAMUEL, ed. *Changing Patterns of Military Politics*. New York: Free Press, 1962.

——————. *The Soldier and the State: The Theory and Politics of Civil-Military Relations*. New York: Random House, 1964.

JANOWITZ, MORRIS. *The Military in the Political Development of New Nations: An Essay in Comparative Analysis*. Chicago: University of Chicago Press, 1964.

——————. *The New Military: Changing Patterns of Organization*. New York: Russell Sage Foundation, 1964.

——————. *The Professional Soldier*. New York: Free Press, 1960.

JOHNSON, CHALMERS. *Revolutionary Change*. Boston: Little, Brown, 1966.

JOHNSON, JOHN J. *The Military and Society in Latin America*. Stanford: Stanford University Press, 1964.

LEE, J. M. *African Armies and Civil Order*. New York: Praeger, 1969.

LEIDEN, CARL, and SCHMITT, KARL M. *The Politics of Violence: Revolution in the Modern World*. Englewood Cliffs, N.J.: Prentice-Hall, 1968.

LIEUWEN, EDWIN. *Arms and Politics in Latin America*. New York: Praeger, 1961.

——————. *Generals vs. Presidents: Neo-Militarism in Latin America*. New York: Praeger, 1964.

McWILLIAMS, WILSON C., ed. *Garrisons and Government: Politics and the Military in New States*. San Francisco: Chandler, 1967.

NKRUMAH, KWAME. *Dark Days in Ghana*. London: Lawrence and Wishart, 1968.

PAYNE, STANLEY G. *Politics and the Military in Modern Spain*. Stanford: Stanford University Press, 1967.

RALSTON, DAVID B., ed. *Soldiers and States*. Boston: Heath, 1967.

SUTTON, JOHN L., and KEMP, GEOFFREY. *Arms to Developing Countries*. Adelphi Papers, no. 28. London: Institute for Strategic Studies, 1966.

VAN DOORN, JACQUES, ed. *Armed Forces and Society: Sociological Essays*. The Hague: Mouton, 1968.

VATIKIOTIS, P. J. *The Egyptian Army in Politics: Pattern for New Nations?* Bloomington: Indiana University Press, 1961.

VERNIER, BERNARD. *Armée et politique au moyen orient*. Paris: Payot, 1966.

WEIKER, WALTER F. *The Turkish Revolution.* Washington, D.C.: Brookings Institution, 1963.

WOOD, DAVID. *The Middle East and the Arab World: The Military Context.* Adelphi Papers, no. 20. London: Institute for Strategic Studies, 1965.

—————. *The Armed Forces of African States.* Adelphi Papers, no. 27. London: Institute for Strategic Studies, 1966.

ZARTMAN, I. WILLIAM. *Problems of New Power: Morocco.* New York: Atherton, 1964.

ZOLBERG, ARISTIDE R. *Creating Political Order: The Party-States of West Africa.* Chicago: Rand McNally, 1966.

ARTICLES

AMANN, PETER. "Revolution: A Redefinition." *Political Science Quarterly* LXXVII (1962), 36–53.

ANKRAH, JOSEPH A. "The Future of the Military in Ghana." *African Forum* II, no. 1 (1966), 5–16.

AUSTIN, DENNIS. "The Underlying Problem of Army Coups d'Etat in Africa." *Optima* XVI, no. 2 (1966), 65–72.

BECHTOLD, PETER. "The Military in Sudanese Politics." *Africa Today* April–May 1968, pp. 23–25.

BESHIR, MOHAMMED O. "The Sudan: A Military Surrender." *Africa Report* December 1964, pp. 3–6.

BIENEN, HENRY. "National Security in Tanganyika after the Mutiny." *Transition* V (1965), 39–46.

BRICE, BELMONT, JR. "The Nature and Role of the Military in Sub-Saharan Africa." *African Forum* II (1966), 57–67.

COLEMAN, JAMES S., and BRICE, BELMONT, JR. "The Role of the Military in Sub-Saharan Africa." In *The Role of the Military in Underdeveloped Countries,* edited by John J. Johnson. Princeton: Princeton University Press, 1962.

COWAN, L. GRAY. "The Military and African Politics." *International Journal* XXI (1966), 289–97.

CROCKER, CHESTER A. "External Military Assistance to Sub-Saharan Africa." *Africa Today* April–May 1968, 15–20.

—————. "France's Changing Military Interests." *Africa Report* June 1968, pp. 16–24, 41.

DALBY, DAVID. "The Military Takeover in Sierra Leone." *World Today* XXI (1967), 354–60.

DUBOIS, VICTOR D. "The Role of the Army in Guinea." *Africa Report* January 1963, pp. 3–5.

DUPUY, TREVOR. "Burma and Its Army: A Contrast in Motivations and Characteristics." *Antioch Review* XX (1960–61), 428–40.

FEIT, EDWARD. "Military Coups and Political Development: Some Lessons from Ghana and Nigeria." *World Politics,* XX, no. 2 (1967–68), 179–93.

FINDLAY, DAVID J. "The Ghana Coup: One Year Later." *Transaction* May 1967, pp. 16–22.

FOLTZ, WILLIAM J. "Military Influences." In *African Diplomacy: Studies in the Determinants of Foreign Policy,* edited by Vernon McKay. New York: Praeger, 1966.

FOSSUM, EGIL. "Factors Influencing the Occurrence of Military Coups d'Etat in Latin America." *Journal of Peace Research* IV (1967), 228–51.

GINWALA, FRENE. "The Tanganyika Mutiny." *World Today* March 1964, pp. 93–97.

GLICKMAN, HARVEY. "The Military in African Politics: A Bibliographic Essay." *African Forum* II, no. 1 (1966), 68–75.

GREENE, FRED. "Toward Understanding Military Coups." *Africa Report* February 1966, pp. 10–14.

GRUNDY, KENNETH W. "Conflicting Images of the Military in Africa." Makerere Short Studies and Reprint Series in Political Science, no. 3. Kampala: East African Publishing House, 1968.

————. "On Machiavelli and the Mercenaries." *Journal of Modern African Studies* VI (1968), 295–310.

GURR, TED. "Psychological Factors in Civil Violence." *World Politics* XX (1967–68), 245–78.

GUTTERIDGE, WILLIAM F. "Military Elites in Ghana and Nigeria." *African Forum* II (1966), 31–41.

HALPERN, MANFRED. "The Army." In *The Politics of Social Change in the Middle East and North Africa,* by Halpern. Princeton: Princeton University Press, 1963.

HARRIS, GEORGE S. "The Role of the Military in Turkish Politics." *Middle East Journal* XIX (1965–66), 54–66, 169–76.

HASAN, YUSUF FADL. "The Sudanese Revolution of October 1964." *Journal of Modern African Studies* V (1967), 491–509.

HOPKINS, KEITH. "Civil-Military Relations in Developing Countries." *British Journal of Sociology* XVII (1966), 165–82.

HOWE, RUSSELL WARREN. "Togo: Four Years of Military Rule." *Africa Report* May 1967, pp. 6–12.

HUNTINGTON, SAMUEL. "Political Development and Political Decay." *World Politics* XVII (1964–65), 386–430.

IDENBURG, P. J. "Political Structural Development in Tropical Africa." *Orbis* XI (1967), 256–70.

JOHNS, DAVID. "Defense and Police Organization in East Africa." Paper presented at the East African Institute of Social Research Conference, December, 1963.

KAMENKA, EUGENE. "The Concept of a Political Revolution." In *Revolution* (Nomos VIII), edited by Carl J. Friedrich. New York: Atherton, 1966.

KILNER, PETER. "Military Government in the Sudan." *World Today* June 1962, pp. 259–68.

KYLE, KEITH. "Mutinies and After." *The Spectator* January 31, 1964, p. 139.

KRAUS, JON. "The Men in Charge." *Africa Report* April 1966, pp. 16–20.

LEMARCHAND, RENE. "Dahomey: Coup within a Coup." *Africa Report* June 1968, pp. 46–54.

LERNER, D., and ROBINSON, R. D. "Swords and Ploughshares: The Turkish Army as a Modernizing Force," *World Politics* XIII (1960–61), 19–44.

LEVINE, VICTOR T. "The Course of Political Violence in Africa." In *French-Speaking Africa: The Search for Identity,* edited by William H. Lewis. New York: Walker, 1965.

_____. "The Trauma of Independence in French-Speaking Africa." *Journal of Developing Areas* II (1968), 211–24.

_____. "The Coup in the Central African Republic." *Africa Today* April–May 1968, pp. 12–14.

LISSAK, MOSHE. "Modernization and Role-Expansion of the Military in Developing Countries: A Comparative Analysis." *Comparative Studies in Society and History* IX, no. 3 (1967), 233–55.

_____. "Selected Literature of Revolutions and Coups d'Etat in the Developing Nations." In *The New Military: Changing Patterns of Organization,* edited by Morris Janowitz. New York: Russell Sage Foundation, 1964.

_____. "Stages of Modernization and Patterns of Military Coups." Paper presented at the Conference on Armed Forces and Society, International Sociological Association, 1967.

MAZRUI, ALI A. "Thoughts on Assassination in Africa." Paper presented at the International Political Science Association, 1967.

_____, and ROTHCHILD, DONALD. "The Soldier and the State in East Africa: Some Theoretical Conclusions on the Army Mutinies of 1964." *Western Political Quarterly* XX (1967), 82–96.

MOORE, RAYMOND A. "The Army as a Vehicle for Social Change in Pakistan." *Journal of Developing Areas* II, no. 2 (1967), 57–74.

MURRAY, ROGER. "Militarism in Africa." *New Left Review* no. 38 (1966), pp. 35–59.

NELKIN, DOROTHY. "The Economic and Social Setting of Military

Takeovers in Africa." *Journal of Asian and African Studies* II (1967), 230–44.

NEWBURY, C. W. "Military Intervention and Political Change in West Africa." *Africa Quarterly* VII (1967), 215–21.

OLUSANYA, G. O. "The Role of Ex-Servicemen in Nigerian Politics." *Journal of Modern African Studies* VI (1968), 221–32.

PAUKER, GUY J. "Southeast Asia as a Problem Area in the Next Decade." *World Politics* XI (1958–59), 325–45.

PERLMUTTER, AMOS. "The Israeli Army in Politics: The Persistence of the Civilian Over the Military." *World Politics* XX (1967–68), 606–43.

PUTNAM, ROBERT D. "Toward Explaining Military Intervention in Latin American Politics." *World Politics* XX (1967–68), 83–110.

PYE, LUCIAN W. "Armies in the Process of Political Modernization." In *The Role of the Military in Underdeveloped Countries,* edited by John J. Johnson. Princeton: Princeton University Press, 1962.

RAPOPORT, DAVID C. "Coup d'Etat: The View of the Men Firing Pistols." In *Revolution* (Nomos VIII) edited by Carl J. Friedrich. New York: Atherton, 1966.

————. "Military and Civil Societies: The Contemporary Significance of a Traditional Subject in Political Theory." *Political Studies* XII (1964), 178–201.

ROTHCHILD, DONALD. "The Effects of Mobilization in British Africa." Institute of African Affairs, reprint no. 2. Pittsburgh: Duquesne University, Institute of African Studies, n.d.

ROULEAU, ERIC. "L'Armée Nationale Congolaise." In *Le Rôle extra-militaire de l'armée dans le tier monde,* edited by Leo Hamon. Paris: Presses Universitaires de France, 1966.

RUSTOW, DANKWART A. "The Army and the Founding of the Turkish Republic." *World Politics* XI (1958–59), 513–52.

————. "Military Regimes." In *A World of Nations: Problems of Political Modernization,* by Rustow. Washington, D.C.: Brookings Institution, 1967.

————. "The Military in Middle Eastern Society and Politics." In *The Military in the Middle East,* edited by S. N. Fisher. Columbus: Ohio State University Press, 1963.

SALE, J. KIRK. "The Generals and the Future of Africa." *The Nation* March 21, 1966, pp. 317–18.

SCHLEH, EUGENE P. S. "The Post-War Careers of Ex-Servicemen in Ghana and Uganda." *Journal of Modern African Studies* VI (1968), 203–20.

SCHNEYDER, PHILLIPPE. "Les Armées Africaines." *Espirit* September 1967, pp. 300–318.

SHEPHERD, GEORGE W., JR. "Seven Days that Shook the World." *Africa Today* December 1964, pp. 10–13.

SKLAR, RICHARD D., and WHITAKER, C. S., JR. "The Federal Republic of Nigeria." In *National Unity and Regionalism in Eight African States,* edited by Gwendolen Carter. Ithaca: Cornell University Press, 1966.

SKURNIK, W. A. E. "Dahomey: The End of a Military Regime." *Africa Today* April–May 1968, pp. 21–22.

STEVENSON, CHARLES. "African Armed Forces." *Military Review* March 1967, p. 20.

STONE, LAWRENCE. "Theories of Revolution." *World Politics* XVIII (1965–66), 159–76.

TERRAY, EMMANUEL. "Les Révolutions congolaise et dahoméenne de 1963: Essai d'interpretation." *Revue française de science politique* XIV (1964), 917–42.

THOMPSON, VIRGINIA. "Dahomey." In *Five African States,* edited by Gwendolen M. Carter. Ithaca: Cornell University Press, 1963.

VAN DEN BERGHE, PIERRE L. "The Role of the Army in Contemporary Africa." *Africa Report* March 1965, pp. 12–18.

VON DER MEHDEN, FRED, and ANDERSON, CHARLES W. "Political Action by the Military in the Developing Areas." *Social Research* XXVIII (1961), 459–70.

WEEKS, GEORGE. "The Armies of Africa." *Africa Report* January 1964, pp. 4–21.

WELCH, CLAUDE E., JR. "Africa's New Rulers." *Africa Today* April–May 1968, pp. 7–11.

_____. "The African Military and Political Development." Paper presented at the 1967 annual meeting of the African Studies Association; to be published in *The Military and Political Development,* edited by Henry Bienen, forthcoming.

_____. "Ghana: The Politics of Military Withdrawal." *Current History* February 1968, pp. 95–100, 113–14.

_____. "Soldier and State in Africa." *Journal of Modern African Studies* V (1967), 305–22.

WILLAME, J. C. "Military Intervention in the Congo." *Africa Report* November 1966, pp. 41–45.

ZOLBERG, ARISTIDE R. "The Structure of Political Conflict in the New States of Tropical Africa." *American Political Science Review* LXII (1968), 43–56.

_____. "A View from the Congo." *World Politics* XIX (1966), 137–49.

Glossary of Acronyms

Names given here in brackets are English translations as used in this book.

ABAKO   Alliance des Ba-Kongo (Congo-Kinshasa)
ADD   Alliance Démocratique Dahoméenne
ALN   [Army of National Liberation] (Algeria)
ANP   [National Peoples Army] (Algeria)
APC   All-People's Congress (Ghana)
          African Peoples Congress (Sierra Leone)
APRP   All People's Republican Party (Ghana)
CMLN   [National Liberation Committee] (Mali)
CND   Convention Nationale Dahoméenne
CNDR   [National Council for the Defense of the Revolution] (Algeria)

CNL	[National Liberation Council] (Congo-Kinshasa)
CNR	[National Revolutionary Council] (Congo-Kinshasa)
CNRA	[National Council of the Algerian Revolution]
CPP	Convention People's Party (Ghana)
CRN	[National Revolutionary Committee] (Congo-Brazzaville)
CVR	Corps des Volontaires de la République (Congo-Kinshasa)
FFS	[Socialist Forces Front] (Algeria)
FLN	Front de Libération Nationale (Algeria)
GAP	Groupement d'Action Populaire (Upper Volta)
GCP	Ghana Congress Party
GOC	General Officer Commanding the Armed Forces (Ghana)
GPRA	[Provisional Government] (Algeria)
KANU	Kenya African National Union
KPU	Kenya People's Union
MAP	Muslim Association Party (Ghana)
MDV	Mouvement Démocratique Voltaique (Upper Volta)
MLN	Mouvement de Libération Nationale (Upper Volta)
MRC	[Military Revolutionary Committee] (Dahomey)
MTLD	Mouvement pour le Triomphe des Libertés Démocratiques (Algeria)
MVC	[Military Vigilance Committee] (Dahomey)
NAL	National Alliance of Liberals (Ghana)
NCA	[National Congolese Army] (Congo-Kinshasa)
NLC	National Liberation Council (Ghana)
NLM	National Liberation Movement (Ghana)
NMR	[National Movement for the Revolution] (Congo-Brazzaville)
NNA	Nigerian National Alliance
NPC	Northern Peoples Congress (Nigeria)
NRC	National Reformation Council (Sierra Leone) [National Renovation Council] (Dahomey)
OAS	[Secret Army Organization] (Algeria)
OAU	Organization of African Unity
PAP	People's Action Party (Ghana)
PDD	Parti Démocratique Dahoméen
PDU	Parti Dahoméen Unifié
POGR	President's Own Guard Regiment (Ghana)
PP	Progress Party (Ghana)
PRA	Parti du Regroupement Africain (Upper Volta)
PSA	Parti Solidaire Africain (Congo-Kinshasa)
PSEMA	Parti Social d'Education des Masses (Upper Volta)

311

RDA   Rassemblement Démocratique Africain (Upper Volta, Dahomey)
RIN   Rassemblement des Impératifs Nationaux (Dahomey)
SLPP   Sierra Leone People's Party
TANU   Tanganyika African National Union
TC   Togoland Congress (Ghana)
TUC   Trades Union Congress (Ghana)
UAMD   Union Africaine et Malgache de Défense (All former French African colonies except Guinea, Mali, and Upper Volta)
UAR   United Arab Republic
UDV   Union Démocratique Voltaique (Upper Volta)
UGCC   United Gold Coast Convention
UGFC   United Ghana Farmers Council
UGTD   Union Générale des Travailleurs du Dahomey
UND   Union Nationale Dahoméenne
UNP   United Nationalist Party (Ghana)
UP   United Party (Ghana)
UPGA   United Progressive Grand Alliance (Nigeria)

Index

Abbas, Ferhat, 239, 242
Abboud, Ibrahim, 2, 23
Abdelghani, Maj., 237, 242 n, 245
Action Group, 22
Adamafio, Tawia, 173
Adandé, Alexandre, 80 n
Adjou, Basile Moumouni, 12
Adotevi, Stanislas Spero, 72, 73, 79, 91 n
Adoula, Cyrille, 131
Aferi, Gen. Nathan, 216
African Peoples Congress (APC, Sierra Leone), 53, 55
Africanization: of civil service, 6, 12; in Congo-Kinshasa, 137; of officer corps, 6, 9, 10, 12, 14, 15, 259; of officer corps, Dahomey and Upper Volta, 100; of officer corps, Ghana, 181–83; of officer corps, Sudan, 260
Afrifa, Brig. Akwasi A., 33, 182 n, 183 n, 186, 186 n, 187, 192, 193, 200, 201, 204, 214, 215, 216
Aho, Philippe, 93 n, 105, 107
Ahomadegbe, Justin Tometin, 71–73, 75–79, 79 n, 90, 91 n, 97 n, 109 n, 110, 112, 113, 120
Ait-Ahmed, Hocine, 241, 248
Akli, Col., 233
Akufo-Addo, 192, 205
Alexander, Gen. H. T., 5
Algeria, 2, 3, 12, 222–49, 256, 265; creation of ALN, 231; creation of ANP, 236; 1965 coup, 242; 1967 attempted coup, 244–45; military attitudes, 247–49; provisional government (GPRA), 229, 231–32; "reconversion," 232; effects of revolution, 224–29; state-building,

227; warlordism, 240–41. *See also* ALN; ANP
Alley, Alphonse, 52, 79, 86, 96, 97, 99, 100 n, 102, 104–7, 109 n, 120, 121
Alliance Démocratique Dahoméenne (ADD), 79
All People's Party (Ghana), 212
ALN (Army of National Liberation, Algeria), 227, 228, 230, 231, 233–36, 239; Executive Coordinating Committee, 231; "reconversion" of, 233 ff
Amlon, Leandre, 79 n, 109 n
Amponsah, Reginald, 192
Amuako-Atta, R. O., 177
Anany, Jerome, 148
Angola, 253, 256
Ankrah, Gen. Joseph A., 31, 33, 39, 85 n, 117, 153, 185, 186 n, 187, 189, 193, 199, 201, 214, 215, 216
ANP (National Peoples Army, Algeria), 226, 235–37, 239, 241, 243, 245; attempt to impose civilian control, 239; 1964 party congress, 240; friction between professionals and *mujahidin,* 247; Political Commissariat, 247; in Six-Day War, 243; social origins, 245; territorial reorganization, 239. *See also* ALN
Anti-Corruption Revolutionary Movement (Sierra Leone), 54, 55
Apithy, Sourou Migan, 71–77, 79, 91 n, 112, 113, 120
Appiah, Joe, 192, 212
Appiah-Danquah, Martin, 171
Aplogan, Valentin Djibode, 74, 76, 79 n
Armed Forces Bureau (Ghana), 184

313

Armed Forces Council (Algeria), 216
Armies: differentiation and specialization, 39; disunity within, 115;
external assistance to, 41; political
interference in, 33; impact on
national unity, 263; technological
and organizational position of,
32; typology of, 254–64. *See also*
Military; individual country list-
ings; appendixes
Army of National Liberation (Congo-
Kinshasa), 222, 230–31
Arthur, Lt. Samuel, 39, 188
Ashanti, 156, 158, 160, 165, 166, 168,
194 n, 212, 255
Ashanti Youth Association, 165
Askaris, 258
Association pour le Maintien de
l'Unité et de la Langue Kikongo,
127
Assogba, Oke, 112
Ataturk, Kemal, 50, 56
Aubame, Jean-Hilaire, 24
Aupiais, Father, 71
Austin, Dennis, 19
Authority, 37–38, 43, 44, 50, 52, 57,
98, 130, 143, 145–56, 150–51, 155, 166,
176. *See also* Legitimacy; Power
Awolowo, Obafemi, 48 n
Azzedine, 241, 248

Baako, Kofi, 183
Bakongo, 129
Bakusa, 133
Baluba, 130, 133
Balunda, 133
Bamba, Emmanuel, 148
"Band-wagon effect," 12, 13, 19
Bangala, 129
Bangala, Col., 149
Barwah, Maj. Gen., 187, 216
Basonge, 130
Batetela, 133
Bayeke, 133
Belgian Congo, 8, 13, 15. *See also*
Congo-Kinshasa
Belgium, 28, 45; colonial policy, 126–
27, 137, 146; military aid to Congo-
Kinshasa, 139
ben Bella, Ahmed, 222, 223, 226, 229,
232–35, 237–43
Bencherif, Ahmed, 242 n
ben Haddou, 237, 242 n
ben Rehen, Larbi, 233, 236, 248
ben Salem, Abderrahman, 240, 242 n
Bendix, Reinhard, 133
Bentum, Benjamin, 196, 197

Biafra, 48, 253. *See also* Nigeria; Ibo
Bilson, John, 212
Bing, Geoffrey, 166
Bitat, Rabah, 241
Black Power Party (Ghana), 212
Boers, 254, 257
Bohiki, Christophe, 74
Boison, J. K., 212
Boissier-Palun, Leon, 112 n, 117
Boni, Nazi, 64, 65, 87
Borna, Bertin, 79 n, 93 n
Botsio, Kojo, 174
Boublider, Nsalah, 242 n, 244
Boujenan, Ahmed, 233, 237, 242 n
Boumaza, 239, 242 n
Boumedienne, Houari, 223, 229, 231,
232, 234, 235, 237–45; relations with
military professionals, 248–49
Boussouf, Abdelhafid, 231
Bouteflika, 239, 243
Boya, Antoine, 79 n
Braimah, J. A., 192
British Togoland, 156, 164, 167, 168.
See also Ghana; Togo
Bruce, Gen. C. C., 216
Busia, Kofi, 163, 190, 192, 193, 204,
206, 212, 213
Burundi, 2, 18, 26

"Caesarism" in Congo-Kinshasa, 143,
146
Cameroon, 8 n, 12, 45
Canada, 139
Center for Civic Education (Ghana),
193
Central African Republic, 2, 25, 27,
70
Central Cooperative Council
(Ghana), 170, 173
Centralization, 36, 51, 63, 66, 73, 119
Chaabani, Mohammed, 233, 237, 240,
241
Chabou, Abdelqader, 242 n
Chadli, Benjedid, 242 n, 245
Charisma, 3, 56, 125–26, 147, 160, 168
Chasme, Joseph Louis, 105, 108 n,
109
Cherif, 239, 242 n, 243
China, Nationalist, 76, 84 n, 85 n
China, Peoples Republic of, 76
Civil service, 4, 30, 46, 48, 49, 55, 56,
59, 65, 66, 77, 112, 143–44
Civilianization of military govern-
ments, 55–58. *See also* Dahomey;
Ghana
Clausewitz, Karl von, 8
"Club of Palace Children," 89 n

Cocoa Purchasing Company (Ghana), 161

Cocoa Marketing Board (Ghana), 195

Collège des Commissaires Généraux (Congo-Kinshasa), 122, 141

Colonial Armies, 7, 8, 258–61

Committee for the Liberation of Maurice Yaméogo, 89 n

Committee on National Reconstruction (Ghana), 191

Comité Revolutionaire (Gabon), 24

Congacou, Tahirou, 79, 100 n

Congo-Brazzaville, 2, 25, 150

Congo-Kinshasa, 2, 8, 9, 15, 26, 33, 41, 45, 56, 57, 230, 256, 263, 265; "Caesarist" bureaucracy, 143–47; 1960 and 1965 coups, 122–23; ideological legitimation, 133–35; role of military, 132–33; 1960 mutiny, 15; declining role of parliament, 144; "patrimonialism," 125–35; shift from Force Publique to National Congolese Army, 137–40; 1964 uprising, 135–36; role of youth, 149–50

Conombo, Joseph, 64, 65

Conseil de l'Entente, 66, 69, 69 n, 70, 74, 76, 88, 97 n, 101

Consultative Committee (Dahomey), 86

Contagion, 26–27, 70

Constituent Assembly (Algeria), 236

Constituent Assembly (Ghana), 205, 208, 217

Convention Nationale Dahoméene (CND), 79 n

Convention People's Party (CPP), 19, 21, 31, 33, 34, 154, 160, 161–66, 166 n, 167–77, 183, 184, 188, 192, 193, 194 n, 200, 203, 207, 212–15, 262; atrophy of, 172; bases of recruitment, 166; ethnic opposition, 169; factionalism within, 174; leadership of, 161; legitimacy of leadership, 160, 163, 168; nature of, 160; post-independence goals, 167; radicalization of, 172–75

Cooperative Alliance (Ghana), 170

Corruption, 30, 31, 46, 50, 53, 54, 56, 59, 143, 172, 188, 196, 213, 214; attitude of NLC, 215

Council of State (Ghana), 216

Coulibaly, Ouezzin, 64, 65

Coups: Algeria, 242; Congo-Kinshasa, 122–23, 141–43; Dahomey, 74, 76–79, 103–7; Ghana, 186–88, Upper Volta, 67–71; causes of, 17–35; institutionalization of, 58

Corps des Volontaires de la République (CVR, Congo-Kinshasa), 144, 147

Dahomey, 2, 13, 25, 27, 29, 45, 48, 51, 54, 56, 255; background to coups, 71–79; 1963 coup, 24, 74; 1965 coup, 76–79; 1967 coup, 39, 103–7; 1968 attempted coup, 120; economic factors, 80–84; effects of military rule, 117–19; government structure, 86; military attitudes, 114–15; military disunity, 103–7; military unity, 96–102; political forces, 89–96; return to civilian rule, 51–53, 96, 110–13, 119–21; unions, 95–96

Danquah, J. B., 164

da Sylva, Karim Urbain, 112 n

de Gaulle, Charles, 76, 84, 97, 98

de Graft Johnson, E. V. C., 212

Degbé, Adrien, 80 n

Deku, A. K., 186

Deutsch, Karl, 20, 38 n

Dombo, S. D., 192

Dorange, Michel, 63, 101 n

Dossa, René, 72, 91 n

Dove-Edwin Commission, report of, 53

Draia, Ahmed, 242 n

Dumont, René, 83

Eaton Hall, 181

East Africa. See Kenya; Tanganyika; Uganda; Zanzibar

Economic develpoment as factor in coups, 47, 49

Egala, Imoru, 212

Egypt. See United Arab Republic

Efomi, Maj., 149

Emerson, Rupert, 4

Entente. See Conseil de l'Entente

Ethiopia, 26, 41, 126, 255, 265

Ethnicity, 19, 23, 48, 49, 54, 71; in African armies, 262; in British Togoland, 164; in Congo-Kinshasa, 129–30, 135, 137; in Dahomey, 104; in Gold Coast, 165; in Sierra Leone, 52

European Development Fund, 85 n

European Economic Community, 82

Ex-Servicemen's Union (Gold Coast), 4 n, 160, 167

Executive Council (Ghana), 193

Expatriate officers, role of, 25

External assistance to African armies, 10. *See also* Belgium; France; Great Britain
Ewe, 164, 167, 186, 200, 213
Eyadema, Etienne, 27, 28

Fage, J. D., 156
Fajuyi, 38
Fanon, Frantz, 128, 136, 222, 227
Farès, Abderrahman, 242
Feit, Edward, 56
Fidayin, 230–31. *See also* Algeria
Finer, S. E., 32, 56
FLN (National Liberation Front, Algeria), 222, 223, 231, 236, 238, 239, 244, 259
Foccart, Jacques, 101 n
Force, 47, 49, 55, 58, 102, 150–51, 184; as characteristic of political systems, 20; in Dahomey and Upper Volta, 115
Force Publique (Belgian Congo), 8, 9 n, 11, 15, 122, 123, 132, 137–41, 258, 260
Fourn, Pierre, 93 n
France, 11, 12 n, 26, 29, 64, 73, 74, 76, 81, 82, 98–101, 114, 222, 256; aid to former dependencies, 100 n; aid to Dahomey, 96; defense treaties with former dependencies, 28; military assistance, 11; trade with Dahomey and Upper Volta, 81
French Equatorial Africa, 11
French Togoland, 8 n, 164
French West Africa, 8, 10, 60, 81

Gabon, 1964 coup, 10, 11, 24, 25
Gallenca, Henri Charles, 85 n
Garango, Tiemoko Marc, 85, 85, 85 n
Garde Républicaine (Dahomey), 103, 115
Gbedemah, Komla, 174, 200, 207, 212, 213
Geertz, Clifford, 19
Generational tensions, 38, 103, 108, 115, 134, 138, 182
Ghana, 2, 9, 19, 21, 27, 29, 30, 33, 48, 66, 70 n, 80, 81, 84 n, 85 n, 110, 253, 256, 262, 263; civil service, 10; Congo crisis, effects of, 183; Constituent Assembly, 205–7; 1966 coup, 186–88; 1967 counter-coup, 39, 118, 216; decline of opposition, 171–72, 1964 constitutional referendum, 175; 1960 presidential election, 171; 1965 parliamentary election, 175; 1969 election, 218–21; economic conditions, 30, 177–79; generational tensions, 182; merchant-professional coalition, 209–13; political participation under NLC, 204–14; radicalization of CPP, 172–75; restoration of civilian rule, 213–21. *See also* Convention People's Party; Gold Coast, National Liberation Council
—military: Air Force, 180; background of officer corps, 182; civil-military relations, changes under Nkrumah, 183–86; civil-military relations, likely patterns, 217; expansion after independence, 180–86; forced retirement of officers, 162, 185; military academy, 181; Navy, 180; probability of future intervention, 215–18; relations between POGR and army, 186
Ghana Bar Association, 207
Ghana Congress Party (GCP), 163, 164
Ghana Democratic Party, 212
Ghana Labour Party, 212
Ghana Youth Council, 206
Gizenga, Antoine, 113, 136
Gold Coast: class-community conflicts, 158–67; 1951 election, 161; 1954 election, 164; 1956 election, 166; growth of CPP, 160–67; 1948 riots, 159. *See also* Ghana
Gowon, Gen. Yakubu, 38
GPRA, 231, 232
Great Britain, 28, 41; ties with Ghanaian army, 216
Groupement d'Action Populaire (GAP), 88
Grunitzky, Nicolas, 16, 17
Guennez, Maj. Mahmoud, 240
Guinea, 12 n, 66, 67, 253
Guissou, Henri, 65
Gutteridge, William F., 6, 9, 26, 28

Hacheme, Jean-Baptiste, 104, 105, 109
Hamah, John Alex, 212
Hansen, R. Adm. David, 216
Harbi, Mohammed, 239 n
Harlley, John W. K., 56, 186, 193, 196, 197, 200, 201, 206, 213
Hassani, Moussa, 241
Hazoume, Paul, 111, 112 n
Herrenvolk Army, 257–58
Hessou, Théodore, 90
Hobbes, Thomas, 5, 21, 37, 43

Hodgkin, Thomas, 126
Houphouet-Boigny, Felix, 63, 64, 66, 67, 69 n, 70, 71, 72, 79, 108 n
Huntington, Samuel P., 35, 37

Ibo, 28, 38, 46
Ileo, Joseph, 142
Indépendants d'Outre-Mer (IOM), 71
Institutionalization, 3, 32, 45, 46, 49, 57, 59, 261–62; of coups, 58
Intellectuals, 54, 72, 92, 127, 138
Intervention: factors promoting, 17–35; types of, 5–17
Ironsi, Gen. J. T. A., 38, 46, 48
Israel, 41, 139
Italy, 139
Ivory Coast, 41, 63, 64, 66, 72, 80, 81, 106 n

Janowitz, Morris, 40
Janssens, Gen. Emile, 14, 15
Johnson, Ferdinand, 108 n, 109 n
Joint Union Committee, 68, 69, 109

Kaboré, Dominique, 94 n
Kabylia: 1963 rebellion, 237–38; revival of dissidence, 240–41
Kalenjin, 41
Kalonji, Albert, 132
Kamerun, 7. See also Cameroon
Kande, Jean-Jacques, 145
Kao, Pascal Kabi Chabi, 108 n
Karboe, A., 192
Kasavubu, Joseph, 23, 122, 123, 127, 141, 142, 183
Kashamura, Anicet, 136
Katanga, 122, 183, 253
Kenya, 12, 253, 255, 263; army of liberation, 256; ethnic factors in army, 41; 1964 mutiny, 254, 259.
Kérékou, Mathieu, 107, 109, 109 n
Khalil, Abdallah, 23
Kimba, Evariste, 148
King's African Rifles, 258, 263
Ki-Zerbo, Joseph, 88
Kotoka, Gen. E. K., 39, 46, 186, 187, 188, 201, 214, 215
Kouandété, Maurice, 47, 48, 55, 61, 107–10, 115, 117, 120, 121
Kraus, Jon, 21, 29, 153
Krim, Belqasim, 231, 234

Lamizana, Sangoule, 27, 28, 68–70, 84, 85, 89, 93, 96–99, 103
Lamptey, Kwesi, 206
Lansana, David, 53

Leclercq, Hughes, 127
Legitimacy, 21, 35, 43, 46–49, 56, 57, 63, 66, 71, 72, 79, 90, 109, 152, 153, 155, 169, 180, 223; and Algerian revolution, 224; conflict over, in Ghana, 207–8; and colonial authority, in Gold Coast, 158; in Congo-Kinshasa, 151; military's conception of, in Dahomey and Upper Volta, 114
Lerner, Daniel, 41
Lévy-Bruhl, Lucien, 129 n
Liberia, 27
Libya, 26
Lipset, Seymour Martin, 47
Lozès, Gabriel, 79 n, 90
Lulua, 130
Lumumba, Patrice, 9, 23, 24, 122, 131, 134, 136, 141, 147, 148, 183
Lumumbism, 147
Lutterodt, William, 212

Maga, Hubert, 24, 71–75, 77, 79, 91 n, 97 n, 101, 109 n, 112, 113, 118, 120
Mahamba, Alexandre, 148
Mali, 2, 66, 81, 118
Malila, Lt. Col., 149
"Manifesto of African Consciousness," 127, 130
Mannheim, Karl, 143
Massamba-Debat, Alphonse, 150
Masson, Governor, 100 n, 101 n
Mba, Leon, 11, 24, 25
Medeghri, 239, 241, 242 n
Menjli, Ali, 232, 242 n
Mensah, Moise, 91
Mensah, Noel, 109 n
Military: attitudes of, 9, 114; protection of institutional interests, 115; self-identification, 32; unity of, 55, 120; withdrawal from political involvement, 50 ff. See also Armies; Algeria; Congo-Kinshasa; Dahomey; Ghana; Sierra Leone; Upper Volta
Military Revolutionary Committee (MRC, Dahomey), 108, 109
Military Vigilance Committee (MVC, Dahomey), 86, 93, 104, 107, 108
Mobutu, Gen. Joseph Desiré, 23, 24, 49, 56, 105, 122, 123, 138, 139, 141–43, 147, 148, 150
Mohammedi, Said, 234, 242 n
Mons, 181
Morocco, 12, 229, 231; war with Algeria, 238
Moro Naba, 64, 70, 88

Mossi, 63, 64, 85, 88, 113
Mouvement Démocratique Voltaique
    (MDV), 64
Mouvement de Libération Nationale
    (MLN, Upper Volta), 68, 84 n, 87–
    89, 92
Mouvement Populaire Africain, 64
Mouvement Populaire de la Révolu-
    tion (MPR), 49
Mouvement de Regroupement Vol-
    taique, 65
Mozambique, 253, 256
Mujahidin. See Algeria
Mulamba, Leonard, 148, 149
Munongo, Godefroid, 133
Musabilin. See Algeria
Muslim Association Party (MAP,
    Ghana), 164, 166
Mustafa Kemal. *See* Ataturk
Mutinies, 6, 11, 14, 25, 27, 146

Nasser, Gamal Abdel, 49, 239
Nation-building, 4, 14, 35, 45, 48, 59,
    153, 170, 227. *See also* State-build-
    ing
National Advisory Committee
    (Ghana), 193
National Alliance of Liberals (NAL,
    Ghana), 212, 213
National Army, 261–62
National Association of Socialist
    Students Organization, 200
"National Committee for the De-
    fense of Democracy," 112
National Congolese Army (NCA),
    123, 132, 133, 137–40, 142, 148–49,
    151
National Council of the Algerian
    Revolution (CNRA), 230, 238
National Council for the Defense of
    the Revolution (CNDR, Algeria),
    241
National Council of Ghana Women,
    200
National integration, 61, 121, 67, 155,
    169. *See also* Nation-building
National Interim Council (Sierra
    Leone), 54
National Liberation Council (NLC,
    Ghana), 152, 187, 189–97, 200, 202,
    204, 206–8, 214, 216; attitudes of,
    189, 203–4, 214–15; attitudes toward
    CPP members, 199–202; ban on
    parties, 204; and chieftancy, 193;
    dependence on civil service, 189;
    economic policies, 190, 197–99;
    establishment of, 188; legitimacy of,

202; and regional and local adminis-
    tration, 190; responsiveness to
    interest groups, 195; and TUC, 196–
    97
National Liberation Movement
    (NLM, Ghana), 165, 166, 212
National Movement for the Revolu-
    tion (NMR, Congo-Brazzaville),
    150
National Peoples Army (ANP, Al-
    geria), 226, 236
National Reformation Council (NRC,
    Sierra Leone), 53–55
National Renovation Committee
    (Dahomey), 86, 92, 93, 95, 103, 108
National Youth Party (Ghana), 212
Nationalist Party (Ghana), 212
Ngalula, Joseph, 133
Nekkache, 239, 241
Niger, 66, 101
Nigeria, 2, 27, 44, 45, 46, 48, 109 n,
    253, 254, 256, 263; January 1966
    coup, 22, 28; July 1966 coup, 58;
    defense pact with Great Britain,
    11; ethnic composition of officer
    corps, 28
Njokwu, 38
Nkrumah, Kwame, 3, 9, 21, 29, 30, 31,
    33, 34, 46, 48, 152, 154, 159–62, 168,
    170–75, 177, 178–80, 183–84, 186–88,
    190, 192, 194 n, 197, 203, 253. *See
    also* Ghana; Convention People's
    Party
Northern People's Party (NPP), 164
Nyerere, Julius, 19, 261

OAS (Secret Army Organization,
    Algeria), 233
Ocran, Col. A. K., 186
Ofori-Atta, William, 192
Ojukwu, Col. Oduwegmu, 38
Okafor, W. A., 38
Okello, John, 29
Okoro, 38
Olympio, Sylvanus, 13, 15, 16, 25, 26,
    59
Omaboe, E. N., 190
Organization of African Unity
    (OAU), 31, 118, 142
Osei-Bonsu, 202
Otu, Gen. S. J. A., 33, 185, 188, 216
ou al-Hajj, 242 n, 244, 248; reconcilia-
    tion with ben Bella, 238
Ouedraogo, Joseph, 63, 64, 65, 68, 69,
    70 n, 89 n
"Oujda Group," 223, 239, 243, 244, 248
Owusu, Victor, 206

Palace Army, 255
Paoletti, Théophile, 78, 79 n
Parsons, Talcott, 22
Parti Dahoméen Unifié (PDU), 72–74
Parti Démocratique Dahoméen (PDD), 24, 75–78, 90
Parti Démocratique de Côte d'Ivoire, 63
Parti Démocratique Unifié (Dahomey), 110
Parti du Regroupement Africaine (PRA, Dahomey), 87–88
Parti National Voltaique (PNV), 65
Parti Republicaine de Liberte (PRL, Upper Volta), 65
Parti Social d'Education des Masses (PSEMA, Upper Volta), 64
Participation, 50, 56, 59, 153
Patrimonialism: in Congo-Kinshasa, 125–35; in Ghana, 176
"Pentecost plot," 148
People's Popular Party (Ghana), 212
Pluralism, 63, 75, 117, 121. See also Ethnicity; Nation-building; Regionalism
Police, 8, 21, 23, 33, 54, 68, 69, 180
Political Bureau (Algeria), 234, 235, 239
Political Committee (Ghana), 192
Political development and military rule, 35–50
Popular Army of Liberation (Congo-Kinshasa), 150
Portuguese Guinea, 253
Power, 150–51; shift from power to force in Ghana, 180
"Power deflation," 22
Professionalism, 32, 34, 35, 49, 55, 152; in Algerian army, 229, 238–39; and 1966 coup in Ghana, 215; in Ghanaian army, 182–83; in NCA, 137–40
President's Own Guard Regiment (POGR, Ghana), 33, 152, 185, 187
Preventive Detention Act, 170
Progress Party (PP, Ghana), 212
Primordial ties, 13, 14, 19, 42, 44, 59. See also Ethnicity
Prudencio, Eustache, 112
Pye, Lucian, 40, 41

Qaid, Ahmed, 232, 239, 241, 242 n, 244, 245
Quaidoo, P. K. K., 212

Raiding Citizen-Army, 254–55
Rapoport, David C., 44

Rassemblement Démocratique Africain (RDA), 64, 65, 71, 87–89
Rassemblement des Impératifs Nationaux (RIN, Dahomey), 76
Regionalism, 28, 46, 48; in Algeria, 223, 237–42, 244–45; in Congo-Kinshasa, 129–32; in Dahomey, 24, 51, 71–79; in Ghana, 156–67, 172, 204, 207–8; in Upper Volta, 63–68. See also Ethnicity; Nation-building; Primordial ties
Republican Party (Ghana), 212
"Revolution of Rising Expectations," 13
Revolutionary Citizen-Army, 256–57
Revolutionary Council (Algeria), 243, 245
Rhodesia, 33, 180
Riggs, Fred W., 39
Robinson, Richard D., 41
Roth, Guenther, 125, 126
Royal West Africa Frontier Force (RWAFF), 6
Rwanda, 26, 255

Saint Cyr, 60
Saka, Jean, 79 n
Salah, Mohammed, 242 n
Sandhurst, 7, 60
"Second independence," 134
"Second-stage" coups, 38, 39
Senegal, 13, 81
Senghor, Léopold Sédar, 112 n
Sierra Leone, 2, 51; 1967 election, 53; military withdrawal, 53–55
Sierra Leone People's Party (SLPP), 53, 55
Sigúe, Nouhoum, 88
Singa, Col., 145
Sinzogan, Benoit Cossi, 104, 105, 107, 121
Skurnik, W. A. E., 24, 47, 51, 60, 61
Socialist Forces Front (FFS, Algeria), 242
Soglo, Gen. Christophe, 24, 27, 48, 51, 52, 74–79, 81, 84, 84 n, 86, 88–91, 95–99, 102–9, 115, 118, 120
Soglo, Nicéphore, 81, 93 n, 108 n
Somalia, 255, 265
Soufi, Salah, 242 n
South Africa, 180, 256, 257, 265
Soviet Union, 33, 184
State-building, 4, 14, 27, 35, 48, 56, 59, 153, 155, 170, 227. See also Nation-building; Regionalism
Stevens, Siaka, 53–55
Sudan, 2, 23, 256

Supreme Council of the Republic (Dahomey), 103
Syndicat des Chefs Coutumiers (Upper Volta), 88
Syndicat National des Commerçants et Industriels du Dahomey, 112 n

Tanganyika, 7; 1964 mutiny, 15, 19, 254
Tanganyika Rifles, 15
Tanganyika African National Union (TANU), 15, 19
Tanzania, 253; National Service, 261
Tayebi, Mohammed, 242 n
Tetegan, Emmanuel, 79 n
Tettegah, John, 170, 173
Thompson, Col. David, 26
Tirailleurs Sénégalais, 258
Tocqueville, Alexis de, 153
Togo, 2, 8, 13, 15, 27, 59, 73, 80, 93 n, 101, 121; 1966 coup, 28; 1967 coup, 17; 1963 mutiny, 15, 262
Togoland. See French Togoland; British Togoland
Togoland Congress (TC), 164, 166
Tota, Noel, 112
Touré, Sékou, 66, 67
Trades Union Congress (TUC, Ghana), 170, 171, 173, 192, 196, 200, 203, 207, 212
Trade unions, 51, 52, 66; in Dahomey, 75, 77, 78, 95–96; in Upper Volta, 94. See also Trades Union Congress; Union Générale des Travailleurs du Dahomey
Tshisekedi, Etienne, 146
Tshombe, Moise, 123, 133, 142, 253
Tunisia, 12, 229, 231
Turkey, 41, 56, 57

Uganda, 1964 mutiny, 254, 259
Union Africaine et Malgache de Défense (UAMD), 11, 101
Union Démocratique Voltaique (UDV), 65
Union Générale des Travailleurs du Dahomey (UGTD), 74, 77, 78
Union Nationale Dahoméenne (UND), 79
United Africa Company, 16
United Arab Republic, 49, 243, 253, 256, 265
United Ghana Farmers' Council (UGFC), 161, 170, 171, 173, 174, 177, 195, 200, 203
United Gold Coast Convention (UGCC), 159, 160, 163

United Nations, 27, 131, 139, 151, 183, 222
United Party (UP, Ghana), 171, 190, 193, 196, 205, 212
United States, 41, 45, 139
Upper Volta, 2, 25, 27, 29; background to 1966 coup, 63–68; reasons for 1966 coup, 68–71; economic problems, 80–82, 84–85; effects of military rule, 117–19; government structure after coup, 85–86; military attitudes, 114–15; military disunity, 103, 115; military unity, 96–102; political forces, 87–89; trade unions, 94

van den Berghe, Pierre L., 137
Veterans, role of, 4 n, 16, 160, 167
Vierin, Jean Baptiste Ganmadualo, 112 n
Vieyra, Christian, 91, 108 n
Voluntary withdrawal, 51–55. See also Dahomey; Ghana

Watusi, 18
Watson Commission, report of, 4 n
Weber, Max, 20, 56, 125, 126, 128, 132, 133, 143, 146, 147, 176
Wilayism. See Algeria; Regionalism
William Ponty School, 118
Willame, Jean-Claude, 8, 23, 30, 33, 123
Wudu, Frank, 212

Yahyaoui, Mohammed Salah, 242 n, 245
Yaméogo, Denis, 66, 67, 69
Yaméogo, Maurice, 64–70, 85, 87, 88, 89 n, 94, 100–103
Yaya, Mede Moussa, 79 n
Yeboah, Lt. Moses, 39
Youlou, Fulbert, 25
Young Farmers League, 173
Young Pioneers, 170, 173, 200

Zanlerigu, Col., 186
Zanzibar, 15, 18, 25, 27, 29
Zartman, I. William, 27, 222
Zbiri, Tahar, 232, 237, 242 n, 243, 244, 245, 248
Zerguini, Mohammed, 245
Ziegler, Jean, 136
Zinsou, Emile D., 52, 55, 83, 108, 117, 118, 120, 121
Zolberg, Aristide R., 13, 18, 19, 21, 65, 125, 155, 170, 176, 180